Development Policy Making

Development Policy Making:

Challenges and Concerns

Apurba Kumar Chattopadhyay
Soumyadip Chattopadhyay

GYAN

ISBN: 978-81-212-2014-9

Published, 2021

Published by

Gyan Publishing House
5, Ansari Road
Daryaganj, New Delhi-110002
Phone: 011-47034999, 9811692060
www.gyanbooks.com
E-mail: books@gyanbooks.com

Printed at: Gyan Press, Delhi.

Contents

Part-III
Agriculture and Rural Development

Part - IV
Health, Education and Basic Services

Preface

'Development Policy Making: Challenges and Concerns' is an edited volume consisting of sixteen chapters selected from the papers presented at the conferences organised by the Department of Economics and Politics of Visva-Bharati (A Central University) under its UGC Special Assistance Programme in 2019 and 2020. These papers critically analyse different policy issues adopted pertaining to environment and sustainability, macroeconomics, agriculture and rural development and finally, health, education and basic services. While majority of the papers analyse policies concerning Indian economy, there are case studies of Bangladesh, Sri Lanka, Ethiopia and Nigeria. It also examines recent policies adopted by the government of India to give stimulus to the Indian economy to pull it out of the economic disaster caused mainly due to COVID-19 pandemic.

The chapters of this volume have been divided into four parts. The first part containing three chapters examine policy issues pertaining to environment and sustainable development both at theoretical and empirical levels. The second part contains four chapters that examine various macroeconomic policies including the recent policy of *Atmanirbhar Bharat Abhiyan*. The third part contains three chapters under agriculture and rural development and finally, part four contains five chapters on health, education and basic services apart from a chapter on crime and socioeconomic condition.

The publication of this volume also reflects a teamwork in advanced research in specific fields as envisaged by the UGC. We are thankful to our colleagues for their assistance in organizing the seminar.

VISVA-BHARATI
Santiniketan
July, 2021

Apurba Kumar Chattopadhyay
Soumyadip Chattopadhyay

Acknowledgements

The book is an outcome of the International Conferences organized by the Department of Economics and Politics, VISVA-BHARATI under the UGC-SAP (DRS-II) programme and held at the Department in January, 2019 and February 2020. We are thankful to the University Grants Commission (UGC) for sponsoring the conferences under the Special Assistance Programme (SAP). Almost all the chapters of the book were presented at the Conferences. We would like to express our gratitude to Shri Chandi Prasad Bhatt, Gandhian Environmentalist, Chipko Movement Leader, recipient of Padma Bhushan and Raman Magsaysay Award who inaugurated the conference on "Natural Resources, Environment and Development" and contributed a chapter to the book. We are also grateful to Professor Bidyut Chakrabarty, Vice-Chancellor, Visva-Bharati, Prof. Ashwini Deshpande, Ashoka University, Prof. Anup Sinha, Chairperson, Bandhan Bank, and Retired Professor, IIM Calcutta, and Prof. Reetika Khera of IIMA for their active participations and patronage. We are also thankful to all the paper presenters who contributed their paper as chapters for the book. We are thankful to our colleagues for their assistance in organizing the conferences.

VISVA-BHARATI
Santiniketan
July 2021

Apurba Kumar Chattopadhyay
Soumyadip Chattopadhyay

List of Contributors

1. **Chandi Prasad Bhatt,** Gandhian Environmentalist, Chipko Movement Leader, recipient of Padma Bhushan, Raman Magsaysay Award and Gandhi Peace Prize. Sarvodya Kender, Mandir Marg, Gopeshwar, Dist. Chamoli, Uttarakhand.
2. **Anup Sinha,** Chairperson, Bandhan Bank, and Retired Professor, IIM Calcutta. E-mail: aksinha@iimcal.ac.in
3. **Runa Sarkar,** Professor, Economics Group, IIM Calcutta, Kolkata. E-mail: runa@iimcal.ac.in
4. **Nilendu Chatterjee,** Department of Economics, Bankim Sardar College, South 24 Parganas, West Bengal.E-mail: nilendu_ chatterjee@ rediffmail.com
5. **Dipak Kundu,** Department of Commerce, Bankim Sardar College, South 24 Parganas, West Bengal
6. **Debabrata Dey,** Department of Commerce, Bankim Sardar College, South 24 Parganas, West Bengal
7. **Biswajit Mandal,** Department of Economics & Politics, Visva-Bharati University, Santiniketan, India. E-mail: Email: biswajiteco@gmail.com
8. **Nilanjan Ghosh,** Observer Research Foundation, Kolkata, India. Email: nilanjanghosh@orfonline.org
9. **Saswati Chaudhuri,** Department of Economics, St. Xavier's College (Autonomous), Kolkata, India. Email: sxcsas@sxccal.edu
10. **Seemantini Chattopadhyay,** Assistant Professor in Economics, Govt. College of Engineering & Textile Technology, Serampore, West Bengal. E-mail:seemantini.de@gmail.com
11. **Solomon Kebede Menza,** Lecturer & Researcher at Wolaita Sodo University, Department of Economics, PhD Candidate @ Arba Minch University, Ethiopia.E-mail: kebedes24@gmail.com or lelisebacha@gmail.com
12. **Bhishan Chandra Barman,** Research Fellow, Department of Economics, University of Rajshahi, Rajshahi 6205, Bangladesh. Email: bhishan.econ@gmail.com

13. **Dr. Md. Abdul Wadud,** Department of Economics, University of Rajshahi, Rajshahi 6205, Bangladesh. Email: wadud68@yahoo.com

14. **Abhijit Pathak,** Assistant Professor, Department of Economics, Dhruba Chand Halder College, Dakshin Barasat, South 24 Parganas, West Bengal, India. E-mail: abhijitdch@gmail.com

15. **Apurba Kumar Chattopadhyay,** Professor in Economics, Department of Economics and Politics, Visva-Bharati, Santiniketan, West Bengal. India. E-mail: apurbak.chattopadhyay@gmail.com

16. **Raj Kumar Kundu,** Assistant Professor, Department of Economics, Sarat Centenary College, University of Burdwan, West Bengal, India. E-mail: rajkumar.kundu75@gmail.com

17. **Bhaskar Majumder,** Professor, G. B. Pant Social Science Institute, Allahabad - 211 019. E-mail: majumderb@rediffmail.com; www.gbpssi.in

18. **Soumyadip Chattopadhyay,** Associate Professor, Department of Economics and Politics, Visva Bharati University India, soumyadip.chattopadhyay@visva-bharati.ac.in

19. **Arjun Kumar,** Director, Impact and Policy Research Institute (IMPRI), New Delhi and China-India Visiting Fellow, Ashoka University, India. arjun.impri@gmail.com

20. **Muktar Bala,** Deaprtment of Economics, Faculty of Management and Social Sciences, Ibrahim Badamasi Babangida University, Lapai, Niger State, Nigeria. Email: muktarbala@yahoo.co.uk

21. **Chayanika Mitra,** Assistant Professor, Department of Economics, St. Xavier's University, Kolkata. Email: chayani kamitra4@gmail.com

22. **Nit Ranjan,** Ph.D. Scholar, CESP/SSS, Jawaharlal Nehru University, New Delhi, India. E-mail: mail2nitranjan@gmail.com

23. **Poulomi Khasnobis,** Ph.D Scholar, Department of Economics, University of Burdwan. E-mail: titlyecono@gmail.com

24. **Soumyanada Dinda,** Professor of Economics, Department of Economics, University of Burdwan, E-mail:sdinda@eco. buruniv.ac.in

1

Development Policy Making: Challenges and Concerns—An Introduction

Apurba Kumar Chattopadhyay,
Soumyadip Chattopadhyay

Development policies are *sine qua non* for development aiming at reduction of poverty and inequality, implementation of fundamental rights and promotion of sustainable development. In 2015, the United Nations has adopted the Agenda-2030 for realising sustainable development goals aiming at the eradication of extreme poverty and ensuring overall wellbeing in an environmentally sustainable manner. In order to achieve these goals governments need to formulate necessary policies. One of the important features of a sound development policy is that it should be amenable to periodic reviews to judge its appropriateness in achieving desired goal. This edited volume includes sixteen papers selected from the papers presented at the conferences organised by the Department of Economics and Politics of Visva-Bharati University (A Central University) under its UGC Special Assistance Programme in 2019 and 2020. These papers critically analyse different policy issues pertaining to environment and sustainability, macroeconomics, agriculture and rural development and finally, health, education and basic services. While majority of the papers analyse policies concerning Indian economy, there are case studies of Bangladesh, Ethiopia and Nigeria. We introduce these papers in following four subsections.

I

The first three chapters following this introductory note deal with environment and sustainability. Chandi Prasad Bhatt in his article, '*Himalayan sensitivity, Environment and Development: Chipko Experiences*'[1] highlights the pivotal role that the Himalaya plays in the

Indian culture and tradition. Its soil, vegetation, water, forests etc. not only influence the human society living in the Himalaya, but also the entire population of the Indian sub-continent. However, excessive human interference in the region over the times has disturbed its ecological balance resulting in recurring devastating floods and landslides in the region. Therefore, he has emphasised that development planning for the region must be undertaken only after ensuring that the fragile ecological balance is not disturbed for the execution of the development plan. He has suggested that the execution of the developmental planning should be carried out in a participatory mode in which the affected society and the local organisations must have a major role to play.

Anup Sinha and Runa Sarkar in their article titled, '*Is the Sustainable Livelihoods Approach towards Development Interventions Truly Sustainable? An Assessment*'[2] assess the Sustainable Livelihood Approach as a means of sustainable development. The authors evaluate this approach critically in the light of its amenability in the growth experience of an economy. They raise an important theoretical question regarding the efficacy of the capitalist market economy 'with its highly individualised incentive structures' in realising sustainable development although they argue that the Sustainable Livelihood Approach is a 'novel and superior strategy to alleviate short-term poverty and inadequate incomes.' Nevertheless, it fails to stand to the scrutiny when looked from the perspectives of the sustainable development. The next article under environment and sustainability is, '*Dependency on Natural Resources and Sustainable Resource Management: A Study of Bankura District*' by Nilendu Chatterjee, Dipak Kundu and Debabrata Dey. It highlights dependence of Bankura district of West Bengal on natural resources and proposes sustainable use of the available resources. It focuses mainly on two natural resources: forestry and drinking water. The article makes use of optimisation model, absolute convergence and contingent valuation method, the results of which have strong implications from the point of view of policy analysis in the study area.

II

The next four articles of this volume concern with macroeconomic perspectives of development policies. The first article in this section, written by Biswajit Mandal, Nilanjan Ghosh and Saswati Chaudhuri is '*Corona Calls for Revival of Globalisation vs. Deglobalisation Debate – Relevance of Atmanirbhar Bharat*'. It has attempted to study the impact of ongoing COVID-19 pandemic globally particularly in the sphere of global value chain, supply disruption, tourism, and productivity shocks. All these may lead most of the countries to move towards inward looking economic policies in coming years. In such a backdrop, the authors attempt to assess the theoretical relevance of Atmanirbhar Bharat Abhiyaan (Self Reliant India) policy adopted in India to cope with the devastating impact of the Covid-19 pandemic. They have predicted that 'the Atmanirbhar Bharat campaign beyond its 'protectionist' layer may just act as an appropriate launching pad to break the shackles of low level equilibrium trap and to move to the next level of development trajectory'. Seemantini Chattopadhyay's article, '*India's Response to COVID-19 and ATMANIRBHAR Package: A Critical Annotation*' also deals with same issue. She scrutinises various aspects of the *Atmanirbhar Bharat Abhiyaan* announced by the government and analyses the effectiveness of the same in dealing with the economic slowdown prevailing in the country. She discusses different components of the economic package with respect to the supply and demand sides of the economy. Further, her study has made a comparative evaluation of the policies announced in other countries to fight the economic crises due to the outbreak of the global pandemic. After analysing various policy options that are in vogue, she advocates strongly in favour of the policy of 'direct cash transfer' as a possible way out of the prevailing economic crisis.

The role of the financial sector in macroeconomic development is very important. Solomon Kebede Menza's paper, '*Empirical Analysis of Long-Run and Short-Run Dynamic Effects of Deposit Rate, Inflation Rate and GDP on Bank Deposit: A Vector Error Correction Model Approach*' examines the long-run and short run dynamic effects of deposit rate, inflation rate and GDP on bank deposit in the context of the commercial bank of Ethiopia (CBE). He has used vector error correction model for his study and has found that among other things, in the long-run on an average inflation rate and GDP have a negative effect on deposit, while deposit rate has a positive effect on the total amount of deposit held by CBE. Therefore, mobilisation of deposits for the CBE should be an important policy option for the government. The next article in this section, '*Impact of E-banking on the Performance of Commercial Banks in Bangladesh: Evidence from Panel Data Analysis*' written by Bhishan Chandra Barman and Md. Abdul Wadud examines the impact of e-banking on the performance of commercial banks in Bangladesh. The study has revealed a positive and statistically significant impact of e-banking on return on assets and net interest margin. Impact of e-banking on return on equity is also found to be positive. Overall, the authors have found that e-banking positively affects the banks' performance. Therefore, they have strongly advocated for required investment to setup overall e-banking technologies in the banks where the e-banking services have not yet been initiated in order to reap higher profitability.

III

There are three articles in this section concerning agriculture and rural development. In the first article, '*Agricultural Credit Growth and Credit Policy in India: A Critical Appraisal*', Abhijit Pathak and Apurba Kumar Chattopadhyay examine the performance of agricultural credit delivery by the commercial banks and critically evaluate the agricultural credit policy adopted by the Reserve Bank of India (RBI). Given the importance of the agriculture sector in Indian economy and its increasing prominence in the backdrop of prevailing pandemic that has badly battered other sectors of the economy, delivery of adequate credit to agriculture has become imperative for the smooth functioning of this sector. The article assesses agricultural credit policy for the period beginning with 1970s decade. The first decade after liberalisation has recorded sharp deceleration of credit growth in agriculture. It is not the shortage of liquidity, but the type of monetary policy accommodation pursued by the RBI during the 90s along with its prudential and regulatory framework that made agricultural credit relatively unworthy to the banking sector. The period from 2001 to 2014 has witnessed recovery, boom and moderation of agricultural credit expansion with annual average credit growth around 24 percent. Nevertheless, the quality of credit to agriculture has remained a cause of concern in this period. The authors have found deceleration of agricultural credit expansion in the post 2015 period.

Irrigation is another very important factor for the development of the agricultural sector. Raj Kumar Kundu and Apurba Kumar Chattopadhyay in their article, '*Looking into the Efficiency and Productivity of Major Irrigation Projects in West Bengal, India with Special Reference to the DVC Irrigation Project*', evaluate two major irrigation projects of West Bengal that cover about 66 percent of total canal irrigated area. The Damodar Valley Project (DVC) and Kangsabati Reservoir Project are structurally different—the DVC irrigation project is a single-barrage-multi-reservoir type project but the Kangsabati irrigation project is a multi-barrage-single-reservoir type project. Their study reveals that the multi-barrage-single-reservoir irrigation projects (Kangsabati) is more efficient than the single-barrage-multi-reservoir irrigation project (DVC). They have also found that the summer (boro) paddy productivity is higher in the plots of the head-reach zone compared to that in tail-end zone because of their respective locations vis-à-vis canal water availability and furthermore, this location factor is important in determining crop pattern and crop diversification in the respective zones.

In his article, '*Living Money-less: A Study of Nyishi Households in Arunachal Pradesh, India*' Bhaskar Majumder highlights uselessness of the money economy for the sustenance of tribal social economy because of the self-engagement of the tribal people in their nature-based economy. A social economy shows human beings engaged in collection from nature delinked from money-based exchange that fulfils needs of households. The Nyishi tribe residing in Papum Pare district in the state of Arunachal Pradesh in India revealed a social economy where livelihood could be sustained through self-engagement of women mostly in forests. The author has found that moneylessness does not obstruct the tribe to ensure livelihood as they are mostly engaged in collection from nature.

IV

The final section of this volume include five articles on health, education and basic services. One of the sustainable development goals mooted by the United Nations is to 'make cities and human settlements inclusive, safe, resilient and sustainable'. Given the fact that the global urban population has already outnumbered the rural population in 2008, the goal assumes immense significance. The population residing in urban areas is also growing steadily in India. It is 34.47 percent in 2019[3] and estimated to be more than 40 percent in 2030 by the UN. Soumyadip Chattopadhyay and Arjun Kumar in their article, '*Financing Amenities for Inclusive and Sustainable Cities in India: Challenges and Prospects*' reviews urban policies earmarked for realising the relevant SDG. They have scrutinised several urban policies like, Smart Cities Mission (SCM), Atal Mission for Rejuvenation and Urban Transformation (AMRUT), The National Heritage Development and Augmentation Yojana (HRIDAY), Pradhan Mantri Awas Yojana (PMAY) - Housing for All (HfA) (Urban), Swachh Bharat Mission (SBM) Urban, etc. They have found that most of the urban policies in India, 'despite having scope for directly connecting with the urban citizen, followed a typical top down approach'. They have argued that for the delivery of adequate as well as affordable urban basic services, the city governments need to work in an expansion or exponential mode, with continuous capacity building and revitalisation of administrative and financial energy. This will call for engagement of specialised institutions and parastatal agencies. They have emphasised on efficient coordination among all the stakeholders through an integrated policy and regulatory environment. The incorporation of voices of the marginalised and their needs and priorities in urban plans is central to achieving inclusive and sustainable cities.

It is well recognised that health and education are essential components of human development. They are also closely related and improving one-category helps to have larger impact on the other. This is because greater health capital improves the return on investments in education and similarly, greater education capital improves the return to investments in health. The next chapter in this section titled, '*Education Production Function: Does Health Matter*?', authored by Muktar Bala seeks to establish this relationship using primary data collected from rural areas of Niger State of Nigeria. His study estimates the effects of children's physical and mental health on their academic performance. The study applies quantile regression to discern whether the health of the children may have differential impacts at different points on the children's performance distribution. It has been found that the children's physical and mental health affect their academic performance, but the effect is specific to the children at the lower and upper tails of the performance distribution. Some of the other factors, such as parental involvement, school type and birth order also influence children's academic performance. Therefore, he has sought policies that would enhance the physical and mental health of the children.

The next paper, '*Gender Bias in Education Expenditure among Religious and Social Groups: A Case Study for Below Class 10 Level in West Bengal*', by Chayanika Mitra explores gender bias in education expenditure among the religious (Hindu, Muslim and Others) and the social groups (SC, ST and General) in West Bengal. Using relevant statistical technique the author has identified gender bias in religious or social groups in West Bengal, India. In the next paper. '*Social Determinants and Inequality in Immunisation in India*', Nit Ranjan has shown that religion and caste system in India continue to have unwarranted association with the immunisation coverage in India. His study uses the NFHS-IV data of 2015-16 and found the existence of inequity by religion and caste in uptake of three basic vaccines-BCG, three doses of DPT and measles, allied in prevailing low level of full immunisation. Extensive immunisation programme over the decade has resulted in rapid improvement in vaccination coverage for such children as well. However, Concentration Index based on mother education, health facilities and wealth quantiles emphasize the existence of inequity among Muslim, Scheduled Caste and Scheduled tribes children.

Poulomi Khasnobis and Soumyanada Dinda in the last paper of this volume titled, '*Crime and Socio- Economic Condition in India during 1990-2017: An Empirical Analysis*', have analysed property crime and economic crime and their determinants in Indian context. Some offenses under Indian Penal Code, such as robbery, dacoity, burglary and theft that inflict damage to property of the victims are termed as Property Crime. On the other hand, cheating, breach of trust and counterfeiting constitute economic crime. The authors have tried to explain those crimes in terms of social factors (education, unemployment, income inequality, migration etc.) and financial factors (such as real rate of interest). The study observes long run relationship between crime and socioeconomic variables with short run dynamics. Based on the result of this study, the authors have suggested some policies to combat the robbery and breach of trust. Since higher inflation increases both robbery and breach of trust, the government is advised to focus on price control to reduced crime. Further, by raising education level, economic crime can be controlled and creation of more jobs or job opportunities would lead to reduce the menace of robbery.

Notes

1. Keynote paper presented at the International Conference organised by the Department of Economics & Politics, Visva-Bharati University, Santiniketan on 19th January, 2019.
2. Invited paper presented at the International Conference organised by the Department of Economics & Politics, Visva-Bharati University, Santiniketan on 3rd February, 2020.
3. https://data.worldbank.org/indicator/SP.URB.TOTL.IN.ZS?locations=IN. Accessed on 2-11-2020.

Part - I
Environment and Sustainability

2

Himalayan Sensitivity, Environment and Development: Chipko Experiences

Chandi Prasad Bhatt

Abstract

Himalaya is at the center of the Indian culture and tradition as it is considered the abode of various natural resources. Its soil, vegetation, water, forests, etc., not only influence the human society living in the Himalaya but also the entire population of the Indian sub-continent. It influences the climate and geography of the larger region of Asia. Its forests are the stabilizing forces which hold the carbon content produced by modern human civilization. However, the Himalaya is a very sensitive mountain; it does not tolerate excessive human interference. It is evident by the ferocious floods of 1970s in the Alaknanda, a tributary of river Ganga, which was aggravated by deforestation. After this, consistent efforts were made to save forests through the Chipko movement. The movement forced the Government to put a ban on commercial felling of trees in the region. Similarly, the catastrophic flood in the tributary of the Ganga River along with Kedarnath in June 2013 devastated the entire region. This calamity in Uttrakhand has compelled all of us to seriously analyse the prevailing situation. Similarly, the 2014-2015 floods in the state of Jammu and Kashmir have forced us to reassess the sustainability of our developmental schemes These floods not only have destroyed the agriculture and economy of the local population but also have seriously affected the hydropower and irrigation schemes. The calamity in the Himalayan region is not only due to its inherent character, but there seems to be a significant contribution by the excessive human intervention. The over expansion of the consumer culture has put tremendous pressure on its natural resources. Therefore, the focus of the development in this region, should be the holistic development of the Himalaya and any such developmental planning, which enhances its fragility, should be discouraged.

Key Words: *Himalaya, Chipko Movement, Deforestation, Environmental Sensitivity, Niti Ayog*

Introduction

"Where the mind is without fear and the head is held high
Where knowledge is free
Where the world has not been broken up into fragments
By narrow domestic walls
Where words come out from the depth of truth
Where tireless striving stretches its arms towards perfection
Where the clear stream of reason has not lost its way
Into the dreary desert sand of dead habit
Where the mind is led forward by thee
Into ever-widening thought and action
Into that heaven of freedom, my Father, let my country awake."

Rabindranath Tagore

This humble prayer of a great enthusiast has been an integral part of the day and night events in forest and environmental promotion camps on the bank of river Alaknanda in the Himalayas for last six decades. I do not remember when and how this composition of Rabindranath Tagoreji, a great literary person, thinker and philosopher, has become a part of our daily prayers, but we get a lot of energy and enthusiasm from these lines. I could not get an opportunity to meet the respected Rabindranath Tagore ji, nor I could get a chance to see and read his literary creation, but we keep on getting energy by his name. Today, I am truly delighted and honoured to find myself amongst scholars, experts and young students in this most reputed and famous temple of education, Visva-Bharati University at Shantiniketan.

I would like to clarify politely that I am neither an academician nor a subject expert. I am a person who is familiar with the villagers in the rural surroundings and a person learning from their experiences for social well-being. We are very ordinary people of Gopeshwar, a small village situated in the heart of the Alaknanda, the main stream of Ganga in Uttarakhand of the Himalayas. I am associated with the Dasoli Gram Swarajaya Mandal, the mother organisation of the Chipko movement.

The Chipko Movement

Chipko was primarily a movement against the unscientific, unjust, and the exploitation of natural resources, fought with Satyagraha, a non-violent weapon of the poor. This movement protected our environment and us.

Chipko movement means sticking to the trees and protecting them from being axed, and declaring that we will cut our back before the tree. This method was started in 1973 during the Chipko movement. It was very simple. This was the reason that people of all villages including young and old, women and children were able to get involved in this movement. This method of struggle did not require any revolutionary or strong person to follow it. The weakest of the weak could adopt this technique and strengthen his power.

In this way Chipko was the first, which conveyed in simple words why 'tree should not be cut?' Chipko placed the matter of land and the concerns of the landholders in front of the government and its officials. Thus, with the struggle to save the trees further, the task of forest conservation and environmental protection also continued along with the increase in greenery and water conservation. The journey of the Ganges, Brahmaputra, and Indus Rivers and the trip on the coastal areas of its tributaries undertaken to know the Himalayas, maturated our understanding and enhanced our knowledge about the interdependence of water, forest, land and the human being.

Our work area has been the Uttarakhand of the Himalayas. In a small area of Uttarakhand, we are working to conserve and improve the environment. We do observe today that the incidence of environmental crisis - such as sea storm, avalanche, flood etc. is increasing rapidly in most parts of the world. Even in our country, such incidents are increasing rapidly, but the biggest side effects of environmental disruption are having on the Himalayas. Today, Himalayan region is synonymous with environmental destruction. Himalayan glaciers are moving behind. The traditional sources of water are drying. Events such as earthquake, landslide, land erosion, and stream changes by rivers are constantly getting faster. Every year millions of people are being devastated by floods, development plans are getting affected and the future of our economic, social, cultural, and spiritual prosperity is being questioned. The effects of the tragedies in the Himalayas are greatly impinging on the welfare of people in the plains. Human relations with the Himalayas have been from the very beginning. Himalaya has been a symbol of Indian faith and development.

Himalaya is the Earth's spine

In Gita, the most respected Hindu scripture, while talking to Arjuna, Shri Krishna addressed Himalaya as 'The Sthavranan Himalayas'. That is, I am the Himalaya Mountains among those who remain stable.

He called the Himalayas the spinal cord of the earth. Himalayas is a stabiliser of the Asia's climate. It is a multinational, multiregional and multicultural mountain range and its biodiversity is a boon for the world. Therefore, after the deep study and research of the *Rishis* and *Munis*, the Himalayas were placed in the centre of Indian Culture and *Manisha*. The Himalaya is also a cultural and spiritual arena. It is not only a prime source of our culture but also the basis of natural resources. The soil, water, vegetation and forests here not only affect human life and environment, but also influence the life-style of the Indian subcontinent. Himalayas is also a reservoir of forests that hold carbon formed by the human society.

The Himalayan Geography and Ecology

The vast Himalayan mountain range from east to west is spread in an area of 2500 km. Politically, India, Pakistan, Nepal, Bhutan, Bangladesh and Myanmar associated in the south, and China (Tibet) in the north are located in the Himalayas. Twelve Indian states are located in the Himalayan region, known as the Indian sub-continent. Arunachal Pradesh in the west, the Jammu and Kashmir and Ladakh in the west, Meghalaya, Mizoram, Nagaland, Manipur, Assam, Tripura, Sikkim, Himachal Pradesh and Uttarakhand and the Darjeeling region of the West Bengal are situated in the High Himalaya and its sub-regions. Approximately 16.2 percent of the total geographical area of India falls in the Himalayan region. Despite the scattered settlement here, approximately six percent of the total population of the country resides in this region.

There is a huge difference in the architecture, climate and soil texture of the Himalayas. Acute topography is the primary cause of diversity of the region. The Himalaya Mountains are so wide as well as diversified. The area consists the depth of the sea to the height of Sagarmatha, Kanchenjunga and Nanda Devi. In the foothills where the high temperatures of the plains are present, hundreds of peaks and one-fourth of the quadrangle are always glaciated, with temperatures below zero degree Celsius.

The Himalayas can be divided into four main parts: Trans Himalaya– The trans-Himalayan area consists of Lahaul- Spiti of Himachal Pradesh, Ladakh region, and a small part of the higher region of Sikkim. This land of the Himalayas is also known as the cold desert. It is popular for its bushy vegetation and the colourful Plateau. Since the beginning of the last century, man- made greenery, primarily populas, and majanu has expanded in these areas. Along with the medicinal plants, these areas also have rare species of wild animals such as snow leopard, musk deer, white bears, murand bharad, Himalayan thar, runda (Himalayan marus hair), monal and red beak crow birds.

Maha Himalayas – This area consists of 92 peaks, whose height is more than 8000 meter. It is spread between 3000 meter to the highest peak of 8000 meter. Most of its peaks are covered during the whole year with ice-cold snow. In the lap of their glaciers stretches to miles and at the same time, velvet buggy is also spread in places. Here the rich nature is reflected from Kai to wild flowers like, Brahmakamal, Fenkamal and medicinal plants such as Atis, Archa, Kadvi, Kedarpati, Google, Jatamasi, Nirvishi, Salampanja, Somlatta etc. This area is famous for the snow leopard, the shellfish and birds like monal. There is abundance of glaciers, which are also the source of many rivers in the country. This area is extremely sensitive. Its bugyaals are famous for pastures.

Middle Himalayas - The area after the Maha-Himalayas is called as the middle Himalayas. This is 1000 meter to 3000 meter wide and its length goes up to 75 kms. After bugyaals the area covered by trees starts. There are various species of Bhojpatra, oak (baanj), buranga kalpa, pangar, etc. The four-leaf forest and the Angular trees, shrubs, creepers, which absorb the rain in their own. Similarly, wild animals and birds also have a whole world in this area. Many streams originate from these forests. Below this is the strip of Bhabar and Shiwalik, which is known for its Himalayan Paradise.

Rainfall - From the point of view of the diversity of the weather, the Himalayas are divided into Eastern, Central and Western zones, where rainfall variation can also be seen. The **Eastern Zone** has the highest rainfall of 2500 mm to 5000 mm. **The Central Zone** has a rainfall from 2000 mm to 2500 mm. In the middle of the Western Zone and Shivalik the average rainfall remains between 1000 to 2000 mm, in the Great Himalayas it is between 600 to 1000 mm and 75 mm in the trans Himalayas. This diversity of climate has inspired the local inhabitants to adopt a different kind of lifestyle; however, nature is the main source of their livelihood and their life cycle. When nature is the primary part of their life, it is natural to have their inclination to protect it. Therefore, the general and intuitive tendency between varieties of variations can be seen from one end to the other that is the reasonably consumed nature and its maximum protection. There are many traditional customs and practices followed by the local people for the protection and promotion of glaciers, bugyaals and forests. Compliance of these eco-friendly practices can still be seen in almost all the villages of Uttarakhand.

Himalaya is at the center of the Indian culture and tradition as it is considered the abode of the various natural resources. Its soil, vegetation, water, forests etc. not only influence the human society living in the Himalaya but the entire population of the Indian sub-continent. It dictates the climate of the Asian sub-continent, and its forests act as filter for the anthropogenic produced carbon dioxide.

The Himalayan River System

Three major rivers emerge from Himalaya: these are Ganga, Brahmaputra and Indus and cover around 43 percent of the geographical area of the country and accounts for 63% of the total river water. Because of this, these rivers are called the fortunes of India as they are used for drinking water, irrigation, power generation and industrial activities.

Out of these rivers, the significance of the Ganga River is well evident. Compare to its significance towards our faith, our existence is more intimately associated with it. The influence of Ganga is spread over 26% area of the country and together with its tributaries, it contribute 25% of the total water budget. The catchment area of Ganga River is spread over nine states and supports around 41% of the total population. The major tributaries of the Ganga are not only the Bhagirathi and Alaknanda rivers, but also Yamuna, Tons, Gori-Dhauli (Sarda-Ghagar) and innumerable tributaries that contribute into it. Uttarakhand-Himachal Pradesh along with the country of Nepal contributes to the Himalayan watershed of the Ganga.

Threats to the River system

Himalaya is a very young mountain; hence, its break and growth are the inherent characteristic of this mountain. It is irresistible to human access and interference. Earthquake, landslides, avalanches, flood, Glacier Lake outburst and obstruction of rivers are inherent to its character. In view of this, the entire Himalaya is calamity prone and every year the frequency and magnitude of the loss of life and property is on rise. For the last six-seven decades, many threats and challenges have been developed for the rivers originating from the Himalayas. The following are the main reasons for that:

(i) The mega developmental projects going on in the Himalayan region.

(ii) Destruction of forests, construction of large projects and the vast expansion of roads in the sensitive areas.

(iii) Expansion of large cities in sensitive areas.
(iv) Increase in the number of population.
(v) Rapid mining of medicinal plants such as wormwood, kutki, atis, etc. from *Bugyaals* and *Himarekha* due to market pressure.
(vi) Mining in sensitive areas along the rivers.
(vii) Lack of compliance for laws made from environmental vision and finally.
(viii) Lack of political will.

For these reasons, Himalaya's sensitivity is increasing day by day. Due to this, continuous increase in the calamities is happening. Now the disasters are happening in every second or third year's intervals. These factors have increased the number of disasters for the Himalayan Rivers and the frequency of their recurrence is increasing day by day. On the other hand, astronomical and climate change is very difficult to control.

For the time being, even if we ignore calamities of 19th and 20th century, by the beginning of 21st century i.e. from 2000 to 2017 every year the terrain witnessed various form of calamity and it is rising linearly. For example, the flood of 2000 in Indus, Satluj and Siyang and Brahmaputra, or the breaching of 2004 Perchu Lake and subsequent flood in Satluj river, 2008 Kosi flood, or the floods in Tista, Manas, Gori, Leh, Ashi Ganga (a tributary of Bhagirathi river) are the floods that occurred during the last 10 to 15 years. All these floods have shown the sensitivity of the Himalaya towards human intervention.

The catastrophic June 2013 flood in the tributary of the Ganga River along with Kedarnath devastated the entire region. This calamity in Uttarakhand has compelled all of us to seriously analyse the prevailing situation. Similarly, the 2014-2015 floods in the former state of Jammu and Kashmir have forced us to reassess the sustainability/stability of our developmental schemes. These floods not only have destroyed the agriculture and economy of the local population but also have seriously affected the hydropower and irrigation schemes. The condition of the Himalaya (over sensitive to slight perturbation) is not only due to its inherent character, but there seems to be a significant contribution towards the observed calamity is due to the excessive human intervention. The over expansion of the consumer culture has put tremendous pressure on its natural resources. Therefore, a combination of natural and human interventions in Himalaya resulted in the serious problems, which are assisting in aggravating various calamities.

Suggestions to Protect Himalayan Ecology

Himalaya plays a major role in regulating the Indian sub-continent's climate. Any disturbance in this region has far-reaching impact on the land and people, who are not only inhabitants of the Himalaya, but also those living far away in the Indo-Gangetic plains. Therefore, there should be equilibrium between the developmental planning, local ecology, felt need of the local people and the fragility of the terrain.

However, the planning and implementation of development activities in the Himalayan regions is not being complied with complicated land structure, sensitive ecology and environment. Therefore, their proper documentation is not available, but on the contrary, it appears to have adverse effects in many areas, and it seems that most of our activities are spoiling our environment rather than promoting development. Determination of policies and programmes related to conservation, assessment and use of natural resources, mainly land, water and forest in the Himalayan regions cannot be determined without taking into account the local requirements and circumstances. That is why there prevails a huge discrepancy and imbalance.

Therefore, there is a need to make proper policy documentation in line with the requirements of local ecology and circumstances. Following are the prerequisites to achieve the above objectives:

(i) The first and foremost goal of development should be the all-round development of the Himalayas and any such activity should be discouraged, which is harmful for increasing the sensitivity of the Himalayan region.

(ii) A brochure should be prepared for making comprehensive assessment of major resources of the Himalayan regions, such as land, water and forest and their proper conservation, promotion and use should be made a part of the development process.

(iii) Implementation should be made with public participation; making effective coordination between the local conditions, people's need and the sensitivity of the area, and ensure effective role of local people's organisations.

(iv) The land use, forest and water policy for Himalayan areas should be focused on the continuous conservation and promotion of these natural resources and their various components, the first and universal authority of their reasonable use should be for local communities and subsequently other societies should get their benefit.

(v) Forest enhancement should focus on enhancing the productivity and concentration of forests, prominently in development programmes.

(vi) In the Himalayan region, agriculture is the traditional source of sustenance. However, the increasing reduction in agricultural areas and their scattered distribution has made it economically unviable. This is one of the major reasons for the migration of the local people. Therefore, there is a need to encourage such crops, which can fetch higher prices, are not damaged by the wild animals, have large demand in the market, easy to transport, and have longevity if kept for longer time. This requires innovation and experiment; hence, there need to be a plan to transmit new technology to the target population.

(vii) The impact of the climate change is quite evident in the Himalayan region. There is a growing concern about the recession of the Himalayan glaciers. There is a need to study the impact of climate change and its effect on the productivity. In addition, a database on this important aspect should be generated so that the comparative study can be undertaken at different times in order to evaluate its impact. Findings of such studies should be made public.

The developmental planning in the Himalaya should, therefore, resonate with its geological consideration and ecological/environmental sensitivity. In this region, the main focus of the development should be the holistic development of the Himalaya and any such developmental planning which enhances its fragility should be discouraged. Himalaya plays a major role in regulating the Indian sub-continent's climate. Any disturbance in this region has far reaching impact on the land and people, who are not only the inhabitants of the Himalaya but also on those living far in the Indo-Gangetic plains. Therefore, there should be equilibrium between the developmental planning, local ecology, felt need of the local people and the fragility of the terrain. In Himalayan region, ecological development should be kept at the center stage while going for the economic development so that ecological balance is maintained. The execution of the developmental planning should be carried out in a participatory mode in which the effected society and the local organisations must have a major role to play.

Institutional Structure

There is no formal institution at the state or national level for the coordinated environmental development in the Himalayan region. This could have formulated and coordinated planning pertaining to various issues in the region, and then implemented them in an organised manner. Such an institutional structure is essential which can formulate the developmental planning, secure financial assistance, help implementation and monitoring of the laws. The institution may also have power to intervene as and when required in consonant with the administrative machinery and make necessary programmes towards understanding the interstate conflicts related to the environmental development, social and economic growth.

In 1982, Government of India constituted a working group committee under Dr. M.S. Swaminathan to study the eco-development program in the Himalayan region. The working group recommended that under the chairpersonship of the Prime Minister, 'eco-development commission' should be constituted. However, the recommendation was not implemented. Considering that, the global climate is changing and the temperature is on rise, it is high time to constitute a high level Himalayan eco-development commission. The Prime Minister or the Vice-chairman of the Niti Aayog can head the commission. The member of the commission could be the Ministers-in-charge of finance, environment, agriculture, energy, transport, and also the concerned chief ministers and Niti Aayog members responsible for the hill region. The commission should be the apex body for the Himalayan region. The commission should have at least one meeting every year during which the report on the state of the Himalaya should be presented in front of the Niti Aayog so that a regional planning and evaluation of the Himalaya could be made.

A working committee should be formed which will work as an eco-development unit. This committee could be headed by a member of the Niti Aayog and comprise of secretaries from various Ministries viz. finance, environment, agriculture, energy, transport, and development commissioner and secretary planning from the Himalayan states should also be part of it. This working committee would keep information, monitor and give suggestions and orders related to short term and long term developmental schemes.

The working committee can assist in the eco-development of Himalaya. This committee should formulate the working plans and in every three months, the progress of the committee should be assessed. This committee can call upon the experts as and when required for consultation. Such an institutional structure can be created from village to state level. It is expected that such an institutional structure will pave the way for the development of the Himalayan region without inflicting any damage on the lifestyle of the local population.

Our last six-decade experiences in the Uttarakhand, the newly established state of the Central Himalayas, which is referred in Gita as a stabilising force, is that Himalaya is at risk due to the human behaviour and its increasing needs and greed. It is a collective crisis for the Indian sub-continent. This crisis is not only linked with the life and livelihood, but also concerned with the crisis of the Indian identity and human existence. We need to understand and bring changes in our behaviour accordingly. This is the message of the Chipko activists from the land of Chipko.

(This paper was presented at the International Conference organised by the Department of Economics & Politics, Visva-Bharati University, Santiniketan in January, 2019 and translated from Hindi by Dr. Prakash Chand, Assistant Professor, Dayal Singh Evening College, University of Delhi)

References

Bhatt, Chandi Prasad (2008), Some Points of Himalayan Environmental Protection, Promotion and Development. ISG newsletter - Indian Society of Geoinfomatics, December.

Bhatt, Chandi Prasad (2015), Himalayan Sensitivity and Present Crisis, Himalaya Popular Lecture Series. G. B. Pant Himalaya Institute of Environment and Development, Kosi Katarmal, Almora (Uttarakhand) 22 April.

Dasgupta, S. P. (1984), Basin Sub-basin Inventory of Water Pollution: The Ganga Basin, Part- 2, Centre for Study of Man and Environment, Central Board for the Preventing and Control of Water Pollution.

Government of India (1982), Report of the Taskforce for the Study of Eco-development in the Himalayan region. Planning Cmmission, New Delhi.

Government of India (2006), Report of the National Forest Commission, Ministry of Environment and Forests, New Delhi.

Pahadi Ramesh (2003), *Dasholi Village Swarajya Mandal* (Basis of Public Empowerment) Aniket Publication, New Delhi.

Uttarakhand Science and Technology Council (2011), Effect of Current Development Process on Environment and Common Man, in the Context of High Himalayas: Recommendations of the Seminar organised on 2-3 June 2011 jointly by Dasheri Village Swarajya Mandal and Uttarakhand Science and Technology Council.

3

Is the Sustainable Livelihoods Approach towards Development Interventions Truly Sustainable? An Assessment

Anup Sinha, Runa Sarkar

Abstract

During the last three decades or so, development interventions have changed significantly. The earlier top-down, state-driven, one cap-fits-all approach has been replaced by a more market friendly, private non-government organisations driven, bottom-up, context determined approach. This approach is often referred to as the Sustainable Livelihoods Approach (SLA). This paper argues that the SLA is a potentially effective microeconomic tool that seeks to enhance income and employment opportunities in poor and rural areas. The approach is consistent with mainstream neoclassical theory that focusses on optimisation through incremental change. The word 'sustainable', in the context of development, is a macroeconomic global concept from which microeconomic intervention designs must follow. The sustainable livelihoods approach, on the other hand, is independent of macro-constraints and can, at best, be a local solution. In SLA, the work 'sustainable' is used in the context of microeconomic continuity rather than the more broad based sustainable development as intergenerational equity. Moreover, we assert that the SLA, like neoclassical theory, is not suitable to guide an economy towards a sustainable development pathway, as it does not recognise the proverbial 'limits to growth'. Does sustainability call for an entirely new debate?

Key Words: *SLA, Sustainable Development, Watershed Development*

1. Introduction

A truly sustainable development intervention is one where the benefits from the intervention continue to persist long after the intervention is withdrawn, not only with respect to increased incomes of the people involved, but also with respect to an improvement in their social and ecological milieu. For this to be possible, the intervention must be able to plug in to the macroeconomic policy framework in a seamless manner, that is, the intervention should be consistent with the nation's growth story.

The Sustainable Livelihoods Approach (SLA) was devised as a mechanism by donor agencies particularly Department for International Development (DFID of the United Kingdom) to ensure that development was locally led, as it was believed that participation is the key to any development intervention being successful. In addition, if the development ideas were to emerge 'bottom up', social and ecological constraints would be embodied in the ideas themselves, since these participants were the long term stakeholders in the project.

In this paper we attempt to assess whether the SLA towards development interventions is truly sustainable. We start by providing a brief review of what the understanding of sustainable development has evolved in the context of development interventions, followed by an overview of the SLA. We then explain how the SLA fits into the neoclassical framework of economic theory, although the approach may not have been developed from a theoretical basis at all. We then critique the SLA. Although there is a lot of literature which has provided criticisms of the SLA, we attempt to critique the SLA from the point of view of how well the SLA fits into the growth story of an economy. This in turn leads us to the final concluding section that questions as to what extent neoclassical economics is helpful in understanding sustainable development.

2. Sustainable Development

Development is looked at as a structural break from an agrarian economy to an industrial-urban society. How this transformation could be brought about was the subject matter of the discipline of Development Economics. In this context the issues pertaining to rural-urban migration, relative wages, and the terms of trade between the two sectors have been discussed as sources of problems that could slow down the pace and extent of industrialisation. During the structural break, transitional problems of livelihoods of the rural poor could arise. For instance the number of jobs in the industrial sector available could be less than the number of job-seekers who wish to migrate to a new life. Or, it could be that despite some opportunities of alternative employment, people may find it too costly to migrate from their roots in the rural economy. Migration and mobility are dependent on a host of complex factors, some of which are structural, others quite personal. Problems of persisting poverty and worsening income distribution, viewed as something that could be addressed by markets and economic policies, have been discussed quite extensively by economists (Narayan and Glinskaya, 2007). The rate of economic growth was the critical number which would ultimately contribute to the resolution of all economic problems.

It was much later in the 1990s that serious questions began to be raised about the sustainability of the process of economic growth in the light of rapid depletion of exhaustible resources, the growing degradation of the natural environment, and threats to the quality of life of all living species (WCED, 1987). Nature as a constraint to economic growth began to be discussed more frequently. For example, Sheppard et. al. (2009, pp. 441) state "Industrialisation, particularly combined with long distance trade, engendered distinctive claim by humans on the earth's biophysical environment. First, industrialisation demands large quantities of cheap energy, available to order. The industrial revolution quickly exceeded the local availability of energy in the forms generally used today: biomass (fuel-wood, charcoal, animal power) and water power. It was rapidly determined that fossil fuels – coal, and later oil and natural gas – provided energy in forms that were easy to access, transportable to where they were needed and capable of producing a lot of energy quickly". On a similar note, Dasgupta (2009, pp. 4977-5046) opines "Are humanity's dealings with nature sustainable? Should one expect the global economic growth that has been experienced over the past five decades to continue in the foreseeable future? Should we be confident that knowledge and human skills will increase in such ways as to lessen our reliance on nature in relation to humanity's growing numbers and rising economic activity? Contemporary discussions on these questions are now several decades old. If they have remained alive and continue to be shrill, it is because two opposing empirical perspectives shape them. On the one hand, if we look at specific examples of natural capital (aquifers, ocean fisheries, tropical forests, the atmosphere as a carbon sink - or *ecosystems*, generally), there is convincing evidence that at the rates at which we currently exploit them they are very likely to change character dramatically for the worse, with little advance notice. Indeed many ecosystems have already collapsed, with short notice".

Another problem that has remained throughout the post-World War II period has been that the pace of industrialisation in many countries was significantly slower and much more problematic than that predicted by mainstream economic theory. The emergence of modern economic growth through the transformation of the agricultural sector remained uneven, incomplete and sporadic (Amin, 1976; Frank, 1978). The experience of economic growth in these developing countries (as opposed to developed countries) was, from the very beginning, marked by widespread poverty, deprivation and inequality (Ahmad et. al., 1991).

The standard response to such problems by policy-makers during the 1960s, 1970s and 1980s was to plan for interventions that would alleviate poverty, much of which was located in rural areas of these economies. Such types of interventions did not have much of an impact in general – hampered by corruption or ill-designed interventions which were not appropriate to the context in which they were being implemented (Lipton, 1977). The implementing agents (usually government) were in many cases singularly inefficient and uninvolved, with no incentive to ensure proper delivery. The involvement of the local people or the direct beneficiaries for whom the project was supposed to be designed was absent. Their acceptance of a project was taken for granted. In this topdown approach to solving social and economic issues, it was believed one solution could be appropriate for all problems. Such an approach in particular and planning systems in general came under critical scrutiny. By the 1990s, the pattern of development interventions shifted (Krugman, 1994). With the collapse of the Soviet Union, there was a resurgence of faith in markets. The role and presence of non-governmental organisations (NGO) increased substantially. Their style of intervention was supposedly more people-based (bottom up), designed for specific contexts, and the creation of jobs (or livelihoods) more sustainable in the use of ecological services. Hence the aggregate, one-size-fits-all approach was replaced by a more decentralised, contextual, microeconomic one where the beneficiaries had some say in the design of local solutions.

However, there was one thing common to both these approaches. There was a tacitly, shared belief underlying the two distinct approaches that ultimately macro-economic growth would be able to solve the problem of modernisation, industrialisation and a higher standard of living for all people in the economy. The problems of rural poverty and unemployment could at best be described as intrinsically transient in character. It was believed that these interventions would keep macroeconomic growth unhindered even if the structural break was not patently evident.

3. Sustainable Livelihoods Approach

Since the 1990s there have been many kinds of development interventions. Most, if not all these interventions, depended on local participation of the people and the leveraging of local markets. The objective was to link resources to people, and people to markets. A commonly used framework (with some variants) for interventions is the well-known SLA. This framework was largely developed by researchers at the Institute of Development Studies (IDS) (Ahmed and Lipton, 1997; Arce, 2003; Bebbington, 1999; Carney, 1998; Chambers and Conway, 1992) and is widely practised in tackling the lack of adequate jobs and incomes arising from the fundamental problem of inadequate or insufficient industrialisation. Knutsson (2006) goes on to elaborate the appeal of SLA as a concept for donor institutions: "Only five years after the formal introduction of the sustainable livelihoods concept by Robert Chambers and Gordon Conway in 1991, important donor institutions such as Care, Oxfam, the United Nations' Development Programme (UNDP), and the UK Department of International Development (DFID) had adopted the *Sustainable Livelihoods Approach* (SLA) as basis for their development programmes and practices". SLA heralded the inclusion of environmental concerns in development programming and a shift away from a static approach to poverty towards one which embraced the role of partnerships of the government with NGOs to combat it (Solesbury, 1999).

The SLA is a comprehensive *framework* for development interventions. It is not a development theory but a problem solving mechanism, suitably contextualised to local conditions. Two things are worth noting about the SLA. First, the entire approach does not view development as a process that unfolds through social and economic changes over time, but rather as something that is the result of appropriate actions. Changes are viewed as essentially quantitative though some qualitative dimensions give the approach a normative flavour. The second aspect of SLA is in the use of the word 'sustainable'. The SLA literature admits that sustainability is a contested term and does not have any precise, accepted definition (de Haan, 2000, de Haan and Zoomers 2005). The framework views sustainability in a dual sense. Sustainable livelihoods are income and employment that can be reproduced over time even in the face of unpredictable and adverse shocks. The other aspect of sustainability is that in creating livelihoods for people, the local environment or ecology (natural capital) is not destroyed. The two taken together is a strong requirement, especially when viewed as an intervention on a small scale –say in the context of a village, or a cluster of a few villages.

Scoones (1998) provides a summary framework of SLA which remains a standard reference. The SLA attempts to integrate theory from various disciplines while taking a systems approach to viewing a developmental problem and combines a variety of methodologies bringing together and coordinating with an assortment of institutions to solve the problem. The most commonly quoted definition of sustainable livelihoods from Chambers and Conway (1992, pp.7) reads: " A livelihood comprises the capabilities, assets (stores, resources, claims and access) and activities required for a means of living: a livelihood is sustainable which can cope with and recover from stress and shocks, maintain or enhance its capabilities and assets and provide sustainable livelihood opportunities for the next generation; and which contributes net benefits to other livelihoods at the local and global levels and in the short and long-terms". The DFID has built its operational strategies around Scoone's framework (Solesbury, 2003). It covers an extensive set of issues and includes both operational aspects of processes and measures of outcomes.

The description of the framework that follows draws heavily from Scoone's paper. It consists of five interrelated stages which are shown in Figure 1. Underlying this framework there is a pre-analytical position that rural livelihoods are inadequate in terms of income and employment. However, livelihoods can be improved with the use of resources available

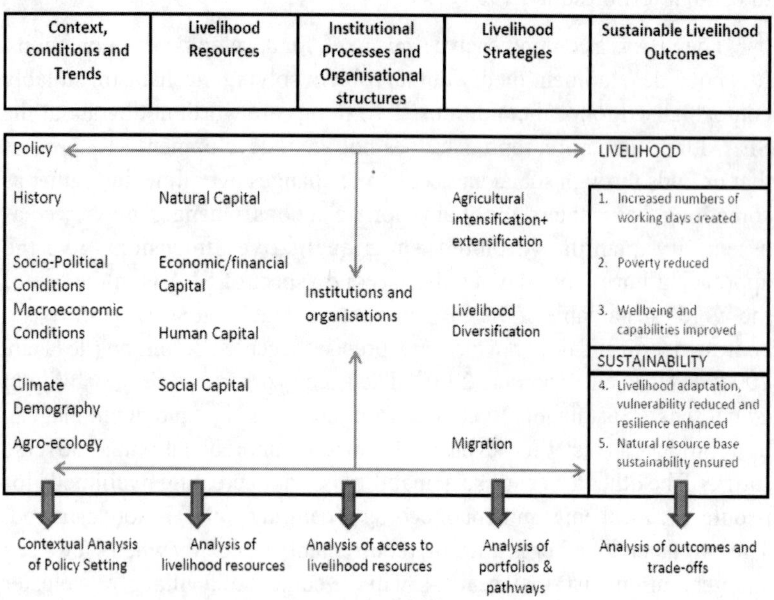

Source: Adapted from Scoones, I. 1998 'Sustainable Rural Livelihoods: A Framework for Analysis'. IDS Working Paper. Brighton: Institute of Development Studies.

Figure 1: A Schematic describing the SLA Framework

in the local environment. The intervention is not a topdown set of instructions from a manual, but something that evolves through the participation of the ultimate beneficiaries of development. Left to their own socioeconomic devices the people would not be able to generate the change themselves. Hence there is a justification for a catalyst that maps the untapped local possibilities and triggers people's participation. Scoones uses the Chambers and Conway (1992) definition of a sustainable livelihood as the capabilities and assets (both material and social) that are required for a living. To be sustainable this living must be capable of exhibiting resilience in the face of shocks. The assets and their uses must not undermine the natural resource base available to the beneficiaries. Hence, there are three requirements: first, the possession of a minimum set of capabilities and assets, second, the capabilities and assets must be adequate, quantitatively, to withstand shocks, and the use of these capabilities and assets must not destroy natural capital.

Before any intervention can be designed and made operational, the framework stresses the importance of understanding the context within which the changes in livelihood strategies are to be brought about. The context is conceived in the widest sense of the term – it includes institutions, local history and politics, socio-economic conditions and demography, as well as, the natural climate and agroecology. Once the context is set, there is a need to analyse the availability of livelihood resources which are essentially the stocks of all productive capital, starting from natural and economic capital to human and social capital. Social institutions determine the sharing and exchanging of productive capital. The task is to design (by involving local people) a new set of feasible and superior economic opportunities that would augment or alter their current portfolio of activities. If any new knowledge or skill is required, it is to be provided by the intervening agency. The framework looks at livelihood strategies in terms of three (broadbanded) pathways through which the new opportunities can alter activity portfolios. These are changes in agricultural practices through more intensive or extensive cultivation, diversification of income earning activities, and migration away from the geography.

Finally, the framework focuses on the outcomes of the development intervention. The outcomes are categorised into two distinct sets. The first set is described as livelihood outcomes and can be measured, or at least observed. It includes, for instance, the increase in persondays of employment created, increase in income (or reduction in poverty) and an improvement in capabilities such as education, or access to health care. The second set is the sustainability indicators and a lot harder to measure or even observe in any systematic fashion. This set includes livelihood adaptation, enhancement of resilience, and creation of a sustainable (non-decreasing) natural resource base.

When assessing a particular activity as a livelihood, the framework stresses the importance of viewing it as a sequence of actions. That sequence would require certain kinds of capital that, in turn would have to be acquired or tradedoff against some existing stock. Another related question in this context is whether the activity is a standalone activity, or part of a cluster of activities that can be pursued together to gain advantages of scope. Finally, there is the issue of access to institutions and resources that is likely to be determined by economic wealth and political power. Many social institutions do not allow universal inclusion on the lines of caste or religion, and access requires greater power or wealth. The process through which the sequence of actions has to be navigated is critical for the success of outcomes. The emphasis on processes in addition to measurable outcomes makes the SLA more people-based (Leach et. al., 1999). Yet, this particular aspect makes it complex and messy. It can mean anything and everything that determines human interactions and exchanges.

The institutions could vary from formal to very informal ones, and they could operate at different levels from the local to the national. Understanding the interactions of, and developing processes to work with (or around) an existing set of institutions can take a long time. Scoones (1998) claims that this general framework is operationally convenient as it provides opportunities for interventions at different levels from the very micro level of a particular economic activity to bigger interventions, involving changes in agricultural practices, off-farm opportunities and migration. Hence, for Scoones, development is about the outcomes of appropriate interventions in the market economy.

4. Applying the SLA to the Implementation of a Watershed Development Project in Odisha

Turton (2000) writes about a DFID project in 4 districts in western Odisha, which contributed to the Government of India's (GoI) effort to eliminate poverty by supporting its watershed development programme, executed in the late 1990s, where elements of the SLA were applied. The project districts were among the poorest in India despite receiving greater than average rainfall, and having higher than average land holdings as compared to the rest of the state. There was a skewed control over land and water in the chosen area, with 10% of the landed community controlling 35% of all natural resources. This 10% also controlled informal credit, transport, input and output markets and migratory labour contracts. Coupled with variable rainfall patterns this led to high prevailing rates of interest, chronic indebtedness and moneylenders controlling both land and bonded labour. In addition, people were accustomed to seeking relief from the government for their survival on a routine basis.

The objective of any watershed development is to increase the productivity of land (both common pool, for grasing or forests and agricultural) in undulated and semi-arid areas. A combination of water conservation and soil re-vegetation measures (in the upper slopes) are deployed to replenish the fertility of soil, which in turn could reduce poverty as the land becomes more productive. Simple structures such as contour bunds and check-dams are built along the watershed to ensure that water is retained after rain falls within this land, so as to recharge the water table, which could contribute to irrigation. Since these measures could result is lesser water flow into the lower lying more fertile lands, owned by more affluent and usually more powerful people, there is a need for government intervention to initiate and supervise the sequencing of watershed rehabilitation activity. Further, the process is highly decentralised with villages preparing a rehabilitation plan to be approved by the implementing agency and villagers signing off the disbursement to contractors in phases as work is completed. This is in recognition of the difficulty faced by poorer people in ensuring that their needs are met in the rehabilitation plans: the extended preparatory period is allocated to 'entry point' activities – generally group-based savings, credit and other activities undertaken by the poor, supplemented by training in the skills necessary for leadership, accounting, conflict resolution and so on. In this way, the intention is to strengthen the capability of poorer groups to press forward their requirements in the potentially more contentious areas of watershed rehabilitation.

The SLA substantially broadened the scope of the watershed development activity to emphasize participation at all levels, catalysed through the deployment of a livelihood support team in each community to build capacity and facilitate negotiation of resource rights for the poor and vulnerable over and above the recommended project deployment mechanisms suggested by the GoI. Turton (2000) says "The key lies in identifying an appropriate mix of 'escape routes' from poverty, drawing in elements of NR-based intensification; activities largely *non* land-based, and labour-based strategies. If this is to be achieved, people's capital assets will have to be strengthened, and vulnerability reduced, in an appropriate sequence." The project started with investing in strengthening capital assets such as domestic water supply and sanitation, and promoting backyard activities for the landless to reduce their vulnerability and build confidence. The more contentious areas of designing the watershed activity followed, by which time the poor and landless had more confidence and basic livelihood security to sustain lengthy negotiations.

Turton (2000) surmises that the SLA broadened the perspective of the team members in Odisha, encouraging them to think deeply about why the poor in that part of the country were struggling to secure a livelihood. Specifically, the capital assets component of the SLA framework helped in integrating insights into the nature of poverty with implications of the potential project approaches. This led to the realisation that improving the natural resource endowment (which is at the centre of any watershed development project) is not enough; it was essential to empower the poor and build capacity to enable their participation in institutional processes. An extended preparatory period of a year was allocated to activities such as group-based savings undertaken by the poor, supplemented by training in leadership, accounting and conflict resolution skills, so as to ensure that the watershed development activity truly empowers them. The team realised the need to be flexible in their approaches allowing local communities to prioritise project interventions, which were often non land based. Further, the need to link into the wider range of social and economic opportunities and government programmes were emphasised by the SLA.

The SLA framework worked well in Odisha to integrate perspectives and understand complex interactions, through which it could highlight the importance of non-land based activities for the poor. The inter-relationships between communities and watersheds and the potential conflict between different livelihood strategies were underlined. It emphasized the need to make external linkages beyond the project area (rural-urban linkages, for example) for the initiative to be truly sustainable. Finally, it recognised the need to achieve a balance between policies at the macroeconomic level and actions at the microeconomic level, recognising that the former relates to long term interventions while the latter can only meet short term immediate needs.

5. SLA as Compatible with Neoclassical Economic Theory

"SLA is an example of an approach founded on good theory driven by an understandable desire to link intervention to evidence, but there can be a tendency for good theory to obscure the equal need for good practice based upon that theory" (Morse et. al., 2009). The emphasis on incremental incomes, asset accumulation, linking individuals to markets and using nature to generate incomes implies that the approach is embedded within a market based economic structure, and is actually quite consistent with mainstream (neoclassical) economic theory. We now critique this body of theory in the context of ecology-economy interactions.

Neoclassical economic theory is based on the logic of allocating scarce resources according to price signals from markets. The principle of analysis is based on understanding incremental (marginal) effects and local stability conditions. There are a number of problems with this approach. It was developed when the abundance of nature was taken for granted. Nature was not only a gigantic gift-hamper which one could dip into for resources (often freely available like fresh water and clean air) but also a gigantic garbage bin where the wastes created in the processes of production and consumption could be dumped without costs. Resource allocation decisions by economic agents –firms (suppliers) and households (demanders) would be on the basis of market prices. The use of marginal analysis gives the notion of an optimal size for each activity carried out by firms and households. There is an optimal production where profits are maximised; there is an optimal consumption where utility is maximised. The notion of optimality comes from acknowledging the presence of constraints imposed by the larger system where the smaller units are embedded. New firms can enter the market and old ones wind up. A similar process of growth and decay exists for households too.

However, while microeconomic units have an optimal scale of operations determining the size, the macro-economy (where the micro units are embedded) has no scale. The value of production can grow indefinitely, measured by GDP. The macro-economy is not seen as embedded in anything at all. It is the whole. Prices determine the relative proportions of resources used, and getting that correct is considered the most important problem the economy has to solve. Neoclassical theories allow for continuous growth of GDP through capital accumulation, growth of the labour force, and technological progress. The neoclassical theory of resource allocation per se does not require economic growth, but growth is seen as a solution to the chronic economic problems a market economy throws up – poverty, unemployment, and distributional inequity. The standard analogies found in discussions on the significance of growth are – a rising tide lifts all boats, or a larger cake means the possibility of a larger slice for all. However, continuous growth has not solved the chronic problems of poverty and unemployment. It has also been claimed that as economic growth takes place and incomes increase, society learns to value natural capital as more than just being instrumental in creating flows of income (Kuznets, 1955; Economist Sep 14, 2013). The improvement in some measures of pollution in developed countries has often resulted simultaneously in more pollution in developing countries as the more polluting industries and technologies have shifted to lower income economies.

Neoclassical theory allows for two qualifications to this analytical vision. First, GDP is actually a value index – the product of price and quantity. The quantity could be that of a tangible product (good) or something not tangible but whose effect is useful (service). If we consider real GDP (at constant prices) growth of GDP could mean either of two things. It could represent an increase in the physical quantity of a product (say computers) or an improvement in its quality. The quality change would be implied by a reduction in material or energy intensity of production or improved performance. In the latter situation the value added of the product improves, that is, the services provided by the computer increases. Since services are embodied in someone or something for some period of time, their expansion also cannot be indefinite (Wernick et. al., 1996).

The second qualification in neoclassical economics is that economic activities have bystander effects on society (externalities) that create a wedge between private costs and benefits on the one hand, and social costs and benefits on the other. These are referred to as instances of market failure. These externalities could be things such as pollution-creating emissions or effluents that cause damage to the environment, as well as damage to human health and property. In such situations, state intervention is required in terms of taxes to include marginal social costs in marginal private costs. The use of marginal analysis clearly looks for local solutions by setting the marginal damage costs of negative externalities equal to the marginal costs of abatement (Kolstad, 2010; Harris, 2006). Hence pollution, determined by this principle, could be positive but set at an optimal level. Scale effects are just not considered (Costanza et. al., 1997). In short, neoclassical environmental economics does not take into account the total impact of the damaging effects of economic activity on ecology and bio-physical limits in any systematic way (Sengupta, 2013). Moreover, marginal analysis is meaningful only for linear systems. Most scientists are of the opinion that ecological systems display non-linear characteristics (Rockström et. al., 2012). All damage to the environment is not reversible. Thresholds may be crossed beyond which the system tips into nonincremental change, and could also completely collapse.

There is some scepticism about GDP being an adequate measure of wellbeing, which has led to the use of a number of alternative measures (Kerschner 2006). When one takes into account the value of the external damages (negative externalities) caused by economic growth, there is evidence indicating that economic growth may have actually reduced wellbeing. Like neoclassical economics, the SLA also does not treat the ecology as a system which might limit growth. The systemic limits that could be imposed by physical constraints or even the possibility of a zero growth society (stationary state) have been extensively discussed by the earlier classical economists from Adam Smith to David Ricardo and John Stuart Mill (Smith, 1801; Ricardo, 1817; Mill, 1888). Other economists like Malthus and Marx looked at the instability of the macro-economy with roots in physical and institutional limits (Malthus, 1993(1798); Marx, 1976). Some modern economists like Daly and Georgescu-Roegen have analysed the biophysical and social constraints to growth more deeply (Daly, 1992, 1996; Georgescu-Roegen, 1971).

6. Is the Sustainable Livelihoods Approach Truly Sustainable?

Livelihoods are about living and ultimately about living well, and should be more than just acquiring assets and earning incomes (Polanyi, 2001; Sen, 2000). This means that people must be able to comprehend the environment in which they live and work. If necessary, they should also be able to challenge the existing rules of the game that regulate the control, distribution and transformation of resources. While the SLA may be an expression of the desire for evidence based interventions and policy design, it still has to operate within a complex mess of other regulations, policies and social circumstances, which undermines its impact at a broader level. The SLA, thus, is not an integrated theory of development (Morse et. al., 2009). Small (2007) concludes that "[a]lthough it draws together a number of themes from current international development thought, it does not integrate these ideas into a theoretically consistent whole. Processes of social change are left undefined. This is particularly problematic for an approach that actively seeks to use and intervene in these processes". By design, SLA has a microeconomic focus. The sum totals of these interventions do not add up to a macroeconomic picture of transformation. It merely reveals a patchwork of activities where some people and some assets are brought together.

If it is not a theory of transformation and it does not contest or question the larger social institutions that govern resource allocation and economic power, then the people-centred approach for providing more income or assets becomes a way of subtle persuasion to accept the macroeconomic situation and work within that framework to maximize individual economic returns. The capability to leverage opportunities, handle conflicts and question the rules of the game is not addressed by SLA. It is evident from figure 1 that 'people' do not enter the scheme of things though they are supposedly at the centre of all activities from the inception of a project to its sustained flow of benefits. When dealing with people, complicated issues of power, class, caste, ethnicity, community and gender become unavoidable. These cannot be subsumed in the black box of local institutions (both formal and informal). These issues are more basic since they contribute to the configuration of power within institutions (Rowland, 1997).

Our critique of SLA so far has been that it is more a corrective tool of intervention than a way of initiating any systematic transformation. It boils down to creating access to markets, making available more credit, altering the input-output mix in agriculture and changing the portfolio of activities in facilitating what could be described as a microcosmic capitalism (Herrera, 2006). This microcosmic capitalism has a number of implications. First, more often than not, these interventions are biased in favour of people who have greater endowments to begin with. Hence, over time, the local distribution of wealth and income actually worsens (Sarkar and Sinha, 2015, Bateman, 2010). This might weaken the overall stability and strength of the local community.

The second implication is that it necessarily ignores the notion of community or collective in a very fundamental sense. The household with its own internal distributional dynamics is no longer taken to be an indivisible unit. Indeed, this is very evident from the fact that most development projects have some activity exclusively designed for women. This trend towards individualisation breaks down the households into men, women and children. Each can have different goals and interests, and pursue different livelihoods. Individual goals and household goals may differ, as may goals across households.

Finally, livelihoods may change because of external opportunities, individual confidence, or new capabilities. This constant weighing of strategy against available options is done through a set of negotiations with oneself as well as with the external environment. The interventions boil down to several short term changes covering a set of individuals without any emergent discernible pattern.

The most important of these inconsistencies can be seen when one views the role that nature and natural capital is supposed to play in the

SLA. Rather than viewing all economic activities and livelihood sources as ultimately embedded in nature, SLA views natural capital as one kind of marketable productive capital that has instrumental value in providing income. This capital can be substituted with other forms of capital, and choices can be made. This view of looking at nature as having a purely instrumental value can be problematic. An example will suffice. Land can have alternative sustainable uses. How is the use, or perhaps the mix of uses, going to be decided? Sarkar and Sinha (2015) discuss a case where the dust from quarrying for granite as an economic activity was playing havoc with a cluster of villages that was trying to integrate its natural resource base in terms of a mutually interrelated set of sustainable activities. It was a classic example of market failure a negative externality. The solution requires looking at ecosystems as a whole rather than drawing the boundary of a project in terms of a village or a cluster of houses. If nature and ecology has to be the basis of sustainability, then any intervention must begin by marking out the appropriate boundary. This is where the knowledge or experience of the development agency might come in useful. Otherwise, merely pointing out to existing opportunities would tantamount to an implicit assumption that the participating people are quite ignorant of their own local economy. The SLA starts with identifying livelihoods and then looks at those which are most sustainable, that is, it looks at the problem from the inside out, whereas sustainability requires that an outside-in approach be taken.

If sustainable development is only about alleviation of poverty for the current generation living on the planet, then the SLA makes sense. The approach moves away from the top down, mechanistic designs that almost "force feed" economic development to the poor. SLA can involve local people; build on their ideas and resources, creating a synergy within which new activities could be started with some help from the organisation coordinating the SLA. Incomes can increase and the vulnerability of the poor to external economic shocks could be reduced. However, sustainable development means something more; the welfare of future generations, the preservation of bio-diversity, the continuous reduction in pollution and the halting of degradation of the natural environment. It is a macroeconomic outcome where all the micro activities need to be consistent with the macro objective of sustainability.

Sustainable development is inherently inter-disciplinary in character. It has to base itself on scientific data, understand complex ecosystems, involve people, influence policy-makers and above all, be able to change society's behaviour towards the natural environment. SLA is undoubtedly interdisciplinary too. However, it is not designed as a part of a complex system of interaction of nature and society. It is more contextual in the sense of understanding local needs and local aspirations only. The evolution of interactive outcomes and the impact on the future of life on the planet is not usually taken into consideration.

Another area where the SLA is different from a more macro strategy of sustainable development is that the former does not focus much on savings. It is more concerned with income generation from new activities with available local resources. However, sustainable development is essentially about savings that will at the least take care of depreciation. The stock of capital that is to be bequeathed to the next generation has to be non-decreasing. Savings can vary with incomes as well as the impatience, or what is technically referred to as the rate of time preference, of individuals. There is nothing in-built in the SLA approach that focuses on savings. Poor people with low and uncertain incomes are typically observed to be more impatient. Tonight's dinner is more important for them than saving something to ensure tomorrow's dinner. In other words, the present outcomes are more important than future ones. On the other hand even if a person is willing to save for himself or his immediate family, it is not likely that he will save for the protection of the welfare of other (possibly unknown) people. This is where society has to discount the future at a rate much lower than that of an individual who saves for personal reasons. These issues are not part of the SLA.

7. Does Sustainability Call for an Entirely New Debate?

There is a more fundamental question that remains, over and above the macro-micro inconsistency that constrains SLA as an adequate strategy for sustainable development. The question is whether a capitalist market economy with its highly individualised incentive structures is at all equipped with institutions and foresight to move on to a pathway of sustainable development. Anything to do with the future revolves around personal gains and losses. Welfare of all living beings (including those yet to be born) never forms a part of any objective function of any agent in a capitalist economy. An implication of this leads to a bigger debate about whether a new system would be required to ensure sustainable development – a more radical integration of ecology and economics, where planning for the future is to be given priority over current needs. Capitalism is based on possessive individualism. It does not have the capacity to generate collective savings for the future of the world. Our inability to do anything significant in tackling the threat of climate change is a good example.

SLA might not have been under the scrutiny of what it does for the future, if the word 'sustainable' had not been used in describing the approach to development. It does pass the test as a novel and arguably superior strategy to alleviate short-term poverty and inadequate incomes. It does not do so when it is put under the lens as a long-term solution to sustainable development.

References

Ahmad, Etisham et al (1991), *Social Security in Developing Countries,* New Delhi: Oxford University Press.

Ahmed, Ismail and Michael Lipton (1997): "Impact of Structural Adjustment on Sustainable Rural Livelihoods: A Review of Literature," *IDS Working Paper,* No. 62, Brighton: Institute of Development Studies.

Amin, Samir (1976): *Unequal Development,* London: Monthly Review Press.

Arce, Alberto (2003): "Value Contestations in Development Interventions: Community Development and Sustainable Livelihood Approaches," *Community Development Journal*, Vol. 38, No. 3, pp. 199–212.

Bateman Milford (2010): Why Doesn't Microfinance *Work? The Destructive Rise of Local Neoliberalism,* New York: Zed Books.

Bebbington, Anthony (1999): "Capitals and Capabilities: A Framework for Analysing Peasant Viability, Rural Livelihoods and Poverty," *World Development,* Vol. 27, No. 12, pp. 2021–44.

Carney, Diane ed. (1998), *Sustainable Rural Livelihoods. What Contribution can we Make?*, Nottingham: Russell Press Ltd.

Chambers, Robert and Gordon R. Conway (1992): "Sustainable Rural Livelihoods: Practical Concepts for the 21st Century," *IDS Discussion Paper*, No. 296, Brighton: Institute of Development Studies.

Costanza, Robert et al (1997): *The Development of Ecological Economics,* Cheltenham,UK: Edward Elgar.

Daly, Herman E. (1992): *Steadystate Economics,* London: Earthscan Publications Ltd.

Daly, Herman E. (1996): *Beyond Growth: The Economics of Sustainable Development,* Boston MA, Beacon Press.

Dasgupta, Partha (2009): The Place of Nature in Economic Development, in Handbook of Development Economics, Vol. 5, edited by Dani Rodrik and Mark Rosenzweig (Amsterdam: North Holland).

deHaan, Leo J. (2000): "Globalisation, Localisation and Sustainable Livelihood," *SociologiaRuralis*, Vol. 40, No. 3, pp. 339–365.

deHaan, Leo J. and AnneliesZoomers (2005): "Exploring the Frontier of Livelihood Research," *Development and Change,* Vol. 36, No. 1, pp. 27–47.

Economist (2013): All Creatures Great and Small, *Hang onBiodiversity Special report,* Sep 14. downloaded from http://www.economist.com/node/21585091/print

Frank, Andre G. (1978): *Dependent Accumulation and Underdevelopment,* London: Macmillan.

GeorgescuRoegen, Nicholas (1971). *The Entropy Law and the Economic Process*, Cambridge MA: Harvard University Press.

Harris, Jonathan M (2006): Environmental and Natural Resource Economics: A Contemporary Approach, 2nd edition, Boston: Houghton Mifflin.

Herrera, Rémy (2006): "The Neoliberal 'Rebirth' of Development Economics", *Monthly Review*, Vol. 58, No. 1, pp. 3850.

Kerschner, Christian.(2006): "The Steady State Economy: The Only Path to a Sustainable Future?," *EconomicaCritica,* downloaded from http://pendientedemigracion.ucm.es/info/ec/jec10/ponencias/410kerschner.pdf

Knutsson, P., Ostwald, M. A (2006): Process-Oriented Sustainable Livelihoods Approach–A Tool for Increased Understanding of Vulnerability, Adaptation and Resilience. *Mitig Adapt Strat Glob Change*, https://doi.org/10.1007/s11027-006-4421-9

Kolstad, Charles (2000): *Environmental Economics*, New York: Oxford University Press.

Krugman, Paul (1994): "The Fall and Rise of Development Economics", Rodwin, L. and D. Schon (eds.), *Rethinking the Development Experience: Essays Provoked by the Work of Albert O. Hirschman*, Washington (D.C.): Brookings Institution, pp. 39-58.

Kuznets, Simon (1955):"Economic Growth and Income Inequality,"*American Economic Review*, Vol. 45, No. 1, pp. 1–28.

Leach, Melissa et al (1999): "Environmental Entitlements: Dynamics and Institutions in Community-based Natural Resource Management," *World Development*, Vol. 27, No. 2, pp. 225-247.

Lipton, Michael (1977): *Why Poor People Stay Poor: A Study of Urban Bias in World Development*, London: Temple Smith.

Malthus, Thomas R. (1993 (1798)): *An Essay on the Principle of Population,* Oxford/New York: Oxford University Press.

Marx, Karl (1976): *Capital Volume 1*, New York: International Publishers.

Mill, John Stuart (1888): *Principles of Political Economy with Some of their Applications to Social Philosophy,* London: Longmans, Green, & Co.

Morse, Stephen et al (2009):"Sustainable Livelihood Approach: A Critical Analysis of Theory and Practice," *Geographical Paper*, No. 189, The University of Reading, UK. downloaded from http://www.reading.ac.uk/web/FILES/geographyandenvironmentalscience/GP189.pdf

Narayan, Deepa and Elena Glinskaya (2007): *Ending Poverty in South Asia : Ideas That Work,* Washington, DC: World Bank.

Polanyi, Karl (2001):*The Great Transformation: the Political and Economic Origins of Our Time,* Boston, MA: Beacon Press.

Ricardo, David (1817): *On the Principles of Political Economy and Taxation. The Works and Correspondence of David Ricardo,* P. Sraffa (ed.). Cambridge: Cambridge University Press.

Rockström, Johanet al(2009): "Planetary Boundaries: Exploring the Safe Operating Space for Humanity,"*Ecology and Society*, Vol. 14, No. 2: 32.

Rowland, Jo (1997): *Questioning Empowerment: Working with Women in Honduras*, Oxford: Oxfam.

Sarkar, Runa and AnupSinha (2015): *Another Development: Participation, Empowerment and Well-being in Rural India,* New Delhi: Routledge.

Scoones, Ian (1998): "Sustainable Rural Livelihoods: A Framework for Analysis," *IDS Discussion Paper*, No. 72, Brighton: Institute of Development Studies.

Sen, Amartya (2000): *Development as Freedom*, New Delhi: Oxford University Press.

Sengupta, Ramprasad (2013): *Ecological Limits and Economic Development: Creating Space,* New Delhi: Oxford University Press.

Sheppard, Eric et al (2009): *World of Difference: Encountering and Contesting Development 2nd edition*, New York: The Guilford Press.

Small, Lee-Ann (2007):"The Sustainable Rural Livelihoods Approach: A Critical Review," *Canadian Journal of Development Studies / Revue canadienned'études du développement*, Vol. 28, No. 1, pp. 27-38.

Smith, Adam (1801): *An Inquiry into the Nature and Causes of the Wealth of Nations*, Paris: Basil.

Solesbury, William (2003): "Sustainable livelihoods: a Case Study of the Evolution of DFID Policy," Working Paper 217, London: Overseas Development Institute. downloaded from http://www.odi.org/sites/odi.org.uk/files/odiassets/publicationsopinionfiles/172.pdf

Solesbury, William. (1999): Sustainable Livelihoods: A Case Study of the Evolution of DFID Policy. OD1Working Paper 217. London: Overseas Development Institute.

Turton, C. (2000). Sustainable Livelihoods and Project Design in India, ODI Working Paper 127, London: Overseas Development Institute.

WCED (1987): *Our Common Future*, Report of the World Commission on Environment and Development, New York: United Nations.

Wernick, I. K. et al (1996): "Materialisation and Dematerialisation: Measures and Trends,"*Daedalus*, Vol. 125, No. 3, pp. 171–198.

4

Dependency on Natural Resources and Sustainable Resource Management: A Study of Bankura District

Nilendu Chatterjee, Dipak Kundu and Debabrata Dey

Abstract

The paper attempts to provide a comprehensive study on the dependency on natural resources of the district of Bankura and provides a guideline to achieve sustainability so far as dependency on natural resources is concerned. It focuses mainly on two natural resources: forestry and drinking water on which people in our study area are heavily dependent. The paper starts with a discussion on few aspects of irrigation and forestry in our study area and after that it considers a profile of our study area, based on field survey, to discuss the socio-economic features of the people residing in that area. The paper also considers some methodological issues in terms of dynamic optimisation model, absolute convergence and contingent valuation method the results of which have strong implications from the point of view of policy analysis in our study area.

Key Words: *Dependency, Sustainability, Dynamic Optimisation, Convergence, Contingent Valuation, Willingness to Pay.*

1. Introduction

The world's drylands are fragile ecosystems due to harsh climatic conditions and growing human pressures. Yet, they constitute some of the world's largest land reserves and provide a wide range of goods and services which are fundamental to the livelihoods of millions of people. The semi-arid and arid regions are situated in the tropical and sub-tropical parts of the world and they account for almost 30% of the world's total area and around 20% of the total population. According to the World Atlas of Desertification (UNEP, 1992), drylands have a ratio of average annual precipitation (P) to potential evapotranspiration (PET) of less than 0.65. In fact, according to the report of Food and Agricultural Organisation (FAO) in 1993, drylands are categorised into hyper arid, arid, semi-arid and dry sub-humid zones not only on the basis of P/PET ratio but also on the basis of rainfall (in mm.). Thus, when P/PET ratio is less than 0.05 and rainfall is less than 200 mm, the dryland is referred to as Hyper-arid. Again when P/PET ratio lies between 0.05 to 0.20 with rainfall less than 200 mm. in winter and 400 mm. in summer, it is considered as arid zone. The next categorisation is Semi-arid zone for which P/PET ratio lies between 0.20 and 0.50 with rainfall less than 200-500 mm. in winter and less than 400-600 mm. in summer. Finally, when P/PET ratio lies between 0.50 and 0.65 with rainfall less than 500-700 mm. in winter and less than 600-800 mm. in summer, it is referred to as Dry sub-humid zone. On the basis of FAO statistics, the percentage share of arid and semi-arid categories combined together are the highest among the total dryland areas of the world.

In India, arid and semi-arid zones are characterised by low to medium mean annual rainfall coupled with high coefficient of variability, large amplitude of fluctuations of temperature, strong wind regions and high potential evaporation. The average annual rainfall of these regions varies between 150 mm and 500 mm along with a coefficient of variation as high as 60% to 70%. The distribution of rainfall is also very erratic.[1] In India out of the total geographical area, almost one-sixth area with 12% of the population belongs to drought prone areas. At present 74 districts, covering 13 states of the country have been identified as drought prone.

The dryland areas of West Bengal comprise of districts like Purulia, Bankura, West Midnapore and a part of Birbhum as per the State Plan of West Bengal, based on the document "State Agriculture Plan for West Bengal"[2]. Part of Bankura district comes under "red laterite soil region" in West Bengal and here crop productivity is limited. FAO's classification for categories of dryland areas are based on P/PET ratio and on rainfall (in mm). The State Plan of West Bengal has considered FAO's classification. Additionally, the plan has classified agro-climatic region based on soil contents. Bankura district can be termed as semi-arid for the nature of its soil and parts of it showing features of aridity.

The dryland area of Bankura is also a part of the *'Jangal Mahal'* area with the feature that people residing in this region are poor and are heavily dependent on natural resources. The two major natural resources on which people of this area are highly dependent are forestry and drinking water. Though they extract these resources for their livelihood, they have the knowledge base to sustain these resources for future. Hence, they maintain a balance between sustainable resource management and extraction of resources in the context of their dependency on natural resources. So a study of the economic behaviour of the people residing in the Bankura becomes essential. However, such a study requires having a quick analysis of the literature that exists in this line.

Though there are quite a substantial number of works on dryland areas in India, here we mention only a few works that are relevant for our present study. One can refer to the works of Gautam and Rao (2007), Ram and Davari (2010), Bhattacharya and Gupta (2010), Saha and Usha (1992), Bouma and Scott (2006) etc. Gautam and Rao (2007) have shown, in detail, about history of rainfed agriculture in India, starting from pre-independence period. They have also discussed about the magnitude of problems of rainfed agriculture, delineating of rainfed farming. Ram and Davari (2010) have considered rain water and soil as the two most important natural resources of dryland resources. They have emphasised on management practices that maximize the usefulness of limited rainwater by imposing relevant conservation measures and land uses matching with the water availability period in India. Bhattacharya and Gupta (2010) have shown the impact of integrated watershed projects in India. They have shown the impact of completed watershed projects on the livelihood of rural population who are associated with the projects. People of arid regions are forced to migrate to the urban areas to avoid the manifold problems of such areas, especially the problem of water. The authors, in their work, have addressed this reality and have recommended the amount of income that a watershed project should generate to avoid the migration. Saha and Usha (1992) have made a study about the role of rural women of drylands in decision-making processes of various socio-economic activities. In decision making, especially, in agriculture, livestock and socio-religious matters, women were consulted by the heads of households. By and large, little differences in decision-making processes between different groups established homogeneous character of the population. Bouma and Scott (2006) have made an assessment of the impact of large-scale investments in soil and water conservation on dryland crop yields in three semi-arid watersheds in India. Investments in soil and water conservation are supposed to contribute to dryland crop yield improvement by rehabilitating the productive capacity of the land. On the basis of farmers' interviews, group meetings and field visits, they have explored the main constraints for dryland crop yield improvement. There are only a few works related to the dependency on natural resources in dryland areas of West Bengal.

The motivation behind the present study generates from the fact that most of the people living in the dryland areas are poor and are heavily dependent on natural resources of the area so that a study on sustainable resource management and extraction of resources is very much relevant. For example, most of the people in the area are aware about harvest of timber and non-timber forest products (NTFP) but they are also aware about the fact that forests are to be protected and conserved for their own sustainable livelihood. Our study area is featured with underdevelopment, poverty and starvation, dependence on natural resources for livelihood, lack of alternative job opportunities and last but not the least frequent political disturbance.[3] So a comprehensive study of the area will help us to suggest appropriate policy to uplift the conditions of the people residing in the region. There is lack of such comprehensive study in the literature and the present paper attempts to fill the lacuna. The present paper deals with a comprehensive study that deals with a collection of issues on dependency on natural resources by the people in the Bankura of West Bengal.

The paper is organised in the following manner. Section 2 deals with a brief outline of the agriculture and forest related infrastructural scenarios in the district of Bankura. A brief profile of the surveyed regions is analyzed in section 3. Some methodological issues to capture dependency on natural resources are explained briefly in Section 4. Finally, the conclusions are derived in Section 5.

2. Agriculture and Forest Related Scenarios Bankura

In order to understand the agricultural scenario of Bankura, we start with some facts and figures related to the irrigation situation in the district of our study, given the fact that there is scarcity of water in our study area. Condition of Bankura is reflected through Table 1.

Table 1: Irrigation of Land from Different Sources in Bankura (in Thousand Hectares) from 1998-99 to 2012-13

Year	*Govt. canal*	*Tank*	*HDTW*	*MDTW*	*LDTW*	*STW*	*RLI*	*ODW*	*Others*	*Total*
1998-99	187.00	44.70	1.79	1.22	14.10	94.06	5.32	4.60	16.81	369.60
1999-2000	205.20	44.60	1.51	1.41	16.20	93.65	5.40	6.10	17.93	392.00
2000-01	151.00	39.50	1.51	1.56	17.40	93.06	5.83	4.30	18.62	332.78
2001-02	183.60	36.20	1.52	1.68	20.30	87.69	5.94	5.20	9.97	352.10
2002-03	152.73	40.46	1.53	1.84	18.96	98.10	3.81	5.86	8.84	332.13

(*Contd...*)

2003-04	109.02	26.74	1.02	1.36	7.49	44.25	4.18	2.66	5.96	202.68
2004-05	109.89	32.35	0.50	1.45	0.68	47.98	7.28	2.17	6.32	208.62
2005-06	176.29	33.11	0.47	1.46	0.70	47.43	5.38	2.52	6.20	273.55
2006-07	180.35	33.47	0.53	1.49	1.35	45.91	5.08	2.49	6.28	276.94
2007-08	195.93	32.76	0.76	2.50	1.14	48.71	9.67	3.36	6.21	301.04
2008-09	180.60	35.18	0.95	2.50	1.14	55.32	11.57	3.58	6.68	297.52
2009-10	152.04	35.02	0.95	2.50	1.14	56.45	10.30	3.43	5.20	267.03
2010-11	26.36	19.29	1.03	2.54	1.16	50.80	6.24	2.01	5.77	115.20
2011-12	183.21	27.80	0.80	2.94	1.42	54.49	8.88	2.42	6.33	288.29
2012-13	153.32	29.19	0.80	2.94	1.42	53.18	19.04	2.37	6.59	268.85

Source: Bureau of Applied Economics and Statistics, Government of West Bengal[4].

Keeping aside the extreme drought of 2010-11, this district has performed fairly well regarding irrigation, although there were few years of poor performance in between good seasons. But, this is far below than the desired level. Let us check the numbers of sources of irrigation in table 2.

Table 2: Irrigation of Land from Different Sources in Bankura (in Numbers)

Year	*Tank*	*HDTW*	*MDTW*	*LDTW*	*STW*	*RLI*	*ODW*	*Others*
1998-99	22328	41	76	118	130	197	1479	6859
1999-00	22438	42	77	147	153	224	1479	3702
2000-01	21351	42	75	171	148	232	1479	751
2001-02	21391	41	85	164	151	232	1479	912
2002-03	21392	38	102	1065[5]	25930[6]	236	7379[7]	969
2003-04	20716	38	104	173	27445	281	6765	791
2004-05	20952	38	104	173	27754	353	7049	1065
2005-06	20957	38	104	173	27785	354	7084	1179
2006-07	20977	38	104	173	27798	355	7106	1190
2007-08	21006	38	125	190	28700	386	7257	1191
2008-09	21006	38	125	190	28870	434	7257	1195
2009-10	21011	38	125	190	28890	436	7272	1191
2010-11	21293	41	127	194	29634	438	6089	1676
2011-12	21343	32	147	237	29700	438	6101	1681
2012-13	21409	32	147	237	29887	473	6119	1736

Source: Bureau of Applied Economics and Statistics, Government of West Bengal.

In the above table 2, we can see that the number of sources of irrigation has varied over the years but the number of tanks has gone down consistently, but, that of other sources have fluctuated year by year, showing ups and downs.

Table 3: Forest Area, Forest Produce, Revenue and Expenditure from Foresrty in Bankura from (2003-04 to 2012-13)

Item	*Unit*	*03-04*	*04-05*	*05-06*	*06-07*	*07-08*	*08-09*	*09-10*	*10-11*	*11-12*	*12-13*
Reserved Forest	Hectare	8004	3889	3889	3889	4449	4449	4449	4572	4572	4572
Protected Forest	,,	131119	131199	131199	131199	132002	132002	132002	136230	136230	136230
Unclasse-d State Forest	,,	9054	7756	7756	7756	2713	2713	2713	2238	2238	2238
Khas Forest	,,	-	-	-	-	-	-	-	-	-	-
Vested Waste Land	,,	-	-	-	-	-	-	-	-	-	-
Forest owned by Corporates	,,	-	-	-	-	-	-	-	-	-	-
Forest owned by Individuals	,,	-	-	-	-	-	-	-	-	-	-
Total	,,	**148177**	**142844**	**142844**	**142844**	**139164**	**139164**	**139164**	**143040**	**143040**	**143040**
Forest produce	Thousand cubic meters										
Timber	,,	4.89	6.287	5.546	5.56	5.011	5.38	4918.41	546.63	840.44	765.51
Non-timber	,,	51.723	46.760	44.686	21.684	6.965	13.99	8945.43	950.23	3597.23	2532.54
Revenue earned	Thousand Rs	15032	14378	30823	30619	59207	68491	148972	170799	181725	210569
Expenditure	,,	70318	60958	105286	142740	203087	182203	543342	631482	487296	158652

Source: Bureau of Applied Economics and Statistics, Government of West Bengal

Next, we shall look into the forestry-oriented conditions. This district has good figures regarding the forest area, its produce and revenue generation. This is shown in table 3.

From the above Table 3 it is apparent that expenditure is much higher than revenue earned. So, here forestry runs in subsidies. Also, the production of Non-timber is very high compared to that of timber. There is absence of private bodies in forest-owner category. So, from these figures it is appearing that there is scope for developing forests in these areas and the government has been doing that by providing subsidies.

3. Brief Profile of Surveyed Areas of Drylands

We have surveyed 300 households in Bankura district. We have categorised the respondents in different income groups. We have classified the entire income range in different groups like ₹ 0-2500, ₹ 2501-5000, ₹ 5001-10000, ₹ 10001-20000 and more than 20000 then, frequencies of people falling in each group with their percentages shown in the Table 4.

Table 4: Different Income Groups of Respondents with Frequency and Percentage

Districts	*Bankura*	
Income Groups (Rs.)	*Frequency*	*Percentage*
0-2500	50	16.66%
2501-5000	150	50%
5001-10000	78	26%
10001-20000	12	4%
More than 20000	10	3.33%

Source: Primary Survey.

Socio-economic condition of the surveyed area is shown in table 5. During our survey, we have observed most of the area is poverty- stricken. As per our survey report the share of BPL is very high than that of APL. It is quite expected for our surveyed backward areas. Regarding religion, we have found the presence of Hindus and Muslims only. Existence of any other religion has been rarely observed. But, as far as 'caste' is concerned, we have found the presence of people of all types of castes.

The condition of education is very pessimistic, as we have observed around 57% of the respondents (or, any family member of that respondent) have not completed elementary education. We have focused on the availability of drinking water facilities for the households of our surveyed area. We can see that none of the households have the facility of drinking water in their houses. It is apparent from the table that the problem of drinking water is an important issue in the drylands of West Bengal.

Table 5: Division and Socio-Economic Conditions of Households of sample survey

District	***Village***	***No. of Households Used for sample survey***		***Nature of Dryland***		
	Susunia	225		Hilly		
	Sewlibona	75		Hilly		
	Total No. of Families Surveyed	No. of APL families		No. of BPL families		
Bankura						
	300	123		177		
		Families "With In house Drinking Water" Facility		Families "Without Drinking Water" Facility		
		0		300		
		No. of respondents Taking water from tube wells		No. of respondents Taking water from ponds/ watersheds/waterfalls		
		210		90		
		No. of Families Using Fuelwood	No. of Families Using Fuelwood and Gas		No. of Families Using Gas	
		212	79		9	
		No. of General Category Respondents	No. of SC Category Respondents	No. of ST Category Respondents		No. of OBC Category Respondents
		95	53	108		44
		No. of illiterates	No. of people studied between class 1 to 7	No. of people completed elementary education (passed class 8)	No. of people studied after elementary education (class 9 to 12)	No. of Graduates and/ or Master degree holders
		56	114	62	56	12

Source: Primary Survey.

Next, if we consider the term 'forest dependency', we find that almost all the people of our study area are forest dependent. Almost all the households use non-timber forest products for their cooking purpose. Even if few of them use 'gas' as the main source of fuel, they also use firewood as an alternative source of fuel but in lesser quantities than those who cannot use gas. So, we have classified the households in three segments- those who use only fuelwood, those who use both fuelwood and gas and those who use only gas. People are heavily forest dependent in the dryland areas of West Bengal. Even during field-survey we have seen that people residing 5-10 miles away from the exact forest, also come to the forest for collecting fuelwood. In our surveyed area, it is very difficult to distinguish who are forest-dependent and who are not. One important thing that needs to be mentioned is that people of these areas are dependent on forest throughout the year. They go to forest throughout the year; maximum households go for 10 to 20 days per month. Very few households, those who are not so much dependent on forest, go for 5 to 7 days per month. They collect fuelwood and few other things like sal leaves, honey, kendu leaves, etc., both for consumption as well as for selling in the market during poor financial condition of the family. Forest products collected mainly for selling in the market – such phenomenon is also observed in West Midnapore. People mainly collect those forest products that are being permitted to collect by the Joint Forest Management Committees (JFMC) and Forest Protection Committees (FPC). To a large extent, they collect these products for consumption purpose. So, the collection of fuel wood out of all types of non-timber forest products (NTFPs) is very high because the committees allow them to collect those products only. More than 95% of the respondents are dependent on forest products for getting their fuels.

Land is generally considered as an indicator for economic wealth of a family. In our survey areas we have seen only 185 families out of 300 possess their own land but the average amount of land holding is very poor. The lowest amount of land held by a family is 1 bigha or 0.1338 hectare or 0.3306 acre[8] and the highest is 6.235 acre.

4. Some Methodological issues to Capture Dependency on Natural Resources

There are various ways on the basis of which one capture dependency on natural resources in the dryland areas. We shall briefly discuss two ways it can be captured. The first one is the dynamic optimisation technique which can be used to analyze such dependency through sensitivity analysis, the second one is the use of absolute Beta Convergence, which is used for checking the nature of growth of income from forestry in this district and the last one is the use of contingent valuation method to value the natural resources on which the stakeholders are dependent. This valuation exercise has strong implications for sustainable livelihood and hence on sustainable resource management. We shall first explain the dynamic version in a descriptive manner and after that we shall provide some elements of applicability of contingent valuation method (CVM) for forestry and drinking water.

4.1 Application of Dynamic Optimisation Technique to Analyze Dependency on Natural Resources

The dynamic model that has been considered is an extension of the work of Gupta (2006). In this paper we just want to present the outline of the model without going to the equational specification. The actual model is shown in the paper by Chatterjee and Gupta (2018).[9] The present model is different from the model of Gupta (2006) in a wide extent. Gupta (2006) has considered the interlinkage between mangrove (forestry) and shrimp (fishery), whereas the present model focuses on the forestry sector only with harvest of timber and NTFP. The purpose is to examine whether (i) a change in the proportion of timber harvest obtained as NTFP or (ii) a change in the intrinsic rate of growth of forest stock or (iii) a change in the discount rate measuring the opportunity cost of forestry gives us some counter-intuitive results. The base values for sensitivity analysis are obtained through calibration (field survey and secondary sources). The structure of the model can be explained in terms of the following points:

- *Objective:* To maximize welfare from extraction of timber and non-timber forest product (NTFP)
- *Constraint:* Net growth of forest stock.
- *Enforcement:* Harvest of timber is mainly under government's control and a part of non-timber as well.
- *Property rights:* Well defined property rights and are managed through the joint forest management (JFM) system.
- *Operation:* Given the fact that the foresters are price-takers, welfare maximisation of the foresters (through the JFM system) is in the form of maximisation of profit.
- *Study Area:* Bankura.
- *Analysis:* Done through Sensitivity Analysis after calibrating for the base values.

The main result of the study, which is contrary to the conventional wisdom, is that for Bankura, an increase in the proportion of timber harvest obtained as NTFP reduces the level of welfare in the study area. Apart from this we find that a reduction in the intrinsic growth rate of forest stock reduces the level of timber cutting and also reduces the availability of NTFP. These two results show the awareness of the forest-fringe people regarding the sustainable use of forest. Finally, we have shown that a change in the discount rate causes insignificant changes in the major study variables, emphasising dependency as well as sustainability of forests.

4.2 Application of Convergence for Checking the Growth of Income from Natural Resources

Now, we would like to focus on a different issue which has also some dynamic flavour. Economic growth and convergence is one of the most discussed fields in economics, as the long-run growth determines the welfare of countries. The word 'convergence' has been used by different economists in different contexts. For example, Baumol (1986) has pointed out that the phenomenon of convergence has an unambiguous meaning which can be interpreted in terms of faster economic growth of late comers to industrialisation so that in the long run they move towards convergence of per-capita product. The phenomenon of convergence has found a life in modern growth economics. A natural starting point for a theoretical discussion of economic growth is the neoclassical growth model developed by Solow (1956) and Swan (1956).

Thus, all economies, over time, may converge in terms of income per head. In economic growth literature the term 'convergence' can be interpreted in two ways. The first kind, also known as 'sigma-convergence', refers to a reduction in the dispersion of levels of income across economies. 'Beta-convergence' on the other hand, occurs when poor economies grow faster than rich ones. Economists say that there is 'conditional beta-convergence' when economies experience 'beta-convergence' but conditional on other variables being held constant.

It is said that 'unconditional beta-convergence' or 'absolute beta-convergence' exists when the growth rate of an economy declines as it approaches its steady state. Thus, when the dispersion of real per capita income across a group of economies falls over time, there is σ-convergence. When the partial correlation between growth in income over time and its initial level is negative, there is β-convergence.[13] Broadly speaking, unconditional convergence occurs when the income gap between two countries decreases irrespective of these countries' "characteristics" (e.g., institutions, policies, technology or even investments). Conditional convergence occurs when the economic gap between two countries that are similar in observable characteristics is becoming narrower over time. Convergence can be considered not only by comparing between countries but also by comparing between regions within a country.

From the point of view of methodology, we have used simple diagrammatic and econometric technique of Least Square method for our analysis of convergence by using various statistical tools.

Our econometric equation, for testing Beta convergence, is of the following form

$$g_{it} = \alpha + \beta Y_{it-1} + u_{it} \quad (1)$$

Equation (1) is used for testing Simple or absolute β convergence. Here, 'g' is the average growth rate of Y, which is our concerned variable (such as income from forest). Here, 'i' refers region or area and 't' refers to time period. From equation 1, Y stands for income from forestry.

For the sake of removing the heterogeneity from the data set, we have converted the actual values of the variables in their log-values. A negative value of β would mean convergence, given that is significant according to statistical tests, where as a positive value means divergence and u_{it} has mean zero, finite variance, σ^2_u, and is independent over t and i.

We have used a panel data set for Bankura for the time period 2002-2012; including the variables Gross district domestic product, growth rate of district domestic product, Net district domestic product from forestry and per capita income. All variables are in constant price. By using net district domestic product from forest, we have computed the growth of income from forest sector.[11] Our analysis has shown that there is absolute Beta convergence in the growth of income forest sector. So, growth rate of income from forestry depicts a falling tendency. Here, NDDP refers to Net District Domestic Product. The finding of Bankura district is described by the following diagram. (Fig. 1).

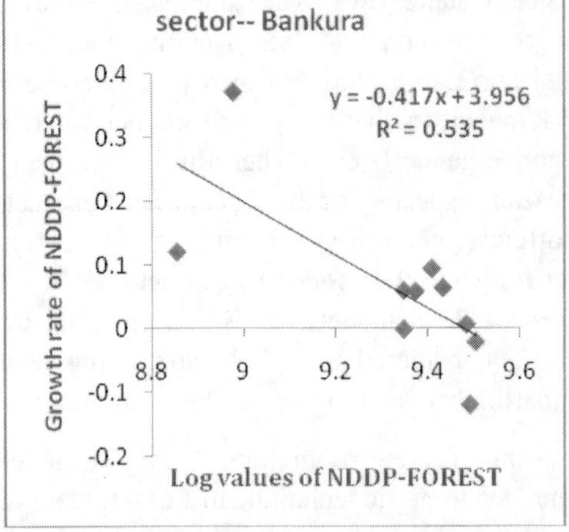

Fig. 1: Absolute β convergence in Bankura 2002-2012.

We have seen absolute Beta convergence, regarding income from forest sector in the study area. One can say that the existence of absolute Beta convergence, in Bankura is quite significant from the point of view of forest management.

4.3 Application of Contingent Valuation Method (CVM) for Valuation of Natural Resources

Economic value of the environment is specified in the background of three important features of environmental goods which are namely, (i) irreversibility, (ii) uncertainty and (iii) uniqueness. We can classify total economic value into two categories: (i) user value (ii) non-user value.

Valuation can simply be defined "as an attempt to put monetary values or to environmental goods and services or natural resources". It is a key exercise in economic analysis and its results provide important information about values of environmental goods and services. This information can be used to influence decisions about wise use and conservation of forests and other ecosystems. The basic aim of valuation is to determine people's preferences by gauging how much they are willing to pay (WTP) for given benefits or certain environmental attributes e.g. keep a forest ecosystem intact. In other words, valuation also tries to gauge how much worse off they would consider themselves to be as a result of changes in the state of the environment such as degradation of a forest.

In the dryland areas of developing countries the conservation of environment should get more priority because in the presence of very few alternative income opportunities, people of such areas rely very heavily on environmental goods, especially on forests, for their livelihoods. Valuation of water is also another important aspect that has been neglected as far as drylands are concerned. Lack of ground water availability and recurrence of droughts hinder agricultural activities. For the same reason, scarcity of drinking water makes living more difficult for the people of drylands.

For the valuation of forest-dependency as well as problem of drinking water, we have used Contingent Valuation Method (CVM). For this purpose we have conducted household surveys without which it is impossible to conduct CVM. In our work, single bounded dichotomous choice has been considered in closed ended referendum. Here one particular bid is shown to each respondent and the responses are in the form of either "yes" or "no", that is, whether he is going to accept the bid or not. Accordingly few statistical tests have been done to derive average willingness to pay.[12]

Contingent valuation surveys were first proposed in theory by Ciriacy-Wantrup (1947) as a method for eliciting market valuation of a non-market good. The first practical application of the technique was performed in 1963 when Davis used surveys to estimate the value hunters and tourists placed on a particular wilderness area. He compared the survey results to an estimation of value based on travel costs and found good correlation with his results. This type of Contingent Valuation (CV) exercise has several drawbacks. In response to criticisms of contingent valuation surveys, a panel of high profile economists (chaired by Nobel Prize laureates Kenneth Arrow and Robert Solow) was convened under the auspices of the National Oceanic and Atmospheric Administration (NOAA) in 1990. The NOAA panel was set up in the early 1990s in the US, to review the CVM. A concrete background for the panel was the controversy surrounding the so called Exxon Valdez incident, with a large oil spill off the Alaska coast, in 1989. In that case, WTP data obtained from CVM studies were brought to court. These studies were contested, and the entire CVM seriously questioned.

The NOAA panel tried to remedy this problem, by providing guidelines for use of the CVM, in particular as court evidence. It issued a report in 1993, which has been widely cited and followed. The guiding principle behind these recommendations was that the survey operator has a high burden of proof to satisfy before the results can be seen as meaningful. Surveys meeting these criteria are very expensive to operate and to ameliorate the expense of conducting surveys the panel recommended a set of reference surveys which future surveys could be compared to and calibrated against. The NOAA panel also felt, in general, that conservative estimates of value were to be preferred and one important consequence of this decision is that they recommended contingent valuation surveys measure willingness to pay to protect the good rather than willingness to accept compensation for the loss of the resource.

As a result, current contingent valuation methodology corrects for these shortcomings, and current empirical testing indicates that such bias and inconsistency has been successfully addressed. In the application of CVM, obtaining of bids is the most important section of the study. At this stage field survey is conducted, generally. A face-to-face interview by well-trained interviewers is needed for effective data collection. Individuals are asked to state their maximum willingness to pay (WTP) or minimum willingness to accept (WTA) for a proposed change in the environmental quality. To quantity the precise amount fruitfully, a number of alternative strategies are applied which are:

(a) Closed ended referendum (b) Open ended referendum

Average WTP calculation for a closed ended referendum is different from that of an open ended bid. In case of open ended bid, since exact information about max WTP is available, the average is calculated by using either arithmetic mean or median. Since the lower bids are more likely than higher bids for environmental goods (for free-riding problem), thus median WTP < mean WTP. But in case of dichotomous choice type closed ended bidding, it is recognised that though the consumer knows his preference completely, it is not totally observable to the researchers. Hence, a Random Utility Model (RUM) is chosen to represent the choice decision where the probability of a "yes" response to a bid can be derived by applying logit estimation technique.

The purpose of using CVM is very clear. Natural resources perform several economic functions on which price cannot be assigned. Even if there are announced property rights related to ownership of the resource, the rights cannot be properly assigned to the owners. Use of CVM helps to resolve these issues. In our study we want to value forest resources and drinking water in the dryland areas of West Bengal. In our study for selection of villages we have followed stratified sampling and for selection of households we have followed partly stratified and partly random sampling. The number of respondents interviewed in the two villages, taken together from Bankura, is 300 and it has seen that the response rate is 100% which is high.

For the above kind of analysis it is important to determine the bid first and then to determine how these bids are to be shown to the respondents. The bids that we have considered are ₹ 2, ₹ 5, ₹ 8, ₹ 10, ₹ 15 and ₹ 25 (in terms of per month) to conserve and sustainably use forestry. The same bids are offered for having "in house facility of drinking water supply".[16] Here the bids are determined after discussing with the local people through pilot surveys which gave us an idea of the maximum and minimum amounts that we should put forward to the respondents as bid amounts. The next step is to identify the "valid" responses out of 200 respondents. For this we have followed a strategy in the final survey. We have categorised the respondents in three bid groups, namely, *low, medium and high*. We have applied single-bound dichotomous choice CV method. The *low* bid group implies bids of ₹ 2 and ₹ 5 per month for having and also to conserve drinking water. For *medium* bid group the bid amounts are ₹ 8 and ₹ 10 per month. For *high* bid group the bid amounts are ₹ 15 and ₹ 25 per month. [14]

Our present survey reflects that 95 respondents out of 300 respondents are not willing to accept the bids and thus we will consider 205 respondents as *"willing"* respondents and 95 respondents as *"non-willing"* for our further analysis. Here 95 *"non-willing"* participants are considered as *"protest bidders"* for the conservation of forestry and for water. We have considered a logit analysis to estimate Willingness to Pay (WTP) for both conservation of forests and drinking water under closed ended referendum. We have also estimated WTP for both conservation of forests and drinking water under open ended referendum.

In case of forestry under close-ended referendum we have found the mean WTP to be ₹ 13.25 per month whereas it is ₹ 6.75 per month for the open-ended referendum. We can find an average of the two mean WTPs and name it as *'true WTP*, in our model. The *'true WTP'* turns out to be ₹ 10 per month. One can say that for the sake of their own livelihood in the long run because of the presence of very few alternative income opportunities, people of Bankura, despite being poverty-stricken, are willing to pay this minimal amount. This amount though appears to be low, is reasonable given the fact that most of the stakeholders in our study area either lives below the poverty line or belongs to the lower income groups.

In case of drinking water under closed-ended referendum we have found the mean WTP to be ₹ 12.80 per month whereas it is ₹ 10.20 per month for the open-ended referendum. The *'true WTP'* turns out to be ₹ 11.50 per month. One can say that for the sake of their own development and to get rid of the problem of drinking water, people of Bankura can bear to pay this amount. This amount once again though appears to be low, is reasonable given the fact that most of the stakeholders in our study area mostly poor. Their WTP for conservation cum sustainable use of forestry and drinking water has important policy implications from the point of development of Bankura. Government should give special emphasis on these issues for developing this area.

The methodology that we have discussed here provides a guideline to the researchers and the policy makers to conduct serious study to understand dependency on natural resources in other parts of the World and also to link it with sustainable resource management.

5. Conclusions

Here, we have made an attempt to integrate the major issues related to dependency on natural resources and their implications on sustainability issues in the Bankura district of West Bengal. This comprehensive study is not actually a survey of existing works rather it provides an analysis of facts and figures along with a guideline regarding the methodologies that can be followed to study the nature of dependency on natural resources. Our study shows that people in the Bankura of West Bengal depend heavily on forestry and suffer from the lack of drinking water, owing to the poor irrigational-agricultural conditions and dryness of the weather. Then we have described few aspects of socio-economic conditions of the district, as we have observed from our field survey. In terms of a dynamic model we have shown that, contrary to the conventional wisdom, how in Bankura (part of dryland areas of the state) an increase in the proportion of timber harvest obtained as NTFP reduces the level of welfare in the region. In terms of our dynamic model we have shown the importance of forestry and hence its conservation (can be interpreted as sustainability of forestry) from the point of view of the people residing in the area. Then, we have shown how the growth of income from forestry in this district has been falling over the years, which an issue of concern for the government and raises the question of conservation-cum-sustainable use of this important natural resource. Lastly, we have shown that how the people of Bankura think about conservation of forestry and drinking water and also the use of these two resources through Contingent Valuation Technique. Thus, we have captured the overall natural resource scenario of Bankura of West Bengal and also we have emphasized on people's perception in their (natural resources) protection and sustainable use. Our study suggests some values for the conservation of resources in terms of their WTP. These figures are really useful for policy analysis to achieve sustainable resource management of natural resources in our study area.

References

Barro, R. J. (1991): 'Economic growth in a cross section of countries', *Quarterly Journal of Economics,* 106(2), 407–443.

Barro, R. J., and Sala-i-Martin, X. (1991): 'Convergence Across States and Regions', *Brookings Chapters on Economic Activity,* 1, 107-58.

Barro, R. J., and Sala-i-Martin, X. (1992): 'Convergence', *Journal of Political Economy,* 100(2), 223–251.

Baumol, W.J. (1986): 'Productivity Growth, Convergence and Welfare: What the Long run Data Show?' *American Economic Review*, 76(5), 1072-85.

Bhattacharya, A. and Gupta, K. (2010): 'Impact of Integrated Watershed Projects on Sustainable Development in India: A Quantitative Approach', A Collaborative Project of Institute for Global Environmental Strategies, Japan & Centre for Human Development and Human Rights, Rabindra Bharati University, Kolkata, India.

Bouma, J.A. and Christopher, C.A. (2006): 'The possibilities for dryland crop yield improvement in India's semi-arid regions-Observations from the field',

CA Discussion Paper 3, International Water Management Institute (IWMI), Hyderabad, India.

Chatterjee, N. (2014): "Willingness to Pay for Drinking Water in Some Selcted Dryland Areas of West Bengal: A Contingent Valuation Approach", Vidyasagar University Journal of Economics, Vol. XIX, 2014-15: 14-37.

Chatterjee, N. (2018): "A Dynamic Model of Forestry for the Dryland Areas of West Bengal", Department of Economics, Rabindra Bharati University, *Economic Affairs,* June, 2018.

Chatterjee, N. (2017): "An Assessment of Infrastructural Facilities in the Dryland Areas of West Bengal" in Ramesh Chandra Das (ed.), *Social, Health, and Environmental Infrastructures for Economic Growth*, IGI Global, USA, 2017.

Chatterjee, N. and Dinda, S. (2016): "Convergence of Forest Resources in Jangalmahal, West Bengal" in Ramesh Chandra Das (ed.), Handbook of Research on Global Indicators of Economic and Political Convergence, IGI Global, USA, 2016.

Ciriacy-Wantrup, S.V. (1947): 'Capital Return from Soil Conservation Practices', *Journal of Farm Economics*. 29: 1189-96.

Davis, R.K. (1963): 'Recreation Planning as an Economic Problem', *Natural Resource Journal*, 3: 239-49.

Gautam, R.C. and Rao, J.C. (2007): "Integrated Water Management: Concepts of Rainfed Agriculture", *mimeo.*

Gupta, K. (2006): 'Mangrove-Fishery Linkages under Alternative Policy Regimes' in Sengupta, N. and Bandyopadhyay, J. (eds.), *Biodiversity and Quality of Life*, McMilan India Ltd., pp. 272-293.

Ram, M. and Davari, M.R. (2010): "Management of Natural Resources for Sustainable Dryland Agriculture", *International Journal of Agriculture and Crop Sciences*, Vol. 2 (1), 9-25.

Saha, D. (2015): 'Some Economic Aspects of Forestry in the Sunderbans', *Unpublished PhD Dissertation*, Department of Economics, Rabindra Bharati University, Kolkata, India.

Saha, D.K. and Usha, R. (1992): 'The role of rural women in Decision making process in Arid Rajasthan', *Annals of Arid Zone*, 31(4), 295-297.

Solow, R. M. (1956): 'A contribution to the theory of economic growth', *Quarterly Journal of Economics,* 70(1), 65–94.

Swan, T. W. (1956): 'Economic growth and capital accumulation', *Economic Record 32*, 334–361.

Notes

1. Status report on hydrology of arid zones of India, 1999-2000, Prepared by National Institute of Hydrology.
2. Prepared by NABARD Consultancy Services Pvt Ltd (NABCONS), West Bengal.
3. Though political disturbance was there a few years back but at present it is under control.

4. HDTW- High Capacity Deep Tubewell, MDTW- Middle Capacity Deep Tubewell, LDTW- Low Capacity Deep Tubewell, STW- Shallow Tubewell, RLI- Riverlift Irrigation, ODW- Open Dug Well.
5. Including Private LDTW.
6. Including Private STW from here onwards.
7. Including Private ODW from here onwards.
8. As per the law in West Bengal.
9. Interested readers are advised to go through the paper by Chatterjee and Gupta (2018).
10. The concepts of Sigma convergence and conditional Beta convergence are adapted from Barro (1991) and Barro and Sala-i-martin (1991, 1992).
11. Interested readers are advised to go through the paper by Chatterjee and Dinda (2015) for a detail analysis of "Convergence of Forest Resources in Jangal Mahal."
12. See Chatterjee (2014) for valuation of drinking water.
13. Here, "in house facility of drinking water supply" also comprises the concept of proper management and use of available drinking water in this area.
14. Interested readers are advised to see Chatterjee (2014) for selection of bids for CVM.

Part - II

Macroeconomic Policies

5

Corona Calls for Revival of Globalisation vs. Deglobalisation Debate – Relevance of *Atmanirbhar Bharat*

Biswajit Mandal, Nilanjan Ghosh and Saswati Chaudhuri

Abstract

This note strives to explore the channels of how worldwide transmission of Corona virus may reignite the debate around the effectiveness of (de)globalisation from the perspective of economic interconnectedness among countries. Taking clue from such economic underpinnings we further move to understand why this pandemic may have long-lasting economic ill effects. The probable conduits are disruption in global value chain, demand shortage originating from supply crisis, tourism, and productivity shocks. All these crucially hinge upon trade in goods, movement of labour, and the quality of health and stock of human capital. Therefore, we argue that the ongoing health calamity is likely to end up with a bigger economic crisis and with an indication towards more insulated economic system in coming years even if we recuperate from Corona catastrophe. In such a backdrop we attempt to assess the theoretical relevance of ***Atmanirbhar Bharat*** *as well.*

Key Words: *Globalisation, Protectionism, Trade War, Self-Reliance, Covid-19*

1. Introduction

The onslaught of massive wide-reaching lockdown calls for brief prologue about what is in the hindsight. It is the outbreak of COVID-19, a new Coronavirus disease which took hold of China in December-end, 2019. This belongs to the same family of viruses that caused the SARS (Severe Acute Respiratory Syndrome) epidemic in 2003. Asian Development Bank (ADB) Brief reported COVID-19 to be less dangerous than SARS that has a mortality rate of 10% while the former's mortality rate might vary among various age cohorts. On an average the death rate in Covid-19 patients ages

80 and over was 10.4%, compared to 5.35% in 70s, 1.51% in patients 60 to 69, 0.37% in 50-59. However, both share the same level of infection rate. The first confirmed case outside mainland China occurred in Thailand, Japan, and South Korea according to the World Health Organisation's first situation report released on 21st January 2020. By January end, amidst thousands of new cases in China, a "public health emergency of international concern" was officially declared by the W.H.O. Subsequently on 12th March, WHO declared COVID-19 as pandemic.

COVID-19 is a war which is mainly waged in the health sector but is going to have a far-reaching impact on the economic front too. The stock market is one of many different factors that economists consider while examining economic health. Stock markets worldwide have knocked rock bottom.

2. The Chinese Sneeze and the World Catches Cold too

One of the most famous phrases about the global economy has been attributed to Matternich, a distinguished 19th-century diplomat. However, his saying was a bit different as he was talking of an era when Europe dominated the world. He came up with the phrase: "When France sneezes, Europe catches a cold" which later changed to America and rightly now to China.

Even though the major symptom of COVID-19 is common cold and flu-like symptom, we are basically more concerned with its economic impact. It does have the potential of slowing down not only the Chinese economy but also the global economy and the tremors are already felt. UNCTAD had spelt it out in clear and simple terms when it announced that "any disruption of China's output is expected to have repercussions elsewhere through regional and global value chains". China, for some decades now, has become the central manufacturing hub of many global business operations and a slowdown in Chinese production will naturally have repercussions in other countries. The intensity of the repercussion would obviously hinge on how dependent the industries of the said country are on Chinese suppliers. Many developing Asian economies like Hong Kong, Mongolia, the Philippines, Singapore, Taipei and Vietnam will be materially affected by the corona outbreak. The primary reason is not only that these economies witness a significant share of Chinese tourists but China is also a major destination of their intermediate and final goods and services.

There are several channels through which the COVID-19 outbreak affect economic activity in China, the rest of developing Asia, and the world. A sharp but temporary decline in domestic consumption is unavoidable in all the outbreak-affected economies. Outbreak would obviously affect people's perceptions regarding future business activity and a probable decline in investment is imperative. A decline in tourism and business travel is the most anticipated channel of disruption of economic activity. World Tourism Organisation throws up interesting figures. They analysed tourist arrivals from China as a share of total arrivals in various countries in 2018. Hong Kong tops the list with 68% of the total tourist arrivals from China. Others high up in the list are Cambodia, Vietnam, Korea, Mongolia, Thailand, and Myanmar. The COVID-19 outbreak would obviously lead to a considerable decline in the Chinese tourists and for those who wanted to take a transit route through China. Each of them would also have a say as the world takes the much dreaded path to the global recession viz. spillovers of weaker demand to other sectors and economies through trade and production linkages; supply-side disruptions to production and trade and effects on health such as increased disease and mortality as well as shifts in healthcare spending.

To stall the Corona march, various economies have taken measures like full border closure. Thus, human mobility has been significantly curbed or constrained. The impact of closures and lockdown/shutdown are something that is not hard to imagine. It would lead to inevitable production disruptions because of forced business closures. Immobility of labour due to various controls would be accompanied by unnecessary economic cost. Lastly, there may also be important long-term economic upshots through COVID-19's health impacts on mortality and morbidity, and through changes in (and diversion of) healthcare.

Thus, various economic policies are framed and international sanctions are imposed to restrict international movement of goods and services, and factors of production including labour. Textbook economics teaches us that such sanctions are accompanied by huge economic costs. This impact would be similar to the one noticed during H1B visa sanctions imposed by the USA government or during BREXIT. Global production or trade in goods and services have been adversely impacted. However, when national policies are responsible for the immobility of labour, a substitute process is also made handy. In this context, production cost rises but the supply chain is not disrupted because production still takes place (may be by domestic labour). Thus, inability to harness the cost advantage that was possible due to availability of cheap foreign labour in pre-COVID era would also lead to a rise in price level along with a fall in demand. This certainly has huge economic impact. However, when the root cause of all restrictions are health-related and that too a contagious one just like the one with COVID-19, the pathways to an alternative production process no longer remains a viable option. When mobility of resources like labour is restrained worldwide, production in a single particular economy does not get affected alone – it affects the global economy at large. We must witness a global price rise for all commodities and services in future. Concurrently we should not forget that 60% of the value of the international trade comes through global value chain while 40% of the global production is contributed by the labour from various countries. Hence when international movement of labour and other factors are restricted, the entire global production system will certainly be badly jostled. This will automatically trigger a global economic crisis. According to an ADB report, high-frequency indicators suggest that production in China as a whole fell to 50%–60% of normal levels. China is a global and regional hub for manufacturing and value chains— many economies export a sizeable amount of intermediate goods to China and other economies use inputs from China in their production. Therefore, these temporary disruptions in China would cause a sudden slip in production and trade in other economies too.

3. Trade Equalises Morbidity?

It seems now that Corona virus outbreak took the corridor of physical proximity of affected countries and human beings. This corroborates the role of trade, travel and migration for whatever reasons in transmitting Corona virus. Hence to contain the severity of this contagious virus several countries restricted two things: trade (movement of goods) is restricted due to low domestic production and less import demand; travel is restricted because of implementing strict social distancing policy.

On the other hand, liberalised trade policy is conventionally assumed to be the most effective policy to foster global development though it allegedly begets divergence and some other perils [Stiglitz (2002); Feenstra and Hanson (1996) etc.]. In a recent book, however, Baldwin (2016) succinctly argued why and how the whole word is again converging. This is further extended in Helpman (2018) to explain why trade is not solely responsible for an increase in two-sided wage inequality among skilled-unskilled workers. So, irrespective of whether we blame or praise, trade is what keeps us bonded, makes us dependent, and eludes us from being self reliant. This thread of bonding is now under severe peril as one cannot deny the deadly contagious nature of the corona virus. Celebrated trade models of gravity equation [Melitz (2007); Head and Mayer (2014) etc.] asserts that apart from cost of production induced commodity price differential there are a bunch of other factors behind rising volume of trade. Correspondingly, they also influence labour migration prospect. Labour migration is again primarily driven by the wage differences between countries. Thus, international labour mobility is frequently considered as a substitute of trade in goods and services as both these two channels, interestingly, aim at global factor price equalisation (Samuelson, 1948). Ironically, Corona virus is taking the same route to ensure morbidity equalisation across the globe. Now, a worldwide complete lockdown promising complete closure of international movement of goods and labour to contain the transmission would naturally lead to widening of income disparity in coming years even if we survive the Corona outbreak.[1]

4. What Next and Why 'NEW'?

The next humungous task researchers would be exposed to is to analyse the statistics of quality of health condition and work ability of all the Corona survivors. We have already emphasised before that health has a sustaining long run effect on human capital and productivity in general. Thus, the possibility of second round productivity shock, first round of which is going on at this juncture, should not be ruled out. And if the global lockdown, which is in force almost across the globe, is the only means to contain the severity of Coronavirus, this again would pilot us to an age old debate of liberalisation versus protectionism entailing the efficacy of a self-reliant economy. In time of global crisis an independent economy can only insulate the domestic economy and society. Thus, the ongoing wave of deglobalisation gets auxiliary impetus with its health and productivity related dimensions.

Thus, amidst the global pandemic and in the wake of the wide reaching containment efforts implemented by the governments in most of the countries,we have gradually entered a new global economic order both domestically and internationally. Globally this phenomenon has been christened as 'new normal' which naturally includes reshaping trade and commerce, social sectors' magnitude, international relation and integration, mobility of capital and human capital, nature of transaction of goods and services and so on. Such intriguing restructure in every dimension of the society and economy in particular forced everyone to think such 'new normal' subsequently compelled the government of India to vouch for 'vocal for local' campaign, which was immediately supported by the 'self-reliant India' or '*Atmanirbhar Bharat*' slogan in conformity with the 'Make in India' initiative of the same government. However, the much-hyped idea of '*Atmanirbhar*' is beyond 'self-sufficiency': '*Atmanirbhar*' also has the scope of production for export which is missing in self sufficiency. Immediately after the '*Atmanirbhar Bharat*' speech is aired by the Prime Minister, it took the entire country by storm and has managed to become a buzzword in the last couple of weeks. But whether the buzzword is a complete bizarre mind-game is yet to be analyzed!

The basic principle of self-reliance is, however, very simple – produce whatever you need, produce whatever you desire to export, and try to arrange for all the inputs you require to carry out production. So, naturally it's a case of 'no-import' but definitely not a 'no-export'. Thus, the question boils down to who would be buying our products as all other countries are also suffering from similar social and economic upheavals. So, in principle, the idea of self-reliance in this era of (de)globalisation is not a very pragmatic idea to dwell upon and it turns out to be uneconomical too as it fails to uphold the tenets of division of labour of David Hume and Adam Smith, comparative cost advantage principle of David Ricardo, love for variety and home market effect of Paul Krugman etc. All these globally acclaimed concepts are in line with globalising the market while the recent campaign of '*Atmanirbhar*' or self-reliance focuses on the opposite of globalisation –protectionism.

5. Protectionism in History

The concept of protectionism had been in vogue before. It is essentially an age-old idea which has significant connotation for the *Corn Law*. And the repeal of the *Corn Law* was perhaps one of the well documented and accepted movements from protectionism to globalisation. The *Corn Law*, in brief, is imposition of tariff on imports of Corn, which led to higher domestic price of Corn in Britain. Thus, profit of agriculture and landlords went up while that of other manufacturing units went down. In addition, to compensate for higher corn price workers demanded higher wage rate. This became the prime reason for decreasing profit in all other sectors, igniting the movement against the *Corn Law* and eventually the British government had to repeal it. The story of *Corn Law* was in the first half of the nineteenth century. Therefore, this naturally begets another question: What was there before?

To start with there was a sort of self-reliant economy though that was essentially in the spirit of self-sufficiency: produce, and consume what is produced. This very concept is succinctly analyzed with a modern look in a recent book – *The Great Convergence* – by Richard Baldwin (2016). He described this phenomenon as *bundling*. This is bundling of production and consumption at the same place – double coincidence of demand. Then came *first-unbundling* between production and consumption. But in reality the idea was creation andaccumulation of more wealth. Trade or exchange was free then, except for transportation cost. Thus, the point of concern is - how to acquire wealth? The simplest answer to this million dollar question is 'sell more and buy less' or 'export more and import less'. This is perhaps the best alternative to war and a convenient pathway to acquire wealth and become richer- popularly known as *Mercantilism*. One can easily understand that the basic essence of both *Mercantilism* and *Corn Law* is same – building huge reserve through trade surplus.

David Hume was, however, very critical of Mercantilist's view. He thought trade surplus is an absolutely temporary phenomenon and would not sustain for a longer period. His apprehension was very basic text book kind of analysis. Huge trade surplus naturally leads to an increase in the purchasing power of the countrymen. This encourages the demand for domestic goods and subsequently price of domestic goods rises. It has two effects: domestic consumers shift to cheaper foreign goods leading to an increase in import; and foreign consumers buy less domestic goods leading to a fall in export. Therefore, trade surplus must shrink and eventually vanish.

Thus, the idea of *Mercantilism* lost its ground. A closer look at both *Mercantilism* and *Corn Law* reveals that these are fundamentally the routes to become powerful both economically and politically. Therefore, it is apparent that the proponents of *Mercantilism* were well aware of the fact that open and free trade has a levelling effect or has the potential to equalise every country economically. In fact, *Mercantilism* is a mix of two extremes: free trade in export and complete protectionism on import.

Later on Adam Smith also criticized *Mercantilism* citing that it goes against efficiency, competition and productivity. And consequently he came up with the idea of *Vent for Surplus*. Surplus land and surplus labour arises in an isolated economy mainly due to narrowness of the domestic market. The only solution to this problem is accessing foreign market and to go for export. But the question remains: where to export? Who will buy? In order to enable others to import they should also be allowed to export their products. This is how trade may lead to growth and development leading to the notion of *export led growth*.

6. Free Trade, Hiccups, and Protectionism again

The main driving forces behind free trade were division of labour, increased competition among agents, expanding the size of the market, and reduction in wastage of resources. All these, in tandem, ensure low cost of production and price of the goods through more efficiency, less monopolisation of the market, and an increase in economies of scale. Therefore, trade was welfare improving. But was everything good with free trade? The unambiguous answer is 'no'.

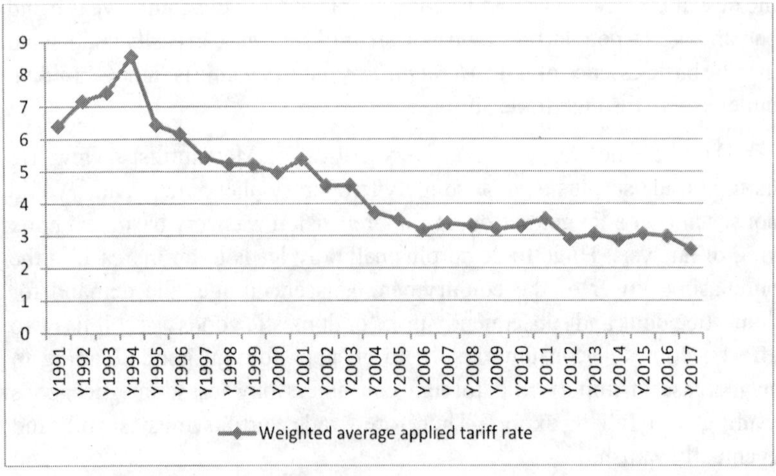

Source: World Bank, UNCTAD, WTO

Fig. 1: World Average Tariff Trend

Trade leading to growth and development is definitely not a zero sum game; it is indeed a positive sum game. In spite of that it creates both winners and losers or some gains more and some gains less. This raises conflict of interest and pressure to shift from free trade regime. This contention got further impetus owing to some basic presumptions supporting free trade as an engine of growth. This includes absence of perfectly competitive market, externalities in both production and consumption, growth in wrong direction indicating immiserisation, exorbitantly high transportation cost, effect on terms of trade etc. On top of all these, an all-round increase in wage disparity between skilled and unskilled workers because of free trade generated another worrying problem.

Accordingly, we gradually moved to a protectionist era with an aim to solve few non-trivial issues like unemployment, trade deficit, setting up of indigenous industries, dependence on other trading countries etc. But unfortunately protectionism also did not yield much desired results.

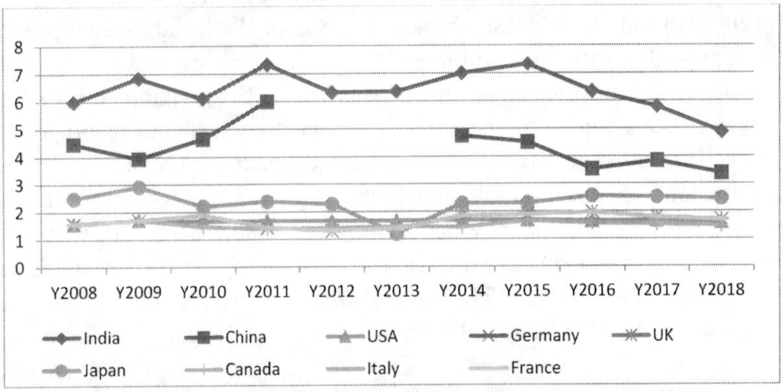

Source: World Bank, UNCTAD, WTO. China's data for some years are not available.

Fig. 2: Average Tariff Trend for Selected Countries

From thereon we had two clear and parallel waves: globalisation and protectionism. Protectionism is not in the form of very high tariff (as evident from the line diagrams) or quota following WTO agreements; but the process of formation of various trading blocs was on. The main motive was to tilt the international terms of trade in favour of its member countries. During that time globalisation mostlytook place through more free movement of goods, labour and capital. This wave of globalisation was driven by a reduction in transportation or trading cost which also helped trade in intermediate goods, outsourcing, global value chain etc. This phase is known as *second-unbundling.*

Gradually we have entered into the epoch of New Globalisation. It is less open, restricted, and limited. We may call it *deglobalisation* or resurgence of protectionism. This sort of opinion is, however, not accurate as protectionism has always been there incessantly in form of customs union, trade blocks. In fact there was Buy American Act, Buy British Campaign, European Union export subsidy etc. Very recently this protectionist approach took a serious turn with Donald Trump, H1B VISA restriction, BREXIT, trade war etc. when we are no longer living in the era of *second-unbundling*. This is the time of *third-unbundling* where cost of communication is negligible, global trade is dominated by service, distance is no more a matter of hindrance for service transaction, 40% of world GDP is produced through global value chain, 60% of global trade accrues to trade in intermediate goods and services.

Recent *deglobalisation* trend has been essentially propelled by three factors: (1) a tendency to shift back the centre of economic power to Asia;

(2) world wealth share of developed countries rose from 20% to 70% during 1820-1990, but recently it slid back to the level of 1900; and (3) an increase in income disparity both within and between countries, and no signs of worldwide factor price equalisation [Baldwin, (2016); Helpman (2018)]. These reasons forced the so called developed countries to resort to an increase in average tariff rate on imported goods, put a restriction on international labour mobility, and controlling inward and outward direct investment. Eventually they had to find out a new name in favour of protectionist arguments as *protectionism* has already been stigmatized as harmful for global welfare. Thus, *deglobalisation* surfaced though this term was used by Walden Bello, a Phillipino sociologist long back in 2005.

7. Trade War and the Golden Opportunity

Is the *Atmanirbhar Bharat* campaign a groundless one that attempts to shift away focus of the nation from the ongoing health crisis and the subsequent unavoidable economic setback? There is no clear answer to this query, though, of course, it diverts attention from some pertinent issues. But that is surely not the only motive behind such puffed up campaign as State guided campaign often induces a sort of *Bandwagon effect* helping it to become a '*movement*', and that works for good cause. During the global lockdown driven supply shock, a *Bandwagon effect* of the type we explained may, in fact, be very handy when the economy is hobbling with the problem of local supply shortage. The scope of self-reliance being much wider than catering only local market, such campaign and a nationwide concerted effort might be very constructive in exploring the export market. This should be done in a relatively cost-effective manner which again emphasises on the principle of comparative cost advantage. During corona pandemic, some countries are forced to retreat from their respective export markets and naturally, those markets are now open to all for competition. This has been originally propelled by USA-China trade war and the loss of China's credibility in the world market. India must appropriate such prospect and for that low-cost production is the major driving force, which India might be able to manage owing to huge pool of cheap labour force. In line with this strategy, not joining hands with other countries in Regional Comprehensive Economic Partnership (RCEP) is not an idiotic decision.

Hence, international lockdown and complete shutting down of labour mobility due to the spread of COVID-19 may turn out to be a boon for the Indian economy. India must capitalise on the scope thrown to her through the combination of demographic dividend, global supply shortage, and a fall in crude oil price in the world market. The *Atmanirbhar Bharat* campaign beyond its 'protectionist' layer may just act as an appropriate launching pad to break the shackles of low level equilibrium trap and to move to the next level of development trajectory.

References

Acemoglu, D., & Johnson, S. (2007). Disease and development: the effect of life expectancy on economic growth. *Journal of Political economy*, *115*(6), 925-985.

Baldwin, R. (2016). *The great convergence*. Harvard University Press.

Becker, G. S. (1962). Investment in human capital: A theoretical analysis. *Journal of political economy*, *70*(5, Part 2), 9-49.

Feenstra, R. C., & Hanson, G. H. (1996). *Globalisation, outsourcing, and wage inequality* (No. w5424). National Bureau of Economic Research.

Grossman, M. (1972).On the concept of health capital and the demand for health. *Journal of Political Economy*, *80*(2), 223-255.

Head, K., & Mayer, T. (2014). Gravity equations: Workhorse, toolkit, and cookbook. In *Handbook of International Economics* (Vol. 4, pp. 131-195). Elsevier.

Helpman, E. (2018). *Globalisation and Inequality*. Harvard University Press.

Kalemli-Ozcan, S., Ryder, H. E., & Weil, D. N. (2000). Mortality decline, human capital investment, and economic growth. *Journal of Development Economics*, *62*(1), 1-23.

Melitz, J. (2007). North, South and distance in the gravity model. *European Economic Review*, *51*(4), 971-991.

Summers, L. H., & Pritchett, L. (1996). Wealthier is healthier. *J Human Resources*, *31*(4), 841-868.

Samuelson, P. A. (1948). International trade and the equalisation of factor prices. *The Economic Journal*, *58*(230), 163-184.

Stiglitz, J. E. (2002). *Globalisation and its Discontents* (Vol. 500). Norton: New York.

UNCTAD (2020): https://unctadstat.unctad.org/wds/ReportFolders/ reportFolders. aspx?sCS_ChosenLang=en, accessed in August, 2020.

Well, D. N. (2007). Accounting for the effect of health on economic growth. *The quarterly journal of economics*, *122*(3), 1265-1306.

World Bank (2020): https://wits.worldbank.org/CountryProfile/en/IND , accessed in August, 2020.

World Trade Organisation (2020): https://www.wto.org/english/res_e/ statis_e/ statis_e.htm, accessed in August, 2020.

Notes

1. Another undeniable economic setback would follow through the conduit of quality of human capital. In this context, health becomes the most predominant factor. Following Becker (1962), Grossman (1972) was among the very few to formally establish the connectedness among health and improvement in health as investment in human capital. Improvement in health not only enhances

productivity immediately, it also adds to the stock of human capital and increases the rate of human capital formation for augmenting productivity in future. Productivity rises in both manual and psychological fronts. Hence the link between health, human capital and economic growth is apparent. Acemoglu et al. (2007), Kalemi-Ozcan et al. (2000), Summers et al. (1996), Well (2007) etc. are some notable works to explore further the adage -healthier is wealthier. But, unfortunately, accessible health infrastructure in various countries are showing signs of waning in their incessant warfare against the pandemic. In what follows is a gradual deteriorating health condition of the society. This obviously calls for a significant amount of government money being justifiably siphoned off for treating Corona patients and for protecting the others. Thus, the governments would be left with no choice but to cutback spending to finance other programmes including health and human capital for future. So, it goes without saying that the niggling question coming to the fore is who is going to substitute human capital? What would happen to mental health, happiness, social capital etc.? These are some worrying difficulties one has to get to grip with even if we pull through the current quandary.

6

India's Response to COVID-19 and *Atmanirbhar* Package: A Critical Annotation

Seemantini Chattopadhyay

Abstract

The Atma Nirbhar Bharat Abhiyan (ANBA) is a combination of reforms, monetary and fiscal measures to combat the on-going economic crises. In particular, the package promises (a) to increase the liquidity by giving collateral free loans to small, medium and micro enterprises and by offering reduced rate of interest by the banks and other financial institutions and (b) to provide direct support to the vulnerable section of the population by transferring money, especially through increasing the allocation in the employment guarantee schemes. Importantly, even before the outbreak of COVID-19 pandemic, Indian economy was already witnessing an economic slowdown. Against this background, the paper examines the various components of the economic package announced with respect to the supply and demand sides of the economy and assesses it's effectiveness in dealing with the economic slowdown in the country. The paper also compares the financial stimulus of ANBA with that in other countries to fight the economic crises following the outbreak of corona virus. As the announcements of the package have been subjected to severe criticism over the real quantum and the prospective effects, an attempt has been made to document the various suggestions offered by the critiques and, accordingly, to prescribe specific measures needed in the short run as well as in the long run for making the program truly effective.

Key Words: *Atmanirbhar, Economic Slowdown, Economic Package, Economic Growth, Liquidity.*

Introduction

Covid-19 and the attendant preventive measures, such as lockdowns, have halted almost all economic activities in most economies across the world and led to a massive humanitarian crisis of unprecedented nature. In India, a nationwide lockdown was announced on 23rd March 2020 to stop the spread of the COVID-19. Accordingly, the whole nation came to a halt till 20th April after which some relaxations were announced to keep a balance between health crisis and economic crisis. Indian economy was already witnessing a slowdown during the pre-pandemic era with increasing unemployment and significant "income crunch" for both rural and urban sectors leading to sharp reduction in aggregate demand in the country. With reduced aggregate demand, there was no sign of fresh investment in the business sector due to the existence of excess capacity and reduced return on the already invested capital (Sen, 2020).

The initial 21-day lockdown was expected to further accelerate the slowdown and jeopardised the economic wellbeing of millions of people, especially the marginalised ones. The unlocking phase started from 20th April, 2020 with gradual relaxation and since then India witnessed

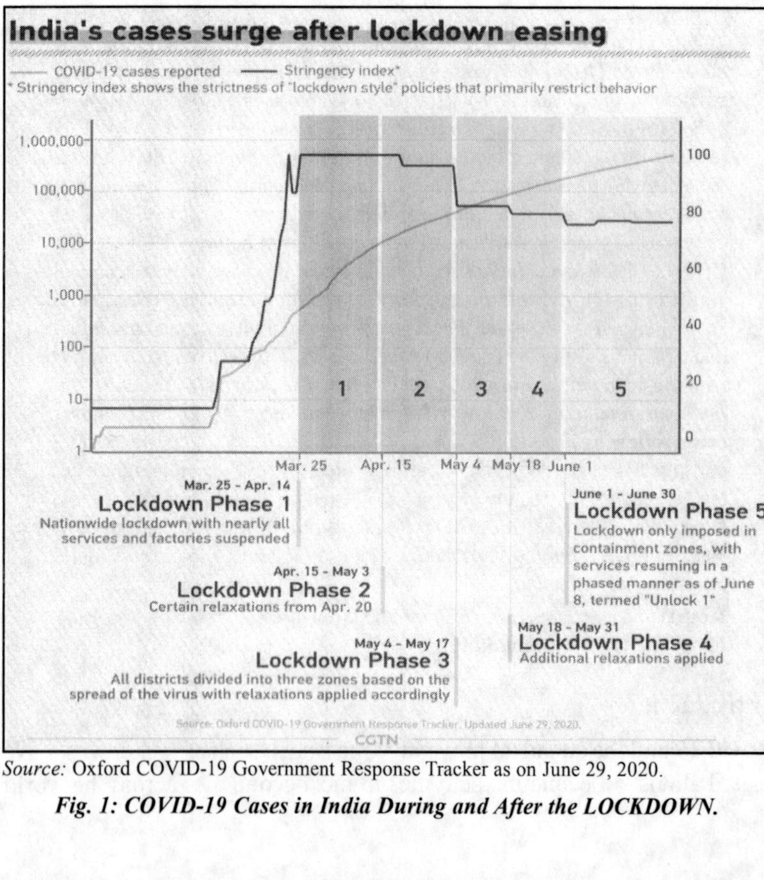

Source: Oxford COVID-19 Government Response Tracker as on June 29, 2020.

Fig. 1: COVID-19 Cases in India During and After the LOCKDOWN.

massive surge in the number of COVID cases (Yiwei, 2020). The first 100,000 cases recorded in 109 days but the next 100,000 cases were added in only 6 days since the relaxation of lockdown took place as evident from the following figure (Figure 1).

A preliminary assessment report of ILO documents the disastrous impact of COVID 19 on employment with expected loss of more than 300 million full-time jobs in the second quarter of 2020 and disruption of economic activities of around 436 million enterprises worldwide (International Labour Organisation, 2020). In conformity with this worldwide trend, unemployment in India started rising sharply since the end March 2020 (Figure 2).

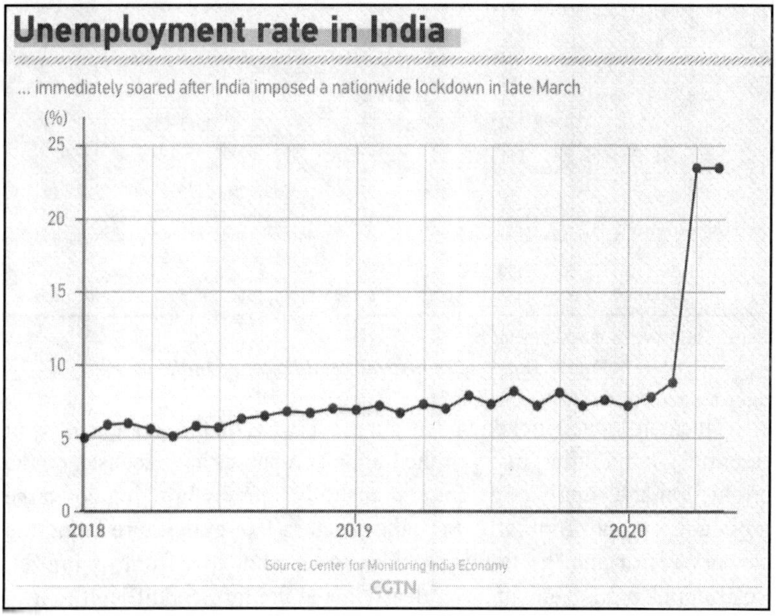

Source: CMIE, 2020.

Fig. 2: Unemployment Rate in India.

Millions of people, especially the daily wage earners, small traders, lost their jobs and even the corporate sector resorted to pay cuts and job termination and the major organisations and start-ups took a deep fall. The stock markets in India recorded the worst losses faced by various institutions in the history of India on the 23rd of March, 2020. India's services business activity index came in at a shocking 5.4 in April, the largest month-to-month contraction since its data collection began over 14 years ago as recorded by IHS Markit. Industrial production, as reported by the Ministry of Statistics and Programme Implementation, dropped sharply when factories were closed under lockdown (Figure 3).

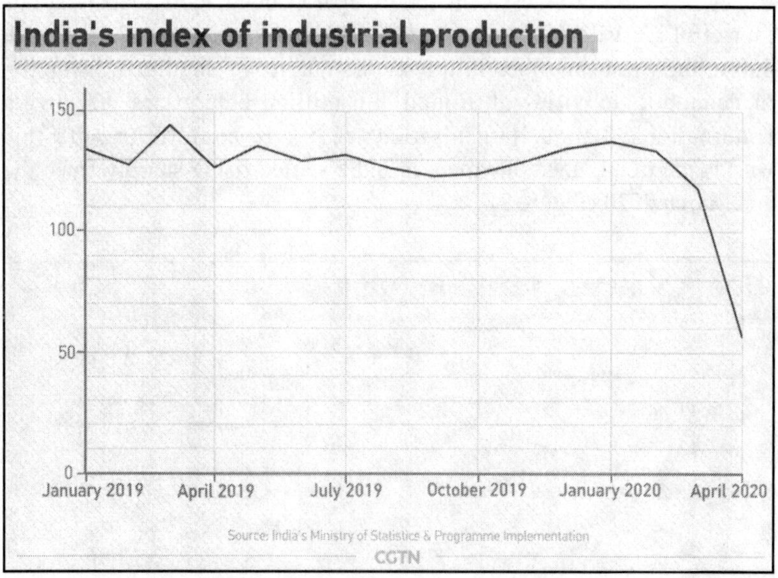

Source: http://www.mospi.gov.in/

Fig. 3: Index of Industrial Production of India

Since prolonged lockdown has put great stress on the supply chains of essential commodities, many of the Indian companies have focused on the production and supply of essential items only, thereby bringing down the production graph. Similarly, the other sectors like agriculture being the primary sector and the tertiary sector are also not free from its impact. Restrictions on movement have clearly made the farmers difficult to take their produce for sale to the markets (Sengupta and Vardhan, 2020). Informal sector, the backbone of Indian economy, is the hardest hit in view of economic activities coming to a total standstill. The workers in informal sector are the most vulnerable ones, having no social security benefits and constitute a major share of the workforce. The lockdown has brought total shutting down of tourism sector. The live events industry has also estimated a loss of more than ₹ 3000 crores (Gupta, 2020). These lockdowns and restrictions on commercial activities and public gatherings are necessarily likely to strongly impact domestic growth. The Centre for Monitoring Indian Economy (CMIE) estimated the overall unemployment rate to surge to 23 percent, with urban unemployment standing at nearly 31 percent.

The Government of India announced the much awaited economic package of ₹ 20 lakh crores, equivalent to 10% of India's GDP, to revive the economy on 12th May 2020. The ATMANIRBHAR BHARAT ABHIYAN (ANBA) has focussed on land, labour, middle income tax payers, industries, Micro, Small and Medium Enterprises (MSMEs) to bring about reforms across all the sectors of the economy to make India self-reliant. Emphasis has been placed on the local resources in catering to the local needs during the lockdown. Self-reliance of India has been assumed to be achieved by relying on its inner potential and making them global. In particular, the ATMANIRBHAR BHARAT was based on five pillars and they are - (i) economy which will have quantum jumps rather incremental changes, (ii) infrastructure representing the modern India, (iii) system, driven by technology to fulfil the dreams of 21st century, (iv) vibrant demography as a source of energy and (v) demand i.e. fully utilising the power of supply as well as demand. Against this background, the paper examines the various components of the economic package announced with respect to the supply and demand sides of the economy and assesses it's effectiveness in dealing with the economic slowdown in the country. The paper also compares the financial stimulus of ANBA with that in other countries to fight the economic crises following the outbreak of corona virus. As the announcements of the package have been subjected to severe criticism over the real quantum and the prospective effects, an attempt has been made to document the various suggestions offered by the critiques and, accordingly, to prescribe specific measures needed in the short run as well as in the long run for making the package truly effective.

Dissecting the Economic Package

The Finance Minister of India gave the detailed account of the ATMANIRBHAR BHARAT ABHIYAN stimulus package in five phases. Although the economic package was being termed as fiscal stimulus and it was claimed to be 10 percent of GDP but actually it was much lesser than that. An allocation of fund is considered to be 'fiscal stimulus' if and only if money goes directly to the hands of the beneficiaries so that they can use it for consumption which will add to the aggregate demand of the economy under consideration. The first announcement, on 13th May, focused mainly on Micro, Small and Medium Enterprises (MSMEs), Non-Banking Financial Companies, Housing Finance Companies and Micro Finance Institutions. The financial assistance provided to them was more of liquidity driven with no immediate effect on the aggregate demand, as it did not transfer cash directly to the hands of beneficiaries. It was more of a loan or a long-term investment whose return would be realised under certain conditions. The pre-pandemic era was already going through a phase of excess capacity and lack of overall demand. Therefore, without provisioning for demand in the present situation, injecting liquidity provision might not bring about the expected return. The provisioning of funds should have been to boost the consumption expenditure to deal with the slackening aggregate demand.

The reduction in Employees' Provident Fund (EPF) rate (about ₹ 6750 crore) have got direct positive impact on the demand as more money will be available in the hands of the employees to spend but the effectiveness of the same depends on the coverage of the EPF scheme (KPMG Report, 2020). Some of the developing countries such as Indonesia and Bangladesh have significantly increased the coverage of schemes after COVID-19. The majority of the workforce in India cannot come under such scheme as they belong to the informal sector having no social security coverage from their employees. The Periodic Labour Force Survey shows that around 50% (52.5% for rural and 47.7% for urban) of the regular wage/salaried employees are not eligible for any kind of social security benefit including EPF (in 2017-18). Therefore, the impact of such stimulus remained doubtful in bringing the expected outcome. If we closely analyse the first tranche of the package, only about 10 percent could be considered as actual fiscal stimulus.

The second tranche came on 14th May, which consisted of free food grains distribution through the state governments to the migrant labourers for three months amounting to ₹ 3500 crore for two months, interest subvention for MUDRA (Micro Units Development and Refinance Agency Ltd.), Shishu loan (₹ 1500 crore), Housing Credit Linked Subsidy Scheme (CLSS) through which the government sought to provide more cash in the hand of people worthy of ₹ 75,000 crore. The fiscal stimulus in this tranche was actually 24.2 percent approximately. Rest of the allocation such as additional working capital through NABARD, additional credit via Kisan Credit Card, special loans to the street vendors did not contribute towards consumption.

The third tranche was mainly allocated to improve the agriculture infrastructure and skill development in allied activities, which was long pending. A portion of which was already allotted in the Union Budget in February 2020. Again, the type of allocation in this tranche would be helpful to strengthen the supply side of the agriculture and allied activities rest aside the demand side constraint faced by the economy in the pandemic situation.

The fourth tranche completely focussed on coal, minerals, defence, power distribution, civil aviation, space and atomic energy sectors which hardly drive the aggregate demand of the economy in the short run. On account of similar logic, viability gap funding worth ₹ 8,100 crore, which was government's investment in infrastructure, provided no immediate incentive to stimulate private consumption spending. Only, allotment of additional ₹ 40,000 crore in Mahatma Gandhi National Rural Employment Guarantee Act (MGNREGA) scheme could bring about the desired change in the prevailing economic crisis.

In essence, the measures taken up in the ATMANIRBHAR BHARAT ABHIYAN project were largely in line of giving a strong supply-side push by boosting the availability of capital on easy terms and putting minimum burden on the exchequer. Direct transfer of cash, the most popular instrument in dealing with such crisis, constituted minimum share of the package. The fiscal stimulus of ₹ 20 lakh crore actually came down to 1.27 percent of GDP (Table 1).

Table 1: Final Calculation of the Fiscal Stimulus

Sl. No.	*Item*	*(Rs. Cr.)*	*Actual fiscal stimulus (Rs. Cr.)*
1.	Part 1	5,94,550	59,550
2.	Part 2	3,10,000	75,000
3.	Part 3	1,50,000	0
4.	Parts 4 and 5	48,100	40,000
	Sub-Total	**11,02,650**	**1,74,550**
5.	Earlier measures including PMGKY	192,800**	62,000+7,800+15,000=84,800
6.	RBI Measures (Actual) (This is entirely liquidity provision, which can only translate into fiscal infusion if government borrows from that provision and distributes as fiscal package)	8,01,603	0
Sub-Total		**9,94,403**	**84,800**
GRAND TOTAL		**20,97,053**	**2,59,350**
In terms of share of GDP		**10.29%**	**1.27%**

Source: Dey and Kundu (2020)

Note: (i) ** ₹ 192,800 crore = 170,000 crore is PMGKY + 7,800 crore as revenue lost due to tax cut + 15,000 crores as PM's announcement for the health sector. (ii) A back-of envelope calculation shows that the total budget commitment for all the measures announced under the 170,000 crore for PMGKY is not more than ₹ 62,000 crore.

The rest were repackaging of some old measures, some new reforms in agriculture and public sector enterprises which was pending for long and appropriation of liquidity measures announced by the RBI. Moreover, the centre agreed to increase the borrowing limits of the states to 5 percent of GSDP from 3 percent of GSDP. But the state could only borrow 0.5 percent unconditionally. One percent would be released in tranches of 0.25 percent each of the following – (i) to reforms in urban local body revenues, (ii) one nation one ration card, (iii) power distribution and (iv) ease of doing business. The balance 0.5 percent would be released upon states' implementation of at least three of the four milestones.

Comparing the ANBA with Economic Packages of other Economies

While there are differences across the countries with respect to the extent of COVID-19 spread, socio-political-economic factors and mode of fiscal policies prescribed by the government, a comparative analysis of the fiscal stimulus, both quantitatively and qualitatively, might help us to review the ATMANIRBHAR package announced by the Indian government and also to get a better perspective of future course of action.

According to an IMF report (October 2020) the additional spending or foregone revenues of India's economic package is 1.2 percent of GDP whereas the same figure for UK is 6.2 percent of 2019 UK GDP; for Germany it is 9.4 percent of their GDP; for Japan it is as high as 11.3 percent of Japan GDP and US declared 12.3 percent of the US GDP. Compared to the additional spending or foregone revenues of developing countries, such as Brazil (6.5 percent of GDP), China (4.1 percent of GDP) and Indonesia (2.4 percent of GDP), India scored quite low (Ghatak and Dhingra, 2020). While comparing the financial support extended to the informal sector workers, small enterprises and mostly affected areas bearing the brunt of the COVID-19, it was observed that Vietnam gave $77 (₹ 5870) per month to the workers who are temporarily laid-off or forced to go on unpaid leave and $43 (₹ 3280) per month to the self-employed and the workers without any social security benefit. Brazil announced $115 (₹ 8760) per month for three months to the workers in the informal sector (54 million workers) (Coutinho and Basole). India might not be in such financially flamboyant state but what it offered i.e., ₹ 500 (around $7) per month to 200 million women and similar kind of direct cash transfer at the state level to the marginalised and most affected workers fell far short of the other comparable economies of the world. Also it was far from meeting the challenges of slackening demand in the country. Many developing countries such as Indonesia, Vietnam, Bangladesh and China announced tax relief in terms of deferments or reduction for small and medium-sized enterprises suffering from COVID-19. These reductions allowed the firms to defer contributions to social security funds which would in turn reduce their operating cost in order to remain afloat in the business. India also announced Employees' Provident Fund support for business and workers and reduction in EPF rates and the 25 percent reduction in TDS/TCS rates for non-salaried payments was a welcome move to increase short term liquidity. Moreover, there was significant expansion of coverage of cash transfer programmes from pre-COVID-19 levels in many developing countries. Bangladesh and Indonesia - increased the number of beneficiaries by 163% and 111%, respectively (Coutinho and Basole, 2020). In Indonesia, cash schemes covered more than 158 million people (or 60% of the population) and also the government of Indonesia created two new unconditional cash schemes to reach 20 million individuals in urban and rural settings excluded from the current social protection measures.

Evaluating the ATMANIRBHAR Package – a Critique

A great economist of his time, Milton Friedman, famously observed, "One of the great mistakes is to judge policies and programmes by their intentions rather than the results". The ATMANIRBHAR BAHARAT ABHIYAN package announced by Indian government to fight the evil of COVID-19 drew both applaud for using very craftily the COVID-19 pandemic crisis to plough through long pending, deep-rooted structural reforms and adverse criticism for its meagerness towards immediate fiscal transfers to boost the falling aggregate demand. On one hand, the government did well in increasing the budget for MGNREGA by two-thirds by adding another ₹ 40,000 crore. With migrant workers now returning to their villages, MGNREGA could be leveraged to keep them occupied with meaningful work for their sustenance. The demand of States for higher borrowings limit was also granted but with clear reform goals that they have to meet. The government also used the opportunity to unleash some much-needed reforms in agriculture marketing (Chauhan, 2020). Also, reduction in the rate of 'Tax Deduction at Source' and 'Tax Collected at Source' for all non-salaried payment to residents by 25 percent of the remaining FY 2020-21 would inject liquidity in the economy. On the other hand, it is observed that majority (almost three-fourth) of the ABA package was about potential liquidity infusion and expected increase in the credit off take at aggregate level. But the potentiality of this liquidity injection would be realised if there is increase in the investment demand which in turn depends on the increase in the aggregate demand for goods and services produced in the economy (Das, 2020). But aggregate demand is directly related to aggregate income, which needs to be enhanced by providing more and more direct transfer of cash through various schemes already floating in the economy. As per the official records 29.84 crore bank accounts are there under Jan Dhan Yojana with 38.35 crore beneficiaries; around 6 crore beneficiaries are there under MGNREGA programme; 8.5 crore account holders are there under PM Kisan schemes and 65 lakh SHGs are there involving almost 7 crore women mostly in rural areas. On an immediate basis demand could be boosted by channelizing funds directly to these accounts (Dey and Kundy, 2020). In order to achieve expected results of the package, many of it's initiatives require efficient coordination between central government, state government and local level government for proper targeting of beneficiaries. The NGOs can play an important role as being the missing link between the provider and the receivers to facilitate different schemes of the government on an immediate basis. The Atmanirbhar Bharat Abhiyan remained silent about the rehabilitation of the migrant labourers. Millions of migrant workers endured immense hardships to trudge back home and are unlikely to return to towns in the foreseeable future. Employment has to be provided to them where they are, for which the MGNREGA in rural areas should be strengthened and also must be designed and extended to urban areas as the problem of COVID – 19 is found to be deeper in urban areas (Das, 2020). On the supply side, the package addressed the finance related issues but missed the crucial issue of supply chain disruption due to the nation-wide lockdown and restriction of movement across the world. Moreover, the corporate revenues reportedly fell by more than 25 percent during the lockdown. They need relief and tax refunds in order to retain payroll and maintain liquidity to bear the operating cost. The government can waive the GST partly for six months period to give them some respite. The plight of the large number of workers in the organised sector facing heavy pay cuts, job losses, a sharp fall in income, and uncertainty attracted little attention in the package.

Further, it has been observed that ₹ 9.73 lakh crore has been allotted for potential liquidity injection, through various measures of RBI, into the banking and financial system and ₹ 6.25 lakh crore to the MSMEs, the farmers by providing collateral free or partially guaranteed easy loans. Approximately, these two accounts for more than 75 percent of the package, which is expected to boost the overall credit off-take of the economy. But increase in aggregate demand for credit depends on increase in aggregate investment which in turn depends on the expected return on the investment project. But return or profitability of an investment solely depends on the aggregate demand in the market. Moreover, the causal relationship between infused liquidity and aggregate demand will be fulfilled if and only if the MSMEs and farmers do not substitute their past debts with easy and collateral free loans. RBI has lowered the repo rate to 4 percent (an all-time low repo rate) and also reduced the reserve ratio to make the path of an easy loan in the market. The resultant effect of increased liquidity in the market must be reflected in increased credit-deposit ratio of all the commercial banks after the announcement of the economic package. But it has been found out that the credit-deposit ratio started falling after March 27, 2020 following the lockdown (Das, 2020). The deposits have been increasing and the credit off-take is falling continuously since the problem lies in dearth of aggregate demand in the economy, not the scarcity of liquidity. Eventually, the agenda of injecting liquidity (constituting more than three-fourth of the Atmanirbhar package) in order to boost the economy out of the pandemic situation is bound to be unsuccessful.

Summing Up

Following a careful analysis of the package and experts' suggestions, it seems that the popularity of direct cash transfer in this pandemic situation cannot be ignored. The various economic packages announced by developed and developing economies discussed in this paper clearly suggest that to revive the economy out of the trap of slackening demand, cash transfer in the hands of the people, bearing the brunt of the shock, is the most effective strategy. This is further corroborated by the World Bank's list of 621 measures across 173 countries out of which half are cash-based. Rests are mostly related to food assistance (23%) or waiver/postponement of financial obligations (25%). Only 2 percent is related to public works (Dey and Kundu, 2020). Such popularity of cash transfers over public works for income support could perhaps in part be attributed to concerns over physical distancing. The supply side of the economy would realise the benefit of the package if only they can accrue the return by selling their products. So, there should be a balance of both supply and demand side of the economy while designing the package. Since we are going through a pandemic situation which has been the cruellest since the Second World War, far fetching reforms and benefits are not something people from different strata of the economy expect from the government. On an immediate basis, the central government as well as state government should encourage rolling out of big infrastructure projects by maintaining social distancing, to boost demand and create employment. The state governments need substantial financial support to fight with the pandemic as the disease is spreading rapidly in most of the states and healthcare system is also suffering from inadequate infrastructure and funds. A quick transfer of various tax and other dues to the states can serve the purpose to some extent. Local level governments (panchayat and municipalities) should be playing pivotal roles to spread awareness about the coronavirus disease as well as ensuring all the endeavours of the higher level government to fight with the current health hazards and consequent economic crises. Self-reliance or Atmanirbhar essentially signifies the importance of local manufacturing, local supply chain, and local market in the time of restricted movements in the national as well as global front. It emphasises on the realisation of inner potentiality which will increase the efficiency and competitiveness of various sectors of the economy in the long run. But in the short run the government needs to embrace multiple mechanisms to revive the economy by boosting aggregate demand. If not, then soon India as a nation will face a larger threat than that of a health pandemic – poverty, destitution, and hunger – signs of which are already visible in many parts of the country.

References

Chauhan, A K (2020): "How does India's recent stimulus package compare with other countries?", https://www.cnbctv18.com/views/how-does-indias-recent-stimulus-package-compare-with-other-countries-5966521.htm.

Coutinho, J. and Basole, A (2020): "India must enhance fiscal support for COVID-19 relief and rebuilding" https://www.thehindu.com/opinion/op-ed/comment-india-must-enhance-fiscal-support-for-covid-19-relief-and-rebuilding/article31373123.ece.

Das, S (2020): "An estimation of required fiscal stimulus to revive the economy in India" https://vikalp.ind.in/2020/05/an-estimation-of-required-fiscal/ May 6.

Das, S (2020): "Why Modi Govt's Atmanirbhar Abhiyan Package would fail" https://www.businesstoday.in/opinion/columns/modi-govt-atmanirbhar-bharat-abhiyan-would-fail-covid19-lockdown-self-reliant-india/story/410133.html, September 1.

Dey, S and Kundu, A (2020): "Atmanirbhar Bharat Abhiyan: Putting the cart before the horse" https://www.ideasforindia.in/topics/money-finance/atmanirbhar-bharat-abhiyan-putting-the-cart-before-the horse.html#:~:text=In%20an%20attempt%20to%20tackle,to%2010%25%20of%20India's%20GDP.

Ghatak, M and Dingra, S (2020): "Comparing Rishi Sunak's Plan For Uk To India's Steps", https://www.ndtv.com/opinion/what-would-rishi-sunak-make-of-indias-economic-plan-2265603.

Gupta, A (2020): "India: Coronavirus (COVID-19) and Indian Economy" https://www.mondaq.com/india/operational-impacts-and-strategy/936014/coronavirus-covid-19-and-indian-economy.

IMF Report (2020): *Fiscal Monitor Database of Country Fiscal Measures in Response to the COVID-19 Pandemic*; IMF Fiscal Affairs Department, October.

KPMG Report (2020): *Potential Impact of COVID-19 on the Indian Economy*, April.

Sen, P (2020): "The Covid-19 shock: Learnings from the Past addressing the Present" https://www.ideasforindia.in/topics/macroeconomics/the-covid-19-shock-learnings-from-the-past-addressing-the-present-i.html, June 5.

Sengupta, R and Vardhan, H (2020): "The pandemic and the package" https://www.ideasforindia.in/topics/macroeconomics/the-pandemic-and-the-package.html, 04 June.

Yiwei, H (2020): "Graphics: How COVID-19 lockdown hit India's economy" https://news.cgtn.com/news/2020-06-30/Graphics-How-COVID-19-lockdown-hit-India-s-economy-RJSmm5Laes/index.html, 30 June.

7

Empirical Analysis of Long-Run and Short-Run Dynamic Effects of Deposit Rate, Inflation Rate and GDP on Bank Deposit: A Vector Error Correction Model Approach

Solomon Kebede Menza

Abstract

This paper empirically examines the long-run and short-run dynamic effects of deposit rate (r), inflation rate (π) and GDP on bank deposit. The study targeted commercial bank of Ethiopia (CBE) because it has been taking a lion's share in terms of deposit amount, which in turn plays a vital role in deposit refunding for investors. To show the long-run and short-run dynamic effects of r, π and GDP on the deposit amount of CBE we took 30 years data from the year 1988 to 2017 from MOFED, CSA, National Bank of Ethiopia and CBE data sets. To achieve the objectives vector error correction model (VECM) was used after checking the possible assumptions of our economic series. The results of ADF test statistics confirms our economic series are stationary at their first difference. This indicates that the variables are integrated of order one, I (1). Johansen's co-integration test suggests one co-integrating relationship between the variables. According to our findings, the coefficient of the error correction term for CBE deposit is statistically significant, and the speed of convergence to equilibrium of approximately 16 percent. Hence, in the short run, deposits are adjusted by 16 percent of the past year's deviation from equilibrium. The joint effect result indicates that except deposit rate all included variables have no significant short-run effect on deposit amount. More specifically, the result of Johansen normalisation restriction shows in the long-run on average inflation rate and GDP have a negative effect on deposit, while deposit rate has a positive effect on the total amount of deposit held by CBE, among other findings. Finally, the government and other concerned bodies should take necessary steps to mobilize deposit in CBE.

Key Words: *Annual Deposit, Vector Error Correction Model, Commercial Bank of Ethiopia.*

1. Introduction

1.1. Background of the Study

The financial sector like insurance companies, banks, micro-finance institutions, saving and credit institutions can play a significant role in the economy of a given nation. As car does not operate with the absence of fuel so does the economy of a given country without financial institutions. This implies that financial institutions are synergies for the economic growth as well as development of a nation. The banking industry accounts for about 82 percent of the total financial sector assets, implying that the financial sector is under developed (NBE, 2015). Thus, banking sector is the largest component of the financial system, and it plays great role on all aspects of the national economy (Falkena et al., 2004).

Currently banks, insurance companies and micro finance institutions (MFIs) constitute the main financial institutions in Ethiopia. The number of operating banks reached 19 as of June 2017 of which 16 are owned privately. The bank branches reached 2,693, with the private sector accounting for 58.1percent. Consequently, the ratio of bank branches to population was reduced to 33,448.2, reflecting an improvement in financial services outreach. Total banking system capital reached ETB 31.5 billion, of which private banks accounted for 56.5 percent. The state-owned commercial bank of Ethiopia (CBE) accounted for 34 percent of banking system capitalisation. Meanwhile, total banking system loan disbursements reached ETB 18.9 billion, of which 55.6 percent was by public banks and the remainder by private banks. About 99.6 percent of the private banks' new loans and 54.5 percent of public banks loans went to the private sector. About 99.8 percent of outstanding private banks loans were claims on private enterprises. While 58.1 percent of public banks outstanding loans (excluding credit to government and inter-bank lending) were claims on public enterprises, 41.9 percent were on private enterprises (NBE, 2017). In addition, from the total capital invested in the banking sector the share of CBE is 34 percent but the share of 16 private banks where only 56.5 percent. This indicates that the role of government owned bank and his playing field are by far different from private owned banks.

Ethiopian banking sector is small in absolute and relative size, which could be characterised by low loan deposit ratios and, as a result, large shares of assets held in the form of government securities (IMF, 2016). There is a general view that monopolistic competition among banks in terms of price and investment opportunity. Meaning, Competition in terms of price is relatively weak in the Ethiopian banking industry (Zerayesus et al., 2003).

Deposit by individuals is a major source to resource mobilisation of CBE in particular and banks in general. Hence, deposits have a strong impact in resource mobilisation of commercial Banks. On the basis of resource mobilisation purpose CBE serve different types of deposit mobilisation strategies. These forms were demand deposit, time deposit, youth deposit, saving deposit, women deposit, and fixed time deposit. As a financial intermediary, CBE can collect a deposit from individuals and lends back to these who need capital for investment (Mohammad and Mahdi, 2010). Therefore, banks play an intermediary role by collecting excess money in the form of deposit and provide a loan for those who need finance. However, there have been cases whereby private companies and small-scale firms complaining about lack of loans and credit facilities, particularly those which were not able to present collateral properties (World Bank, 2011). In addition, as of the study by Abay (2010) Ethiopia's rate of domestic saving has been very low as of the standard of Sub-Saharan countries.

1.2 Statement of The Problem

According to Franklin et al. (2011) banks perform various roles in the economy. For instance, they improve the information gap between borrowers and investors by monitoring the latter and ensuring an appropriate use of the depositors' endowment. They provide inter-temporal smoothing of risk that cannot be diversified at a given point in a time as well as insurance to depositors against unexpected consumption shocks. Due to the mismatch between the maturity of their assets and liabilities, nevertheless banks are subject to the possibility of runs and systematic risk. Similarly, the role of banking sector in the Ethiopian economy is to revolve deposits from the general public investors on interest bases. This shows that depositors are the major stakeholders of banks in deposit mobilisation strategies (Mahdi, 2008).

Furthermore, banks mobilise, allocate and invest much of society's savings. Households, government and businesses are mainly using banks to save their money to get loan for their project undertakings. According to Kelvin (2001), in most cases commercial banks hold more assets than any other financial institutions. In a nutshell the role of commercial banks are facilitating growth and development in the economy. Savings mobilisation becomes the most important strategy for the economy when economic growth is planned within the framework of targets with maximum reliance on internal resources (Roy, 2003). Roy reflecting the contemporary situation of Ethiopia showed that most of the mega projects, including the Grand Ethiopian Renaissance Dam, are financed by internal resources, deposit is now much more significant than ever in Ethiopia.

On the last decades the size of Ethiopian economy has been shown an improvement and accommodating different FDI coupled with the accessibility of banks and banking information systems among dwellers of Ethiopia which have an important impact on the deposit growth of banks.This raises questions on the capacity of commercial banks in enhancing its deposit bases thereby to enhance liquidity services (Hibret, 2015). In addition, IMF and WB strategic process of financial sector liberalisation intensified competitions among different commercial banks in Ethiopia by following akin forms of deposit mobilisations.

Examining macroeconomic factors effect on the deposit amount and growth would help policy-makers as of in preparing deposit mobilisation strategies. Deposit mobilisation is the major services of commercial banks. Currently in Ethiopia, the pace of the banking system to mobilise adequate resources would not be sufficient, given the large fund requirement of the economy that would certainly result in liquidity gap. This might be due to the fact that majority of people in Ethiopia are using traditional way of saving, holding money in cash and asset forms particularly in country-sides.Thus, the deposit mobilisation practice among commercial banks both government and private owned banks, are not as such accessible at grass root levels (Alemayehu, 2015).

Majority of studies focused from the side of household saving behaviours by giving low attentions for deposit mobilisation in banks. Few scholars had conducted an empirical study on factors affecting deposit mobilisation in Ethiopia. Accordingly, the major variables that affect deposit of banks include inflation rate, interest rate, exchange rate, demographic change (population growth) and branch expansion, among others. According to the findings of Wubetu (2012) branch expansion had positive and significant effect on total deposit whereas deposit interest rate and inflation rate were statistically insignificant affecting deposit. As opposed to this finding, Tizita (2014) reported that branch expansion has negative effect on private saving in the short term. She also concluded that inflation rate influenced private saving negatively and significantly. As per the finding of Tizita level of real per capita income and urbanisation ratio has significant positive effect on private savings.

According to Andinet (2016), inflation rate has a negative and insignificant effect, while interest rate had a positive and significant effect on commercial bank deposit. Contrary the finding of Giragn (2015) found that inflation rate has a positive and statistically significant effect on bank deposit amount. Even though, the direction of the movement between inflation rate and deposit are positive, statistically insignificant according to the study conducted on CBE by Shemsu (2015). Similarly, the effect of interest rate on the total deposit of banks had a mixed result as of the study by Andinet (2016), Shemsu (2014), Dereje (2017) and Wubit (2012).

The above statements are indicating that majority of scholars had conducted research on deposit mobilisation focusing on commercial banks, both private and government jointly to identify factors that affects commercial bank deposits. In addition, majority of the studies conducted in Ethiopia are observing cross-sectional data, and some others examined time series data by mixing micro level factors with macro level factors to examine factors that determines bank deposit. Accordingly, there has been inconsistency in their findings. This might be due to their methodological approach, the type of data, and the time span coverage under their study. Hence, this study is conducted to narrow the gap of these controversial results by applying vector error correction model and examining only major macro-level factors, and considering only commercial bank of Ethiopia because of the fact that majority of Ethiopians had an account from this bank. Moreover, the study analyses based on secondary data covering a time span from 1988-2017 for 30 years' annual data.

1.3 Objectives of the Study

The general objective of this study is to examine the long-run and short-run dynamic effects of deposit rate, inflation rate and GDP on bank deposit of commercial bank of Ethiopia. While the specific objectives of the study are:

1. To identify the existence of long-run dynamics relationship between deposit amount of CBE and inflation rate, deposit rate, GDP, and their reverse causations.
2. To identify the short run dynamics between deposit amount of CBE and inflation rate, deposit rate, GDP, and their reverse causations.
3. To identify the speed of adjustment of deposits from their past year dis-equilibrium given the role of GDP, inflation rate and deposit rate.

1.4 Research Questions

The main research questions that are addressed in this study are:

1. Does macroeconomic factors like GDP, inflation rate, and deposit (interest) rate, significantly affects total deposit of CBE?
2. What are the short-run and long-run relationship as well as causation between deposit of CBE and its determinant factors?
3. What is the speed of adjustment of deposit to return to its equilibrium level?

2. Methodology of the Study

2.1 Research Design

To examine the linkage of deposit amount of CBE with respect to different macro-level variables, the researcher used quantitative research design by examining a time series data for about 30 years.

2.2 Data Source, Type and Method of Data Collection

This study used secondary data collected from different organisations like National Bank of Ethiopia, CBE, MoFED and CSA data sets. The target population under review of secondary data macroeconomic factor related with bank deposit over the period covering from 1988 to 2017 as of annual data. The macro level variables, deposit amount, deposit rate, inflation rate, and GDP, are compiled from the data base of different organisations like National Bank of Ethiopia (NBE), Ministry of Finance and Economic Development (MOFED), Central Statistics Authority (CSA) and CBE.

2.3 Method of Data Analysis

The study used both descriptive and empirical methods of analysis by using Stata 14 version. The yearly data of deposit amount, and GDP are transformed into natural logarithms form and the rest are taking their actually yearly data as it is in a linear form.

The economic series data was checked for the existence of stationarity of the variables at level form by using Augmented Dickey Fuller (ADF) test to use least square estimation technique of vector autoregressive (VAR) model. However, the result of unit test shows that all variables are not stationary at level form, hence we checked stationarity of the variables at first difference, $I_{(1)}$. If the data are stationary at first difference, then we proceed with co-integration test. Co-integration is a necessary condition for the existence of a long run equilibrium relationship between variables having unit roots. In testing for co-integration, we have chosen the Johansen Maximum Likelihood method, for which optimal lag order is selected by employing Akaike Information Criterion (AIC), Hannan-Quinn Information Criterion (HQ), Final Prediction Error (FPE), and Schwarz Information Criterion (SC). The test procedure for ADF test is applied on the following model:

$$\Delta Y_t = \alpha + \beta_t + \partial Y_{t-1} + \gamma_1 \Delta Y_{t-1} + \cdots + \gamma_{p-1} \Delta Y_{t-p+1} + \varepsilon_t \qquad \ldots(i)$$

The unit root test is then conducted with the null hypothesis (H_0) of $\partial = 0$ against the alternative hypothesis(H_1) of $\partial < 0$.

If we obtain at least one co-integrating relationship among our variables, we can proceed to carry out Vector Error Correction Model (VECM) that pinpoints about the speed of adjustment to long run equilibrium avoiding the spurious regression problem (Engle and Granger, 1987). Diagnostic test have been carried out to the estimated VECM model by employing Jarque-Bera (J-B) test for normally distributed disturbances, Lagrange Multiplier (LM) test for residual auto-correlation, stability conditions of the VEC estimates and White Test with cross products for heteroscedasticity. We can specify the VEC model as follows:

$$\Delta Y_t = \pi Y_{t-k} + \tau_1 \Delta Y_{t-1} + \tau_2 \Delta Y_{t-2} + \tau_3 \Delta Y_{t-3} + \cdots + \tau_{k-1} \Delta Y_{t-k-1} + U_t$$

$$\text{Where, } \pi = \left(\textstyle\sum_{i=1}^{k} \beta_i\right) - I_n \quad , and \tau_i = \left(\textstyle\sum_{i=1}^{j} \beta_i\right) - I_n \qquad \ldots(ii)$$

The long-run cointegrating matrix of Π determines the number of cointegrating vectors, whereby it guides us whether to use VEC model or not. The cointegration regression only considers the long-run relationship between our economic series, while the vector error correction model is developed to measure any dynamic adjustments between the first differences of economic series. we can define the error correction term as:

$$\varepsilon_t = Y_t - \beta X_t \qquad \ldots(iii)$$

Where β is the cointegrating coefficient, and ε_t is the error term from the regression of Y_t on X_t. Then the vector Error Correction Model is simply defined as:

$$\Delta Y_t = \alpha \varepsilon_{t-1} + \gamma \Delta X_t + U_t \qquad \ldots(iv)$$

Hence, the first difference of Y_t can be explained by the lagged ε_{t-1} and ΔX_t. And ε_{t-1} indicates the one period lagged values of the residuals from estimation of equilibrium error term, or in other hand, a disequilibrium error term occurred in the previous period. In addition, it indicates the speed of adjustment towards the long-run values, thereby it offers an added explanatory variable to explain ΔY_t.

It is possible to extend the above single equation vector error correction model to multivariate systems of equations. According to this paper deposit amount, average deposit rate, inflation rate and GDP are our endogenous variables. Thus, the VEC model can be written as:

$$\Delta Deposit_t = \beta_0 + \beta_1 \Delta Deposit_{t-1} + +\beta_2 \Delta Deporate_{t-1} + \beta_3 \Delta Inflanrate_{t-1} + \beta_4 \Delta GDP_{t-1} + U_{1t} \quad \text{...(5)}$$

$$\Delta Deporate_t = \alpha_0 + \alpha_1 \Delta Deposit_{t-1} + \alpha_2 \Delta Deporate_{t-1} + \alpha_3 \Delta Inflanrate_{t-1} + \alpha_4 \Delta GDP_{t-1} + U_{2t} \quad \text{...(6)}$$

$$\Delta Inflanrate_t = \delta_0 + \delta_1 \Delta Deposit_{t-1} + \delta_2 \Delta Deporate_{t-1} + \delta_3 \Delta Inflanrate_{t-1} + \delta_4 \Delta GDP_{t-1} + U_{3t} \quad \text{...(7)}$$

$$\Delta GDP_t = \gamma_0 + \gamma_1 \Delta Deposit_{t-1} + \gamma_2 \Delta Deporate_{t-1} + \gamma_3 \Delta Inflanrate_{t-1} + \gamma_4 \Delta GDP_{t-1} + U_{4t} \quad \text{...(8)}$$

where ECTt-1 is the lagged error correction term leaving from the long-run co-integrating relations between these four variables. Thus, what we are observing is the vector error correction model is basically a VAR model in its first difference form with the addition of a vector of co-integrating residuals.

3. Results and Discussions

3.1 Descriptive Data Analysis

According to our data set, the mean values of deposit, GDP, average deposit rate and inflation rate are 62.027, 63.78333, 6.4 and 9.65, respectively. According to Friedman and Woodford (2011) the optimum inflation rate is the one which is in between 2 to 3percent when interest rate is assumed to take zero value. Hence, as of Friedman the existing mean value of inflation rate is normal and does not affect the economy adversely as compared to the mean value of deposit (interest) rate. Whereas the minimum values of deposit, GDP, average deposit rate and inflation rate are 3.495, 17.5, 3.5 and -5.75, respectively. In addition, the maximum values of deposit, GDP, average deposit rate and inflation rate are 364, 200.6, 10 and 33.54, respectively (as shown in Table 3.1).

Table 3.1: Descriptive Statistics of the Variables

Variable	*Obs*	*Mean*	*Std. Dev.*	*Min*	*Max*
Deposit in billions (Birr)	30	62.02673	93.57285	3.495	364
Deposit rate	30	6.400333	1.61146	3.5	10
Inflation rate	30	9.65577	9.356703	-5.755335	33.5414
GDP in billions of USD	30	23.03453	21.40697	6.927	80.561

Source: Own computation via Stata 14, 2018.

3.2 Performance of CBE

CBE plays a catalytic role in the economic progress and development of the country. In terms of technology also it is the first bank in Ethiopia to introduce automated teller machine (ATM) service for local users. As a result, the bank has more than 15.9 million account holders in the year 2016/2017 and it takes the lion's share as compared to total private banks in the country. It has strong correspondent relationship with more than 50 renowned foreign banks, including the Commerz Bank AG (German banking and financial services), Royal Bank of Canada, City Bank (financial services multinational Citigroup at New York), HSBC Bank (multinational banking services, headquarter at London, UK) and others. CBE has a SWIFT bilateral arrangement with more than 700 others banks across the world. CBE has also reliable and long-standing relationships with many internationally acclaimed banks throughout the world. As a result, the bank's asset is increasing growing in the past ten years. Large share of deposit of the bank is mainly from privates and individuals. Others like cooperatives, public enterprises and agencies, domestic banks and other financial institutions, central and local governments and foreign banks have their own share in total bank deposits. The banks total deposit growth trend since in 1985 is shown in Figure 3.1 below.

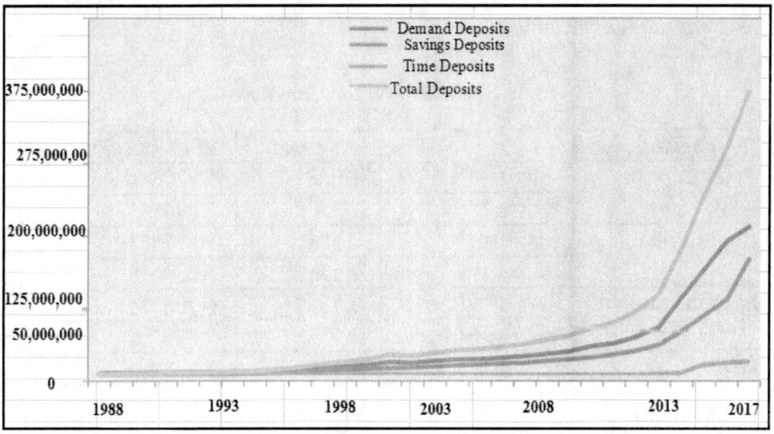

Source: Author's computation, data from CBE.

Fig. 1: Trends of Deposit Amount by Deposit Type.

As the figure shows, the demand deposit is much greater than saving and time deposits. The negative real interest rate may compel the depositors to put their money in demand deposit type. All deposit types have been showing a rapid increase in current years particularly since 2010. The deposit amount of the bank has been steadily growing and it reached 242.497billion, 288.605 billion, 364 billion for the year 2015, 2016 and 2017, respectively, and even reached 451 billion for the year 2018. It may be due to rapid expansion of banks branch network over the country, increase of per-capita income of the society thereby a growth in saving amount and rapid economic growth of the country.

3.3 Econometric Tests and Data Analysis

3.3.1 The unit root test

Table 3.2 shows the results of augmented dickey fuller (ADF) test statistics by using trend and without trend of variables. As for the analysis of long run relationship between the variables the economic time series must fulfil stationarity assumption. According to ADF result all variables except inflation rate with trend and without trend, are non-stationary at level form. Hence, we fail to reject the null hypothesis of non-stationarity, whereas by taking the first difference of all variables and applying the ADF test with and without trend; the series become stationary as shown below in Table 3.2. This indicates that the variables are integrated of order one, I (1) and they may exhibit some long run linear combination, and indicating the use of vector error correction (VEC) model provided that co-integration exists among the variables.

Table 3.2: ADF Test for Unit Root.

Variables		*At Level*	*At First difference*
Total Deposit	With Trend	-1.088	-5.820***
	Without Trend	1.328	-5.490***
Deposit rate	With Trend	-2.585	-5.527***
	Without Trend	-2.371	-5.639***
Inflation rate	With Trend	-3.758**	-6.906***
	Without Trend	-3.652*	-7.023 ***
GDP	With Trend	-1.130	-3.573 *
	Without Trend	1.725	-2.845***

Note: ***, **, and * are p< 0.01, 0.05, and 0.1, respectively.

Source: Stata 14 output from annual data set, 2018.

3.3.2 Optimum lag length

To determine the optimum lag length of the economic series we used the FPE, SBIC, AIC and HQIC statistical outputs. Accordingly, the SBIC test indicates the optimum lag length as 1, and FPE test result recommends optimum lag length as 3 years. While AIC and HQIC suggests that the appropriate lag length is four. Thus, the appropriate lag length that is selected in our analysis is four as of most of the criteria recommends (Table 3.3).

Table 3.3: Lag Length Selection

Lag	*FPE*	*AIC*	*HQIC*	*SBIC*
0.	15.8675	14.1156	14.1714	14.3092
1.	.013715	7.04287	7.32155	8.01063*
2.	.008663	6.48346	6.98508	8.22544
3.	.008109*	6.14231	6.86688	8.6585
4.	.010069	5.72811*	6.67563*	9.01851

Note: * lag order selected by the criterion.

Source: Stata 14 output from annual data set, 2018.

3.3.3 *Identifying the existence of co-integration*

To identify the existence of co-integration among the economic series we used one of the log-likelihood ratio tests, i.e. the trace statistics via Johansen tests for co-integration. The test result indicates the existence of one co-integrating vectors which are reported in Table 3.4 below. The presence of co-integration assures the existence of a stable and long run relationship among variables.

Table 3.4: Johansen Tests for Cointegration

Trend: constant		***Sample: 6 - 30***		***No. of obs= 25***	***Lags = 4***
Maximum rank	***Parms***	***LL***	***eigenvalue***	***trace statistic***	***5percent Critical value***
0.	52	-52.574259		56.9686	47.21
1.	59	-35.868074	0.73723	23.5562*	29.68
2.	64	-28.87806	0.42833	9.5762	15.41
3.	67	-24.772704	0.27995	1.3655	3.76
4.	68	-24.089965	0.05315		

Source: Stata 14 output from annual data sets, 2018.

3.4 *Vector Error Correction Model Result*

Due to the existence of co-integration among variables we proceed to examine the vector error correction model and the result is displayed below in Table 3.5. The summary statistics for model adequacy are displayed for each equation in the form of coefficient of determination and the probability values supplementing the adequacy of our specified model.

The VECM allows the long-run behaviour of our endogenous variables to converge to their long-run equilibrium relationship while allowing a wide range of short-run dynamics. The result of error correction model for both short-run and long-run causality are reported in Table 3.6. Row 18 in

Table 3.5: Vector Error Correction Model

Sample: 6 – 30		*Number of obs=25*			
		AIC		= 7.589446	
Log likelihood =	-35.86807	HQIC		= 8.387278	
Det(Sigma_ml) =	.0002072	SBIC		= 10.46599	
Equation	Parms	RMSE	R-sq	chi2	P>chi2
D_ddeposit	14	.14117	0.7393	31.19621	0.0052
D_ddeporate	14	1.57849	0.7606	34.95366	0.0015
D_dinflanrate	14	8.27037	0.9039	103.519	0.0000
D_dlnGDP	14	.105521	0.7051	26.30286	0.0237

Source: Stata 14 output from annual data set, 2018.

Table 3.6 shows the error correction term (ECT)) for the equations as logarithm of deposit, inflation rate, deposit rate and logarithm of GDP as equation (1), (2), (3) and equation (4), respectively. Accordingly, the coefficient of the error correction term for deposit variable carries the correct sign and statistically significant at 5 percent, with the speed of convergence to equilibrium of approximately 16 percent. Hence, in the short-run, deposits are adjusted by 16 percent of the past year's deviation from equilibrium. This confirms the stability of the system. This is in line with the finding of Lomuto (2008) whose result indicates the existence of long-run relationship between deposit and deposit rate in the case of Kenyan commercial bank deposit growth. In addition, Lumutos finding supplements long-run relationship between lags of deposit with the total amount of deposit growth. Others like Nathanael (2014) study conducted in Nigeria assures the existence of long-run relationship running from interest rate, and general price level as rate of inflation to bank deposit amount. Similarly, the findings of Siaw and Lawer (2015) of Ghana identified that in the short-run bank deposit is adversely affected by inflation rate.

Table 3.6: Vector Error-Correction Model for Four Equations

Sample: 6 – 30		*Number*	*of*	*obs*	=	*25*
		AIC			=	2.312165
Log likelihood =	46.09794	**HQIC**			=	3.326358
Det(Sigmaml) =	2.94e-07	**SBIC**			=	5.968792
Equation	Parms	**RMSE**	**R-sq**	**chi2**		**P>chi2**
D_deposit	18	.116376	0.9097	70.49972		0.0000
D_deporate	18	1.7323	0.5969	10.36394		0.9194
D_inflanrate	18	9.5258	0.7884	26.08497		0.0978
D_lnGDP	18	.11393	0.8552	41.32972		0.0014

Short-run causation	***Equation***			
	***D(lnDeposit)* (1)**	***D(inflationR)* (2)**	***D(deporate)* (3)**	***D(lnGDP)* (4)**
deposit_LD.	-.7237127 (0.141)	10.0935(0.802)	-2.9690(0.685)	.33820 (0.482)
deposit_L2D.	-.0546656 (0.900)	-2.7187(0.939)	-4.1986(0.519)	.076 (0.860)
deposit_L3D.	.428353 (0.179)	-49.5(0.06*)	2.383(0.616)	-.5604(0.073*)

(Contd...)

deposit_L4D.	.1469852 (0.669)	-7.9376(0.778)	.442517(0.931)	.211715(0.530)
Inflanrate_LD.	-.0270485(0.097*)	.035833(0.979)	.024633(0.919)	.015761(0.323)
Inflanrate_L2D	-.0305624(0.068*)	-.12944(0.925)	-.088303(0.724)	.007596(0.644)
Inflanrate_L3D	-.0189932 (0.095)	.237443(0.799)	-.002692(0.987)	.009023(0.418)
Inflanrate_L4D	-.0107661 (0.126)	-.03986(0.945)	-.069334(0.508)	.004641(0.500)
Deporate_LD.	.11463(0.007***)	-4.9136(0.156)	.1165171(0.853)	-.056067(0.175)
Deporate_L2D.	.085059(0.015**)	-.80468(0.778)	.1704979(0.743)	.00884(0.796)
Deporate_L3D.	.0113331(0.745)	.8207091(0.77)	.3176906(0.540)	.0024575(0.943)
Deporate_L4D.	-.0092137(0.739)	2.467874(0.27)	-.015504(0.970)	.0246468(0.363)
lnGDP_LD.	.4412341 (0.275)	-14.718(0.656)	-8.25428(0.170)	.359291 (0.363)
lnGDP_L2D.	.9507194(0.086*)	-5.9789(0.895)	8.261288(0.316)	-.132897(0.806)
lnGDP_L3D.	.1690467 (0.717)	-16.389(0.667)	-2.52023(0.716)	-.402704(0.377)
lnGDP_L4D.	.0908698 (0.823)	45.7298(0.170)	6.222811(0.305)	.462407 (0.246)
Long-run ECT(-1)	-0.1572471 (0.026**)	-2.152231 (0.710)	-0.334512 (0.751)	-0.0578816 (0.404)

Note: Probability values are in parenthesis and the rest are coefficients

***, ** and * indicates 1 percent, 5 percent and 10 percent level of significance respectively.

Source: Stata 14 output from annual data set, 2018.

However, the coefficient of the error correction term for deposit rate, inflation rate and GDP is having the expected sign yet statistically insignificant. Hence no need of further interpretation.

Furthermore, the finding shows that there is a short-run unidirectional causality running from the first and second lag of inflation rate and deposit rate, and second lag of logarithm of GDP to total amount of deposit held by CBE. This finding is consistent to the finding of Otu L. and Peter A. (2015) in examining determinants of Bank deposits in Ghana, which shows that there exists a short-run relationship between inflation rate and deposit. Our study also shows that there is a short-run unidirectional causality running from the third lag of logarithm of deposit to inflation rate. In addition, there exists a short-run unidirectional causality running from the third lag of logarithm of deposit to logarithm of GDP. The result confirms the theory that an increase in inflation rate causes tightening of the monetary policy, which increases the risk-free deposit in banks, this in turn causes a shift from investments in different economic sectors to the safer and less risky savings in a bank. In addition, according to Table 3.6, there exists bidirectional causality among inflation rate at 1st and 2nd lag and deposit at 3rd lag. Similarly, there exists bidirectional causality among GDP at 2nd lag and deposit at 3rd lag. While there exists unidirectional causality running from deposit rate to bank deposit.

Moreover, I conducted joint effect of the lagged values of each explanatory variable on the deposit amount of CBE to show whether there exists a short-run joint effect of the lag of the variables. Since our target variable is the deposit amount of CBE, I examined the joint effects of lags to show the existence of a short-run causality running from other variables to deposit. Thus, according to the table below: the finding indicates that except deposit rate all included variables have no short-run effect on deposit amount. Since the p-value of our test statistics for deposit rate is around 0.0428 which is less than 5 percent, we reject the null hypothesis and conclude that there exists a short-run causation running from deposit rate to deposit amount of CBE. Since the p-values for the lags of inflation rate, GDP and deposit are greater than 5 percent level of significance we accept the null hypothesis (Table 3.7), the coefficients are not significantly different from zero.

Table 3.7: Short-run Joint Effect of the Lags of Each Variable on Deposit

H_0: LD.deporate=	L2D.deporate = L3D.deporate = L4D.deporate = 0
	chi2(4) = 9.86
	Prob > chi2 = 0.0428
H_0: LD.inflanrate=	L2D.inflanrate= L3D.inflanrate= L4D.inflanrate= 0
	chi2(4) = 3.46
	Prob > chi2 = 0.4842
H_0: LD.lnGDP=	L2D.lnGDP = L3D.lnGDP = L4D.lnGDP = 0
	chi2(4) = 6.08
	Prob > chi2 = 0.1932
H_0: LD.deposit =	L2D.deposit = L3D.deposit = L4D.deposit = 0
	chi2(4) = 3.37
	Prob > chi2 = 0.4974

Source: Stata 14 output from annual data set, 2018.

The result of Johansen normalisation restriction in Table 3.8 shows the long-run effect of other variables on deposit amount of CBE. The sign of the coefficients is reversed in the long-run. Keeping other factors remain constant, inflation rate and GDP have a negative effect on deposit, while deposit rate has a positive effect on the total amount of deposit held CBE. More specifically, in the long-run on average as deposit rate increases by a percent, we expect approximately 42 percent increment in the deposit amount, citrus paribus. This might be due to the fact that economic agents are rational as of their positive expectation from long term return from their deposit. This finding is identical to the finding of Lomuto (2008) in the Kenyan commercial bank deposit growth study. Similarly, in the long-run on an average, when GDP increases by a percent, deposit amount will decline by 93 percent, keeping other factors remain constant. Whereas, in the long-run on an average an increase of inflation rate by a percent results a 15 percent decline in the total amount of deposit, keeping the effect of others remain constant (Table 3.8). This is due to the fact that economic agents as a whole are taking their money out of banks to cover their higher expenses at inflationary periods. This finding is consistent with the findings of Muhammad F. et al. (2011), Athukorala and Long P. (2003), and Otu L. and Peter A. (2015). Our finding is also in line with the findings of Siaw and Lawer (2015) of Ghana which identified that in the long-run bank deposit is negatively affected by inflation rate and but inconsistent with the effect of deposit interest rate on bank deposit.

Table 3.8: Johansen Normalisation Restriction for Long-run Dynamics

Beta	*Coef.*	*Std. Err.*	*z*	*P>z*	*[95percent Conf.*	*Interval]*
_ce1						
Deposit	1	.	.	.	.	.
deporate	-.417954	.0136487	30.62	0.000	.391203	.444705
inflanrate	.1532944	.0055234	-27.75	0.000	-.16412	-.1424688
lnGDP	.9313516	.0566879	16.43	0.000	.8202454	1.042458
_cons	-30.18998	.	.	.	.	.

Source: Stata 14 output from annual data set, 2018.

3.5 Diagnostic Checks Analysis

To check the validity of our models, we conducted different diagnostic checks that includes Lagrange-multiplier (LM) test for serial correlation of the error term, Jarque-Bera test for normality and the stability test for misspecifications. The result in Table 3.9 indicates that we are accepting the null hypothesis that states there is no auto-correlation problem due to the p-value is greater than 5 percent level of significance. And similarly, since the p-values in the normality test are greater than 5 percent, indicating that we accept the null hypothesis of normally distributed error term. The diagnostics tests indicate the considered model to be well specified.

Table 3.9: LM Test for Serial Correlation, and Jarque-Bera Test for Normality

I. Lagrange-multiplier test for serial correlation of the error term			
	H_0: no autocorrelation at lag order		
Lag	***chi2***	***df***	***Prob > chi2***
1.	38.3437	49	0.86378
2.	37.6263	49	0.88168
II. Jarque-Bera test for normality			
	H_0: Residuals are normally distributed		
Equation	***chi2***	***df***	***Prob > chi2***
D_ddeposit	5.815	2	0.05462
D_inflanrate	0.298	2	0.86172
D_ddeporate	1.499	2	0.47261
D_ddlnGDP	1.856	2	0.39532
ALL	9.468	8	0.31142

Source: Stata 14 output from annual data set, 2018.

Parameter stability test result is shown below in Figure 3.2 which plots the eigenvalues of the companion matrix with the real component on the x-axis and the imaginary component on the y-axis. The figure also displays the stability of our specified model as of the units are within the circle.

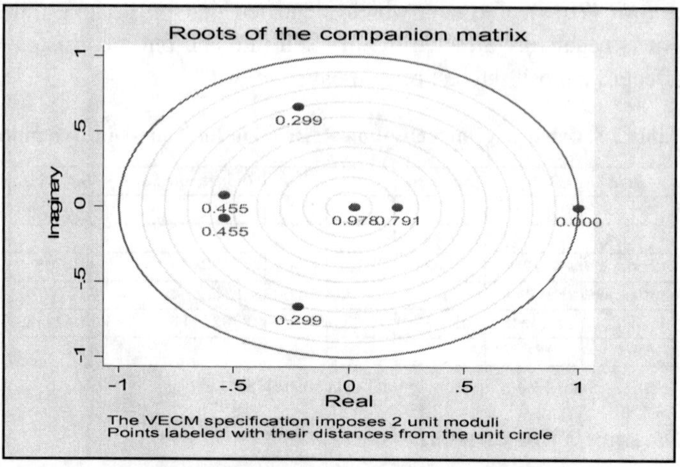

Source: Stata 14 output from annual data set, 2018.

Figure 4.2: Stability Test Output

4. Conclusions and Recommendations

4.1 Conclusions

This study examined the long-run and short-run dynamic effects of deposit rate, inflation rate and GDP on bank deposit. Different post-estimation tests and diagnostic tests were conducted to examine the economic series of our variables. To examine their relationships Error Correction Model was employed and accordingly there exists a long-run causality running from deposit rate, interest rate, and GDP to CBE deposit amount. The finding shows that there is a short-run unidirectional causality running from the first and second lag of inflation rate and deposit rate, and second lag of logarithm of GDP to total amount of deposit held by CBE. Our study also shows that there is a short-run unidirectional causality running from the third lag of logarithm of deposit to inflation rate. In addition, there exists a short-run unidirectional causality running from the third lag of logarithm of deposit to logarithm of GDP.

In addition, there exists bidirectional causality among inflation rate and deposit. Similarly, there exists bidirectional causality among GDP and deposit. While there exists unidirectional causality running from deposit rate to bank deposit. Moreover, we conducted joint effect of the lagged values of each explanatory variable on the deposit amount of CBE to show whether there exists a short-run joint effect of the lag of the variables. The joint effect result indicates that except deposit rate all included variables have no significant short-run effect on deposit amount. More specifically, the result of Johansen normalisation restriction shows in the long-run on average inflation rate and GDP have a negative effect on deposit, while deposit rate has a positive effect on the total amount of deposit held by CBE.

4.2 Recommendations

According to the findings of this study the following major recommendations are forwarded:

- The concerned body specially the national bank of Ethiopia should reconsider the minimum amount of deposit (saving) rate as of indicated in our finding deposit rate can play a pivotal role in bank deposit amount.
- The concerned bodies like national bank of Ethiopia and the government should stabilize the general price index via different policy tools and there by enhance bank deposit.
- The government, national bank of Ethiopia and other concerned bodies should take necessary steps to mobilize deposit in CBE specifically and in all other banks generally.
- The researcher recommends others to conduct in related topic by increasing the time frame and including other macroeconomic factors that affect deposit amount of CBE.

References

Alemayehu, G. (2015).'Will the Government of Ethiopia's policy ot saving mobilisation be successful? The lesson from the African Evidence. Mudaye Neway, 5 (2).

Athukorala, P.-C. and T. Long Pang (2003). Determinants of household saving in Taiwan: Growth, demography and public policy, Journal of Development Studies, 39(5), 65-88.

Bahredin Awol (2016). Determinants of commercial banks deposit growth (Evidence from Ethiopia), Degree of Masters Thesis, Addis Ababa University.

Bond, R. (1971). Deposit Composition and Commercial Bank Earnings. The Journal of Finance, 26(1), 39-50. doi:10.2307/2325739.

Christopher, D. Carroll and Miles S. Kimball (2007, June 12). Precautionary Saving and Precautionary Wealth, Retrieved from http://www.econ2.jhu.edu/people/ccarroll/PalgravePrecautionary.pdf

Davinaga, R. (2010). Theoretical Framework of Profitability as Applied to Commercial Bank in Malaysia, European Journal of Economics, Finance and Administrative Sciences, 74 (97), 63–66.

Dereje Hailemariam Amene (2017). Determinants of Deposit in Ethiopian Private Commercial Banks, Addis Ababa University.

Desinga, R. (1975). Deposit Mobilisation by Co-operative Banks, A Comparison with Scheduled Commercial Banks. Economic and Political Weekly, 10(29), 1098-1100.

Erna, R., and Ekki, S. (2004). Factors Affecting Mudaraba Deposits in Indonesia. Working Paper in Economics and Development Studies Padjadjaran University, Indonesia.

Evan, G. T., and Philip, E. S. (2006). Managing Bank Liquidity Risk: How Deposit-Loan Synergies Vary with Market Conditions, Federal Reserve Bank of New York.

Falkena, H., Davel, J., Hawkins, P., Llwellyn, D., Luus, C., Masilela, E., Parr, G., Piennar, J. and Shaw, H. (2004). Competition in South African Banking. Task group report for the national treasury and the South African Reserve Bank.

Franklin, A., Otchere, I., and Senbet, L.(2011). African financial system: a review: a Review of Development Finance, 1(2), 79-113.

Giragn,G. (2015). Determinants of Deposit Mobilisation and Related Costs of Commercial Banks in Ethiopia, Addis Ababa University.

Haron, S.. Azmi, W. Nursofiza, W. and Shafie, S. (2006). Deposit determinants of Commecial Banks in Malaysia. The quarterly journal of Indian Institute of Finance, 20 (0970-3772), 531-551.

Hibret, B. (2015). Determinate of commercial Bank's deposit growth in Ethiopia: case study on the commercial Bank, Addis Ababa University.

Hirindu, K. and Kushani, P. (2017). The Factors Effecting on Bank Profitability. International Journal of Scientific and Research Publications, 7(2250-3153), 212-216.

John, H. Boyd and David E. Runkle (1993). Size and Performance of Banking Firms: Testing the Predictions of Theory, Journal of Monetary Economics, 31 (issue 1), 47-67.

Kelvin, A. (2001). The Role of Commercial Banks in Financing Growth and Economic Development in Trinidad and Tobago and the Caribbeans: a perspective from the Royal Bank of Trinidad and Tobago, Central Bank of Belize.

Ketema Getachew Bogale (2017). Determinants of Commercial Banks Deposit Mobilisation In Ethiopia, St Marr'y Universtity, Institute of MBA in Accounting and Finance.

Lomuto, J. K. (2008). Determinants of Kenyan Commercial Banks Deposit Growth. University of Nairobi, retrieved from http://erepository.uonbi.ac.ke/bitstream/handle/11295/17109/Lomuto%20Joel%20K_Determinants%20of%20Kenyan%20Commercial%20Banks%20Deposits%20Growth.pdf?sequence=3.

Mahdi Salehi (2008). The Role of Financial Intermediaries in Capital Market, Zanjan University, Zanjan, Iran, Zagreb International Review of Economics and Business, 11(1), 97-109.

Mahendra, V. P. (2005). Impact of Self-Help Groups on Formal Banking Habits. Journal of Economic and Political Weekly, 40 (17).

Mamo, E. (2017). An Investigation of Determinants of Deposit Mobilisation in Commercial Banks of Ethiopia. Research on Humanities and Social Sciences, 7(2224-5766), 55-64.

Mohammad, N., and Mahdi, S. (2010). The Role of Inflation in Financial Repression: Evidence from Iran World Applied Sciences Journal, 6 (1818-4952), 653-661.

Muhammad, F. M., and Amir, R. (2013). Commercial Banks Liquidity in Pakistan: Firm Specific and Macroeconomic Factors. Romanian Economic Journal, retrieved from http://www.rejournal.eu/sites/rejournal.versatech.ro/files/articole/2013-06.

National Bank of Ethiopia, (2009). Monetary Policy Framework. Retrieved from https://www.nbe.govet/pdf/Monetary_Policy_Framework_of_Ethiopiamain_edited.pdf

National Bank of Ethiopia, (2015). Annual Report 2014/1. Retrieved from http://www.nbebank.com/pdf/annualbulletin/Annual%20Report%2020142015/Annual%20Report%202014-15.pdf

Ngula, I. (2012). Determinants of Deposit Mobilisation and Its Role in Economic in Ghana, Retrieved from http://hdl.handle.net/123456789/4950.

Nwanko, F., Ewuim, N. and Asoya, N. P. (2013). Effects of Co-operatives on the Savings Behaviour of Members in Oyi Local Goverment Area, Sahoo Anambra state, Nigeria. African Research Review.

Olga, K. and Rim, E. (2013). Determinants of Non-Resident Deposits in Commercial Banks: Empirical Evidence from Lebanon, International Journal of Economics and Finance, 5(12), 135-150, DOI:10.5539/ijef.v5n12p135

Otu Larbi-Siaw and Peter Angmor Lawer (2015). Determinants of Bank Deposits in Ghana: A Cointegration Approach. Asian Journal of Economics and Empirical Research, 2 (2409-2622), 1-7.

Shemsu, B. (2015). Determinants of Commercial Bank Deposits In Ethiopia: a case of Commercial Bank of Ethiopia, Addis Ababa University.

Shettar, R. M., and Sheshgiri, S. M. (2014). Deposit Mobilisation in Socio-Economic Impact: A case study of union bank of India., IOSR Journal of Engineering (IOSRJEN), 4 (2278 -8719, 21-26.

Tsengabirhan, W. A. (2010). Domestic Resource Mobilisation in Sub-Saharan Africa: The Case of Ethiopia. Retrieved from http://www.nsi-ins.ca/wp-content/uploads/2010/06/DRMEthiopiaFINALPOST.pdf

Tuyishime, R., Memba F. and Mbera Z. (2015). The Effects of Deposits Mobilisation on Financial Performance in Commercial Banks in Rwanda, A Case of Equity Bank Rwanda Limited. International Journal of Small Business and Entrepreneurship Research, 3 (No. 6), 44-71.

Verbeek, JM (2004). A Guide to Modern Econometrics, 2nd edition., John Wiley and Sons Ltd, Erasmus University Rotterdam.

Wooldridge, J.M (2000). Introductory Economics, 2nd Edition. Cambridge, MA. MIT Press.

Wubetu Elias Gemedu (2012). Factors Determining Commercial Bank Deposit: An Empirical Study on Commercial Bank of Ethiopia, Addis Ababa University.

8

Impact of E-banking on the Performance of Commercial Banks in Bangladesh: Evidence from Panel Data Analysis

Bhishan Chandra Barman and
Md. Abdul Wadud

Abstract

Electronic banking (e-banking) is one of the most important technologies and communication systems that have gained popularity in banking industry. This study examines the impact of e-banking on the performance of commercial banks in Bangladesh.

We measure the performance of banks in terms of three ratios- return on equity (ROE), return on assets (ROA) and net interest margin (NIM). We use panel data, which consist of 12 commercial banks, and 10 years data during the period from 2009 to 2018. We select 12 from 58 commercial banks applying stratified random sampling method, 3 banks are state-owned commercial banks and 9 banks are private commercial banks among 12 selected banks. We apply fixed effects model (FEM) and random effects model (REM) and run regressions for three performance indicators of ROE, ROA and NIM. We use ROE, ROA and NIM as dependent variables and number of years of experience of adopting e-banking as independent variable. Bank-specific variables - capital adequacy, bank size, liquidity, credit risk, earnings per share and expenses management and macroeconomic variables-economic growth proxied by real GDP growth rate and inflation rate - as control variables in order to control their effects on bank performance. We perform Hausman test to select the appropriate model between FEM and REM, and REM model is found to the appropriate one for this dataset. This research further applies generalised method of moments (GMM) to investigate the relationship between the e-banking and banks' performance after controlling within group and between group heterogeneity effects.

Results from REM econometric estimations show positive and significant impact of e-banking on return on assets (ROA) and net interest margin (NIM) at 5% and 10% levels of significance respectively. Impact of e-banking on return on equity (ROE), although insignificant, is found to be positive. Estimation results of GMM model report a significant positive impact of e-banking on banks' performance in terms of return on equity (ROE) and return on assets (ROA) at 5% and 10% levels of significance respectively. Results further indicate that e-banking has had favourable impact on net interest margin (NIM), but this impact is not yet significant. Overall, findings reveal that electronic banking positively affects the banks' performance. Effects of the bank-specific and macroeconomic variables on banks' performance are found to be mixed. We notice that the higher is the experience of e-banking, the greater extent and significance is the performance of the banks. Policies leading to the better management and delivery of e-banking services would contribute to the improvement of banks' performance and hence profitability. Furthermore, we can draw conclusion that since all the commercial banks in Bangladesh have not yet ensured all sorts of e-banking services, banks management should invest more to setup overall e-banking technologies in their banks as well as arrange to provide updated knowledge about using e-banking to their employees and clients in order to reap higher profitability.

Key Words: *E-Banking, Return on Equity, Return on Assets, Net Interest Margin, Banks' Performance.*

1. Introduction

Technology is changing day by day and making our life easier. The technological improvement is noticeable in every sector in developed countries as well as developing countries like Bangladesh. Now-a-days banking and business sectors are highly influenced by Information and Communication Technology (ICT) that are known as e-banking and e-business respectively. However, at present, there are almost all banks that adopt e-banking technology that affects their performance.

E-banking is a concept related to banks which includes Automated Teller Machines (ATM), Credit Cards, Debit Cards, Electronic Funds Transfer (EFT) System, Mobile Banking, Internet Banking, Tele-banking, Home banking, Cheques Truncation Payment System. Through the above instruments, banks perform their e-banking services. E-banking technology is very convenient and relevant to use for both banks and their customers. E-banking refers to the system that enables bank's customers to access accounts and general information on bank's products and services through the electronic means like using telecommunications networks, web technology, other electronic devices, and computers' cellular phones. Now e-banking is a global phenomenon. It is a sheltered, quick, simple and proficient electronic service to do web-based banking services, 24 hours a day, and 7 days per week. It is a type of banking where assets are moved through a trade of electronic signals as opposed to through a trade of money, checks, or different sorts of paper documents. Whenever someone takes out cash from an Automated Teller Machine (ATM) or pays for foodstuffs using a debit card the funds are moved through electronic banking.

The transitional period in the financial system of Bangladesh has been going through since this system is moving from the conventional financial framework to the web-based banking system. This indicates that gradually electronic banking is getting its importance in Bangladesh. There are two ways through which banks can offer e-banking, brick-to-click banking which offer online banking along with the physical sites where customers can visit, and virtual banking which offers online banking without the physical site (Rahman, 2016). Although the concept of e-banking is not so old in Bangladesh, it has a high potentiality on the whole banking sector (Ahmed *et al.,* 2011). Carrying cash, as cards are used for shopping, are reduced by e-banking, and it is not necessary to maintain huge documents for banking functions in e-banking, deposit money from ATM booths and customers feel insecurity from hijacker to withdraw (Sadekin and Shaikh, 2016).

In Bangladesh, several private commercial banks (PCBs) and foreign commercial banks (FCBs) now offer limited services of online banking, internet banking and tele-banking facilities to their customers working within the branches of the individual bank in a closed network environment. In the early 1990s, the FCBs play a pioneering role in introducing e-banking with the adoption of modern technology in retail banking. While, in the late 1990s, the state-owned commercial banks (SCBs) and private commercial banks (PCBs) come forward to adopt e-banking services. There are now many banks that provide e-banking services in Bangladesh. The adoption of e-banking highly affects the performance of banks, that is, banks' profit, and banks' risk are affected greatly by adopting the e-banking to the respective banks. Hence, there is a relationship (positive/negative) between the adoption of e-banking and the performance of banks.

Empirical studies reveal that there is a positive impact of e-banking on performance of banks. Some of them are as follows: E-banking begins to contribute positively to bank performance in terms of ROA and NIM with a time lag of two years while a negative impact is observed in the first year of adoption. (Oyewole *et al.,* 2013). The adoption of e-banking enhances the performances of the banking industry due to increased efficiency and productivity (Abdullai and Micheni, 2018). E-banking has strong and significance marginal effects on return on assets (ROA) in the Kenyan banking sector and there is a positive association between e-banking and bank performance (Aduda and Kingoo, 2012). E-banking contributes to the positive performance of banks as witnessed by the bank of Kigali (Ngango *et al.*, 2015), there is a significant change in the banks' performance due to adopt e-banking over the years (Sarker *et al.*, 2015).

But on the other hand, some similar studies reveal that there is a negative impact of e-banking on the banks' performance. Some of them are as follows: adoption of internet banking harms bank profitability after 2 years of adoption as internet banking increases competition and lowers interest income (Onay and Ozsoz, 2011). There is no significant effect of e-banking services on the profitability of recent adopters' banks in terms of ROE and ROA that means there is a high cost associated with applying these services. But it is significantly affected by e-banking services in case of interest margin (Khrawish and Al-sa'di, 2011). Electronic banking has not significantly improved the return on assets of Nigerian banks (Abaenewe *et al.*, 2013). So clearly, there are mixed shreds of evidence about the impact of e-banking on banks' performance.

There, at present, are 57 scheduled commercial banks in Bangladesh (Bangladesh bank, 2018) and most of them have adopted e-banking in the forms of internet banking, mobile banking, SMS banking, ATM, tele-banking, among others. It is, therefore, important for bankers, supervisors, bank regulators and researchers to understand how e-banking affects the performance of commercial banks in Bangladesh. Few researches are conducted considering e-banking in Bangladesh which are mostly descriptive in nature. Hence, the main purpose of this paper is to fill this significant gap by providing a systematic analysis of the impact of e-banking on the performance of commercial banks in Bangladesh. The study selects 12 commercial banks that have adopted the e-banking system over the different periods. Using necessary data and information, we examine the performance of the selected commercial banks in Bangladesh after adopting e-banking. Applying econometric models the study finds empirical findings that have greater significance for developing world like Bangladesh. The study would help the management and policy-makers to pursue such policies to growth e-banking system which ultimately brings long term benefits for the whole banking industry of Bangladesh. Finally, the study helps other academic researchers as a source of reference when they would conduct a research on e-banking.

2. Review of Literature

2.1 Concept of e-banking

Electronic banking is known as e-banking. It is a revolution in the banking industry which makes the bankers and its customers' life easy and fast. Generally, e-banking is the service of traditional banking activities by using different types of electronic devices such as Computer, Mobile, Telephone, Automated Teller Machine (ATM), Point of Sale (POS), Terminal machine etc. Electronic banking is also known as Electronic Funds Transfer (EFT) which is usually the use of electronic means to transfer funds from one account to another, instead of by check or cash. Electronic banking can also be defined as a variety of platforms such as internet banking or (online banking), TV-based banking, mobile banking, and PC banking or (offline banking) whereby customers access these services using an intelligent electronic device, like a Personal Computer (PC), Automated Teller Machine (ATM), Personal Digital Assistant (PDA), Point of Sale (POS), and Touch-Tone Telephone (Alagheband, 2006). E-banking is a system through which financial service providers, customers, individuals, and businesses can access their accounts, do transactions and obtain the latest information on financial products and services from public or private networks, such as the internet. The term e-banking can be explained in a different from different perspectives. Nonetheless, researchers across the world have made extensive efforts to provide a precise and all-inclusive concept of e-banking" (Siddik *et al.,* 2016).

2.2 Previous Empirical Studies

Yang *et al.* (2017) investigate whether e-banking really improves bank performance or not, in China. Empirical results reveal that e-banking can improve Chinese bank performance in terms of ROE, ROA, and OM. While e-banking has a slight impact on Chinese bank performance with respect to NIM and efficiency ratio. Oyewole *et al.* (2013) examine the banking sector in Nigeria's 'E-banking and Bank Performance'. The study applies pooled OLS estimations which indicate that e-banking begins to contribute positively to bank performance in terms of ROA and NIM with a time lag of two years while a negative impact is observed in the first year of adoption. Dinh *et al.* (2015) measure the impacts of internet banking on bank performance in Vietnam. The results show that there is an impact of internet banking on bank profitability through an increase of income from services activities. But the impact level is low around a lag time of over 3 years. Hossein (2013) examines the effect of e-banking on bank profitability regarding some selected Asian countries. The results indicate that internet banking starts contributing to banks' ROE with a time lag of three years while, a negative impact is observed for one year lagged. Siddik *et al.* (2015) investigate the impacts of e-banking on the performance of banks in a developing economy based on empirical evidence from Bangladesh who find that e-banking has a positive contribution to banks' return on equity with a time lag of two years but a negative impact is found in the first year of adoption. Sumra *et al.* (2011) explore the impact of e-banking on the profitability of Pakistani banks covering 12 banks across Pakistan and the results of the study show that e-banking has increased the profitability of banks; it has enabled the banks to meet their costs and earn profits. Acharya *et al.* (2008) examine the impact of online banking intensity on the financial performance of community banks using a combination of primary and secondary data and the results of the analysis indicate that the increasing the use of the internet as an additional channel of marketing banking services has significantly improved the nancial performance of community banks. Hernando and Nieto (2007) take into account a quantitative analysis of the impact of the internet on banks' financial performance, who find that there is an improvement in banks' profitability, which becomes significant after one and a half years in terms of ROA and after three years in terms of ROE.

On the contrary, Malhotra and Singh (2009) conduct a study regarding the impact of internet banking on bank performance and risk from the Indian experience and the results of the study reveal that there does not have any significant relationship between the profitability and offering of internet banking. But, there is a significant and negative association with the risk profile of the banks in internet banking. Al-Smadi and Al-Wabel (2011) analyzes the impact of e-banking on the performance of Jordanian banks. The results of the study show that the costs associating with adopting e-banking are still higher than revenues from provision provided by electronic services. Abaenewe *et al.* (2013) analyze the relationship between the profitability performance of Nigerian banks and the full adoption of the electronic banking system. The result of the study implies that electronic banking has not significantly improved the returns on assets of Nigerian banks.

There are some lackings in the earlier literature which need to be taken into account to conduct a further study for examining the impact of e-banking on the performance of banks'. Few studies considering the impact of e-banking on the performance of commercial banks in Bangladesh have been conducted and in most cases the earlier studies are descriptive in nature. The regression techniques such as, fixed effects model (FEM), random effects model (REM) along with generalised method of moments (GMM) have not been used to estimate the relationship between e-banking and the performance of banks in earlier studies. This study performs such crucial (FEM or REM and GMM) regression techniques to examine the impact of e-banking on the performance of commercial banks in Bangladesh. And no studies (national as well as international) have been found which have valued e-banking in terms of the number of experience years of adopting e-banking by banks. Since, most of the banks in developed and developing countries have already adopted e-banking technology, it is relevant to conduct a research to establish the impact of e-banking considering the number of experience years by banks. This study is conducted to estimate how much influences the performance of banks after adopting e-banking using econometric models. This study is an effort to fill these gaps that are found in earlier studies.

3. Research Methodology

3.1 Data Sources and Description

We collect two types of data which are primary data and secondary data. The primary data are collected through personal visiting to the selected banks' branches at Rajshahi, Bangladesh. We take interviews directly to the branch managers using questionnaire. We collect data for first adopting year of e-banking. We select 12 commercial banks among 57 scheduled commercial banks in Bangladesh (Bangladesh Bank, 2018). Out of 12 commercial banks; 3 are the state-owned commercial banks (SCBs) and 9 are the private commercial banks (PCBs). Secondary data are collected from the respective bank's annual report covering the period from 2009 to 2018. Finally, we collect macroeconomic data (GDP growth and inflation rate) from 'World Data Atlas' website during the period from 2009 to 2018.

The study uses panel data. Because the panel data have the advantage of providing more informative data as it consists of both the cross-sectional information, which captures individual variability, and the time-series information, which captures dynamic adjustment. The collected panel data are analyzed by using descriptive statistics and fixed effects model (FEM), random effects model (REM) and system generalised method of moments (GMM) techniques.

3.2 Variables Selection

3.2.1 Dependent Variables

In this research, we make an attempt to empirically investigate the impact of e-banking on the performance of commercial banks in Bangladesh. So, we take the banks' performance as the dependent variable. We use three proxy variables for the bank's performance. Among these three proxy variables, a commonly used proxy is return on equity (ROE). Al-Smadi and Al-Wabel (2011), Siddik *et al.* (2016), Abaenewe *et al.* (2013), and DeYoung *et al.* (2007) use this proxy the performance of banks. Return on equity (ROE) measures the return earned on common stockholders' investment. It explains how effectively shareholder's funds are being used by the management of the bank. To compute ROE, we calculate net profit after taxations divided by total shareholder's equity.

Another important measure of the bank's performance is return on asset (ROA) which deals with how effective the management of banks is in producing profits with its available assets. Dey (2014), Abaeenewe *et al.* (2013), Khrawish and Al-Sa'di (2011), Oyewole *et al.* (2013), and Siddik *et al.* (2016) use this measure. Sufian and Chong (2008) point out that ROA depends on the bank's policy decisions as well as on uncontrollable factors relating to the economy and government regulations. We calculate profit after taxations divided by total assets to compute ROA.

Various scholars around the world use another measure apart from ROE and ROA, namely, net interest margin (NIM), as a proxy of bank's performance. Government intervention might inflate ROE which may lead to inconsistent results (Onay *et al.,* 2008; Siddik *et al.,* 2016, and Malhotra and Singh, 2009). A third measure, NIM, might be used to measure the performance of banks to avoid such inconsistent results. We also use NIM as a measure of bank's performance. The higher level of NIM of a bank, the more the bank's profitability is (Raharjo *et al.,* 2014). We get NIM from net interest income divided by total assets, and net interest income is the difference between interest income and interest expense of the bank. We employ all three proxy variables ROE, ROA, and NIM to measure the banks' performance in order to attain a comprehensive result of bank performance.

3.2.2 Independent Variable

This research is conducted to explore the relationship between e-banking and banks' performance. Therefore, e-banking is considered as the sole independent variable. E-banking takes a value from the number of experienced years of adopting e-banking by respective commercial banks, where the sample banks have at least 8 years experiences of adopting e-banking technology up to 2018. As most of the commercial banks in Bangladesh have already added the e-banking system in their banks, this study makes an attempt to explore whether the performances of commercial banks in Bangladesh are really influenced by the e-banking system or not. Siddik *et al.* (2016), Oyewole *et al.* (2013), Mapharing and Basuhi (2017), and Yang *et al.* (2018) report that e-banking starts to contribute positively on banks performance after a few years of adopting this indicates that the higher the number of experience of adopting e-banking, the greater the profitability of banks. The coefficient of the e-banking explains the impact of e-banking on the bank's performance and the e-banking indicates the possible association between e-banking and bank's performance. A positive sign is expected for e-banking.

3.2.3 Control Variables

It is necessary to control other variables that have been used in the literature as possible determinants of banks' performance in order to isolate the effect of e-banking on performance. We expect two sets of control variables which are expected to influence banks' performance: the bank-specific and the macroeconomic determinants. In this study, the set of bank-specific variables are capital adequacy (CPATL), bank size (SZE), liquidity (LQDTY), credit risk (CRRK), earnings per share (EPS), and expenses management (EXPMNT). An important determinant of a bank's performance is capital adequacy which plays a vital role in supporting the safety and soundness of banks (Flamini *et al.,* 2009). The banks which are with higher capital to the assets ratio could be considered relatively safer in the event of loss or liquidation. Naceur and Goaied (2001)show a relationship between capital and profitability of a bank which explains that a bank with a higher capital to assets ratio needs lower external financing, as external financing thereby reducing excessive cost; therefore, the bank will experience higher profitability. As a proxy of bank capital (CAPTL), we use the ratio of equity capital to total assets and expect a positive sign for this variable.

As a control variable, the size (SZE) of the bank is included to account for size-related economies and diseconomies of scale. Due to economies of scale, modern financial intermediation theory predicts the efficiency benefits related to bank's size which could imply that larger banks may experience higher (Flamini *et al.,* 2009).There are large banks which have greater loans, product diversification and associability to asset markets, and which may not be available for smaller banks (Guru *et al.,*2000). To measure the size, we compute the total assets in Billion Taka of banks.

Liquidity (LQDTY) indicates how much a bank is able to meet the short term obligations. Liquid assets are often associated with the lower rate of return. Hence, the more the liquid assets are, the lower the rate of return. Guru *et al.* (2000) and Siddik *et al.* (2016) establish that high liquidity would affect the bank's profitability negatively. On the contrary, Samad (2015) finds a significant positive relationship between liquidity and bank profitability. In order to measure liquidity (LQDTY), we use the ratio of total loans to total deposits.

Credit risk is another important determinant of bank's performance. If credit risk increases, bank profitability decreases. Therefore, by minimising the credit risk level through improving their appropriate lending policies, banks can improve profitability (Al-Smadi and Al-Wabel, 2011 and Siddik *et al.,* 2016). We use the ratio of nonperforming loans to total loans to measure credit risk (CRRK). Since, there is a negative relationship between the credit risk and the bank's profitability, a negative sign is expected for this variable.

Earnings per share (EPS) is an important determinant of bank performance and it is calculated as a bank's profit divided by the outstanding shares of its common stock. There is a positive relationship between EPS & ROA, EPS & ROE, EPS & Net Profit, (Saeed and Tahir, 2015). Hence, the higher a bank's EPS, the more profitable it is considered. We use the ratio of a bank's profit to the outstanding shares of its common stock to measure the EPS. A positive sign is expected for this variable.

Another significant determinant of banks' performance is expenses management (EXPMNT). Naifer (2010) and Al-Smadi and Al-Wabel (2011) find that the higher the expenses management, the lower the bank's profit. Hence, there is a negative relationship between expenses management (EXPMNT) and the bank's profitability. We use the ratio of total operating expenses to total operating income as a proxy for expenses management (EXPMNT) and expect a negative sign for this variable.

Moreover, besides the above bank-specific variables, there are two macroeconomic variables: economic growth (RGDP) and inflation rate (INF), which are used as control variables. Economic growth has impacts on the bank's performance. Athanasoglou *et al.* (2008) establish that during economic slowdowns, bank's lending could reduce and deteriorate credit quality which in turn lowers the performance of the bank. On the contrary, during economic booms, an economic condition where all sectors of an economy perform well, demand for a loan could increase which may widen the interest margin of the bank. There is a significant positive relationship between economic growth and the profitability of the bank (Trujillo-Ponce, 2013). We measure economic growth by GDP growth and we expect a positive sign for this variable.

Table 1: Summary of Variables Used in this Study and their Specification

Variables			***Legend***	***Measurement***	***Expected Sign***
Dependent Variables		Return on Equity	ROE	Net profit (after tax) / total equity	N/A
		Return on Asset	ROA	Net profit (after tax) / total assets	N/A
		Net Interest Margin	NIM	(Interest incomes-interest expenses) / total assets	N/A
Independent variable		Electronic Banking	EBANK	The number of experience years of adopting e-banking by selected banks	+
Control variables	Bank-specific variables	Capital Adequacy	CAPTL	Equity capital / total assets	+
		Bank Size	SZE	Total assets	+ / -
		Liquidity	LQDTY	Total loans / total deposits	+ / -
		Credit Risk	CRRK	Nonperforming loans / total loans	–
		Earnings per Share	EPS	(Net income-Preferred dividends) / Weighted average common shares outstanding	+
		Expenses Management	EXPMNT	Total operating expenses / total operating incomes	–
	Macroeconomic variables	Economic Growth	RGDP	Real GDP growth rate	+
		Inflation Rate	INF	Current period inflation rate	+

According to Flamini *et al.* (2009), the impact of inflation on the bank's performance relies on whether the inflation rate in the future is anticipated or not. When the inflation is anticipated and interest rates are adjusted thus, resulting in revenue, which may have a positive impact on the bank's profitability. While due to imperfect interest rate adjustment an unanticipated change could raise costs. Trujillo-Ponce (2013) shows a positive relationship between inflation and ROA of banks. To measure the inflation rate (INF), we use the current inflation rate of the country. A positive sign is expected for this variable. The calculating procedures and the explanations of these variables are summarised in Table 1.

3.3 Methodology and Model Specification

To determine the relative importance of independent and each control variable in influencing the banks' performance, Random Effects Model (REM) / Fixed Effects Model (FEM), and Generalised Method of Moments (GMM) are applied.

The term 'fixed effects estimator' which is also known as the within estimator, is used to refer to an estimator for the coefficient in the regression model including those fixed effects (one time-invariant intercept for each subject) in panel data. Any unobserved variables that are constant over time but vary between individuals by explicitly including a separate intercept term for each individual in the regression equation are controlled by a fixed effects model. The basic equation for the fixed effects model (FEM) is:

$$Y_{it} = \alpha_i + \beta_1 X_{it} + u_{it} \quad [For\ t = 1, \ldots, T \text{ and } i = 1, \ldots, N] \qquad \ldots(1)$$

Where, Y_{it}=the dependent variable observed for individual i and time t; X_{it}= the independent variable (the time variant $1 \times k$ repressor vector); β_1= the coefficient for independent variable (the $k \times 1$ matrix of parameters); α_i = the unknown intercept for individual effect; u_{it} = the error term.

A statistical model where the model parameters are random is called a random effects model which is also known as variance components model. When the heterogeneity is constant over time and not correlated with independent variables, random effects models play a vital role in controlling for unobserved heterogeneity. The basic equation for random effects model (REM) is:

$$Y_{it} = \alpha_0 + \beta_1 X_{it} + \mu_i + \varepsilon_{it} \qquad \ldots(2)$$

Where, Y_{it}= the dependent variable for individual i and time t; X_{it}= the explanatory variable for individual$i$ and time t; β_1= the coefficient of explanatory variable; μ_i= the individual time-invariant effect of i; ε_{it}= the error term; α_0= the constant/intercept term.

The term μ_i is added in random effects model but this term is absent in case of fixed effects model. The μ's of different individuals are independent, have mean of zero, and their distribution is assumed to be not too far away from normality. The μ_i is time-invariant across individuals.

In general, in case of the banking literature, Pooled OLS, Fixed Effects and/or Random Effects models are employed for panel data. However, a difficulty arises with these models when a lagged dependent variable (or possibly other regressors) is important, particularly in the context of a few time periods and many observations (Nickell, 1981). The coefficients may also be seriously biased if the regressors are correlated with the lagged dependent variable to some degree (Heffernan and Fu, 2014). To solve this problem, the dynamic panel data analysis based on the generalised method of moments (GMM) is used mostly. The GMM provides solutions to the problems of endogeneity of the variables, reverse causality, simultaneity bias and omitted variables. The reduced form estimating equation for each performance measured by employing the system GMM approach equation is defined as follows:

$$Y_{it} = \alpha_0 + \gamma_1 Y_{it-1} + \beta_1 X_{it} + \mu_i + \nu_{it} \quad ...(3)$$

Where, Y_{it}= the dependent variable for individual i and time t; Y_{it-1}= the lag dependent variable for individual i and time t; X_{it}= the explanatory variable for individual i and time t; γ_1= the lag coefficient of explanatory variable; μ_i = unobserved individual time-invariant effect; ν_{it}= the error term; α_0= the constant term.

The assumption in OLS for a panel data requires that the intercept and the slope are the same for all the *i*. If samples (banks) are homogenous in terms of individuality, this method is valid. But if the sample is somehow different for the dependent variable, the Pooled OLS is not valid because of individual heterogeneity. Whereas, panel data allows for individual slope and thus allows for individual intercept. Therefore, we ignore Pooled OLS to analyze the data in our study.

The fixed effects method (FEM) and random effects method (REM) are taken to estimate the relationship between the dependent and explanatory variables. In order to obtain more appropriate and relevant estimates, the generalised method of moments (GMM) is also applied to establish the relationship between dependent and explanatory variables.

The functional forms of the econometric models for REM are as follows:

$$\text{Model 1: } ROE_{it} = \beta_0 + \beta_1 EBANK_{it} + \beta_2 CAPTL_{it} + \beta_3 SZE_{it} + \beta_4 LQDTY_{it} + \beta_5 CRRK_{it} + \beta_6 EPS_{it} + \beta_7 EXPMNT_{it} + \beta_8 RGDP_{it} + \beta_9 INF_{it} + \varepsilon_{it} \quad ...(4)$$

$$\text{Model 1: } ROA_{it} = \beta_0 + \beta_1 EBANK_{it} + \beta_2 CAPTL_{it} + \beta_3 SZE_{it} + \beta_4 LQDTY_{it} + \beta_5 CRRK_{it} + \beta_6 EPS_{it} + \beta_7 EXPMNT_{it} + \beta_8 RGDP_{it} + \beta_9 INF_{it} + \varepsilon_{it} \quad ...(5)$$

$$\text{Model 1: } NIM_{it} = \beta_0 + \beta_1 EBANK_{it} + \beta_2 CAPTL_{it} + \beta_3 SZE_{it} + \beta_4 LQDTY_{it} + \beta_5 CRRK_{it} + \beta_6 EPS_{it} + \beta_7 EXPMNT_{it} + \beta_8 RGDP_{it} + \beta_9 INF_{it} + \varepsilon_{it} \quad ...(6)$$

Where, ROE_{it} = return on equity of Bank *i* for year *t*; ROA_{it} = return on assets of Bank *i* for year *t*; NIM_{it} = net interest margin of Bank *i* for year *t*; $EBANK_{it}$=number of experience years of adopting e-banking of Bank *i* for year *t*; $CAPTL_{it}$ = capital adequacy ratio of Bank *i* for year *t*; SZE_{it} = total asset size of Bank *i* for year *t*; $LQDTY_{it}$= liquidity of Bank *i* for year *t*; $CRRK_{it}$= credit risk of Bank *i* for year *t*; EPS_{it} = earnings per share of Bank *i* for year *t*; $EXPMNT_{it}$ = expenses management of Bank *i* for year *t*; $RGDP_{it}$ = GDP growth rate for year *t*; INF_{it}= inflation rate for year *t*; *t* = time period (years); *i*= cross-sectional observations (Banks); β_0= intercept / constant term; $\beta_{1,......,}\beta_9$= coefficients; ε_{it} = error term.

For FEM and system GMM, as are indicated in equations (2) and (3), individual time-invariant effect term and unobserved individual time-invariant effect term are added to equations (4), (5) and (6) respectively for econometric estimation.

4. Empirical Results and Discussions

4.1 Descriptive Statistics

Table 2 shows the descriptive statistics for all dependent, independent and control variables. The number of observations is 120 for all the variables. The average value is 0.083, the maximum value is 0.399, the minimum value is -2.599 and the value of standard deviation is 0.321 in case of return on equity (ROE). There is a higher variation in the data set of ROE, because some banks are employed more capital which increases the bank's ROE. In the case of return on assets (ROA), the mean, maximum, minimum and standard deviation values are 0.011, 0.155, -0.073 and 0.021 respectively.

Table 2: Descriptive Statistics of Variables

Variable	*Obs*	*Mean*	*Std. Dev.*	*Min*	*Max*
ROE	120	0.0826522	0.3196081	-2.599	0.399
ROA	120	0.0106322	0.0212529	-0.0729	0.155
NIM	120	0.0235083	0.0205116	-0.0162	0.204
EBANK	120	11.41667	5.887722	0	24
CAPTL	120	0.0953467	0.1150157	0.0189	0.804
SZE	120	222.8013	155.5747	5.32	866.05
LQDTY	120	0.8550583	0.1255691	0.538	1.153
CRRK	120	0.1734624	0.3948826	-0.000702	3.822
EPS	120	19.04317	30.8315	0.95	187.8
EXPMNT	120	0.6421583	1.560923	0.235	17.444
RGDP	120	6.57	0.7242033	5.3	7.7
INF	120	6.96	1.945752	4.9	11.5

And we have a maximum value of 0.204, a minimum value of -0.016, an average value of 0.024 and a standard deviation of 0.021 in case of net interest margin (NIM). There is only one independent variable which is indicated by EBANK (the number of experienced years of adopting e-banking for the selected banks). In the case of EBANK, the minimum value is 0 because at least one bank adopts the e-banking system after 2009. The maximum value is 24 which indicates that there is at least one bank (selected) who has 14 years experienced of adopting e-banking before 2009. The average year is 11.42 and the standard deviation is 5.89 because the banks accept the e-banking system in different periods. The summary and descriptive statistics of control variables including bank-specific variables and macroeconomic variables are as follows for the CAPTL (capital adequacy), we get the maximum value of 0.804, the minimum value of 0.019, the mean value of 0.095 and the standard deviation of 0.115. In the case of SZE (total assets), the mean is 222.8013, the maximum size is 866.05, the minimum size is 5.32 and the standard deviation is 155.5747. We have the maximum value of 1.153, the minimum value of 0.538, the average value of 0.855 and the standard deviation of 0.126 for LQDTY.

For CRRK (credit risk), the maximum credit risk is 3.822, the minimum credit risk is -0.0007, the mean of credit risk is 0.173 and the variation of credit risk is 0.395. In the case of EPS (earnings per share in BDT), we get the values of 187.8, 0.95, 19.04 and 30.83 for maximum, minimum, average and standard deviation respectively. The variation of EPS is higher because of the uncertainty of profit of shares for different periods in different banks. The minimum value is 0.235, the maximum is 17.44, the mean value is 0.642 and the value of standard deviation is 1.56 for EXPMNT.

In the case of RGDP (real GDP growth rate), the maximum growth rate is 7.7, the minimum growth rate is 5.3, the average growth rate is 6.57 and the variation of growth rate is 0.724. And finally, we have the minimum inflation rate is 4.9, the maximum inflation rate is 11.5, the average inflation rate is 6.96 and the standard deviation is 1.95 for INF (current inflation rate). From above Table 2, EBANK and SZE have the higher standard deviation 5.89 and 155.5747. The SZE and EPS have the maximum values of 866.05 and 187.8 compared to the other variables. And ROE and ROA have the lower minimum values which are -2.599 and -0.0729 respectively among all other variables.

4.2 Correlation Analysis

Correlation analysis is a widely used statistical evaluation technique to find out the degree of relationship between two explanatory variables.

Correlation results are shown in Table 3. The correlation matrix (Table 3) shows the degree of relationship between the explanatory variables. Here, the largest value of correlation coefficient is 0.565 between earnings per share (EPS) and credit risk (CRRK). Therefore, in our correlation analysis, there is not the case of perfect positive or perfect negative correlation. The low correlation coefficient indicates that there is no multicollinearity problem. According to Gujarati (2004), if the pair-wise correlation coefficient between two explanatory variables is high, say, in excess of 0.8, then multicollinearity may be a serious problem.

Table 3: Matrix of Correlations between Independent Variables

Variables	*EBANK*	*CAPTL*	*SZE*	*LQDTY*	*CRRK*	*EPS*	*EXPMNT*	*RGDP*	*INF*
EBANK	1.000								
CAPTL	-0.050	1.000							
SZE	-0.039	-0.260	1.000						
LQDTY	0.352	-0.115	-0.353	1.000					
CRRK	-0.185	0.002	0.178	-0.148	1.000				
EPS	-0.440	-0.052	0.120	-0.379	0.565	1.000			
EXPMNT	-0.051	0.041	-0.009	-0.008	-0.034	0.017	1.000		
RGDP	0.448	0.087	0.436	0.270	0.048	-0.383	0.071	1.000	
INF	-0.220	-0.059	-0.199	-0.024	-0.087	0.046	-0.069	-0.223	1.000

But in our analysis, the highest correlation coefficient is 0.565 which is lower than 0.8. So, the problem of multicollinearity seems not to be appeared.

4.3 Hausman's (1978) Specification Test

Hausman test is beneficial to differentiate between fixed effects model and random effects model. Hausman test helps to take the decision to choose between random effects model (REM) and fixed effects model (FEM). If the Hausman test rejects the null hypothesis, then the random effects is biased and fixed effects is the appropriate estimation procedure. But, if the null hypothesis is accepted, then the random effects model is more appropriate than the fixed effects model. The hypotheses are:

Null: Random effects is appropriate

Alternative: Fixed effects is appropriate

Table 4: Output of Hausman's Specification Test

Hausman Test	*Model 1: ROE*	*Model 2: ROA*	*Model 3: NIM*
χ^2	5.18	15.12	10.27
Probability> χ^2	0.7383	0.0568	0.2466

Table 4 shows the output of the Hausman test for three dependent variables ROE, ROA, and NIM. In these three cases, the null hypothesis is accepted as the Probability>÷^{2}values in all models are more than 5%. This indicates that the random effects model is appropriate rather than the fixed effects model. So, it is relevant to estimate the three models (ROE, ROA, and NIM) by using random effects model (REM).

4.4 Regression Results

4.4.1 Results of Random Effects Model (REM)

From the REM regression results for Model 1, Model 2, and Model 3 shown in Table 5, it is seen that the independent variable EBANK (electronic banking) for Model 1 has a positive coefficient of 0.0015491which is statistically insignificant Although sample banks have experiences (at least 8 years) of adopting e-banking technology, the impact of e-banking on banks' ROE is not statistically significant. The e-banking for Model 2 has a positive impact on Bangladeshi commercial banks' return on assets. There is statistically significant [at 5% significance level (p-value=0.046)] effect of EBANK on the Bangladeshi banks' ROA.

Table 5: Results of Random Effects Model for ROE, ROA and NIM

Explanatory Variable	*Model 1: ROE*		*Model 2: ROA*		*Model 3: NIM*	
	Coefficient (p-value)	*t-value*	*Coefficient (p-value)*	*t-value*	*Coefficient (p-value)*	*t-value*
EBANK	0.0015491 (0.559)	0.58	0.0007695** (0.046)	2.00	0.0008613* (0.069)	1.82
CAPTL	0.190468* (0.059)	1.89	0.0320802* (0.067)	1.83	0.0009097 (0.962)	0.05
SZE	0.0000205 (0.840)	0.20	0.0000104 (0.554)	0.59	-0.000009 (0.638)	-0.47
LQDTY	0.0517016 (0.623)	0.48	0.0248017 (0.180)	1.34	0.021654 (0.289)	1.06
CRRK	-0.8137615*** (0.000)	-28.03	-0.023955*** (0.000)	-4.43	-0.0017063 (0.761)	-0.30
EPS	0.001689*** (0.000)	3.83	0.0001166 (0.147)	1.45	-0.0000157 (0.852)	-0.19
EXPMNT	-0.018239*** (0.002)	-3.15	-0.0016404 (0.126)	-1.53	-0.0019282* (0.084)	-1.73
RGDP	-0.0255544 (0.249)	-1.15	-0.0051722 (0.189)	-1.31	-0.0047732 (0.257)	-1.13
INF	0.0138459*** (0.004)	2.87	0.0031145*** (0.001)	3.47	0.0026621*** (0.004)	2.87
Constant	0.1902609 (0.120)	1.55	-0.0094543 (0.676)	-0.42	0.0117511 (0.618)	0.50
Overall R^2	0.9050		0.3400		0.2158	
R^2 between	0.8089		0.5345		0.4844	
R^2within	0.9216		0.2873		0.1224	
Wald χ^2	1165.37		54.55		23.89	
Prob>χ^2	0.0000		0.0000		0.0045	

Note: *, ** and *** indicate 10, 5 and 1 percent significance levels respectively.

If the number of years of experience of adopting e-banking by commercial banks in Bangladesh increases, the banks' ROA improves, and thus, the profits of commercial banks in Bangladesh also improve. The coefficient of EBANK is 0.0007695 which shows that 0.0007695 unit increase in banks' ROA resulting from 1 year increase in experience of adopting e-banking by banks, holding all other variables constant. Therefore, the higher the number of experience years of adopting e-banking by commercial banks, the greater the banks' ROA that lead to higher profitability of banks. This result is similar to studies by Yang *et al.* (2018), Oyewole *et al.* (2013), Aduda and Kingoo, (2012), Ngango *et al.* (2015), and Akram and Allam, (2010) who find that e-banking has a positive and significant effect on profitability in terms of ROA for studied banks.

Again, e-banking for Model 3 has a positive and statistically significant [at 10% significance level (p-value=0.069)] impact on Bangladeshi commercial banks' net interest margin (NIM). If the number of experienced years of adopting e-banking by commercial banks increases, the banks' NIM improves and thus, the profits of commercial banks also enhances. Therefore, the higher the experience of adopting e-banking by commercial banks, the greater is the banks' NIM which leads to higher profitability of banks. This result is similar to the studies by Oyewole *et al.* (2013), and Khrawish and Al-Sa'di (2011) who report that e-banking has a positive and significant effect on profitability in terms of NIM.

Capital adequacy has a positive and statistically significant impact on the banks' ROE. This result is consistent with studies by Rahman *et al.*(2015), Tam *et al.*(2017), Siddik *et al.* (2016), Oyewole *et al.* (2013), San and Heng (2013), Ongore and Kusa (2013), Malhotra and Singh (2009), Bogale (2019), Petria *el al.* (2015), and Obamuyi (2013) who find that there is positive significant relationship between capital adequacy and banks' ROA. Capital adequacy is positively related to banks' NIM with the coefficient value of 0.0009097 but the relationship between them is not statistically significant.

Credit risk has a negative and statistically significant. This result is similar to the findings by Athanasoglou *et al.* (2008), Flamini *et al.* (2009), Al-Smadi and Al-wabel (2011), Siddik *et al.* (2016), Tam *et al.*(2017), Oyewole *et al.* (2013), and Petria *el al.* (2015) who find credit risk has a negative and insignificant impact on the banks' NIM.

Earnings per share (EPS) has a significant positive relation with banks' return on equity. Saeed and Tahir (2015) also observe the same findings. Again, there is insignificant relationship between EPS and, banks' ROA and NIM. Expenses management has negative and significant impact on the banks' performance in terms of ROE and NIM but insignificant impact on the banks' ROA.

Inflation has a significant negative impact on the banks' performance in terms of ROE, ROA and NIM. This result is similar to the finding of the studies by Goddard *et al.* (2004), Tam *et al.* (2017), and Malhotra and Singh (2009).

4.4.2 Results of Generalised Method of Moments (GMM)

Results of System GMM (shown in Table 6) indicate that e-banking has a significant positive impact on the performance of commercial banks in Bangladesh in terms of ROE and ROA. The similar result has also been found by Siddik *et al.* (2016), Yang *et al.* (2018), Hernando and Nieto (2007), Mapharing and Basuhi (2017), Oyewole *et al.* (2013), Aduda and Kingoo (2012), Ngango *et al.* (2015), and Akram and Allam, (2010). But an insignificant positive impact on the performance of banks in terms of NIM.

Capital adequacy has a significant positive impact on the performance of commercial banks in Bangladesh in terms of ROE and ROA. This result is similar to the findings by Rahman *et al.* (2015), Tam *et al.* (2017), Siddik *et al.* (2016), Oyewole *et al.* (2013), San and Heng (2013), Ongore and Kusa (2013), and Malhotra and Singh (2009). A significant negative impact of credit risk on the banks' performance is observed in terms of ROE and ROA.

Table 6: Results of System GMM for ROE, ROA and NIM

Variable	*Model 1: ROE*		*Model 2: ROA*		*Model 3: NIM*	
	Coefficient (p-value)	*t-value*	*Coefficient (p-value)*	*t-value*	*Coefficient (p-value)*	*t-value*
ROE (L1)	0.0425878* (0.077)	1.77				
ROA (L1)			0.1517179* (0.067)	1.83		
NIM (L1)					0.031797 (0.696)	0.39
EBANK	0.0135162** (0.013)	2.50	0.0021237* (0.070)	1.81	0.0008155 (0.419)	0.81
CAPTL	0.3087813*** (0.008)	2.67	0.0520488** (0.034)	2.13	0.0087379 (0.757)	0.31
SZE	0.0000354 (0.738)	0.34	0.0000162 (0.477)	0.71	-0.0000226 (0.409)	-0.82

(Contd...)

LQDTY	-0.0257614 (0.837)	-0.20	-0.0180384 (0.545)	-0.61	0.0281673 (0.357)	0.92
CRRK	-0.8490924*** (0.000)	-28.07	- 0.0291878*** (0.000)	-4.69	0.0023072 (0.738)	0.34
EPS	0.0021956*** (0.000)	4.07	0.0003322*** (0.004)	2.88	-0.0001133 (0.351)	-0.93
EXPMNT	-0.010391** (0.048)	-1.98	-0.0007874 (0.505)	-0.67	-0.0009219 (0.374)	-0.89
RGDP	-0.0336271 (0.197)	-1.29	0.0015587 (0.783)	0.28	0.0002506 (0.968)	0.04
INF	0.0296007*** (0.000)	4.30	0.0057674*** (0.000)	4.28	0.004061*** (0.008)	2.64
Constant	0.0260238 (0.846)	0.19	-0.0615263** (0.034)	-2.12	-0.0358093 (0.269)	-1.11
Sargan test (p-value)	79.4223 (0.0006)		33.7009 (0.8443)		23.7238 (0.9925)	
Wald χ^2	1833.66		74.49		21.28	
Prob>χ^2	0.0000		0.0000		0.0000	

Note: *, ** and *** indicate 10, 5 and 1 percent significance levels respectively.

Earnings per share has a significant positive effect on the banks' ROE and ROA is observed. There is a significant negative relationship between expenses management and commercial banks' performance in terms of ROE. Inflation has a significant positive impact on the performance of commercial banks in Bangladesh for all the three measures ROE, ROA and NIM. Athanasoglou *et al.* (2008), and Chinoda (2014) report the similar result. Summary of all results and their observed impacts are shown in Table 7.

Table 7: Summary and Comparison of Results with Expectations

Explanatory variables	*Expected Sign*	*Actual Impact*		*Hypothesis Accepted/ Rejected*
		REM Results	*GMM Results*	
EBANK	+	+ on ROE + on ROA** + on NIM*	+ on ROE** + on ROA* + on NIM	Accepted
CAPTL	+	+ on ROE* + on ROA* + on NIM	+ on ROE*** + on ROA** + on NIM	Accepted
SZE	+/-	+ on ROE + on ROA - on NIM	+ on ROE + on ROA - on NIM	No conclusion
LQDTY	+/-	+ on ROE + on ROA + on NIM	- on ROE - on ROA + on NIM	No conclusion

(*Contd...*)

CRRK	-	- on ROE*** - on ROA*** - on NIM	- on ROE*** - on ROA*** + on NIM	Accepted
EPS	+	+ on ROE*** + on ROA - on NIM	+ on ROE*** + on ROA*** - on NIM	Accepted
EXPMNT	-	- on ROE*** - on ROA - on NIM*	- on ROE** - on ROA - on NIM	Accepted
RGDP	+	- on ROE - on ROA - on NIM	- on ROE + on ROA + on NIM	No conclusion
INF	+	+ on ROE*** + on ROA*** + on NIM***	+ on ROE*** + on ROA*** + on NIM***	Accepted

Note: *, ** and *** indicate 10, 5 and 1 percent significance levels respectively.

5. Conclusions

There are various factors that affect the performance of commercial banks in Bangladesh, e-banking is one of them. Empirical results ensure some findings of earlier researches that e-banking has a gradual positive impact on the performance of banks. The findings of this study are more comprehensive than earlier literature since this study considers three different measures namely, return on equity (ROE), return on assets (ROA) and net interest margin (NIM) to measure the performance of banks and employs two different regression technique namely, REM and system GMM to estimate the relationship between electronic banking and other variables of commercial banks in Bangladesh. Most of the earlier literatures have used a single indicator to measure the banks' performance and a single regression approach to estimate the impact of electronic banking.

This study is evolved from the researchers' aim of investigating the impact of electronic banking technology on the performance of commercial banks in Bangladesh. There are 12 commercial banks which have been selected for this study covering the period from 2009 to 2018. The study brings to pass by constructing a balanced panel regression model based on random effects and system GMM.

Our major findings indicate that e-banking has a positive and significant impact on the performance of commercial banks in Bangladesh in terms of ROA and NIM with the significance levels at 5% and 10% respectively. By employing system GMM, the e-banking has a positive and significant impact on the performance of commercial banks in terms of ROE and ROA with the significance levels at 5% and 10% respectively. E-banking is valued by considering the first adopting year with any form of e-banking services by respective commercial banks in Bangladesh. It is recommended that banks should adopt all forms of e-banking system to improve their performance. Since all the commercial banks in Bangladesh have not yet ensured e-banking services, this study also suggests that banks management should invest more to setup overall e-banking technologies in their banks as well as arrange to provide perfect knowledge about using e-banking to their employees and clients in order to receive higher profitability. The regression results reveal that total of six explanatory variables out of nine have significant impacts on the banks' performance in Bangladesh with a positive or negative direction; bank size, liquidity and economic growth are statistically insignificant to affect commercial banks' performance in Bangladesh. Although we find a positive significant impact of e-banking on the performance of commercial banks in Bangladesh measured by ROE, ROA and NIM. We believe that future researchers will pay more concentration to confirm our findings by conducting the research on the same issue.

References

Abaenewe, Z. C., Ogbulu, O. M. and Ndugbu, M. O. (2013). Electronic banking and bank performance in Nigeria. *West African Journal of Industrial and Academic Research*, 6(1): 171–187.

Acharya, R. N., Kagan, A. and Linam, S. R. (2008). Online banking applications and community bank performance. *The International Journal of Bank Marketing*, 26(6): 418-439.

Aduda, J. and Kingoo, N. (2012). The relationship between electronic banking and financial performance among commercial banks in Kenya. *Journal of Finance and Investment Analysis*, 1(3): 99–118.

Ahmed, S. M. S., Rayhan, S. J., Islam, M. A. and Mahjabin, S. (2011). Problems and prospects of mobile banking in Bangladesh. *Journal of Information Engineering and Applications*, 1(6): 16-35.

Akram, J. K. and Allam, M. H. (2010). The Impact of Information Technology on improving Banking Performance Matrix: Jordanian Banks as Case Study. *EuropeanMediterranean and Middle Eastern Conference on Information System*, April 12th –13th, Abu Dhabi, UAE.

Alagheband, P. (2006). Adoption of electronic banking services by Iranian customers. *Master Thesis, Lulea University of Technology,* retrieve from: http://www.epubl.Itu.se/1653-0187/2006/49/LTU-PB-EX-0649-SE.pdf

Al-Smadi, M. O. and Al-Wabel, S. A. (2011). The impact of e-banking on the performance of Jordanian banks. *Journal of Internet Banking and Commerce*, 16(2): 1–10.

Athanasoglou, P. P., Brissimis, S. N., and Delis, M. D. (2008). Bank-specific, industry-specific and macroeconomic determinants of bank profitability. *Journal of International Financial Markets, Institutions and Money*, 18(2): 121–136.

Bogale, Y. W. (2019). Factors Affecting Profitability of Banks: Empirical Evidence from Ethiopian Private Commercial Banks. *Journal of Investment and Management*, 8(1): 8-15.

Blundell, R. and Bond, S. (1998). Initial conditions and moment restrictions in dynamic panel data models. *Journal of Econometrics*, 87(1): 115-143.

Chinoda, T. (2014). The Determinants of Commercial Banks Profitability in Zimbabwe (2009-2014). *IOSR Journal of Economics and Finance*, 5(6): 69-80.

Dey, M. (2014). Profitability of commercial banks in Bangladesh: a multivariate analysis. *IOSR Journal of Business and Management*, 16(4): 92–95.

DeYoung, R., Lang, W. W. and Nolle, D. L. (2007). How the internet affects output and performance at community banks. *Journal of Banking & Finance*, 31(4): 1033–1060.

Dinh, V., Le, U. and Le, P. (2015). Measuring the impacts of internet banking to bank performance: Evidence from Vietnam. *Journal of Internet Banking and Commerce*, 20(2): 1-14.

Flamini, V., Schumacher, L. and McDonald, C. A. (2009). The determinants of commercial bank profitability in Sub-Saharan Africa. IMF Working paper No. 09/15. International Monetary Fund. Hall, M.; Weiss, L. 1967. Firm size and profitability. *The Review of Economics and Statistics*, 49(3): 319–331.

Goddard, J.A., Molyneux, P. and Wilson, J. (2004). The profitability of European banks: a cross-sectional and dynamic panel analysis. *The Manchester School* 72, 363– 381.

Guru, B. K., Staunton, J. and Balashanmugam, B. (2000). Determinants of commercial bank profitability in Malaysia. *Asian Academy of Management Journal*, 5(2): 1-22.

Gujarati, D. N. (2004). Basic Econometrics, 4th Edition, Tata Mc-Graw-Hill Publishing Company Limited, New Delhi, India.

Hefferman, S. A. and Fu, X. (2014). Determinants of financial performance in Chinese banking. *Applied Financial Economics*, 20(20): 1585-1600.

Hefferman, S. A. and Fu, X. (2014). Determinants of financial performance in Chinese banking. *Applied Financial Economics*, 20(20): 1585-1600.

Hossein, S. M. (2013). Consideration the effect of E-Banking on Bank Profitability; Case Study Selected Asian Countries. *Journal of Economics and Sustainable Development*, 4(11): 112-117.

Hausman, J. A. (1978). Specification Tests in Econometrics. *Econometrica,*46 (6): 1251–1271.

Khrawish, H. A. and Al-Sa'di, N. M. (2011). The impact of e-banking on bank profitability: evidence from Jordan. *Middle Eastern Finance and Economics*, 13: 142–158.

Malhotra, P. and Singh, B. (2009). The impact of internet banking on bank performance and risk: the Indian experience. *Eurasian Journal of Business and Economics*, 2(4): 43–62.

Mapharing, M. and Basuhi, E. (2017). Electronic Banking and Bank Performance: Botswana Context. *Journal of Accounting, Business and Finance Research*, 1(1): 84-93.

Naceur, S. B. and Goaied, M. (2001). The determinants of the Tunisian deposit banks' performance. *Applied Financial Economics*, 11(3): 317–319.

Naifer, N. (2010). The determinants of bank performance: an analysis of theory and practice in the case of an emerging market. *International Journal of Business Environment*, 3(4): 460-470.

Ngango, A., Mbabazize, D. M. and Shukla, D. J. (2015). E-Banking and Performance of Commercial Banks in Rwanda a Case of Bank of Kigali. *European Journal of Accounting Auditing and Finance Research*, 3(4): 25-57.

Nickell, S. (1981). Biases in dynamic models with fixed effects. *Econometrica*, 49: 1417–1426.

Obamuyi, T. M. (2013). Determinants of Banks' Profitability in a Developing Economy: Evidence from Nigeria. *Organisations and Markets in Emerging Economies*, 4(2): 97-111.

Onay, C. and Ozsoz, E. (2013). The impact of internet-banking on brick and mortar branches: the case of Turkey. *Journal of Financial Services Research*, 44(2): 187–204.

Ongore, V. O. and Kusa, G. B. (2013). Determinants of Financial Performance of Commercial Banks in Kenya. *International Journal of Economics and Financial Issues*, 3(1): 237-252.

Oyewole, O. S., Abba, M. and El-maude, J. G. (2013). E-banking and bank performance: Evidence from Nigeria. *International Journal of Scientific Engineering and Technology*, 2(8): 766-771.

Pteria, N., Capraru, B. and Ihnatove, I. (2015). Determinants of banks' profitability: evidence from EU 27 banking systems. *Procedia Economics and Finance*, 20: 518 – 524.

Raharjo, P. G., Hakim, D. B., Manurung, A. H. and Maulana, T. N. (2014). The determinant of commercial banks' interest margin in Indonesia: an analysis of fixed effect panel regression. *International Journal of Economics and Financial Issues*, 4(2): 295–308.

Rahman, M. M., Hamid, M. K. and Khan, M. A. M. (2015). Determinants of Bank Profitability: Empirical Evidence from Bangladesh. *International Journal of Business and Management*, 10(8): 135-150.

Rahman, B. (2016). Influence of E-banking Services towards the Profitability of Commercial Banks in Bangladesh: Some Observations. *ASA University Review*, 10(2): 59-73.

Sadekin, M. S. and Shaikh, M. A. H. (2016). Effect of E-Banking on Banking Sector of Bangladesh. *International Journal of Economics, Finance and Management Sciences*, 4(3): 93-97.

Saeed, J. T. and Tahir, J. H. (2015). Relationship between Earning Per Share and Bank Profitability. *International Journal of Novel Research in Humanity and Social Sciences*, 2(2): 4-13.

Samad, A. (2015). Determinants of bank profitability: Empirical evidence from Bangladesh commercial banks. *International Journal of Financial Research*, 6(3): 173 -179.

San, O. T. and Heng, T. B. (2013). Factors affecting the profitability of Malaysian commercial banks. *African Journal of Business Management*, 7(8): 649-660.

Sargan, J. D. (1958). The Estimation of Economic Relationships Using Instrumental Variables. *Econometrica*. 26 (3): 393–415.

Sarker, M. N. I., Islam, M. S. and Rahman, M. M. (2015). Effects of electronic banking on performance of banks in Bangladesh. *International Journal of Applied Research*, 1(1): 28-34.

Siddik, M. N. A., Sun, G., Kabiraj, S., Shanmugan, J. and Yanjuan, C. (2016). Impacts of E-Banking on Performance of Banks in a Developing Economy: Empirical Evidence From Bangladesh. *Journal of Business Economics and Management*, 17(6): 1066-1080.

Sufian, F. and Chong, R. R. (2008). Determinant of bank profitability in a developing economy: empirical evidence from the Philippines. *Asian Academy of Management Journal of Accounting and Finance*, 4(2): 91–112.

Sumra, S. H., Manzoor, M. K., Sumra, H. H. and Abbas, M. (2011). The Impact of E-Banking on the Profitability of Banks: A Study of Pakistani Banks. *Journal of Public Administration and Governance*, 1(1): 31-38.

Tam, L. T., Trang, P. X. and Hanh, L. N. (2017). Determinants of Bank Profitability: The Case of Commercial Banks Listed on the Vietnam's Stock Exchange. *Journal of Business Sciences (JBS)*, 1(2): 1-12.

TrujilloPonce, A. (2013). What determines the profitability of banks? Evidence from Spain. *Accounting & Finance*, 53(2): 561–586.

Yang, S., Li, Z., Ma, Y. and Chen, X. (2018). Does Electronic Banking Really Improve Bank Performance? Evidence in China. *International Journal of Economics and Finance*, 10(2): 82-94.

Part-III
Agriculture and Rural Development

9

Agricultural Credit Growth and Credit Policy in India: A Critical Appraisal

Abhijit Pathak and
Apurba Kumar Chattopadhyay

Abstract

The performance of agricultural sector is hugely important for the Indian economy. The progress of this sector depends on many factors including agricultural credit. Delivery of adequate credit to agricultural is imperative for the smooth functioning of this sector. This paper has attempted to examine the performance of agricultural credit delivery by the commercial banks and critically evaluate the agricultural credit policy adopted by the Reserve Bank of India (RBI). This paper has found that the experience of credit growth in agriculture in the post-liberalisation period is vastly different from that of the 1970s and 1980s. The first decade after liberalisation has recorded sharp deceleration to single digit credit growth in agriculture. It is not the shortage of liquidity, but the type of monetary policy accommodation pursued by the RBI during the 90s along with its prudential and regulatory framework that made agricultural credit relatively unworthy to the banking sector. The period from 2001 to 2014 has witnessed recovery, boom and moderation of agricultural credit expansion with annual average credit growth around 24 percent. But the quality of credit to agriculture has remained a cause of concern in this period. Agricultural credit expansion has decelerated sharply in the last five years since 2015. This is an alarming situation. The latest enhancement of sub-targets for small and marginal farmers from the present 8 percent to 10 percent gradually, beginning from the year 2021-22 is an indication of the gravity of agricultural credit crisis in India.

Key Words: *Agricultural Credit, Small and Marginal Farmers, Priority Sector Lending, Indebtedness.*

1. Introduction

Agriculture is an important sector for the Indian economy. On the one hand, it is the source of employment and livelihood of majority of the population and on the other hand, it ensures availability of food to hundred and thirty crore Indians. It has been vindicated during the present COVID-19 pandemic and its consequent impact on the economy that the relevance of the agricultural sector in India can never be undermined by its declining share in the gross value added (GVA) of the economy. The continuity of production of food grains and vegetables from this sector during the COVID-19 crisis has not only maintained more than adequate supply of food and ensured food security for the huge population in India but also buttressed the economy largely from a free fall situation.

Indian agriculture is engulfed with problems including small land holding patterns, technology constraint, low-productivity, high costs of inputs, non-remunerative prices, low income, faulty government policies and inadequate marketing facilities. However, poor delivery of agricultural credit has always remained an important bottleneck for this sector in India for a very long period. Delivery of agricultural credit is a critical input for the smooth functioning of this sector. Therefore, agricultural credit policy has always received top priority in the hierarchy of credit policies and overall economic policies in India in the post-independence period. Agricultural credit received its biggest thrust after the commencement of the nationalisation of commercial banks in India from the beginning of the 1970s. Bank credit to agriculture registered a phenomenal expansion in the post bank nationalisation period in terms of both quantity and outreach of credit with the spread of branches of the public sector banks to the rural areas in India. This scenario changed drastically in the post-liberalisation period when the competition within the banking sector forced public sector banks to abandon the model of 'social banking'. The change in the attitude of the public sector banks badly affected the rural economy and particularly farmers. The 'small ticket' crop loans of the farmers or the agricultural credit as a whole slid down the priority lists of the public sector banks that control 80 percent of the banking business in India. On many occasions, commercial banks failed to meet their target of lending to the 'priority sector', which includes 'agriculture' as its largest constituent. The number of rural branches of commercial banks and total number of loan accounts for agricultural credit recorded a decline in the 1990s (Shetty, 2005). Instead of forcing banks to comply with priority sector lending (PSL), banks were allowed to bypass their lending obligations through various channels. The introduction of Rural Infrastructure Development Fund (RIDF) to meet their shortfalls in priority sector lending to agriculture is one such example.

We have completed almost thirty years since the introduction of liberalisation policy in India. This is an opportune time to appraise the credit delivery to agricultural sector in India. This paper has attempted to examine the performance of agricultural credit delivery by the commercial banks in the post-liberalisation period. Simultaneously, this paper will make an endeavour to critically evaluate the types of agricultural credit policy adopted by the Reserve Bank of India (RBI) and its impact on the quantitative and qualitative changes of credit delivery to the agricultural sector by the commercial banks over this period. We have organised this paper in five sections. In the second section, we will examine the present status of Indian agriculture and institutional credit at the macro level. In the next section, we will deliberate on the delivery of agricultural credit in the post-liberalisation period in different phases and record the important findings. In the fourth section, we will try to assess the recent policy changes of the Reserve Bank of India pertaining to credit to agriculture under (PSL). It will be followed by concluding remarks in the final section.

2. Status of Indian Agriculture and Institutional Credit

Agricultural sector has undergone massive changes in the last fifty years. A brief description on the present status of the agricultural sector in India will provide us an idea about the evolving nature of credit needs and requirements of this sector and the appropriate response from the banking sector. According to the 'national account statistics' data published by the Central Statistical Organisation (CSO) of the Government of India (GOI), the share of agriculture to gross domestic product (GDP) has gradually declined from as high as 40.6 percent in 1972-73 to 14.4 percent in 2018-19. The low productivity growth in agricultural sector may primarily be attributed for such a secular decline. The latest estimate of International Labour Organisation (ILO) for 2018 has recorded a decline in the share of agricultural employment to total employment to around 44 percent. According to the reports of employment unemployment survey of National Sample Survey Organisation (NSSO) of GOI (68th round in 2011-2012 and earlier surveys reports for earlier rounds of surveys) this share was 73.9 percent , 63.9 percent, 60.2 percent, 56.5 percent and 48.9 percent in the years 1972-73, 1993-94, 1999-2000, 2004-05 and 2011-12 respectively. The above statistics show that the dependence on agriculture for employment did not decline to the extent of its share in GDP. The growth of other sectors did not create much employment and therefore dependence on agriculture could not decline in spite of its poor productivity growth. Agriculture remains the major source of employment in India. The COVID-19 crisis has re-established the significance of this sector.

According to the agricultural Census 2015-16, the marginal farmers and small farmers hold 68.5 percent and 17.6 percent of total operational holding in India. Taken together they account for almost 86 percent of the total holdings. Most of the increase over the last 50 years has come from increase in marginal holdings. The share of marginal holdings has increased gradually from around 50 percent in 1970. The share of operational holdings by small farmers has actually recorded a declined since 1990-91. The operated area under the marginal farmers is only around 24 percent of the total operated area while they possess 68.5 percent of the operational holding. This scenario is much better for the small farmers. They constitute around 23 percent of the operated area and their share of operated area is gradually increasing since 1970-71, even when their share in total operational holdings is actually declining since 1990-91. Therefore, even though we mention small and marginal farmers as a category in the literature particularly in the criteria set out for delivery of credit, the evolution of their holding patterns and operated areas over the last 50 years have dissimilarities. The small farmers have actually been able to hold and consolidate their positions in comparison to all other category (semi, medium and large farmers) of farmers in India. However, the increasing marginalisation of holdings is a general trend in Indian agriculture. The average size of land holding has gradually declined from 2.28 hectares in 1970-71 to 1.08 hectares in 2015-16. Within fifty years, average land holdings in agriculture have been reduced by 50 percent. Given the presence of large number of small and marginal farmers and their low average size of holdings, it was a necessity for the banking system to formulate innovative measures to address the changing demand patterns of the small and marginal farmers and particularly for marginal farmers.

The data regarding debt and investment is collected by the All India Debt Investment Survey (AIDIS) conducted by NSSO. The report of the latest AIDIS survey (70th round survey in 2013) was published in 2014. The earlier survey for the same purpose was conducted in 2002, 1991, 1981, 1971 and 1961. The data on rural indebtedness from the report of AIDIS survey has clearly indicated that there was a marked reduction in the indebtedness among the cultivators in the first decade after bank nationalisation. The indebtedness amongst cultivators reduced from a high of 46.1 percent in 1971 to 22.3 percent in 1981 (Table 1). The rapid spread of rural branches of the commercial banks and the growth of agricultural credit in the 1970s helped in the reduction of indebtedness amongst cultivators in India (Robin and Rohini, 2005; Binswanger and Khandker, 1992). However, the slowing down of growth of agricultural credit during the second half of 1980s resulted in an increase in indebtedness amongst the cultivators to 25.9 percent. The decade of poor agricultural growth in 1990s resulted in an increase in the indebtedness amongst farmers to 29.7 percent in 2002. The 70th round survey of the NSSO on Debt and investment in India in 2013 found that incidence of indebtedness among the rural cultivators reached to 46 percent in 2013, almost at the same level of the 1970s. The high growth of agricultural credit by the commercial banks during the period 2002 to 2013 failed to reduce the indebtedness amongst farmers as achieved during 1970s. Many people may argue that increasing debt may not be a sign of distress as increase in debt may have resulted in higher asset accumulation. Therefore, debt assets ratio (DAR) can give us a better picture. The analysis of debt asset ratios also vindicate that the DAR among the rural cultivators declined from a level of 4.13 in 1971 to 1.61 in 1991. But since 1991 onwards, the DAR of rural cultivators have increased sharply to 2.47 in 2002 and remained almost at the same level in 2013 (Table 1). This clearly indicates that high credit growth in the post-liberalisation period has not been able to create many assets for the cultivators as happened in 1970s. The AIDIS 2013 report has also found that at the all-India level, indebtedness amongst cultivator households (46%) was much higher than non-cultivator households (29%).

Table 1: Debt Asset Ratio and Incidence of Indebtedness among Cultivators of Rural India

Year	*IOI*	*DAR*
1971	46.1	4.13
1981	22.3	1.8
1991	25.9	1.61
2002	29.7	2.47
2013	45.9	2.46

Source: Key Indicators of Debt and Investment in India, NSSO 70th round, December 2013.

According to the report of the AIDIS 2013, the share of institutional credit which increased from 32 percent in 1971 to 66.3 percent in 1991 declined to 61 percent in 2002 and recovered marginally to 64 percent in 2013. As a consequence, the cultivators are forced to take loan from non-institutional sources. Therefore, the share of credit availed by the cultivators from non-institutional sources which was reduced from 68 percent to 33.7 percent in 1991, increased to 39 percent in 2002. It remained as high as 36 percent even in 2013. But most interestingly, amongst the sources of non-institutional credit, share of money lenders which was only 17.2 percent in 1981 has gradually increased to 26.8 percent in 1991 and further to 26.8 percent and 29.6 percent in 2002 and 2013 respectively (Table 2). Given the high rates of interest charged by the moneylenders in comparison to the interest rate charged by the scheduled commercial banks (SCBs) which also include the facilities of interest rate subvention (and interest rate benefit for prompt repayment) schemes of the government, it is unlikely that cultivators will prefer credit from moneylenders unless they are deprived of institutional credit. The retreat of institutional credit and thereby the increasing occupation of that space by the rural moneylenders in the post-liberalisation period is indicated in the figures mentioned above. This vindicates that achievement in the field of agricultural credit during 1970-1990 withered away in the first 10 years of liberalisation and could never be retrieved thereafter in spite of phenomenal credit growth for at least a decade and more since the beginning of this century (Table 2).

Table 2: Institutional and Non-Institutional Credit to Farmers

Sources of Credit	*1951*	*1961*	*1971*	*1981*	*1991*	*2002*	*2013*
Institutional	**10.2**	**20.9**	**32**	**56.2**	**66.3**	**61.1**	**64**
Government		6.2		4	5.7	1.7	1.3
Co-operative Banks and	6.2	12.5		27.6	23.6	30.2	28.9
Commercial Banks	4	2.2		23.8	35.2	26.3	30.7
Insurance and Providend Fund				0.8	0.7	0.5	0.1
Other Agencies					1.1	2.4	3
Non-Instititional Rural Credit	**89.8**	**79.1**	**68**	**43.8**	**33.7**	**38.9**	**36**
Money Lenders	39.8	25.3		17.2	17.5	26.8	29.6
Relatives, Friends				11.5	4.6	6.2	4.3
Traders, Commission Agents				5.8	2.2	2.6	
Land Lords	21.4	15		3.6	3.7	0.9	0.4
Others	28.6	38.8		5.7	5.7	2.4	1.7
Total	100	100	100	100	100	100	100

Source: All India Rural Credit Survey (1954); All India Debt and Investment Survey, Various Issues.

3. Delivery of Agricultural Credit in the Post-liberalisation Period in Different Phases

The nationalisation of the fourteen major commercial banks in July 1969 led to a considerable reorientation of bank lending, especially to the priority sectors of the economy, which had not previously received sufficient attention from the commercial banks. It gave an impetus to the process of reallocation of banking resources to suit the socio-economic needs of the country in which agricultural credit was a major constituent. The phenomenal increase in agricultural credit and outreach of banks are well documented in the literature (Shetty, 2006).

The description of agricultural credit is very different in the post-liberalisation period in India. We have divided this post- liberalisation period in three phases. The first phase coincides almost with the first decade of liberalisation i.e., 1991-2000. This is a period of deceleration in agricultural credit growth. The second phase is for the period 2001-2014. In this period, agricultural credit registered phenomenal growth but without much achievement. The last phase is the period from 2014 onwards to present times. In this phase, both deceleration in agricultural credit growth and quality of credit delivery has become a cause of major concern for this sector.

Phase I (1991-2000)

The Indian banking and financial market adopted the path of gradual de-regulation from the beginning of the 1990s. Accordingly, most of the interest rates were regulated including those subsidised loans directed towards sectors like agriculture. The introduction of new prudential norms for the Indian banking sector as a part of financial sector reform from the beginning of 1990s made it almost mandatory for the commercial banks in India to set aside a part of their assets against loans to certain sectors including agriculture (with higher risk associated with the loan). This made loans to these sectors costlier. The competitive banking environment along with the thrust on compliance to the newly introduced prudential norms made credit to sectors like agriculture less attractive. These prudential norms were not consistent with the earlier approach of 'social banking' followed by the banking sector in India. 'Social banking' approach was essential for provisioning of adequate credit to agriculture and small scale industries in India. The shift in objectives of the public sector banks from social banking to competitive banking were reflected in the poor delivery of credit to agriculture even to the public sector banks in India (Shetty, 2006, 2005). The status of agricultural loans under PSL was even worse for the private sector banks. The PSL criteria in India have made it mandatory for banks to provide 18 percent of their net bank credit to agriculture. But the Economic Surveys published by GOI in the 90s (various issues) reveal that the aggregate credit to agriculture by public sector banks (PSB) accounted for 14-16 percent of net bank credit (NBC) on average in 90s. The corresponding figure for the private sector banks (PVSB) were 8-10 percent only. The decline in agricultural credit and its figures are also alarming. This situation continued till the beginning of this century. According to economic survey 2001-02, aggregate credit to agriculture by PSBs accounted for 15.7 percent of NBC at end-March 2001, compared to 15.8 percent in the corresponding period of the previous year. The figures for PVSB were 9.6 percent and 9.1 percent respectively. The share of agriculture in gross bank credit, which had gone up steadily from 8.0 percent in 1972 to 8.9 percent in 1975, 13 percent in 1980, 16 percent in 1985 and 16.2 percent in 1990, came down equally steadily to 13.5 percent in 1994, 11.7 percent in 1996, 11.6 percent in 1998 and 11.5 percent in 1999 (HBS, RBI, 2019) (Chart 1A). In most of the years in the 1990s agricultural credits registered a single digit credit growth. The annual average growth during 1991 to 1995 was as low as 8.5 percent. Agricultural credit growth was relatively higher in the second half of 1990s. The annual average rate of growth of total finance to agriculture from the commercial banks recorded a growth of 10.7 percent between 1990 and 2000. Within agricultural finance, indirect finance registered an annual average growth of 13.0 percent while direct finance to agriculture stagnated at 10.4 percent only for this decade (Table 3).

Table 3: The Average Annual Growth of Credit to Agriculture

Period	*Average Growth of Total Agricultural Finance*	*Average Growth of Direct Agricultural Finance*	*Average Growth of Indirect Agricultural Finance*
1971-80	28	38	29
1981-85	23	25	17
1985-1990	14	15	8
1991-1995	8	8	11
1995-1999	13	12	16
2000-2004	19	16	38
2005-2009	32	33	30
2009-2014	21	22	15
2014-2019	10	11	2

Source: Basic Statistical Returns of SCBs in India (various issues), RBI.

As mentioned earlier, banks found it costly and unattractive to lend to the agricultural sector in the post-liberalisation period. In the absence of any thrust from the government, they were not under any pressure to enhance credit growth to agriculture. As a large section of the banks were falling short of meeting the PSL limit for the agricultural sector, RBI adopted the path of dilution of norms of PSL for agricultural credit. The government and RBI were not in a position to do away with the sub-target of agricultural credit of 18 percent under PSL realising the credit need of the agricultural sector as well as the political repercussions of such a move. Therefore, they adopted the path of dilution of norms for PSL lending. This started with the bifurcation of the agricultural credit under PSL between direct and indirect finance to agriculture (1993), changing the reference point for calculation of PSL from net bank credit to adjusted net bank credit (1995) and introduction of RIDF deposits to meet the shortfall in PSL target by commercial banks. We will discuss about these shifts in PSL criteria below. These measures were accompanied and followed by inclusion of a number of items and credit categories under direct and indirect finance to agriculture so that banks can fulfil their PSL targets relatively easily. These inclusions continued almost for two decades (BOX 1). Though majority of the inclusion took place after 2000 but the process of inclusion started in 1993 and some important items were included in this phase too for both direct and indirect finance to agriculture. Some of the high value credit categories which were included in the indirect finance category in 1990s and at the initial years of this century were swiftly shifted to direct finance category later. The vacant places created due to their shifting to direct finance form indirect finance category were duly filled by some new credit items in the latter category. All these changes resulted in both reductions in quantum of direct finance as well as quality of credit to the agricultural sector.

The All-India Rural Credit Review Committee submitted its report in July 1969. The Committee recommended direct financing of cultivators by commercial banks but did not rule out indirect financing through suppliers of inputs or those engaged in marketing or processing the produce. Within direct finance to agriculture, a short-term credit or a credit for seasonal agricultural operations has accounted for a significant share. The short-term loans to agriculture are referred to as the "crop loans", as they are advanced for crop cultivation against the hypothecation of the crop to be cultivated by the farmer. The crop loans are provided as cash or in kind, such as the supply of fertilisers and seeds. Apart from the crop loans, direct finance also includes credit for medium- and long-term investment in agriculture. Indirect finance to agriculture includes agricultural production and investment related activities that commercial banks were expected to finance were distribution of fertilizer and other inputs, marketing of agricultural produce, including government procurement operations; and the entire expanding infrastructure of processing, loans to electricity boards, storage and transportation. The indirect credit is important in the sense that it supports in building infrastructure and facilities that subsequently helps agricultural production, storage, marketing and business. These are also essential for emergence of a vibrant agricultural sector in India.

Commercial banks had begun to provide direct and indirect finance to farmers/agriculture even earlier than 1970s. The BSR data published by the RBI since 1971-72 used to report both types of credit provided by the commercial banks while only direct finance to agriculture was accounted under PSL to agriculture. Indirect finance was never a part of the PSL. Therefore, the sub-target of agricultural credit of 18 percent under PSL was solely accounted for direct finance to agriculture. This sub-target of 18 percent agricultural credit was bifurcated in October 1993 to a minimum of 13.5 percent for direct loans and a maximum of 4.5 percent for indirect loans. The lending over 4.5 percent under indirect credit to agriculture was not considered within 18 percent PSL to agriculture but it was recognised within overall PSL limits of 40 percent. This was the beginning of the dilution of the norms for credit to agriculture in India.

The definition of net bank credit as a reference point was modified from March 1995 to adjusted net bank credit (ANBC). The deposits mobilised by banks through FCNR (foreign currency non-resident) and non-resident non-repairable deposit accounts can now be deducted from the base of net bank credit. This will make the base smaller and thereby the absolute credit requirement for meeting the PSL target.

Banks were allowed to deposit a part of their shortfall in PSL target in agricultural credit in the Rural Infrastructure and Development Fund (RIDF) from 1997 onwards. PSL was calculated on the basis of net bank credit of the commercial banks. These were preceded by changes in the branch expansion policies by the RBI at the end of 1980s, which required compulsory opening of rural branches for opening of urban branches in India. To facilitate commercial banks from failing to meet the PSL target, the Rural Infrastructure Development Fund (RIDF) was established with National Agricultural Bank for Rural Development (NABARD) in 1995-96. Banks were asked to contribute in the deposit accounts of RIDF to compensate for their shortfall in the 18% PSL target for agriculture credit. It was argued that it will help to finance short run and long run credit need of agriculture as this fund will be made available to state governments to support investments in building agricultural infrastructure in the state. In other words, commercial banks were given this RIDF escape route in fulfilling the agricultural credit target under the priority sector only to the extent of 1.5% of ANBC so that they do not escape social obligations beyond a point. This further helped banks to receive a guaranteed return against their deposits in RIDF rather than involving itself in providing uncertain 'small ticket' loans to peasantry as well as provisioning additional money against these loans. RIDF was considered under indirect finance to agriculture.

In view of the credit crisis in mid 90s, special agricultural credit plans (SACP) were initiated since 1994-95 with a lead bank in a district.

This programme has not achieved much success till date. As per recommendations of the R.V. Gupta Committee Report in 1997, the then Union Finance Minister announced the KCC Scheme in 1999. This scheme helped in expansion in agricultural credit in the second half of 90s to some extent. After the introduction of RIDF and Kissan Credit Card (KCC) schemes in the second half of the 90s, total agricultural finance recorded an annual average growth of around 13 percent.

The general interest rate in the economy remained higher in the 90s compared to the previous period after the deregulation of most of the interest rates in the economy in the post liberalisation period. The agriculture sector that was an earlier recipient of subsidised finance had to face higher interest rates compared to the earlier period in the aftermath of the financial sector liberalisation in India. This happened not because of the shortage of liquidity in the banking system but because of the kind of deliberate accommodations made by the RBI through its monetary policy to keep the interest rates higher to attract foreign debt investment in India (Patnaik, 2005). Towards this end, the RBI sold huge amount of government securities through open market operations (OMO) in the market (Annual Report, RBI, 2000) to keep the domestic interest rates higher in the economy. Commercial banks also had incentives in higher investment in government securities rather than lending to sectors like agriculture mainly for the following two reasons - (a) Interest rates paid on government securities were attractive, (b) Requirements of higher provisioning under the new prudential norms made agricultural credit costlier and unattractive. Furthermore, there was no thrust from the government to increase agricultural credit either. All these finally resulted in holding of government securities higher than the stipulated SLR requirements by commercial banks in the 90s (HMS, RBI, 2006). Accordingly, credit to agriculture recorded a decline in this period.

Thus, there was no constraint of resources with the banking sector for lending to the agricultural sector. The type of monetary and credit policy accommodation pursued by the RBI during the 90s along with its prudential and regulatory framework made agricultural credit relatively unworthy to the banking sector. This finally resulted in holding of higher government securities by the banking sector than the stipulated SLR limit while credit to agriculture systemically underperformed. All these developments along with an overall poor economic growth resulted in a deceleration of agricultural credit growth in the first decade of liberalisation.

Phase II (2001-2014)

The deceleration in growth of agricultural credit reversed from the beginning of 2000. The average rate of growth of agricultural credit during 2000 to 2004 was 19 percent. In June 2004, the government announced a 'comprehensive credit policy' to increase agricultural credit annually by 30 percent to double the amount of credit growth to this sector. The following three years registered agricultural credit growth above the target level of 30 percent and to be precise the average credit growth during these three years (2005, 2006 and 2007) was 36 percent. The credit growth ebbed from this high peak in 2008 but the average rate of credit growth continued to be around 20 percent till 2014. The deceleration of credit growth to agriculture to as low as 12.9 percent in 2008 may be a reflection of the implementation of the agricultural debt waiver and debt relief schemes announced in 2008 as banks were asked to refrain from giving further credit to the farmers till the settlement of their debt under the debt waiver schemes (RBI 2019). Still the expansion in credit in these two years remained higher compared to the best years of 1990s. The credit growth again started picking up from 2010 and it continued to be above 20 percent till 2014 (Table 4). The trend in direct finance to agriculture was always in tandem with the overall credit expansion to agriculture apart from a few years like 2002 and 2004 when sudden spur in growth in indirect finance to agriculture dominated the credit growth. But in spite of such phenomenal credit expansion for a decade and half which outperformed the credit growth in the post-nationalisation period, spread of institutional credit remained almost stagnant at the level of spread in 2002. This is a complete contrast to our experience of the 1970s where expansion of agricultural credit was accompanied by an increase in the reach of institutional credit and decline in indebtedness of farmers.

Table 4: The Average Annual Growth of Credit to Agriculture

Period	*Average Growth of Total Agricultural Finance*	*Average Growth of Direct Agricultural Finance*	*Average Growth of Indirect Agricultural Finance*
2001-2004	18.9	15.6	37.9
2005-2007	36.3	35.8	38.7
2008-2014	20.4	22.6	13.5
Overall (2001-2014)	23.4	23.4	25.9

Source: Basic Statistical Returns of SCBs in India (various issues), RBI.

So, the question arises where has the credit gone and who received the credit? Here the answer probably lies in the bending and modifying norms and classifications of agricultural credit under PSL by the RBI. The RBI started this process in 90s only but it received momentum from the beginning of this century. These modifications by RBI were mainly aimed to ease the pressure of the commercial banks to meet their PSL targets obviating the need to provide genuine credit to the peasantry, particularly to the small and marginal farmers. The sharp increase in the growth in indirect finance to agriculture from 2001 to 2007 was a special phenomenon in this phase. Indirect finance to agriculture registered an annual average growth of 38 percent during 2001-2007. We have already discussed that indirect credit to agriculture was included in PSL up to 4.5 percent within the 18 percent minimum requirement of agricultural credit within PSL criteria. Now, through this route, a series of items indirectly related to development of cultivation were first included under the indirect finance to agriculture and then many of these items were even shifted under direct credit to agriculture (BOX 1). Items were included in both direct finance and indirect finance categories (Ramkumar and Chavan 2007). Accordingly, the growth of indirect finance and its share in total agricultural credit increased sharply from the beginning of 2001. The direct finance category was also impacted by the incorporation of new items and enhancements of their credit limit in this phase. Many of those new components introduced under indirect finance to agriculture were gradually shifted to direct finance category. For example, the loans up to ₹ 2 crore per borrower for agricultural and allied activities which were earlier considered under indirect finance were shifted to direct finance to agriculture from 2012 onwards. Growth in indirect finance as a share of total finance have registered sharp decline in agricultural finance after 2010 (Chart 1B). The increase in the tariff rates of the rural electrical

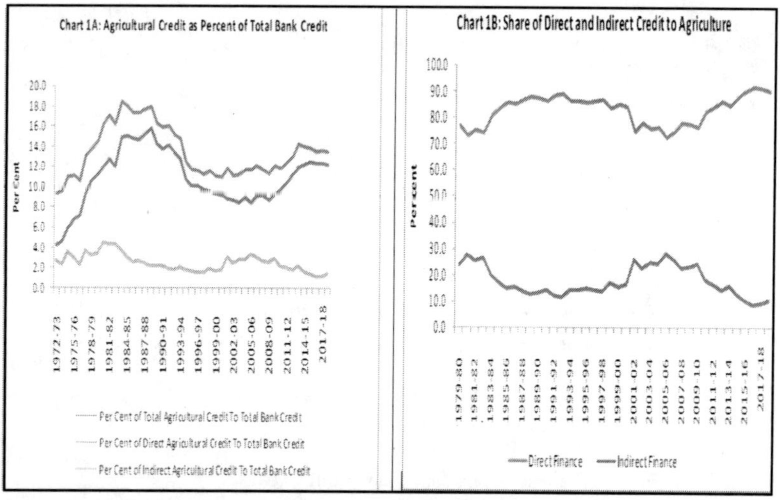

Source: Basic Statistical Returns of SCBs in India (various issues), RBI.

Chart 1: Agricultural Credit

distribution companies after 2010 reduced their need for credit that reduced indirect finance to agriculture to a large extent. This decline may partly be attributed to the ebbing of the startling growth performance of the Indian economy in the aftermath of the international financial crisis. It may be observed that indirect finance has largely been influenced by the overall economic growth in India as period of high growth in indirect finance almost coincides with the periods of higher economic growth. The growth of direct finance continued at an annual average growth rate of around 23.4 percent from 2001 to 2014. But quality of credit to agriculture has remained a cause of concern in this period. The inclusions of these items have made the data comparability difficult and upwardly biased.

The Reserve Bank data on scheduled commercial Banks' direct finance to farmers in the form of 'crop loan' are provided according to the size of land holding. It includes both short-term and long-term loan disbursements. In their data they have defined farmers holding up to 2.5 acre of land as small farmers, 2.5-5 acre as medium farmer and farmers holding and more than 5 acre of land holding as large farmers. The loan per account data clearly indicates how the large farmers receive more 'crop loan' per account than the small farmers (Chart 2).

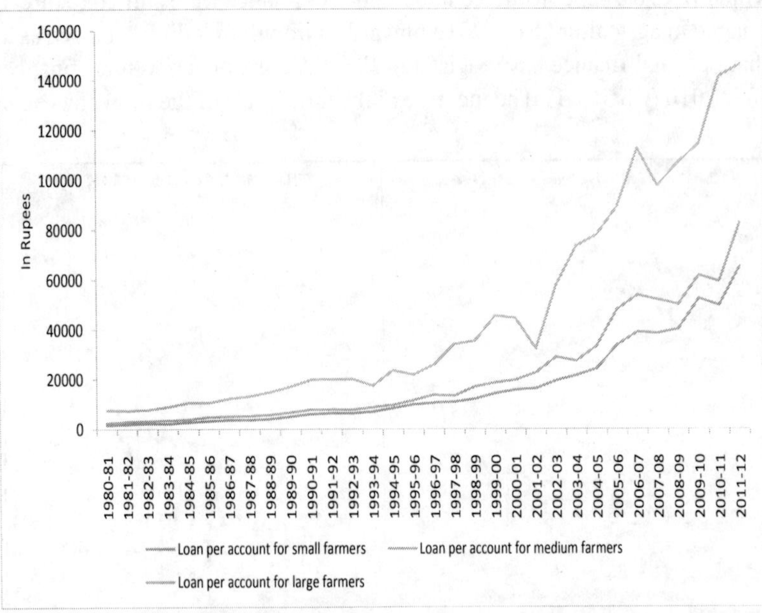

Source: Hand Book of Statistics on Indian Economy 2014, RBI.

Chart 2: Loan Per Account of Farmers

BOX 1: Evolution of Priority Sector Lending Targets and Classifications for Agricultural Finance from 1993 to 2013

1993

Indirect finance became a part of PSL. One fourth of the 18 percent agricultural credit under PSL to agriculture was stipulated for indirect finance. Indirect finance over and above of this limit was allowed to be considered under other priority sector lending in calculation of overall 40 percent target of PSL.

1994

Inclusion: Indirect Finance

Financing dealers /sellers of inputs of fertilisers, pesticides, seeds, cattle feed, poultry feed, agricultural implements and other inputs for agricultural and allied agricultural activities up to 5 lakh. It included activities like poultry feeding, bee keeping etc. These limits were revised and enhanced many time. The upper limit was enhanced to ₹ 15 lakh in 2001, ₹ 15 lakhs in 2001, ₹ 25 lakh in 2002, ₹ 40 lakh in 2006, 1crore in 2012 and finally to ₹ 5 crore from April 1, 2013.

1995

The net bank credit criterion which was so far followed as the basis of calculations was replaced by adjusted net bank credit (ANBC). FCNR deposits and non-resident non-repairable deposit accounts were allowed to be deducted from the base of net bank credit.

1996

Inclusion: Indirect Finance

The loan to dealers in drip irrigation systems, sprinkler irrigation systems and agricultural machinery were considered as indirect finance. The credit limit to these dealers was raised from ₹ 10 lakh per borrower in 1996 to ₹ 20 lakh in 2002 and further ₹ 30 lakh 2004. Further, loans to all input dealers, irrespective of their location, were treated as eligible here. Earlier only loans to dealers in urban and semi-urban areas were considered here.

1997

Inclusion: Direct Finance

Short-term loans to traditional plantation for all size holdings were included under direct finance to agriculture. Later non-traditional plantation and horticulture was included under this category.

2001

Inclusion: Direct Finance

(i) Advances against pledge/hypothecation of agricultural produce revised upward up to 1 lakh crore under crop loan and period extended up to 6 months. This limit was enhanced subsequently to 5 lakh in 2002, 7 lakh in 2007 and finally to 50 lakhs in 2013. From 2007 this loan was extended to all agricultural loans sought by individual farmers, (ii) loans for transport of agricultural inputs and farm transport, (iii) purchase of generator set for agricultural purposes, (iv) loans to farmers for establishment of cold storage in rural areas for storing agricultural products, (v) loans for development of waste land and (v) establishment of bio gas plant by individual farmers.

(Contd...)

Inclusion: Indirect Finance

(i) Deposits under RIDF from banks maintained with NABARD, (ii) 50% of the refinance granted by sponsor banks to RRBs (discontinued from 2002), (iii) loans to SEB for system improvement scheme under special project (SI-SPA), (iv) subscription of bonds issued by Rural Electrification Corporation (REC) for financing pump set in rural and semi-urban areas under SI-SPA (discontinued from 2002), (v) subscription to bonds issued by NABARD for financing agriculture/ allied activities, (vi) loans to hire-purchase for distribution of agricultural machinery etc (vii) loans from banks to non-banking financial companies (NBFCs) for on lending to agricultural activities were included under indirect finance (discontinued from April 1, 2011), (viii) loan to Arthiyas for meeting their working capital need on account of lending to agriculture, (ix) loan to farmers to purchase share of sugar mills and co-operative sugar mills (discontinued from 2011), (x) loan to National Co-operative Development Council (NCDC) for on-lending to the co-operative sector for agricultural credit.

2002

Inclusion: Direct Finance

(i) Loans to small and marginal farmers for purchase of land for agricultural purposes and (ii) financing Agriclinics and Agribusiness Centres by agricultural graduates.

2004

Inclusion: Indirect Finance

(i) Investment by banks in securitised assets which represent direct finance to agriculture and (ii) investment by banks in securitised assets which represent indirect finance to agriculture and (iii) loans for construction and running of storage facilities anywhere.

2006

Inclusion: Indirect Finance

(i) Loans to state electricity board for reimbursing the expenditure already incurred for providing low tension electricity connection for energising their wells, (ii) fifty percent of the credit outstanding loans for general purposes under general credit card (GCC), (iii) loans to farmers through Primary Agricultural Credit Societies (PACS), Farmers' Service Societies (FSS) and Large-sized Adivasi Multi Purpose Societies (LAMPS) Credit for financing the distribution of fertilisers, pesticides, seeds, etc. (iv) loans up to ₹ 40 lakh granted for financing distribution of inputs for the allied activities such as, cattle feed, poultry feed, etc.

2007

Inclusion: Direct Finance

(i) Loans to Self Help Groups (SHGs) and Joint Liability Group (JLGs), (ii) loans to distressed farmers indebted to non-institutional lenders against appropriate securities, (iii) finance up to 1 crore to corporate, partnership firms and institutions for agriculture and allied activities, (iv) one-third of loan to the entities in excess of ₹ 1 crore in aggregate

(*Contd*...)

Inclusion: Indirect Finance

(i) Finance for setting up agribusiness, (ii) two-third of loans to entities in excess of ₹ 1 crore in aggregate per borrower for agricultural and allied activities, (iii) loans to agro processing units up to ₹ 10 crore (iv) loans granted to NGOs/ MFIs for on-lending to individual farmers or their SHGs/JLGs.

2009

Inclusion: Direct Finance

Both traditional and non-traditional plantation became part of crop loan and it included horticulture too. The upper limit for this crop loan was extended to ₹ 1 crore.

2010

Inclusion: Indirect Finance

(i) Loans given to RRBs for on-lending to agricultural and allied sector which was introduced in 2001 and discontinued from 2000 was again made eligible under indirect finance, (ii) Overdrafts, up to ₹ 25,000 per account, granted against no-frill accounts in rural and semi urban areas.

2012

Inclusion: Direct Finance

(i) Loans to farmers under Kisan Credit Card (KCC) scheme (ii) export credit to farmers for exporting their own produce, (ii) all of the loans given to corporate, partnership farms and institutions for agriculture and allied activities below 2 crore, (iii) loans to farmers through Primary Agricultural Credit Societies (PACS), Farmers' Service Societies (FSS) and Large-sized Adivasi Multi Purpose Societies (LAMPS) was considered under direct finance. This was earlier considered under indirect finance.

Inclusion: Indirect Finance

All of the loans given to corporate, partnership farms and institutions for agriculture and allied activities in excess of ₹ 2 crore in aggregate per borrower.

Inclusion: Indirect Finance

(i) Loans up to ₹ 5 crore to Producer Companies set up exclusively by only small and marginal farmers under Part IXA of Companies Act, 1956 for agricultural and allied activities, (ii) export credit to corporate, partnership firms and institutions for exporting their own farm produce.

Source: RBI 2019a, Ramkumar and Chavan 2007, RBI Master Circulars on PSL Targets and Classification (2005-2015).

Phase III (2015 - 2019)

Agricultural credit entered a new phase after 2014. In this phase, agricultural credit growth registered a sharp decline. Both direct and indirect finance to agriculture witnessed decline. However, decline in case of indirect finance was more pronounced than direct finance to agriculture. The average annual growth rates of direct finance and indirect finance during 2015-19 were 11.3 percent and 2.4 percent respectively. Volatility in indirect finance has remained a key character for this category in the past 20 years but this is the phase where indirect finance has registered even a negative growth in consecutive three years beginning from 2015-16 (Table 5).

Table 5: The Average Annual Growth of Credit to Agriculture

Period	*Average Growth of Total Agricultural Finance*	*Average Growth of Direct Agricultural Finance*	*Average Growth of Indirect Agricultural Finance*
2014-2015	7.4	11.8	-15.8
2015-2016	10.2	12.8	-8.8
2016-2017	8.	10.1	-8.3
2017-2018	11.2	10.8	16.1
2018-2019	12.5	10.9	29.0
Overall (2014-15 to 2018-19)	9.9	10.9	2.4

Source: Basic Statistical Returns of SCBs in India (various issues), RBI.

This decline may be attributed to declines in credit taken from state electricity boards with regular increase in their tariff rates in many states and the market linking of fertiliser prices. Other major reasons are that from April 2007 onwards one-third of loans given to corporate, partnership firms and institutions for agricultural and allied activities which was earlier treated under 'indirect finance' were shifted under 'direct finance' category. From October 2012 onwards, all credit to the above category below ₹ 2 crore were considered fully under 'direct finance'. The deceleration of global economy and the decline of prices of primary commodities in the world market since 2007-08 onwards may also have dented the corporate expansion of agriculture in India and thereby deceleration of 'indirect credit'. The growth of direct finance to agriculture in recent years has remained almost at the same level of 1990s. Public sector banks meet their requirement lending targets under PSL norms during 2014-2019 while private sector banks as a whole fall by 1.5 percent to maintain the 18 percent sub-target for agricultural lending (RBI, 2019b). The deceleration in agricultural credit growth may also partially be explained by the increasing NPA of the banking sector, loss incurred by PSBs due to humongous loan evasion by corporate, and deficiency in capital. But largely the deceleration of growth of agricultural credit in this period is a reflection of the fact that the banking sector is generally averse to agricultural lending and will not take this up unless and until it is promulgated by the government or RBI. In this period, intensification of agrarian crisis also necessitated implementation of a series of agricultural debt waiver schemes by various state governments during this period (RBI, 2019a). The agricultural credit policy for this phase has undergone structural changes and has been discussed in the next section.

4. Assessment of Recent Policy Changes of the RBI Pertaining to Credit to Agriculture under PSL

The discussion of direct and indirect finance to agriculture also became somewhat irrelevant after 2014 as the RBI dispensed with the criteria of direct finance and indirect finance to agriculture from July 2015 and instead moved to a new set of norms for agricultural credit under PSL. However, according to RBI, the reporting system of the RBI has continued to report direct and indirect finance to agriculture in accordance with the prevailing reporting system of 2014-15. The shift of the stance of RBI on the PSL to agriculture was based on an internal working group report of the RBI which recommended the proposed changes in the PSL norms (RBI, 2019). This group submitted its report on March 1, 2015 and accordingly RBI came out with the new set of norms for agricultural lending in July 2015. These norms were introduced from the session 2015-2016. In the new set of rules the overall PSL sub-limit of agricultural credit remained at 18 percent as earlier but the criteria of direct and indirect finance to agriculture was removed from the PSL to agriculture by the RBI. Within the 18 percent target for agriculture, a target of 8 percent of adjusted net bank credit (ANBC) was prescribed for small and marginal farmers. Commercial banks were asked to achieve the new criteria in a phased manner i.e., 7 percent by March 2016 and 8 percent by March 2017. The new norms dispensed with direct and indirect finance to agriculture and instead divided agricultural credit into three categories. The lending to agriculture sector has been defined to include: (i) Farm Credit that will include short-term crop loans and medium/long-term credit to farmers, (ii) Agriculture Infrastructure and (iii) Ancillary Activities. A careful look will find that items included under 'Farm Credit' is nothing but items mentioned the direct finance including loan to corporate farmers and other organisations involved in agriculture as well as allied activities (loan up to 2 crore) as mentioned in the 2014 master circular of the RBI. The items of indirect finance were distributed between 'Agriculture Infrastructure' and 'Ancillary Activities'. Bank loans to food and agro processing units became part of agricultural credit. The rest 10 percent of the agricultural credit under PSL was actually open to all kinds of credit related to agriculture. Realising these loopholes, the RBI directed domestic commercial banks in 2016 and small finance banks in 2019 to ensure that the overall lending to non-corporate farmers does not fall below the system wide average of the last three years achievement. The applicable system wide average figure for computing achievement under PSL for the financial years 2017-18, 2018-19 and 2019-20 was 11.78, 11.99 and 12.11 percent respectively. The RBI advised banks to make all efforts to reach the level of 13.5 percent direct lending to the beneficiaries who earlier constituted the direct agriculture sector too. So, finally the whole issue is too complex to understand and there are not sufficient data to decipher whether banks are complying to all these norms properly or not.

For the purpose of computation of 8 percent sub-target for small and marginal farmers (SMFs), farmers with landholding of up to 1 hectare land were declared as marginal farmers and farmers with a landholding of more than 1 hectare and up to 2 hectares were declared as small farmers. Other than SMFs, credit to landless agricultural labourers, tenant farmers, oral lessees and share-croppers, whose share of landholding is within the limits prescribed for SMF were also included in this category. Credit to Self Help Groups (SHGs) or Joint Liability Groups (JLGs), i.e. groups of individual small and marginal farmers directly engaged in Agriculture and Allied Activities were also included here. The inclusion of SHG, JLGs diluted the creation of the sub-category for the 8 percent targeted credit to SMF farmers in India. Furthermore, loans to farmers' producer companies of individual farmers, and co-operatives of farmers directly engaged in Agriculture and Allied Activities, where the membership of SMFs is not less than 75 percent by number and whose land-holding share is also not less than 75 percent of the total land-holding were also a part of this category.

The RBI came out with another internal working group report to review the issue of agricultural credit in September 2019 against the backdrop of a sharp decline in credit for the last 5 years. The scarcity of farm credit was building pressure on the RBI particularly in a situation when the economy was sliding towards a lower growth trajectory and symptoms of economic recession was becoming increasingly prominent. It is true that at the aggregate level, banks have been able to achieve sub-target of SMFs. But large numbers of SMFs are not covered by commercial banks. According to RBI working group reports, as per PSL return (2015-16), the number of accounts under SMFs category are 5.13 crore while the number of SMFs in India are around 12.56 crore (RBI, 2019a). This implies that large numbers of SMFs are not covered by the commercial banking system. Moreover, based on the past data if the present trend continues, the operational holdings under SMFs are going to increase in future. The RBI working group report has also indicated in this direction. Accordingly, to meet the credit need of the peasantry, RBI has decided to fix the sub-target for agricultural credit to small and marginal farmers to 9 percent, 9.5 percent and 10 percent gradually in the financial years 2021-22, 2022-23 and 2023-24 respectively.

V. Conclusion

Delivery of agricultural credit is a critical input for the smooth functioning of this sector. Therefore, agricultural credit policy has always received top priority in the hierarchy of credit policy and overall economic policy in India in the post-independence period. This paper has found that the experience of credit growth in agriculture in the post-liberalisation period is vastly different from that of the 1970s and 1980s. The first decade after liberalisation has recorded sharp deceleration to single digit credit growth in agriculture. It is not the shortage of liquidity, but the type of monetary policy accommodation pursued by the RBI during the 90s along with its prudential and regulatory framework that made agricultural credit relatively unworthy to the banking sector. The period from 2001 to 2014 has witnessed recovery, boom and moderation of agricultural credit expansion with annual average credit growth around 23.4 percent. Therefore, on average this period recorded a significant credit expansion. The sharp increase in the growth in indirect finance to agriculture from 2001 to 2007 was a special phenomenon in this phase. First the inclusion of indirect finance to agriculture under the PSL criteria of agricultural credit and subsequently inclusion of various credit items through modifications of norms within direct and indirect finance remained the hall mark of agricultural credit policy in this period. Therefore, quality of credit to agriculture has remained a cause of concern in this period. Agricultural credit expansion has decelerated sharply in the last five years. This is a serious concern for this sector. The latest enhancement of sub-targets for small and marginal farmers from the present 8 percent to 10 percent gradually, beginning from the year 2021-22 is an indication of the gravity of agricultural credit crisis in India. The inclination of credit delivery initiatives in the post-liberalisation era has inherent proclivity towards large and corporate farmers. The mere increase in the target of lending to SMFs from 8 percent to 10 percent will not help much. If the government is serious about its objective of doubling income of farmers by 2022 or in the foreseeable future, it will have to take serious initiatives at the earliest.

References

Burgess, Robin and Pande, Rohini (2005). 'Do Rural Banks Matter? Evidence from the Indian Social Banking Experiment', *American Economic Review*, June 2005.

GOI (2013). 'Key Indicators of Debt and Investment in India' NSS 70th Round, Ministry of Statistics and Programme Implementation, Governmnet of India.

Hans Binswanger and Shahidur Khandker (1992). 'The Impact of Formal Finance on Rural Economy of India', Working Paper No. 949, World Bank, 1992.

Patnaik, Prabhat (2005). 'Financial Liberalisation and Credit Policy', in 'Financial Liberalisation and Rural Credit in India' edited by V.K. Ramchandran and Madhura Swaminathan, Tulika Books, New Delhi.

Ramkumar, R and Chavan, Pallavi (2007). 'Revival of Agricultural Credit in the 2000s: An Explanation', *Economic and Political Weekly*, December 29, 2007.

RBI (2006). 'Annual Report 2000-2001', RBI, Mumbai, August, 2001.

RBI (2006). 'Hand Book of Monetary Statistics of India', RBI, Mumbai, March, 2006.

RBI (2019). 'Hand Book of Statistics on Indian Economy 2018-19', RBI, Mumbai. September, 2019. www.rbi.org.in. Last accessed on 25.01.2020.

RBI (2020). 'Basis Statistical Returns of Scheduled Commercial Banks in India – March 2019', RBI, Mumbai. Accessed from RBI Online Database on Indian Economy. https://dbie.rbi.org.in/DBIE/dbie.rbi?site=publications. Last Accessed on 03.06.2020.

Reserve Bank of India (2015). 'Report of the Internal Working Group (IWG) to Revisit the Existing Priority Sector Lending Guidelines', www.rbi.org.in, Last accessed on 12.2.2019.

Reserve Bank of India (2019a). 'Report on the Internal Working Group to Review Agricultural Credit', Reserve Bank of India, Mumbai, September, 2019. www.rbi.org.in. Last accessed on 25.1.2020.

Reserve Bank of India (2019b). 'Report on Trend and Progress in India 20181-19', December 2019, Mumbai.

Shetty, S.L (2005). 'Regional, Sectoral and Functional Distribution of Bank Credit', in 'Financial Liberalisation and Rural Credit in India' edited by V .K. Ramchandran and Madhura Swaminathan, Tulika Books, New Delhi.

Shetty, S L (2006). 'Policy Responses to the Failure of Formal Banking Institutions to Expand Credit Delivery for Agriculture and Non-Farm Informal Sectors: The Ground Reality and Task Ahead', Monthly Seminar Series on India's Financial Sector, ICRIER, November, New Delhi.

10

Looking into the Efficiency and Productivity of Major Irrigation Projects in West Bengal, India with Special Reference to the DVC Irrigation Project

Raj Kumar Kundu and
Apurba Kumar Chattopadhyay

Abstract

In West Bengal, about 66 percent of total canal irrigated area has been covered by the Damodar Valley Project (DVC) and Kangsabati Reservoir Project. These two major irrigation projects are structurally different—the DVC irrigation project is a single-barrage-multi-reservoir type project but the Kangsabati irrigation project is a multi-barrage-single-reservoir type project. The objectives of this study have been to make a comparative analysis of the irrigation efficiency of these two types of major irrigation projects and also to find out the possible reasons for their variations over time. We have also attempted to make a zone-wise (head-reach, middle-reach and tail-end-zones) comparative analysis of the irrigation performance in the DVC command area using primary data collected during 2013-14 through field survey. This study reveals that the multi-barrage-single-reservoir irrigation projects (Kangsabati) is more efficient than the single-barrage-multi-reservoir irrigation project (DVC). Further, it has been found that the summer (boro) paddy productivity is higher in the plots of the head-reach zone compared to that in tail-end zone because of their respective locations vis-à-vis canal water availability and furthermore, this location factor is important in determining crop pattern and crop diversification in the respective zones.

Key Words: *Irrigation Efficiency, Potential Created and Utilised, Water Supply, Productivity Variation.*

1. Introduction

Agricultural growth in India is greatly dependent on the monsoon rainfall because it is largely rain-fed. Irrigation, thus, is an important input for increasing agricultural productivity and it is required at different critical stages of plant growth. What is true for the country as a whole is also true for the state of West Bengal. The surface irrigation and ground water irrigation are the two available sources of irrigation. In West Bengal, the ground water irrigation potential was only 16 percent up to 1982 (Boyce, 1987), which increased to about 56.08 percent in 2007 (Ray, *et. al.*, 2009). On the other hand, in 1975-76 canals irrigated area was 47.6 percent (Rawal, 2001), which declined to about 23.78 percent in 2007(Ray, *et. al.*, 2009). These explain declining importance of surface water for irrigation purpose. However, it has been emphasised by the researchers that excessive dependence on groundwater has caused depletion of ground water at a rate greater than the rate of its recharge. This has threatened the water table and also has raised questions about the sustainability of such use in the long run (Dhawan, 1987; Gulati, et al, 2005; Chattopadhyay, 2014). These studies further emphasised on the conjunctive use of both ground water and surface water (whose main constituents are canals) for the purpose of irrigation.

West Bengal has seven major irrigation projects. Among these irrigation projects, Teesta and Subarnarekha Barrage projects have not yet been completed. Damodar Valley Project, the Kangsabati Reservoir Project, the Mayurakshi Reservoir Project, Hinglow Reservoir Project and the Medinipur Canal are the other major projects. The reservoirs or the dams of the projects in South Bengal are located either along the western border of the State or beyond that i.e. within the territory of the adjacent State of Jharkhand.

Among the major irrigation projects, the Damodar Valley Corporation (DVC) project and the Kangsabati Reservoir Project together have covered about 66 percent of total canal irrigated area of West Bengal in 2009-10. Further, these two major irrigation projects are structurally different in that while the DVC irrigation project is a single-barrage-multi-reservoir type project; the Kangsabati irrigation project is a multi-barrage-single-reservoir type. We have taken up these two major irrigation projects for our study for these two reasons. The DVC project has five reservoirs (Tilaiya, Maithon, Panchet, Konar, and Tenughat) and one barrage (Durgapur) while the Kangsabati project has three barrages (Silabati, Bhairabanki, and Tarafeni) and one reservoir or dam (Mukutmanipur). The net irrigated area of DVC project is 3.94lakh ha (covering parts of Burdwan, Hooghly, Howrah and Bankura districts) and the net irrigated area of the Kangsabati project is about 3.41 lakh ha (covering Bankura, West Midinipur and Hooghly districts). We have examined these two major irrigation projects in terms of (a) irrigation efficiency, (b) depth of water supply,

(c) nature of irrigation in all seasons and (d) performance of Command Area Development Authority (CADA). The period of our study is 1980-81 to 2009-10. Further, by using primary data collected from the command area of the DVC project which is the largest among the major projects in West Bengal, we have tried to explain zonal variations in farm productivity and cropping pattern [in respect of head reach (HR), middle reach (MR) and tail end (TE) zones of canal course].

We have structured our article in terms of the following sub-sections. We discuss comparative performance of these two major irrigation projects of West Bengal in Section II and in Section III we will make an appraisal of zone-wise irrigation performance and water use efficiency of the DVC project; and finally, in Section IV we make concluding observations.

2. Comparative Performance of the two Major Irrigation Projects

In this section we make a comparative study of the DVC project which is a single-barrage-multi-reservoir type project with the Kangsabati Reservoir Project which is a multi-barrage-single-reservoir type project in terms of irrigation efficiency (IE) and depth of water supply per ha, in different seasons by using secondary data for the period 1980-81 to 2009-10. Irrigation efficiency of any project is calculated in terms of utilisation and creation of irrigation potential of the concerned project. Thus, Irrigation efficiency = [(irrigation potential utilised ÷ irrigation potential created) × 100] (GoWB, 2013a). We have presented the computed values of irrigation efficiency of these two major projects in Figure-1. It reveals that irrigation efficiency (IE) is higher for the Kangsabati irrigation project, during most of the period of our study compared to the DVC project.[1] Further, in the Kangsabati project, IE has been increasing at a faster rate till 1999-00 and then it is gradually declining but still remains at the higher level compared to that of DVC project. We may now seek to explain the reasons behind higher IE of the Kangsabati irrigation project.

The irrigation efficiency of any irrigation project depends on two factors: (i) gross water supply and (ii) construction of field channels in the command area of the concerned project. That the gross water supply (GWS) is a positive and significant factor of IE of any project can be shown using a single linear regression model: IE = f (GWS). When we run this model separately to the time series data of DVC and Kangsabati irrigation projects the regression coefficients of GWS are found to be positive and statistically significant in both cases.[2] On the other hand, several studies have revealed that under-utilisation of irrigation potential (or low irrigation efficiency) is due to lack of sufficient field channels in the command area of the concerned irrigation project (Kumar, 1978; GOI, 1972; Pant, 1992; Vaidyanathan, 1999 and Viswanathan 2001). Now we can explain why Kangsabati irrigation project is more efficient than DVC in respect of IE by using these two factors.

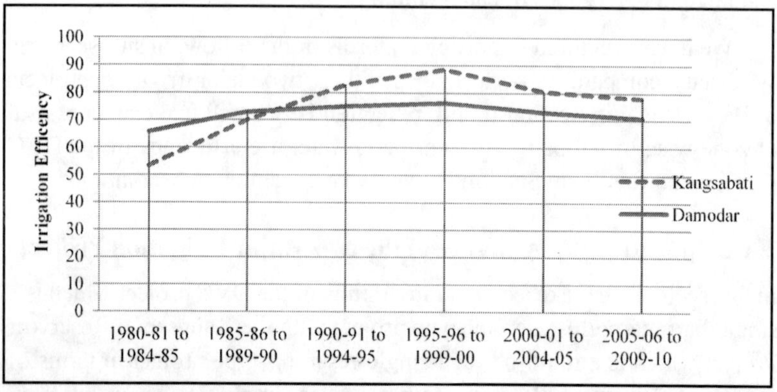

Source: Annual Report of CADA of DVC and Kangsabati Reservoir Project, Govt. of West Bengal (2011-12).

Figure 1: Overall Irrigation Efficiency of Two Major Irrigation Projects during1980-81 to 2009-10.

Water Supply: From the available data (Table 1) we have found that the depth of water supply per ha of the Kangsabati Project is greater than the DVC Project (about 17 percent) during *rabi* & *boro* seasons when the demand for irrigation water is maximum as there is no scope of having normal rainfall. This make the Kangsabati project relatively more irrigation efficient. It may, however, be noted that during the *kharif* or monsoon season the depth of water supply per ha is higher in DVC project (about 45 percent). But, lower depth of water supply per ha in any command area during monsoon does not cause concern because of availability of rain water. This explains differences in the irrigation efficiencies between two major irrigation projects.

Further, the structural differences of the two water projects also make Kangsabati Project more efficient than the DVC which may be explained in terms of the dynamic use of rain water. The Kangsabati project is a multi-barrage-single-reservoir type and thus it can store monsoon rain water in the existing barrages. This stored rain water is distributed as *kharif* irrigation which requires release of less water from Mukutmanipur reservoir. In this way multi-barrage-single-reservoir type irrigation project may be able to store higher level of water in the connected reservoir for *rabi* &

boro seasons and provides higher amount of water for irrigation purpose. It is to be noted that percolation rate of river connected with barrage is relatively higher than reservoirs. On the other hand, the Damodar irrigation project is a multi-reservoir-single-barrage type for which procedures for storage of rain-water and release of it are completely different. In the latter case, rain water gets stored in dams and then distributed through the barrage in need or under compulsion. This implies that dynamic-use-of-rain-water for irrigation is substantially higher in the Kangsabati project than DVC project. It is to be noted that for dynamic use of rain water Kangsabati project has been providing about 25.02 percent more irrigation water than their actual storage capacities, while for DVC project this is only about 17.90 percent[3]. There are certain other factors which resulted in lower IE of the DVC projects. They are: (i) Kangsabati project is entirely meant for irrigation purpose while DVC project is for both power generation and irrigation purpose; (ii) During last 30 years no new reservoir was constructed by DVC but 16 new thermal power plants have been built up (GOI, 2013); (iii) the water supply for industrial and municipal uses has also increased rapidly during last couple of years[4].

Table 1: Depth of Water Supply in the Damodar and Kangsabati Irrigation Projects

Year	*Kharif (Cu. M / Ha)*		*Rabi & Boro (Cu. M / Ha)*	
	Kangsabati	*Damodar*	*Kangsabati*	*Damodar*
1980-81 to 1984-85	3100	6288.15	10933	8562.49
1985-86 to 1989-90	3920	5448.56	11950	8125.37
1990-91 to 1994-95	2800	4901.32	7060	9747.37
1995-96 to 1999-00	3750	4556.47	10100	8916.58
2000-01 to 2004-05	3120	4687.35	8625	8033.72
2005-06 to 2009-10	3340	3221.24	11200	7764.31
Average	3338	4851	9978	8525

Source: Annual Report of CADA of DVC and Kangsabati Reservoir Project, Govt. of West Bengal (2011-12).

Field channel area: In a study relating to Hirakud irrigation project, Kumar (1978), has found that field channels have significant role in increasing the overall irrigated area and raising cropping intensity. Further, Pant (1992) in his study in the command area of Sharda Sahayak irrigation project has found that absence of efficient field channels and field drains within the command of outlet have been responsible for underutilisation of irrigation potential and on-farm development is marginal. In the Kangsabati project field channel area is comparatively higher in both absolute (70,811.3 ha till 2009-10) and relative senses (20.78 percent of net irrigated area) (GoWB, 2014) than the DVC project (47,300 ha and 12.01 percent, respectively, till 2009-10) (GoWB, 2013). These imply that field channel area has played a significant role to enhance irrigation efficiency or performance of the Kangsabati project compared to that of DVC project.

3. Zone wise irrigation performance and water use efficiency of the DVC project

In this section, we have tried to examine zone-wise irrigation performance on farm productivity in the summer season and irrigation efficiency of this project as revealed by crop pattern in different segments of the canal course. For the purpose of primary survey we selected samples from the Left Bank Main Canal command area of DVC that has originated from Durgapur Barrage. It covers three districts of West Bengal namely, Burdwan, Hooghly and Howrah. The entire area has been divided into three zones, namely, Head Reach (HR), Middle Reach (MR) and Tail-end (TE) zones. These divisions have been made on the basis of water availability and physical structure of canal network and follow the procedure adopted in previous studies pertaining to DVC canal network (IIMC, 2008; Kundu and Chattopadhyay, 2017).

In our study area, summer paddy (*boro*) has been the main crop during summer and it is cultivated in most of the arable land in HR and MR zones of the canal course but in the TE zone less than 40 percent of land is used for *boro* paddy production. This follows the pattern of availability of the irrigation water in the land corresponding to different zones of the canal course. Thus, while the plots of land served by HR zone and large part of the MR zone get required canal water for irrigation there are always uncertainty about the availability of canal water in the TE zone. The data from our primary survey has revealed that productivity of *boro* paddy is the highest in the HR segment and it is lowest in the TE segment. Previous studies have also revealed similar outcome (GOI, 2003; Hussain, 2004). Further, we have used the multiple-regression model to ascertain if the supply of canal water has been a major factor in determining differences in productivity across lands corresponding to different zones of the canal network. Regression results are presented in the Appendix Table 1. It clearly reveals that supply of canal water is highly significant factor to explain differences of productivity across different zones. Other important factors are type of the soils, participation of adult family members, cost of other factors of production and techniques of production.

It may be noted that the farmers in the TE zone incurs substantial cost on underground irrigation to neutralise the uncertainty and uneven supply of canal water. Excessive storage of canal water by the farmers in the HR and MR zones making use of their location advantages vis-à-vis TE farmers has led to the uneven distribution of water and thereby making the latter farmers dependent on other costlier sources of irrigation. This inefficient management of canal water is one of the factors which explain lower *boro* paddy productivity in the TE zone.

Further, this uneven distribution of canal water leads to create different types of cropping pattern across HR, MR and TE zones of the DVC command area, which is shown in Table 2. From this table we can observe that about 92 percent and 73 percent of gross cultivated land has been used for paddy cultivation only in the HR and MR areas, respectively. While in the TE area this figure is about 44 percent and remaining part of land is used to produce less water intensive crops like, potato (29%), *til* (12%), vegetables (7%), mustard (3%) and other crops (ground nut, pulses, etc.) (5%). This indicates that location advantages of the farmers in the HR and MR zones lead to over use of canal water and cultivation of water intensive crop like paddy while TE farmers are compelled to use major portion of their land for production of less water intensive crops. Wade (1976) in his study have reached similar conclusion. This means, water use efficiency is relatively lower in the HR and MR zones compared to TE zone.

Table 2: Inter-segments Variation of Cropping Pattern in the DVC Command Area

(Area in hectare)

Types of crop area	*Head Reach*	*Middle Reach*	*Tail-end*
kharif Paddy	133.40	112.97	79.44
boro Paddy	92.91	76.03	18.34
Potato	0.93	44.12	63.65
Mustard	16.60	6.53	5.62
Wheat	1.87	0.00	0.00
Til	0.00	15.39	26.14
Jute	0.00	0.00	4.00
Vegetable	0.00	3.64	15.45
Ground nut	0.00	0.00	1.28
Pulses	0.00	0.00	0.11
Others #	0.00	0.00	7.35
Gross cultivated area	245.71	258.68	221.38
Net cultivated area	135.13	113.56	82.54
Cropping intensity (%)	181.83	227.79	268.21
Crop diversification*	0.51	0.64	0.74

Notes: # Others consist of fruit (cucumber and water-melon), turmeric, etc.

* It has been calculated based on Transformed Herfindahl Index formula[5].

Source: Primary Survey.

Our study has revealed the following reasons for uneven water distribution of canal water in different segments of the canal course (HR, MR and TE zones): (i) Area under field channels is relatively higher in the TE area compared to the HR area which results in greater seepage loss in the HR area compared to TE area; (ii) Further, due to lack of proper management by the authority there occurs huge loss of precious irrigation water through unmanaged canal outlets mainly in the HR area; (iii) The method of flood irrigation is adopted for paddy cultivation, where each plot needs to be irrigated before passing onto the subsequent plots. This results in wastage of water since a part of the flooded plots might not be used for cultivation that season or around the same time. Had there been more field channels in the HR area; this wastage of canal water could be avoided; (iv) It may be noted that if plots are flooded by the farmers themselves at the time of paddy cultivation, the amount of water use would be relatively lower than when irrigation water is supplied by the irrigation authority who generally does not have knowledge about quantum of water requirements at different stages of plant growth within huge command area for irrigation; (v) Further, the huge length of channel network proves to be a classic example of managerial diseconomies of scale to deliver water successfully till the end point of the channel network; (vi) Furthermore, absence of continuous supervision of water delivery in the channel network also leads to uneven distribution of irrigation water.

4. Concluding Observations

Our study has revealed that multi-barrage-single-reservoir (MBSR) type irrigation project is relatively better than single-barrage-multi-reservoir (SBMR) type irrigation project in respect of irrigation efficiency or potential utilisation of their targeted area of irrigation. We have also found that expansion of gross field channel area play a significant role in enhancing irrigation efficiency in the command area. Further, dynamic use of rain water is considerably higher in the MBSR type of project compared to the SBMR type project. Therefore, when additional water is required for cultivation (i.e., in the *rabi & boro* season), depth of water supply per hectare is higher in the MBSR type project than SBMR project. Thus, DVC project is required to build additional barrage to improve irrigation efficiency, dynamic use of rain water and depth of water supply per hectare in winter and summer (*rabi & boro)* seasons.

Our analysis of primary survey data collected from the DVC command area reveals that water availability is relatively higher in the HR zone compared to the MR and TE zones. This has influenced the cropping pattern in the three segments of the canal course. As a result, the TE farmers use their land to produce less water intensive crops while the farmers of HR area mainly cultivate water intensive crops. This implies that water use efficiency is relatively lower in the HR and MR zones compared to TE zone. Further, average summer paddy productivity is relatively higher in the HR area followed by MR and TE areas. This variation is also due to uneven water distribution of canal water among farmers in the HR, MR and TE zones. Thus, DVC is required to improve management in the DVC canal network during water delivery and also it is required to construct additional field channel area to distribute canal water equally among farmers in the HR, MR and TE zones. Further, there is an urgent need of transforming old method of irrigation (flood irrigation) to new method of irrigation (SRI, drip, spring, etc).

References

Boyce, J. K. (1987): *Agrarian Impasse in Bengal: Agricultural Growth in Bangladesh and West Bengal*, 1949-1980, Oxford University Press, New York.

Chattopadhyay, Apurba Kumar (2014); 'Water Resources in India: Some Issues in Irrigation Management' in S Pan (ed.), *Economic Reforms and Common Property Resources: Issues and Challenges*, Regal Publications, New Delhi, pp. 140-53.

Dhawan, B.D. (1987): "Water Management in the Mula Command: A Study in Productivity Impact of Canal Water", *Indian Journal of Agricultural Economics,* Vol. 42, No. 1, Jan-Mar. p. 51.

GOI (1972): *Report of the Irrigation Commission*, Vol. I, Ministry of Irrigation and Power, Government of India, New Delhi.

GOI (2003): "Tail-enders and Other Deprived in the Canal Water Distribution", Planning Commission, Government of India, December-6, dsc@satyam.net.in, pp. 5 & 18.

GOI (2013): *Storage Status of Important Reservoirs in the Country*, Central Water Commission, Ministry of Water Resources, New Delhi.

Government of West Bengal (GoWB) (2013): *Annual Report 2011-12*, Damodar Valley Command Area Development Authority (DVCADA), Purta-Bhavana, Burdwan, Water Resource Investigation & Development Department.

Government of West Bengal (GoWB) (2013a): *Annual Report 2009-10 & 2010-11*, Mayurakshi Command Area Development Authority (MCADA), Suri, Birbhum, Water Resource Investigation & Development Department.

Government of West Bengal (GoWB) (2014): *Annual Report 2010-11*, Kangsabati Command Area Development Authority (KCADA), Birbhum, Water Resource Investigation & Development Department.

Gulati, A, *et al* (2005): *Institutional Reform in Indian Irrigation*, International Food Policy Research Institute, SAGE Publications, New Delhi, p. 78-79, 130.

Hussain, Intizar (Ed) (2004): *Pro-poor Intervention Strategies in Irrigated Agriculture in Asia*, Country Report India, International Water Management Institute, ADB, Colombo, Sri Lanka.

IIM (Indian Institute of Management) Calcutta (2008): *IPC-IPU Gap Analysis in West Bengal and the North-East*, Final Report, October pp. 10-28.

Kumar, P (1978): *Economics of Water Management: A Study of Field Channels*, Heritage Publications, New Delhi.

Kundu, R. K. and A K Chattopadhyay (2017): "Analysing Varying Crop Productivity in Canal Irrigation: A Case Study of Damodar Valley Corporation (DVC) in West Bengal", *Indian Journal of Agricultural Economics*, Vol. 72, No. 4, October-December, pp. 513-534.

Kundu, R. K. and A K Chattopadhyay (2018), "Spatio-temporal variations of Crop Diversification: A block-level study in West Bengal", *Economic and Political Weekly*, Vol. 53, No. 21, pp. 58-64.

Pant, N. (1992): *Irrigation and Agriculture Development (in a CADA)*, Ashish Publishing House, New Delhi – 110026.

Rawal, V. (2001): "Irrigation Statistics in West Bengal", *Economic and Political Weekly*, Vol. 36, No. 27, July 7.

Ray, A. and Shekhar, S. (2009): "Ground Water Issues and Development Strategies in West Bengal", *Bhu-Jal News*, West Bengal Special Issue, Central Ground Water Board, Ministry of Water Resource, Government of India, Vol. 24, No. 1, June-March.

Vaidyanathan, A. (1999): *Water Resources Management: Institutions and Irrigation Development in India*, New Delhi: Oxford University Press.

Viswanathan, P.K. (2001): *Economics of On-Farm Development: A Study of Major Irrigation Projects in Kerala*, Ph. D. Thesis submitted to the Department of Economics, University of Mysore, Mysore, Ecological Economics Unit, Institute for Social and Economic Change, Bangalore – 560072.

Wade, R (1976): "Performance of Irrigation Projects," *Economic and Political Weekly*, Vol. 11, No. 3, Jan. 17, pp. 63-66.

Notes

1. Gross irrigation efficiency of Kangsabity, and DVC Projects during 1980-81 to 2009-10.

Irrigation Projects	*1980-81 to 1984-85*	*1985-86 to 1989-90*	*1990-91 to 1994-95*	*1995-96 to 1999-00*	*2000-01 to 2004-05*	*2005-06 to 2009-10*	*Average*
Kangsabati	53.35	69.89	82.88	88.39	80.42	77.92	75.47
Damodar	65.64	72.95	75.03	76.33	72.83	70.73	72.25

Source: Annual Report of CADA of DVC and Kangsabati Projects, Govt. of West Bengal (2011-12).

2. The regression coefficients of GWS are 0.06* (0.01) and 4.89*** (2.80), respectively for DVC and Kangsabati Projects. The asterisks '*' and '***' indicate 1% and 10% level of significance, respectively and values in parentheses are corresponding standard errors.

3. The storage capacity of five reservoirs of the DVC project for irrigation and power generation purpose is about 1829.33 MCM (GoWB, 2013). The storage capacity of Kangsabati reservoir is about 917 MCM where storable water is used only for irrigation. The yearly average water supplies for irrigation from these projects are about 2066.83 MCM and 1146.39 MCM, respectively. Additionally, DVC provided 90MCM water for power generation purpose in 2009-10. The calculation of dynamic use of rain water of DVC project is $[(2066.83 + 90) \div 1829.33] \times 100 = 117.90$ i.e., 17.90 percent more than their actual storage capacity.
4. The DVC water supply for industrial and municipal uses increased from 73.35 MCM to 1408.77 MCM during 2005-06 and 2015-16 (DVC Annual Report 2005-06, p.44 and 2015-16, p. 37). Further, the present water supply for industrial and municipal uses is more than half of average water supply per year for irrigation (2066.83 MCM).
5. For a detailed discussion of the nature and extent of crop diversification in the study area, please see, Kundu and Chattopadhyay (2018).

Appendix

Table 1: Regression Results Explaining Zonal Differences of the Summer Paddy (*Boro*) Productivity

Explanatory Variables	*Values of Regression Coefficients*			
	All zones	*Inter-zonal*		
		Head Reach (HR)	*Middle Reach (MR)*	*Tail-end (TE)*
Participation rate of adult family member in agriculture (X^{PRA})	3.76* (0.56)	4.35* (1.33)	4.14* (0.77)	4.43* (0.87)
Soil types (D^{ST}) (1- sticky, 0 – loamy)	3.74* (0.60)	-	2.10** (0.75)	-
percentage of canal water availability (X^{CWA})	0.24* (0.01)	0.26* (0.04)	0.22* (0.01)	0.19* (0.05)
Technique of paddy cultivation SRI ($D^{TC\text{-}SRI}$): (SRI=1 and 0, otherwise)	11.24* (1.40)	-	-	10.51* (1.49)
Fertilizers cost (X^{FC})	0.04 (0.03)	0.08 (0.06)	0.01 (0.04)	-0.05 (0.06)
Seed cost (X^{SC})	0.23** (0.09)	0.13 (0.17)	0.17 (0.16)	0.27*** (0.15)
Pesticides cost (X^{PC})	0.02 (0.06)	0.005 (0.07)	0.09 (0.12)	0.30 (0.19)
Constant	10.91* (1.61)	12.86* (3.45)	13.60* (2.98)	9.75** (4.54)
R^2	0.76	0.53	0.79	0.86
Adj R^2	0.75	0.51	0.78	0.84
F value	88.63*	18.78*	48.15*	30.22*
Observation	204	88	81	35
Irrigation cost (X^{IC}) #	-0.50* (0.06)	-2.36* (0.52)	-1.44* (0.23)	0.59** (0.28)

Note: Here (-) means no change of the respective value of variable in the respective areas and *, ** and *** imply statistical significance at 1%, 5% and 10% levels, respectively.

The linear regression model is: $Y_j^s = \alpha_s + \beta_{ks}(\sum_{j=1}^{ns} X_i + \sum_{j=1}^{ns} D_i) + u_j$

Where Y_j indicates summer paddy productivity (kg/*katha*) in the s = zone (all zones, HR, MR and TE). j = 1, 2, 3,..., n indicate number of observation (204, 88, 81 and 35 respectively for different zones). Independent variables and regression results are given in the above Appendix Table 1. Regression coefficient of fertiliser cost is positive in HR (0.04) and MR (0.01) zones but it is negative in the TE zone. In the TE area, impact of fertiliser cost is negative because about 69% plots are used to cultivate *boro* paddy after potato production and there is a tendency to apply less fertiliser (since farmers apply huge amount of fertiliser per unit of land for growing potato and part of it stays in the field) while the farmers apply relatively higher amount of fertiliser in those plots which are used only for paddy cultivation (both *kharif* and *boro*).

Irrigation cost (X^{IC}) is not an explanatory variable in our model since it produces multicolinearity problems with other variables. This row depicts the result of single linear regression model (last row of the above table), where irrigation cost is the only explanatory variable.

Source: Primary Survey.

11

Living Money-less: A Study of Nyishi Households in Arunachal Pradesh, India

Bhaskar Majumder

Abstract

A social economy shows human beings engaged in collection from nature delinked from money-based exchange that fulfils needs of households. The Nyishi tribe residing in Papum Pare district in the state of Arunachal Pradesh in India revealed a social economy where livelihood was sustained through self-engagement of women mostly in forests. The single question that we propose in this paper is whether development can be money-less; our argument is in the affirmation where moneylessness did not obstruct the tribe to ensure livelihood as they were mostly engaged in collection from nature. The paper explains how the women in Nyishi tribe in the district remained engaged in the social economy for sustainable livelihood. The paper pleads for least intervention by the state in this social economy.

Key Words: *Livelihood, Nyishi Tribe, Social Economy, Moneyless Development.*

Introduction

An economy buds through a social arrangement of individuals sharing natural resources in an interdependent relation. The economy takes birth in the womb of the society from which it gradually distances itself. A social formation of human beings at its nascent stage is understood by a tiny group of people working together with a common purpose like hunting in the forests in the primitive era. The evolution ultimately brought about a perception that took forests as something to be preserved by the custodian of resources and kept distanced from human living and livelihood. The custodian's control over nature gradually eroded the symbiotic man-nature relationship.

The self-engagement of people shows formation and functioning of a social economy that is also a kind of nature-based economy as practiced by the communities (Nitsch, 1990). We do not include in our analysis cooperatives, non-government organisations, philanthropic organisations, missionaries of charity, self-help groups, and foundations of corporate houses to explain the functioning of the social economy. The activities like begging, stealing, borrowing are excluded from our canvas of self-engagement. The social economy in our frame is unstructured that gets revealed by the way the communities voluntarily participate in their daily life where the activities are visible to the non-participants willing to observe. The self-engagement, thus, is outside own house and open for public scrutiny. There is no Act in India to guide such a social economy but it continues inter-generationally. The social economy functions intra-household as well as extra-household.

Self-Engagement

The self-engagement of the working population in India is essentially to secure livelihood of the households. It shows almost all members of a household engaged in works much before completion of stipulated years of schooling. Such works are unpredictable and hence the workers move around, often directionless. While this moving around is seen as migration, often by default linked with positive wage-differential, the major chunk of the workers remain self-engaged on the wasteland with no work-cum-wage security. These workers include the self-engaged waste pickers, vegetable vendors, and the workers standing on labour squares on urban roads for any odd job to earn any positive wage rate. The borderline between being self-engaged and being hired is also often blurred for it may be based on wage-information or wage-uninformed search for jobs.

The activities in self-engagement are mostly manual labour based and mainly for home consumption. The usable tools are first-stage transformation of materials collected from nature to use in re-collection from nature. Survival of the household has no single strategy; many times the person does not know what to collect or sell the next day. If the household member has no exchangeable assets, no land to cultivate and no relevant education to sell labour power by being employed, the person himself gets engaged on the wasteland. If he had an outstanding debt, then the major part of the goods or services that he produces through self-engagement goes to loan repayment, if the goods and services that he produced had money-equivalence.

For the asset-poor, home itself often becomes an economic space assuming a liveable home exists for the household. It is not home-based labour hired by any external agency, but the very works that the household women get engaged in, that ensure livelihood. These include fuel, technique of cooking, micro storage of food-fuel, repetitive uses of private utilities, and multiple uses of the private utility in alternative uses. The portfolio of the poor is not a stock of products at any particular point of time for the products continue to change by shape, quality and uses.

We have two viewpoints to visualise this phenomenon of self-engagement of women as workers, one under compulsion and the other under choice. Self-engagement of women in particular is both intra-household and outside house – these two go parallel. This is because many of the materials collected from CPRs by them add utility to household members including construction of the house itself. The women, for example, are self-engaged in grass cutting, collecting, feeding cattle to ultimately get milk for self-consumption at home and for sale. We need to explore ground reality thus.

The purpose of this paper is to explore the social living of the people in the state of Arunachal Pradesh in India. The often invisibility and dislocation of the tribes that constitute most of the population in the state made us question how they lived on their own. The purpose of the paper was to find out their self-engagement as workers for their livelihood.

We explored self-engagement of women in Nyishi tribe in the state of Arunachal Pradesh in India. The households were not on the scale of poverty for their livelihood was radically different from poverty as cardinally measured in mainstream literature. The rest of the paper is structured as follows. In Section I, we present review of literature in brief that includes Policies and Acts of the Government of India focused on forests as well as India's forest cover by states. In Section II we present the methodology, sample and the study zone. In Section III, we elaborate on the forest-based living of the Nyishi tribe. In Section IV, we examine the role of Nyishi women in livelihood security of the households. In Section V, we see self-engagement of Nyishi women as self-employment. Finally, in Section VI, we sum up.

1. Review of Literature

'In the Roman context, the term "tribe" was used to refer to a state of barbarism, but also to indicate a tributary relationship between a group and the imperial State, with whom gifts and tributes were exchanged....Later, the idea of the tribe as people living in "primitive" conditions became dominant' (GoI, 2014:51). In India, the term "tribe" is often used to denote "*jana*" or communities of people as different from '*jati*' or hierarchical caste system of social organisation (GoI, 2014:51).

The NCEUS, Government of India, failed to distinguish between self-employment as a paid activity and self-engagement as an unpaid activity, and hence, missed the distinction between labour in self-employment and works in self-engagement (GoI, NCEUS: 85). A Committee was constituted by the Government of India on June 10, 1994 that accepted the community, rather than an administrative unit like a village, as the basic unit of the system of self-governance in tribal areas. A habitation was the natural unit of the community. At the level of Gram Sabha, the traditional institution of the people, that is the community as a whole was recognised that would function based on consensus and without any formal structure at that level (Sharma, 1995: 22-23).

We present briefly the Policies as well as Acts and Conventions of the Government of India related to forests.

Post-Independence India

National Forest Policy, 1952: The Policy pledged to set up sanctuaries and national parks for preservation of wildlife. The Policy accepted the state as the authority at the cost of the forest-based communities that was legitimised by national interest (Jewitt, 2004: 72). The post-colonial policies of the government of India de facto followed the British India's colonial policies related to forests for the Government was concerned for national interest and not the unrecorded customary forest-rights of the local communities.

Forest Conservation Act, 1980: Based on the 1878 Forest Act, copying almost all the sections of the Act, India's forest policy was formulated and came as the draft Forest Act, 1980. The rights of the Adivasis over forests ceased to exist following this. The Adivasis became India's internal "Others".

The impact of India's Forest Conservation Policy, 1980 imposed a rival relationship between man and nature based on the perception that the forest dwellers were anti-preservation of forests and Himalayan bio-diversity. This posed a threat to the livelihood security of the forest dwellers in the Himalayan region. In the period prior to forest legislations, the idea of poverty and deprivation was an alien concept as tribes lived in harmony with nature sustaining their livelihood.

The Biological Diversity Act, 2002: This Act provided for 'conservation of biological diversity, sustainable use of its components and fair and equitable sharing of the benefits arising out of the use of biological resources, knowledge and for matters connected therewith or incidental thereto' (GoI, The Gazette of India Extraordinary, Part II, Section I). The Act acknowledged India's rich biological diversity and associated traditional and contemporary knowledge. India is a party to the United Nations Convention on Biological Diversity signed on June 5, 1992.

The tribes as users of biological resources were nowhere mentioned in these criteria.

Forest Rights Act, 2006: The Draft of the Act was proposed in the Parliament in 2005, finally passed in 2006 and came into effect on January 01, 2008. The Act recognised the customary rights of the households in forests and no proof was needed for cultivating land up to four hectares per household. Following this Act, the forest dwellers had the right to collect non-timber forest produce. The Act also empowered these dwellers to protect and conserve forests where they had been living.

National Environment Policy, 2006: The Policy suggested appropriate land use planning and cultivation of traditional varieties of crops and horticulture by promotion of organic farming. The Policy suggested promotion of 'sustainable tourism....within the carrying capacity of the mountain ecology'.

Forests Perceived in India's Plans

The 11th Five Year Plan of the Government of India (GoI) linked forests to livelihood and focused on strengthening participatory processes. The National Afforestation, Eco-restoration, and Eco-development Board (NAEEB) was formed. It was argued that the Gram Sabhas and the traditional institutions in the North-East could act as community forestry institutions. Joint Forest Management (JFM) Committees were supposed to recognize the existing Van Panchayat and other community forestry institutions (GoI, Planning Commission, 2007-2012, pp. 66-67).

The Planning Commission of the 12th Five Year Plan of the Government of India opined that, 'The National Forestry Information System should enable networking with States for tracking changes in forest development, harvesting, trade and utilisation scenario with particular focus on issues of ownership and rights under Scheduled Tribes and Other Traditional Forest Dwellers (Recognition of Forest Rights) Act' (GoI, Planning Commission, 2013, Vol. 1:218).

Forest Cover in India

Nature provides the space for self-engagement. We focus here only on forests. The forest cover as a percentage of total area in India was 15.7 that was marginally less than that of Asia as a continent and was far behind world average. Per capita forest in India was far below not only Asian average but more so below world average (State of World Forest, FAO, 1999).

India ranked 10th in forest area as percentage of global forest area, accounting for only 2 percent; India's forest area as a percentage of country area fixed her rank at 9th at par with China in 2015. The top ten countries accounted for 67 percent of global forest area in 2015 (Table 3).

The Indian Himalayan Region (IHR) covers 16.2 percent of India's geographic area; the forest cover in IHR represented twice its proportion in geographic share. There were, however, no changes in forest cover in IHR over 2007-2011 as percentage of India's geographic cover. In parallel, we present percentage share of the twelve states in total geographic area in IHR (Tables 1 and 2).

Table 1: Contribution of the IHR to the Total Forest Cover of India, 2007-2011

Region/Country	*Geographic Area (%)*	*2007 (%)*	*2009 (%)*	*2011 (%)*
IHR	16.2	32.3	32.04	33.5
India	100.0	21.0	21.0	21.2

Source: GoI, Planning Commission (for year 2007); Forest Survey of India (for years 2009, 2011); State of Forest Report, Dehradun.

Table 2: Share of Geographic Area of States in Indian Himalayan Region, 2002

Sl. No.	*State/Region*	*% Share of Geographic Area in the IHR*
1.	Jammu & Kashmir	41.65
2.	Arunachal Pradesh	15.69
3.	Himachal Pradesh	10.43
4.	Uttarakhand	10.02
5.	Meghalaya	4.20
6.	Manipur	4.18
7.	Mizoram	3.95
8.	Nagaland	3.11
9.	Assam Hills	2.87
10.	Tripura	1.97
11.	Sikkim	1.33
12.	West Bengal Hills	0.59

Note: IHR: Indian Himalayan Region. We did not get data post-2002.

Source: Office of the Registrar General of India, Ministry of Home Affairs, GoI.

The forest cover as percent of geographic area of the state in the IHR varied over the 12 states. It was basically seven sisters of the north-east India that provided most of the forest cover as percentage of respective state geographic area. The state of Arunachal Pradesh showed forest cover as around 80.0 percent of state geographic area during 2005 to 2013 that declined in 2017 (Table 3).

Table 3: Forest Cover of States in Indian Himalayan Region (As % of Sate Geographic Area)

State/Region	*2005*	*2007*	*2011*	*2013*	*2017*
Jammu & Kashmir	9.57	10.21	10.14	10.14	9.10
Arunachal Pradesh	80.93	80.43	80.50	80.39	61.39
Himachal Pradesh	25.81	26.35	26.37	26.37	66.52
Uttarakhand	45.70	45.80	45.80	45.82	71.05
Meghalaya	75.74	77.23	77.02	77.08	42.34
Manipur	76.53	77.40	76.54	76.10	78.01
Mizoram	88.63	91.27	90.68	90.38	26.26
Nagaland	82.75	81.21	80.33	78.68	52.01
Assam Hills	35.25	35.30	35:28	35.28	34.21
Tripura	77.77	76.99	76.07	75.01	60.02
Sikkim	45.97	47.31	47.34	47.32	82.31
West Bengal Hills	13.99	14.64	14.64	18.93	13.38

Source: Forest Survey of India, State of Forest Report, 2005, 2009, 2011, 2013, Dehradun.

2. Methodology, Sample, and Study Zone

We selected the state of Arunachal Pradesh based on its forest cover that was more that 80.0 percent of the geographic area of the state till 2013; this percentage, however, showed a sharp decline to 61.39 percent in 2017. Among all the 12 states on the Indian Himalayan Region (IHR), the state of Arunachal Pradesh was ahead of the other states by forest cover excepting two very small states, namely, Mizoram and Nagaland. This ranking was also up to 2013.

We selected one district, Papum-Pare, of a total of 16 districts in Arunachal Pradesh inhabited mostly by tribes. The district ranks first by size of total population and size of ST population by districts. Of total number of districts in the state that was 13 in 2014, Papum Pare had lowest ST population by percentage of total population by districts (Table 4).

The total population of the district Papum Pare was 12.76 percent of total population in Arunachal Pradesh in 2011 that was a little higher than that of 2001. The total Nyishi population in the state in 2011 was

Table 4: Districts of Arunachal Pradesh with ST Population more than 50.0 Percent

Sl. No.	*District Name*	*No. of Households*	*Total Population*	*ST Population*	*% of ST*
1.	Kuurung Kumey	15037	92076	90764	98.6
2.	Upper Subansiri	15869	83448	78323	93.9
3.	East Kameng	14508	78690	72400	92.0
4.	Tirap	20611	111975	98372	87.9
5.	Lower Subansiri	15249	83030	72911	87.8
6.	West Siang	21231	112274	92783	82.6
7.	Upper Siang	7324	35320	28468	80.6
8.	Anjaw	4612	21167	16451	77.7
9.	Dibang Valley	1952	8004	5701	71.2
10.	Eastr Siang	19107	99214	69979	70.5
11.	Tawang	10062	49977	34811	69.7
12.	Papum Pare	35730	176573	117216	66.4

Source: GoI, Ministry of Tribal Affairs, 2014, May, p. 418.

18.05 percent of state total population that was much higher than that of 2001. The total Nyishi population in Papum Pare district in 2011 as percentage of Nyishi total population in the state of Arunachal Pradesh was 29.97 that showed a sharp decline from 46.40 in 2001 (Table 5 & Appendix Table 1).

Table 5: Selected Indicators of State Arunachal Pradesh and District Papum Pare

Selected Indicators/Census Year	*2011*	*2001*
Total Population (AP)	1,383,727	1,097,968
Total Population of PP as % of AP	12.76	11.11
Nyishi Total population in AP as % of AP Total Population	18.05	7.98
Nyishi Total population of PP as % of Nyishi Total Population of AP	29.97	46.40#

by mother tongue; AP: Arunachal Pradesh, PP: Papum Pare.

Source: Office of the Registrar General, India.

Of total population in major STs in Arunachal Pradesh, Nyishi tribe constituted 12.43 percent in 2001. The other STs had varying percentages in major STs in the state (Table 6).

The Nyishi language belongs to the Sino-Tibetan family; however, the origin is disputed. Of total Nyishi population in Arunachal Pradesh in 2001, Papum Pare district had 34.72 percent classified by mother tongue. The non-Nyishi population in the state mostly included Nepali, Adi, Adi Gallong, Monpa, Bengali, Hindi and Assamese; the rest of the population were few in number but multi-lingual (Appendix Table 2). *Nyi* refers to a man and *shi* refers to being. Thus, Nyishi means a human being. The tribe is spread over many districts in Arunachal Pradesh plus some districts in the bordering state of Assam.

Table 6: Population of Major STs in Arunachal Pradesh, Census 2001

Sl. No.	*Name of Major STs*	*Population*
1	All STs	7,05,158 (100.0)
2	Nyishi/Nissi	87,656 (12.43)
3	Adi	32,582 (4.62)
4	Adi Gallong	48,126 (6.82)
5	Adi Minyong	33,984 (4.82)
6	Adi Padam	11,625 (1.65)
7	Dafla	45,276 (6.42)
8	Monpa	41,983 (5.95)
9	Tagin	39,091 (5.54)
10	Wancho	47,788 (6.78)
11	Galong	27,239 (3.86)
12	Others	2,89,808 (41.09)

Source: Office of the Registrar General, India.

Table 7: Households Selected from District, Blocks and Villages in Arunachal Pradesh

State	*District*	*Block*	*Village*	*Total Households*	*Households Covered*	
					Number	*%*
Arunachal Pradesh	Papum Pare	Sagalee	Sangri	28	14	50.0
			Lang Dang	35	12	34.3
			Rachi	28	11	39.3
		Balijan	Rakap	40	16	40.0
			Jote	44	09	36.4
			Puma	55	16	29.1
		Kimin	Lower Jumi	20	10	50.0
			Kakoi 2	70	16	22.9
Total Number	**01**	**03**	**08**	**320**	**104**	**32.5**

Note: We could not cover all the five blocks for time-cum-budget constraint. We could not cover CD Block Doimukh and Mengio.

The number of villages from three Blocks were 302 i.e. Sagalee (162 Villages), Kimin (35 Villages), and Balijan (105 Villages).

The selection of villages was based on the habitations of the Nyishi tribe distanced reasonably from concrete roads. There was no a priori decision to cover only 8 villages – what we could cover was a total of 8 villages on stipulated days of field visits. Similarly, there was no a priori decision to cover 104 households – what we tried was to converse with reasonable number of members from households from each selected village.

Source: Field Survey, November-December 2018.

The district Papum Pare has five development blocks. Because of time-cum-budget constraint, we covered only three blocks, namely, Sagali, Balijan and Kimin in the district dispersed by geography; because of the same constraint, we covered a total of only eight villages well distributed by blocks; we conversed with 104 households that constituted 32.5 percent of all the households residing in the selected villages (Table 7).

We did not administer any structured schedule on the sample households. We conducted Group Discussions in the houses of the households including those of *Gaon Buda* who was the local Councillor selected by the community and acknowledged by the state. The number and location of Group Discussions (GDs) were not pre-fixed – those evolved because of curiosity among the respondents who assembled to share their experiences. Both male and female members of households participated in the conversations. Thus, the conversations included personal interviews and group discussions. We also had conversations with women of different ages carrying bundles of grasses-leaves on their head on the boundary of the forests adjoining public roads as well as entry point of their houses. We took help of local facilitators in our primary survey to overcome linguistic gaps and in approaching areas that often seemed inaccessible.

3. Forest-Based Livelihood of Nyishi Households

The Nyishi tribe was forest-dependent to meet basic needs. For this tribe, hills-forests-habitats-houses were inseparable. Unlike wet cultivation, the tribe practiced Jhum (shifting cultivation) inside forests after cleaning the demarcated area to cultivate paddy. Thus, forests were not destroyed for cultivation. They protected the forests independent of any knowledge about state laws. The hunting in forests was done by the tribe in groups – the persons collectively decided the time of hunting. This meant that they had to keep forests intact in view of the frequency of hunting. The members of the Nyishi households kept bows and arrows and other equipments to hunt animals for meat. They used to hunt wild boar, monkeys, mice, goat, and deer in the forests. Wild animals like tigers, elephants, wild boar roamed within forests and did not invade residential areas implying continuing carrying capacity of the forests.

Bamboo-based Livelihood

Bamboo as a grass grew naturally in abundance in the forests. It grew in cluster – unplanned. Bamboo was a major component of forests in the selected district. The unnumbered pieces of bamboos on the hills of the district could be easily replenished by natural growth even after some mature bamboos were chopped off by the households of the adjoining areas. Bamboo had twin purposes: consumption and construction. In construction works, bamboo was used to make floor and walls of the house, boundary walls outside house to mark the private space. In consumption, bamboo shoot was preserved as soft cake and dried particles; soft cake was used in cooking, and dried particles were for tongue-tied anytime for chewing. The dried particles of bamboo shoots tasted like dried ginger. Bamboo as soft cake preserved in water in a bottle with cap closed had an acid effect that was understood as soon as the bottle was uncapped. It was a delicious food preserved in a number of forms like (i) shoot pulp kept in quarter-filled water in an air tight jar, (ii) dried shoot in very tiny pieces, and many other forms. The Nyishi tribe regularly consumed bamboo shoots preserved in different forms prepared as vegetables.

In livestock, most of the households had chicken. The Nyishi tribe prepared 'bamboo shoot-chicken' as a delicacy served on leaf plates for occasional consumption during festivals and with guests. They collected bamboo shoots from forests. The bamboo shoot in chicken soup looked like potato finger chips. The food was prepared boiling chicken-bamboo in water-salt-chilli-turmeric. The households did not store chicken-meat.

Bamboos were of different diameter, from very narrow (non-hollow type) to as cylindrical as seven-inch in diameter. The thickest bamboos were made in parts, each part around 20 inches in length with bottom-end closed to carry water collected from the mountains. Bamboo tubes were used to collect and carry water, cook food in bamboo vessels, bamboo mugs used to drink water, and bamboo container to store goods. Apart from these, bamboos were used to make arrows, room floor, musical instruments, agricultural tools, and baskets.

4. Livelihood Security: Role of Nyishi Women

The women were central to collect most of the natural resources to consume unprocessed or to transform those resources to manufacture household utilities, or cook as food, and animal feed. The relationship between women and forests was symbiotic. Women used to enter in groups into forests during day, collected non-timber forest produce and came back after hours spent. It was silent work by self-engagement. Nobody hired them on wage basis. Women had natural freedom to move out of house to extract vegetables and roots and fruits from forests and bring wood-leaves-grasses for fuel and housing materials. Women generally got self-engaged in groups for collection from nature. Freedom of women ensured food security at home, caring for children and gave men time for hunting-cultivation-fishing.

All women remained engaged in collection and extraction throughout the year; many times it was time-utilising like in animal grazing and livestock caring; they did not express fatigue in voluntary group works that they considered time-engaging. Some of the women members of households made clothes from berks of trees, knitted/weaved clothes, they coloured clothes black in stripe from one type of berks of banana trees found on the hills. The tribe could identify the specific banana trees required to get berks for colouring clothes. They made U-shape carrier from dried pumpkin of different size to keep vegetables. The women members of the households used to crush paddy manually in a top-open cylinder-shape wooden bowl. Meat was dried and preserved by women. They made potteries from clay at zero material cost. They practiced these based on inherited knowledge that is not to be understood as primitive. There was no gender-specificity in works. However, the women decided what activities they would be engaged in (Box 1).

Box 1: Activities of Self-Engaged Nyishi Women

Women	***Activities***
Social	Collecting water, fodder, cooking and related works, serving food at home, looking after children, keeping animal shed, meat drying and preservation.
Economic	Animal husbandry, stitching and tailoring at home, basket making, occasional sale of fruits and vegetables, support in cultivation and collection of roots and fruits.

Source: Field Survey, November-December, 2018.

Livelihood of Nyishi Tribe

The Nyishi tribe sustained their livelihood in satiety-based social equilibrium. Poverty was not in the psychology of the tribe; they mostly lived in non-material mode distanced from non-satiety based individual utility maximisation. It was community living where indigenous knowledge worked in their symbiotic relationship with nature. The indigenous knowledge that the tribe had was unrecorded for absence of any script (Flow Chart 1).

The Nyishi households consumed mostly from collection – it was need-based. Works followed from their self-engagement, mostly in groups, in hunting, sowing, harvesting, digging, fishing etc. Nyishi life was collective and not in a comparative mode. The practice of storage was absent except paddy and dried meat. All were non-vegetarians though they used to eat

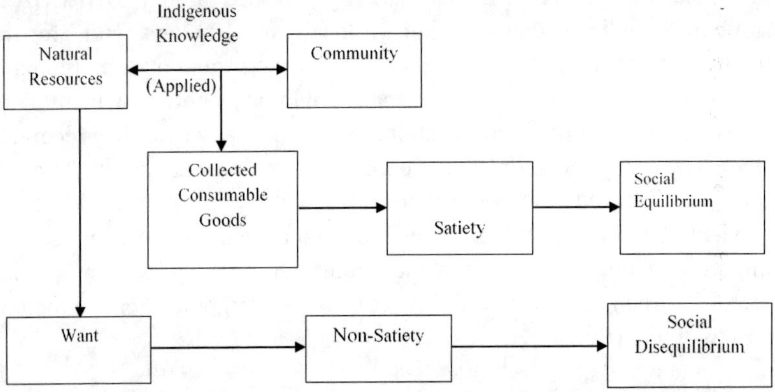

Flow Chart 1: Social Equilibrium of Nyishi Tribe in Arunachal Pradesh

vegetables and roots (collected/cultivated) adequately. The major food were rice, meat, vegetables (different leaves, roots, pumpkin), and bamboo shoot. The households fulfilled their need in a non-comparative mode. Famine was never heard of in Nyishi's life in the memorable past; in absence of adequate paddy, or to overcome deficit, they discovered roots of different types to extract and consume. As conveyed by the households, they were not poor for they could satisfy their basic needs from nature (Box 2).

Box 2: Livelihood Support of Nyishi Households

Livelihood Support	***Items***	***Provided by***	***Time/Sustainability***
Private Utilities	Food, Housing Materials, Livestock	Self-labour, collective labour	Both short-term & long-term
Public Utilities	Roads, Electricity, LPG, Water	Government	Both short-term & long-term
Public Space	Hills-Forests-Rivers	Nature	Eternal

Source: Field Survey, November-December 2018.

Estimating the income of the household of the Nyishi tribe is premature for most of their livelihood support was from self-engagement of women; self-engagement found its own socio-geo-economic space, major components of which were collection from CPRs and keeping livestock. CPRs and livestock were also inseparable. Forests provided space for animal grazing mostly guided by women and forests provided animal feed at home. Thus, women, CPRs and livestock were inseparable. Food security had two main components, one Jhum cultivation where paddy was grown after cleaning land inside forests mostly by men while the complementary food like vegetables were collected/extracted by women. Hunting was male group behaviour that provided meat. Meat was dried and preserved at home by women. The dried meat was preserved for the year.

Of late, administered labour market got formed through MNREGA in some of the villages that were known locally as '100 days work' for the members of the households engaged. The workers, both male and female, engaged in construction/repair of roads could not report how many days they had been working since past one year and what wages they received. Because of very recent introduction of the work programme in the areas that we observed, the wage-income earned by the households from MNREGA did not supplement their livelihood much. The youth started migrating mainly for education and opportunity to get jobs in the service sector in urban areas within the state; however, migration-related income was marginal (Box 3).

Box 3: Income by Types and Sources for Nyishi Households

Activities	*Income*
Private/Collective	
Self-Engagement of women	In kind
Cultivation by men	In kind (Jhum)
Hunting (Occasional) by men	In kind
Collection from CPRs by women	In kind
Livestock rearing mostly by women	Mostly in kind
Petty Business	Not much reported$
Migration (Job search)	In cash (Marginal)
State-Administered	
MNREGA	Wage income (Supplementary)
PDS	Real income enhancing

In some difficult regions, the sample households were represented by Group Discussions.

$ The Tamin Block in the selected district has a double boundary with Lakhimpur district of Assam where Nyishi people used to go to sell fruits and vegetables. The Tamin Block had also a large tea estate that produced high flavour tea for sale.

Source: Field Survey, November-December, 2018.

The domains of self-engagement of Nyishi households were forests-mountains apart from their own home. The home-based works were not delinked from collection works outside (Box 4).

Box 4: Domains of Self-Engagement by Nyishi Women

Components	*Items*	*Sources/Location*
Collection	Vegetables-roots-fruits, grasses-leaves-NTFPs, Water	Forests, Mountains
Cooking	Food	Home
Storage	Water, fuel-wood, animal-feed	Home and adjoining space
Animal rearing	Feeding animals, grazing	Animal shed at home, forests
Child caring	Food, clothing, sleeping	Home

Source: Field Survey, November-December, 2018.

Point Self-Engagement and Period Self-Engagement

What we present here is self-engagement of Nyishi women at a point of time and over a period of time. There is, however, no strict separation between the two types for the point self-engagement may also get spread over a period depending on the nature of work. Nyishi women got self-engaged at home and outside implying time-engagement that was both point engagement and period engagement. Point engagement was specific for the particular point of time on a day and period engagement was on time interval over days. For example, collection from CPRs was period engagement (Table 8).

Table 8: Time Engagement per Day of Nyishi Women

Age	*Activity*	*Time/Tenure per day*
Below 15	Schooling, home-assistance	Morning
15-45	Home-maker, Collection from CPRs	5 a.m. to 8 a.m.; 9 a.m. to 12 noon#
Above 45	Home-maker	5 a.m. to 10 p.m.*

Note: It was not possible to calculate individual time spent by components for some activities were person-specific and some collective. It was also not possible to calculate intra-household time in components and time engaged outside house.

We did not ask women their age; so it was a guess. We could not also link age with marriage.

* We did not question about the leisure time of women.

Flexible time engaged in caring for children and domestic animals, cleaning animal shed, arranging collected forest resources.

Source: Field Survey, November-December, 2018.

The Nyishi women were self-engaged in collection from CPRs where most of the collected materials served multi-purpose. For example, (i) water collected served the purpose of drinking by household members and domestic animals, cooking food, cleaning utensils and clothes, (ii) leaves collected helped as housing material as well as animal feed, (iii) fuel-wood collected was for daily cooking as well as drying meat infrequently and arranging fire outside house for all as a climatic-cultural practice (Box 5).

Box 5: Collection of Livelihood Support from CPRs by Nyishi Women

Collection	*Source*
Water	*Shrot* (Mountain)
Leaves	Forests
Fuel-wood	Forests
Animal-feed	Forests
Grasses	Forests
Roots, bamboo shoot, vegetables (food)	Forest-land
Shrot: Natural flow of water	

Source: Field Survey, November-December, 2018.

Time Utilisation

More often than not the time spent by women in India is considered as unproductive labour. The major reason may be that their self-engagement is either not noticed or not paid; also their works are seen as routine or taken for granted. One historical reason may be patriarchy; the other could be pre-conceived notion in the male-dominated society that the women are unfit for labour that suits the men even before experimenting that the women could perform many of those 'masculine activities'. The conceptual problem is, in self-engagement it is works and not labour, the latter is paid as wage-labour in time rate or piece rate while the former is unpaid.

So far as household works are concerned, who decides to pay and to who is not manifest. The man as the head of the household in patriarchy may be incapacitated to pay for the works of the women members; if at all those works are recognised, are recognised as routine works often perceived as fait accompli for women. Non-payment leads to non-acknowledgement. The public domain as a work space for women are more troublesome for women may not be allowed to work in factory at night and so on. But this taboo cannot go against the recognition of women as workers.

In case of Nyishi women engaged in multiple activities in sustaining livelihood, the above obscurity by paid or unpaid labour, superior or inferior labour, was not much relevant. Also, it was not linked with any short period like a month. The social time did not get readily converted into economic time for the Nyishi women workers.

Income in Cash and Kind of Nyishi Households: Contribution of Women

Conventionally, livelihood security is based on economic well-being that, in turn, rests on income to be spent per period. Income is not only in money (cash) but also in kind. In case of Nyishi tribe it was mostly in kind for two major reasons: (i) it was because of the self-engagement of women, and (ii) income in cash was transitory. The following may elaborate our argument:

Household Income = Income in Cash + Income in Kind

Income in Cash = Income from sale of goods collected/produced + Income from MNREGA works.

Income in Kind = Income from self-engagement + Income from CPRs + Income from Livestock.

We derived the following (Field Survey, 2018):

- Income from MNREGA was transitory and supplementary in nature.
- Migration-related remittances were marginal.
- Migration was mostly intra-state.
- Income in cash was transitory and hence could not project income per month or per year.
- PDS enhanced real income if there were functioning Fair Price Shops (FPSs) and households had access to it and had money to buy items distributed through the FPSs.
- Income in kind mostly ensured the livelihood security of the Nyishi households.
- It will be premature to cardinally calculate the components of income in cash and income in kind.

We focused on women who had been the key actors in livelihood security of households for we observed self-engagement of women for collection from CPRs and maintaining livestock that were the main pillars of livelihood. The intra-household self-engagement of women being voluntary labour, the income earned on this account was hypothetical. The self-engagement of women in collection of water for multi-purposes like drinking, cooking, animal feeding from *shrot* (natural flow of water from mountains) was unaccounted income. Actually, it was real income of the household; hence, what percentage of household income Nyishi women contributed was a non-question. It was not possible to readily convert the non-money income of the household into money income.

5. Self-Engagement: An Alternative Way of Looking at Self-Employment

The alternative avenues of self-employment ignore self-engagement though the latter plays a major role in livelihood security of households in major regions of India.

The characteristics of self-engagement included the following:

1. It was not wage-labour.
2. The self-engagement was not backed by any institutional frame.
3. The self-engagement was in forests-hills-rivers, that is, in nature.
4. It was collective self-engagement mostly by women.
5. Women were not asked to get engaged; they decided it on their own.

6. Self-engagement was community-linked.
7. Self-engagement revealed social formation.

Strength in Self-Engagement

1. The resource base remains protected at users' custody.
2. Community decides time and uses of resources per household.
3. Resources remain visible over generations.
4. Livelihood remains simple and more equal.
5. State Acts are hardly needed for protection of life-saving resources.

Constraints in Self-Engagement

1. It is women-centered engagement.
2. It is based on availability of CPRs.
3. It is operative in hills-forests.

Some Implications

1. Self-engagement was delinked from pricing.
2. Self-engagement sustained livelihood of the households.
3. The livelihood of the community was non-conflicting for it was collective work.
4. The rate of unemployment was irrelevant in self-engagement.
5. Livelihood through self-engagement was money-neutral and hence, inflation-deflation neutral.

Market Formation in the budding

1. Market formation, often state-sponsored or state-administered, started transforming the social formation into economic formation.
2. Administered labour market like MNREGA opened up cash habits of workers by their conversion into wage-laborers.
3. State welfare mechanism like PDS required households to have money to buy from FPSs to enhance real income.
4. Education-weighted migration started showing economic formation.
5. Inter-generational gap started manifesting itself through infrastructure (state-sponsored), technology, and migration.

State Question

In the midst of community living of the tribe in nature, the state is seen as the 'other'. This 'other' becomes dominant as the custodian of natural resources, as distinct from nature. The state acts in two basic ways, one is through Acts that show what people are authorised to do, the other is forming space like market facilitating people to act. The first one is institutional and the second one is market; the first one included administered markets also. The ground reality is, between institutions and market, there is a social space where people act voluntarily. This space is community space where traditions and customary rights operate. In our understanding, social space is different from economic space for the latter may be geography-neutral while the former is not. The Nyishi tribe was obsessed with living in nature like forests-hills-rivers seen as their social space. The Nyishi women were in collection mode independent of any state laws. The Nyishi women utilised time by self-engagement. Till the year 2006 the state did not acknowledge the centuries-old customary rights of the communities in forests. Unless alternative livelihood space is provided that suits the communities, as revealed by the communities, this meant denying Article 21 of the Constitution of India, that is, right to life.

The state in India is distanced from the natural members of the society for the differences in initial conditions by education and control over land apart from historical injustice inflicted on the socially distanced. The state needs to encapsulate all the population within its sovereign geographic space and hence sets up institutions for their welfare and development. Self-engagement revealed choice-based self-determination for the Nyishi tribe in Arunachal Pradesh. Unless that comes into conflict with choice of others, there is no reason why the government should stop the practices of self-engagement. The problem remains if the state will be willing to allow community control over natural resources.

6. Summing Up

In forest-based living of the Nyishi tribe, women played the central role by being self-engaged. The natural growth of grasses, including bamboo, provided elastic space for the women to enter into forests to collect basic needs. In a general complementary relationship between men and women in Nyishi households, we found women encompassed all works intra-household and outside house that maintained the micro social equilibrium.

Homogeneity of the Nyishi tribe in Arunachal Pradesh was natural-cultural. We observed the following:

- Nature provided the pedestal of living for the Nyishi tribe through collection.

- Inherited skill helped the households to prepare goods for domestic use, mostly bamboo-made.
- Living was based on basic needs.
- Collective living was practiced in forests and on hills through collection, cultivation and hunting.
- Women played a major role in ensuring livelihood security of the households.
- Living of the Nyishi tribe was in the real economy and not in the monetised economy.
- Intra-Nyishi tribe conflicts in access to and uses of forest resources were absent.
- The Nyishi tribe felt uncomfortable to live outside the hills-forests and distanced them from sound and demonstration as in city-based living.

The 'Inner Line Permit' was introduced during British India for the region called Arunachal Pradesh to restrict people from outside to enter the state. The 'Permit' continues at present though some people from adjoining states enter through hilly terrain for short-duration trade. It seemed to be a judicious decision of the state of India to allow the tribes live undisturbed on the hills-forests. It was a one-way restriction. The inhabitants of the hills were allowed to move in either direction with no requirement of such permit (Furer-Haimendorf, 1982: 288). The tribes so far remained reluctant to come out to the plain land to be 'Mainstream'.

In keeping with the above, we plead for least intervention by the government in the forest-based livelihood of the Nyishi tribe. The livelihood of Nyishi tribe was far from money-centric. The tribe had stable livelihood by self-engagement. It was mostly self-engagement of women based on collection from forests-hills. The social economy of the tribe is well served if the tribe is allowed self-determination rather than dragged into the stream that it keeps distance from.

Acknowledgement

The paper is an offshoot of the research project 'Integration of Indigenous Knowledge for Sustainable Livelihood Support from Forests in the Himalayan Forest Belts' under Indo-Japan Research Programme sponsored by the ICSSR, GoI.

References

Baruah, S. (2005). Durable Disorder, Understanding the Politics of Northeast India, Oxford University Press, New Delhi.

Chalam, K.S. (2017). Social Economy of Development in India, Sage Publication, New Delhi.

Furer-Haimendorf, C. von, (1982). Tribes of India, The Struggle for Survival, Oxford Univ. Press, Delhi.

GoI, NCEUS. 2008. Report on Conditions of Work and Promotion of Livelihoods in the Unorganised Sector, Academic Foundation, New Delhi.

GoI, Planning Commission, Eleventh Five Year Plan, 2007-2012, New Delhi.

GoI, Planning Commission, Twelfth Five Year Plan, 2012-2017, New Delhi.

GoI, Ministry of Tribal Affairs, (2014), May, Report of the High Level Committee on Socio-Economic, Health and Educational Status of Tribal Communities of India.

Jewitt, Sarah, (2004). 'Mothering Earth? Gender and Environmental Protection in Jharkhand, India' in Corbridge, S. et al, 'Jharkhand, Environment, Development, Ethnicity', Oxford Univ. Press.

Nitsch, Thomas. (1990). Social Economics: The First 200 Years. In *Social Economics: Retrospect and Prospect*, (ed). Mark Lutz. Boston: Kluwer.

Polanyi, K. (2001). The Great Transformation: the Political and Economic Origins of Our Time. Boston, Mass., Beacon Press.

Sharma, B.D., (1995). Whither Tribal Areas?, Sahyog Pustak Kutir, New Delhi.

Appendix

Table 1: Selected Indicators of State Arunachal Pradesh and District Papum Pare

Selected Indicators/Census Year	*2011*	*2001*
Total Population (AP)	1,383,727	1,097,968
Total Population of PP as % of AP	12.76	11.11
Population Growth (AP) in Decadal %	26.03	26.21
Population Growth (PP) in Decadal %	44.73	67.56
Nyishi Total population (AP)	2,49,824	87,656
Nyishi Total population in AP as % of AP Total Population	18.05	7.98
Nyishi Total population (PP)	74,885	40,676#
Nyishi Total population of PP as % of Nyishi Total Population of AP	29.97	46.40

by mother tongue.

Source: Office of the Registrar General, India.

Part - IV

Health, Education and Basic Services

13

Financing Amenities for Inclusive and Sustainable Cities in India: Challenges and Prospects

Soumyadip Chattopadhyay and
Arjun Kumar

Abstract

Inaccessibility of basic services by a large proportion of urban households in India, especially the households located in slums, small-size class of towns/cities and backward states and those belonging to the lower socio-economic strata has rendered the SDGs unfulfilled and thus requires immediate policy action. Review of the relevant urban policies reveals that most of them, despite having scope for directly connecting with the urban citizen, followed a typical top down approach. Policies have facilitated increasing dominance of private actors and their interests in formulation and implementation of urban plans. Participatory avenues have been found to be restricted to the upper- and middle-class people whose visions largely reflect that of the consultant driven city administration. City governments are devoid of any real decision-making power and lack financial resources and perform only as implementing agencies of the central and state urban plan and policies. This paper argues that for delivering adequate as well as affordable urban basic services, the city governments need to work in an expansion or exponential mode, with continuous capacity building and revitalisation of administrative and financial energy, which will require roping in of specialised institutions and para-statal agencies. Efficient coordination is required among all the stakeholders through an integrated policy and regulatory environment.

Key Words: *Urban Basic Services, Urban Finance, JNNURM, Smart Cities, India.*

1. Background

Cities are engines of economic growth, but managing complexity, increasing efficiency, reducing the expenses, and improving quality of life have been the foremost challenges of large-scale urbanisation. The Universal Declaration of Human Rights of the United Nations (1948), the Millennium Development Goals (MDGs) (2000) and the recently adopted Sustainable Development Goals (SDGs)[1] (2015) explicitly acknowledge the importance of the right to decent standard of living and making cities inclusive, safe, resilient and sustainable. India is urbanizing[2] and Indian cities were estimated to have contributed more than 60 percent of the GDP and about 80 percent of the total tax revenue (McKinsey and Company, 2010). The challenge facing India's planners and policy-makers is how to provide adequate urban infrastructure and services to the citizens and to make the Indian cities contribute as they should to economic growth.

However, widespread deficits in physical infrastructure and municipal amenities and consequent perpetuation of socio-economic inequities not only jeopardise the quality of life of urban populace but also undermine the potential of Indian cities as an agency of economic development. The World Bank (2015) report recognised "urbanisation in South Asia and in India has been messy and hidden", which is reflected in the widespread existence of slums and sprawl that give rise to hidden urbanisation, particularly on the city-peripheries. A plethora of studies indicate intercity as well as intra city disparities in availability of urban basic services with the coverage being far from satisfactory (Mitra and Nagar, 2018; Kundu and Banerjee, 2018; Bhan and Jana, 2015; HPEC, 2011). Further, it has been observed that service coverage increased systematically with the size class of the cities and intra category disparities were higher for smaller cities (Chattopadhyay and Das, 2018; Kundu *et al.*, 1999). Availability and accessibility of water, sanitation and hygiene in largest six urban agglomerations of India demonstrate inequality both within and between cities (Saroj *et al.*, forthcoming). Moreover, the availability and accessibility of urban services is even more precarious for the migrants, citizens belonging to the socially marginalised groups and the poor households (Kundu *et al.*, 2018). Hence, it is as a serious cause of concern for the India, and as this article argues, becomes an important case for urgent action.

The deplorable state of urban services is typically attributed to poor financial health, lack of planning and weak institutional capacities which are in turn linked to the absence of effective governance structures of the Indian cities (Ahluwalia, 2017; Rao and Bird, 2014; Sridhar and Reddy, 2010). Scholars have highlighted the disproportionate infrastructural investments across urban spaces, cognitive insensitivity of the states and their para-statal institutions towards small and medium towns, with simultaneous failure of private sector partnerships to prove themselves as viable alternatives (Kundu et al., 1999; Kundu, 2006; Kumar, 2013; Kundu, A., 2014; Kundu D., 2014). Hence the buck stops at the level of state and local governments, having the responsibility of providing affordable housing and basic amenities to all (Kundu *et al.*, 1999) and to tackle the phenomenon of exclusionary urbanisation (Kundu, 2014; Kundu, 2011). Further, it has also been evidenced that amid modest increase in public spending on slum improvement, there has been a simultaneous increase in the exclusionary practices such as evictions, in order to '*cleanse' the cities and enhance their image among prospective investors*' (UN- Habitat: 2014). Under the Smart City Mission, private consultants have assumed central position in designing the smart city proposals that are shaped by 'globalised' aspirations of urban smartness and by the upper and middle classes, leaving behind the voices and needs of poor and marginalised citizens (Ghosh and Arora, 2019). Thus, besides socio-economic exclusions, policy-making efforts have trailed behind with the inefficient top-down policy implementation in India.

Against this background, it becomes imperative to examine the various policies of the government and the persistent challenges towards building inclusive and sustainable cities in India, with a focus on basic amenities. The next section assesses the needs and dynamics of the demand-side of the situation of urban households' amenities, along with the financial estimates. The third section documents the recent policies related to transformation of urban governance and their implications for access to basic amenities. The fourth section examines the challenges and prospects in financing cities' amenities. The fifth section summarizes the main arguments and recommends policy directions that will be relevant for India.

2. State of Amenities, Service Level Benchmarking and Financial Estimates

The Technical Group on Urban Housing Shortage, 2012-17 (TG-12) estimated the number of urban households to be 81.35 million and the urban housing shortage to be 18.78 million, in 2012. Economically weaker sections (EWS) and lower income groups (LIG) households were the major sections in these shortages, with the congestion factor cognizably high (Kumar, 2015a). The Table 1 shows the levels of deprivation of the households during 2001 and 2011. While there has been an improvement in the availability of the amenities such as drinking water, sanitation, electricity and drainage arrangement, etc. by the urban households in proportional terms since 2001, yet as the statistics below show, there has been a stark rise in the deprivation in absolute numbers (except for access to electricity in the house, where there was a fall in the absolute number of deprived households).

Table 1: Deprivation in Access to Important Basic Amenities by the Household during 2001 and 2011 in Urban India

	Levels		*2001 – 2011 (Changes)*		
	2011	*2001*	*Numbers (millions)*	*as proportion of total households during 2001 (in %)*	*Annual compounded (in %)*
Number of Households (in millions) *in %*	78.9	53.7	25.2	*46.9*	
Number of Households Not having Availability of Drinking Water within the premise (Near the premise and Away) (in millions)	22.7	18.6	4.1		
as proportion of total HHs (in %)	*28.8*	*34.6*		*22.3*	*-1.82*
Number of Households Not having Latrine Facility within the premise (Public and Open latrine use) (in millions)	14.7	14.1	0.5		
as proportion of total HHs (in %)	*18.6*	*26.3*		*3.9*	*-3.40*
Number of Households Not having Electricity in the house (Kerosene, Other sources and no lighting) (in millions)	5.8	6.7	-0.9		
as proportion of total HHs (in %)	*7.3*	*12.4*		*-13.5*	*-5.16*
Number of Households Not having Closed Drainage Connectivity for Waste Water Outlet (Open drainage and No drainage) (in millions)	43.8	35.2	8.6		
as proportion of total HHs (in %)	*55.5*	*65.5*		*24.4*	*-1.64*

Note: Annual compounded growth rate is calculated based upon percentage in 2011 over percentage in 2001 of levels of deprivation of corresponding housing amenities.

Source: House listing and Housing Census Data, Census of India, 2001 and 2011.

Further, Table 2 and Table 3 demonstrate that households located in slums and in small and medium towns and cities, and in backward regions and those belonging to the poor (lower strata of consumption expenditure classes), scheduled tribe, scheduled caste and wage labourers (casual labourers) lagged behind in as far as the availability of amenities in the house was concerned (Kundu *et al.*, 1999; Kumar, 2013; Kumar, 2015b). Previous literature on the theme have pointed out that the problem of

Table 2: Deprivation in Access to Important Basic Amenities by the Household in Urban Slums and Urban India during 2011 (in %)

	Urban Slums	*Urban India*
Number of Households (in Millions)	13.75	78.87
Households Not having Availability of Drinking Water within the premise	43.3	28.8
Households Not having Latrine Facility within the premise	34.0	18.6
Households Not having Electricity in the house	9.5	7.3
Households Not having Closed Drainage Connectivity for Waste Water Outlet	63.1	55.5

Source: Primary Census Abstract for Slums, Census of India, 2011. Slums reported in 4041 STs, for details see Census.

Table 3: Deprivation of Few Important Basic Amenities by the Household among Various Size class of Towns/Cities during 1993 and 2008-09 in Urban India (levels are in % and changes in annual compound growth rate)

	Small Towns	**Medium Towns**	**Large Towns**	**Urban Areas**
No Facility of Drinking Water in the House				
Levels in 1993	*44.6*	*41.0*	*28.4*	*39.2*
Levels in 2008-09	*31.6*	*22.5*	*15.6*	*22.9*
Annual Change, 1993 to 2008-09	*-2.2*	*-3.7*	*-3.7*	*-3.3*
No Latrine Facility in the House				
Levels in 1993	*42.7*	*36.0*	*29.9*	*36.6*
Levels in 2008-09	*26.5*	*14.7*	*15.3*	*17.7*
Annual Change, 1993 to 2008-09	*-3.0*	*-5.5*	*-4.2*	*-4.5*
No Electricity Use for domestic Purposes in the House				
Levels in 1993	*25.2*	*18.7*	*8.9*	*18.4*
Levels in 2008-09	*7.0*	*3.6*	*1.4*	*3.9*
Annual Change, 1993 to 2008-09	*-7.8*	*-9.9*	*-11.3*	*-9.4*
Open, Katcha and No Drainage Arrangement in the House				
Levels in 1993	*51.7*	*40.5*	*18.5*	*38.8*
Levels in 2008-09	*34.1*	*22.0*	*5.2*	*20.6*
Annual Change, 1993 to 2008-09	*-2.6*	*-3.8*	*-7.7*	*-3.9*

Note: The classifications used here for the analysis of different size classes of towns/ cities, from NSS data during 1993 and 2008/9, are: Small towns- population less than 50,000; Medium towns- population more than 50,000 and less than 1 million; and, Large towns- population more than 1 million.

Source: Author's Calculation using National Sample Survey, Household Conditions Rounds, unit record data for the respective years.

delivery of basic amenities is also linked with other challenging issues such as densification, rapid urbanisation and migration, socio-spatial situated-ness (location or spaces of informal/illegal settlements, slums, city class size, backward states, hilly terrains, etc.), institutional, resources and capacity constraints, and so on.

Qualitative assessment of the basic services shows that the minimum standards required to be maintained in the delivery of basic services such as water supply, sanitation and solid waste management are still below the norms (Mathur *et al.*, 2007), which presses on the need of increased accountability for delivery of services. It is hence not surprising that the various reform agenda of the Union Government have emphasised upon shifting the focus from infrastructure creation to delivery of service outcomes, for instance, the concept of Service Level Benchmarking (SLB), which involves a systematic and continuous measuring and monitoring of the performance of service providers, in order to ensure better services to people. Launched by the Ministry of Urban Development (MoUD), the SLB initiative seeks to (i) identify a minimum set of standard performance parameters for the water and sanitation sector that are commonly understood and used by all stakeholders across the country; (ii) define a common minimum framework for monitoring and reporting on these indicators and (iii) set out guidelines on how to operationalise this framework in a phased manner (GoI, 2008). In 2019, an attempt has been made to construct the Municipal Performance Index (MPI) for 100 smart cities and other million plus population cities to examine the sectoral performance of these cities across a set of five verticals – service, finance, technology, planning and governance (MoHUA, 2019). In particular, the MPI signifies an outcome-based approach to assess the use of municipal resources and subsequently to devise strategies for achieving broader developmental outcomes including the sustainable development goals.

Further, the MoUD constituted the High Powered Expert Committee (HPEC) to estimate the investment requirements for urban infrastructure service. In their Report on "*Indian Urban Infrastructure and Services*", the HPEC selected the service norms for basic amenities (based on the MoUD's SLB). Given the desirability of the service level standards, it has been observed that the achievement of these still remain a distant dream. For example, in sharp contrast to the SLB's goals of 100% individual pipe water supply to all the households, 24x7 water supply for all the cities, and per capita consumption norms for 135 litre per capita per day (lpcd) for all the cities, the Census 2011 showed some staggering results. Around 70% of urban households had piped water supply (around 62% having access to treated and rest 8% having untreated water supply). Several studies have shown that the continuity of water supply in most of the cities is for around 1-6 hours a day, with the per capita consumptions varying from 63 to around 200 lpcd across different cities (HPEC, 2011).

Census 2011 also showed that around 15 million urban households do not have latrine facilities within the premise. As against the objectives of the SLB, the composition by type of latrine facility were: 81.4% of the households had latrine facility within the premises (i) Water Closet- 72.6% (piped sewer system- 32.7%, septic tank- 38.2%, other systems- 1.7%); 7.1% of the households had pit latrine- (with slab/ ventilated improved pit- 6.4%, without slab/ open pit- 0.7%); 1.7 % of the households had other latrine- 1.7% (night soil disposed into open drain- 1.2%, night soil removed by human- 0.3%, night soil serviced by animals- 0.2%)) and 18.6% of the households had no access to latrine facilities within the premise (public latrines- 6% and open defecation- 12.6%). Also, the 2015 report of the WHO-UNICEF Joint Monitoring Programme (JMP) for Water Supply and Sanitation suggested that while the situation of water supply in India had improved substantially yet there has been moderate progress in sanitation facilities in the country and much remained to be done to attain the aspirations of open defecation free and hygienic cities.

In case of urban solid waste management, around 70-90% of the solid waste is collected and transported. But issues remain in the proper disposal, segregation and treatment of the solid wastes. 'Waste to Wealth' programmes modelled on public–private partnerships (PPPs) have mixed results in different cities (Rajkot was successful while Lucknow was not). Also, around 50% of the households had underground drainage facilities in 2011, and the goal of 100% coverage of drainage network throughout the length of the road on both its sides for all the cities and 100% collection and treatment of waste water remain a mirage. Thus, overall, the status of urban amenities along with their SLBs in urban India has not been satisfactory, with acute problems in informal/illegal spaces, slums and squatter settlements.

Considering the SLBs as the goal, the HPEC estimated the investment requirements for urban infrastructure services over 20 years (2012-2031) at 2009-10 prices (based on the per capita investment cost by sector and computation of the service backlog). It estimated that the average investment per person for the eight sectors of urban infrastructure (water supply, sewerage, solid waste, urban roads, urban transport, traffic management system, storm water drains and street lighting) at all India level was estimated to be ₹ 43,386 and ₹ 1,806 for capital investment and Operation and Maintenance (O&M) cost respectively. The details are listed in the following table:

Table 4: Per Capita Investment Cost Requirement

Urban Sectors	*Per Capita Investment Cost by Sector (in Rs)*	*Per Capita O & M Cost by Sector (in Rs)*
Water Supply	5099	501
Sewerage	4704	286
Solid Waste	391	155
Urban Roads	22974	397
Urban Transport	5380	371
Traffic Management System	945	34
Strom Water Drains	3526	53
Street Lighting	366	8
Total	43386	1806

Note: Average cost at 2009-10 prices.
Source: HPEC, 2011.

The HPEC also estimated that ₹ 39.2 lakh crore was required for urban infrastructure (capital expenditure or CapEx) which included ₹ 34.1 lakh crore for asset creation (out of which the investment for the eight major sectors was ₹ 31 lakh crore, ₹ 4.1 lakh crore for renewal and redevelopment including slums and ₹ 1 lakh crore for capacity building).

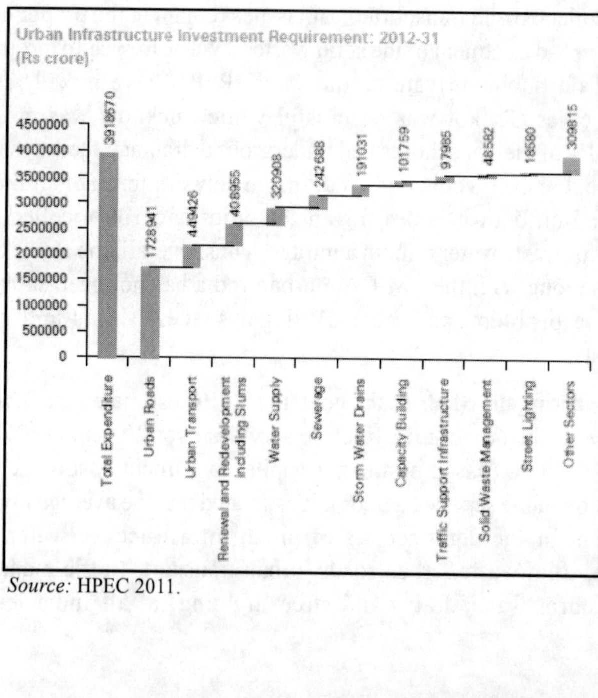

Source: HPEC 2011.

The investment estimates for the eight sectors of urban infrastructure for the 20-year period from 2012 to 2031 amounted to ₹ 31 lakh crore at 2009-10 prices. Sectors delivering urban services such as water supply, sewerage, solid waste management, and storm water drains accounted for 26 percent (₹ 8 lakh crore) of the total investment requirement. The estimates indicate a higher investment requirement for water than sewerage, because provision was made for up gradation of the distribution network for continuous water supply (₹ 88,000 crore) and metering of water connections (₹ 21,500 crore).

In essence, the estimates prepared by the HPEC based on the proposed service standards indicated that almost 40 percent of the total investment for infrastructure was required to address the unmet demand for these services. The cumulative gap of urban service delivery over the last several years had to be compensated by larger investments in the decades to come. The HPEC also noted that metropolitan cities (classified as IA and IB, i.e. cities with population over 1 million), with almost 43 percent of the total urban population by 2031, would require about 50 percent of the total investment. Class IC cities, i.e. cities with population between 100,000 and 1 million, would require about 30 percent of the investment, reflecting the potential growth of India's small and medium cities. The investment requirement for urban infrastructure for all towns (Classes II to IV+, i.e. with population less than 100,000) would be about 20 percent of the total. It must be noted that separate provisions for urban infrastructure services for the urban poor has not been provided because this was already included in the overall estimates, with the HPEC's decision to *not* to differentiate between services for the poor and the non-poor.

The Report of the Sub-Committee on Financing Urban Infrastructure in the 12th Plan estimated the investment for affordable housing (including slums) to be 8.5 lakh crore (for both slums and non-slums areas; for new construction and up gradation; including infrastructure cost of around ₹ 2 lakh crores) (GoI, 2012). Given the total investment estimate of ₹ 34.1 lakh crore for urban infrastructure and considering that 25 percent of the urban population lives in slums, this yields ₹ 8.5 lakh crore for slum population, assuming universal standards for all, as well as universal provision for access and mobility. Since the majority of the urban poor live in Class I cities and require comparatively higher investments, the investment share targeted towards the urban poor may even be higher than ₹ 8.5 lakh crore. The HPEC was of the view that the proposed levels of investment for the urban poor were critical for building inclusive cities.

The proposed investment in urban infrastructure, renewal and redevelopment including slums, and capacity building, implies that by 2021-22, annual investment required would be 1.14 percent of GDP, amounting to ₹ 1.79 lakh crore. Thereafter, both GDP and urban infrastructure investment are projected to grow at 8 percent per annum so that by the terminal year (2031-32), the urban infrastructure investment would still remain at 1.14 percent of GDP, with the level of investment reaching to ₹ 3.86 lakh crore.

The requirement for O&M was separately estimated by HPEC which was ₹ 19.9 lakh crore (OpEx), out of which around ₹ 11 lakh crore was for services. The O&M cost considered for the estimation exercise included the cost of O&M of physical assets, staff, and related administrative cost for the respective sectors. The O&M computation took into account both the cost of O&M of existing assets as well as of new assets that would be created over the 20-year period.

Table 5: Operation and Maintenance Expenditure by Sector (Rs Crore at 2009-10 prices)

Sector	*Total*
Water Supply	546095
Sewerage	236964
Solid Waste	273906
Urban Roads	375267
Strom Water Drains	34612
Urban Transport	304386
Traffic Support Infrastructure	36690
Street Lighting	4717
Total of core sectors	1812638
Total of all sectors	1993902

Source: HPEC, 2011.

The estimated annual O&M expenditure was expected to rise from ₹ 35,516 crore in 2012-13 (0.45 percent of GDP) to ₹ 2.08 lakh crore by 2031-32 (0.61 percent of GDP). Of the ₹ 18.1 lakh crore for the eight sectors, O&M cost of urban transport and urban roads amounted to ₹ 6.8 lakh crore (38 percent of the total), followed by ₹ 5.5 lakh crore for water supply (30 percent of the total).

Another estimate by McKinsey Global Institute (MGI) in 2010 revealed that India needed $ 1.2 trillion in capital expenditure and $1 trillion in operating expenditure over next 20 years (2010-2030 at 2008 prices). Within capital expenditure, almost half of the amount was necessary to erase India's existing infrastructure backlog in its cities and rest were needed for their future needs. The share of water, sewerage, solid waste and storm water drains were around 20% of the CapEx and rest was for roads, mass transit and affordable housing (MGI, 2010).

3. Transformation in Urban Governance and Provision of Urban Services: Review of Some Recent Policy Initiatives

Historically, Indian cities experience incoherent urban policies and their tardy implementation coupled with significant underinvestment (Chattopadhyay, 2017). Urban governance, being state subject, provides state governments considerable discretion over implementation of urban development plan and policies. All these have contributed significantly to the deteriorating conditions of Indian cities. The central government introduced the Jawaharlal Nehru Urban Renewal Mission (JNNURM) in 2005 to improve the country's urban infrastructure, provide affordable housing and basic services for it's urban poor and reform the urban governance. The JNNURM catered to the non-mission towns and cities through two components, namely the Urban Infrastructure Development Scheme for Small and Medium Towns (UIDSSMT) and the Integrated Housing and Slum Development Programme (IHSDP).

Most crucial feature of JNNURM was to tie up the release of fund under the schemes to the cities with the successful implementation of a set of reforms at the state and municipal level. A close reading of the reform conditions attests central government's attempt to revamp the municipal governance by infusing participation, transparency and accountability in governance structure and promoting the public-private partnership and principle of cost recovery to make the cities sustainable. However, the actual implementation of all these objectives virtually contributed to centralisation of municipal governance with severe implications for provision of urban services. The JNNURM imposed one-size-fit-all reform conditionalities. Many of them, e.g., achieving 85 percent collection efficiency of property tax, levy of user charges with full cost recovery, introduction of double entry accounting system aimed to improve the fiscal health of the cities. But, cities in India have limited taxing instruments as they can levy and collect only those taxes that are specified by the state government. So the fiscal empowerment of the city government remains a myth and this, in turn, limits their capacity to provide basic services. Involvement of consultants and lack of citizen participation in preparation of the city development plan made the plan inattentive to the needs and priorities of common people. With the approval and monitoring of the CDPs by multiple agencies often with overlapping mandates, the implementation became all the more cumbersome. In many cases, JNNURM prioritised market-oriented policies and cost recovery in the name of efficiency and city competitiveness and that too at the cost of fulfilling basic needs of the urban poor. In spite of little or no interest from the private sector to invest on basic services like water supply, sanitation etc. the public-private partnership remained the preferred model. Although, water supply, sewerage and SWM and transport sector accounted for 83 percent of the sanctioned funds, only 30 percent of the sanctioned funds were released with transport projects recorded maximum utilisation of 50.5 percent (Avashia and Garg, 2016). On the one hand, this indicates that Indian cities potential lies in making intervention in the essential urban services which nonetheless requires strengthening of local capacity. But consultant driven policy making undermined local capacity building. On the other hand, lack of financial capabilities of the city governments in generating matching revenue contribution led to delay in release of central fund. The overall outcome has been disappointing with commercially oriented infrastructure development, exacerbation of intra and intercity inequalities, weakening of municipal capacities and increasing tendencies towards centralisation of municipal governance (Sadoway *et al.*, 2018).

With change of guards at the Union Government, three important schemes replaced the JNNURM, namely, the Smart Cities Mission (SCM), the Atal Mission for Rejuvenation and Urban Transformation (AMRUT), and the National Heritage City Development and Augmentation Yojana (HRIDAY). The Pradhan Mantri Awas Yojana- Housing for All (Urban) (PMAY HfA Urban), Swachh Bharat Mission (SBM) Urban, Ujwal Bharat (which aims to realise the vision of 24×7 Affordable Power for all and also using new and renewable energy), affordable and clean cooking fuel and energy, adequate water supply and pricing, Digital India among other programmes have also been launched and put into action as it is true that comprehensive development occurs in areas by integrating the physical, institutional, social and economic infrastructure. Many of the sectoral schemes of the Government converge in this goal, although the path is different. At the planning stage itself, it is expected that cities must seek convergence in the Smart City Plan with AMRUT, SBM Urban, HRIDAY, Digital India, Skill development, PMAY HfA Urban, construction of Museums funded by the Culture Department and other programmes connected to social infrastructure such as Health, Education and Culture.

The SCM and AMRUT have made a set of mandatory reforms (milestones and timelines) for ULBs to access the funds. Many of these reforms' measures pertain to achieving improvements in the service delivery and governance. The SCM focuses on SBM Urban to make the city open defecation free and hygienic and also on 10% of power from solar energy projects to focus on renewable energy. The AMRUT have also detailed these and include improvement in levy and collection of user charges, energy and water audit, SBM Urban and so on.

Smart Cities Mission (SCM)[3]

The objective of the SCM is to promote cities that provide core infrastructure and give a decent quality of life to its citizens, a clean and sustainable environment and application of 'Smart' Solutions. The focus is on sustainable and inclusive development and the idea is to look at compact areas, create a replicable model which will act like a ***light house*** to other aspiring cities. It is meant to set examples that can be replicated both within and outside the Smart City, catalysing the creation of similar Smart Cities in various regions and parts of the country (GoI, 2015c).

With citizen being at the core of the Mission, the key features of a Smart City is the intersection between competitiveness, capital and sustainability, which have the capacity to provide good infrastructure and quality of life such as water, sanitation, reliable utility services, healthcare; attract investments; transparent processes that make it easy to run commercial activities, and others. The operational procedures for Smart Cities are: (a) Citizen Reference Framework, (b) Smart City Development Plan (i) GIS mapping, (ii) spatial mapping, (iii) Information and communications technology (ICT) mapping, (iv) Master Plan), and (c) Environmental Sustainability Plan (ESP).

The strategic components of area-based development in the Smart Cities Mission are City Improvement (***Retrofitting***[4]), City Renewal (***Redevelopment***[5]) and City Extension (***Greenfield development***[6]) plus a ***Pan-city***[7] initiative in which ***Smart Solutions*** are applied for covering larger parts of the city. For North Eastern and Himalayan States, the area proposed to be developed would be one-half of what is prescribed for any of the alternative models - retrofitting, redevelopment or green-field development. Application of Smart Solutions would enable cities to use technology, information and data to improve infrastructure and services. Pan City development envisages the application of selected Smart Solutions to the existing city-wide infrastructure.

The implementation and progress of the SCM so far has important implications for building inclusive and sustainable cities in India. The central government utilised "India Smart Cities Challenge" to select cities for smart city development based on objective criteria and the merit of smart city proposals. As of now, all the 100 cities under the SCM has been selected and the Mission will influence a total population of more than 99 million. Apart from the merits of the city proposals, equal weightage of the urban population of the state and the number of the towns in the states have been used as selection criteria for choice of cities from each state. These, in general, resulted in larger states getting more smart cities (e.g. ten cities for Maharashtra). As exception, Arunachal Pradesh has been allocated two smart cities. Given, the matching funding requirement for financing smart cities from the state government, this has forced the state with smaller proportion of urban population, even lower than Assam, to allocate funds for SCM that otherwise could have been used to meeting the rural infrastructure needs (Das, 2019). Even after four years of the Mission's inception, the physical progress has been disappointing. As on July 25, 2019, only 18 percent of Smart City projects have been completed; work orders have been issued for 37 percent projects; tenders have been issued for 16 percent projects and 29 percent of proposed projects are still at the detailed project report stage (Deka, 2019). Moreover, progress of the mission has been unequal as 54 percent of the completed projects have come from just four states - Karnataka, Madhya Pradesh, Gujarat and Uttar Pradesh (Deka, 2019). At the city level, ten cities (New Delhi, Belagavi, Surat, Indore, Varanasi, Raipur, Tumakuru, Vadodara, Ajmer and Ahmedabad) account for 48 percent of the completed projects under the Mission (Deka, 2019).

MoUD largely determines the objective, scope, organisational plans, financing and the monitoring mechanism for the 100 smart cities. As the city selection under SCM is based on city's competence and smartness of the proposal, state actors engage themselves in competitive mode to attract capital investment as well as create new institutions that are directly controlled by state (regional) institutions to manage the new state space. Special Purpose Vehicles (SPVs), headed by a CEO and regulated by the Companies Act 2013, have been in charge of mission implementation. Most importantly, under the Companies Act 2013, these SPVs are incorporated as a "limited company" with options for private sectors to take equity in the "limited company" with the argument of making itself "self-sustainable". Mode of infusing corporate governance for efficient management and implementation of urban plan under the SCM largely follows the legacy of

JNNURM, *albeit* with one key difference. Instead of focussing on a specific urban sector, the SPVs are mandated to control the management and implementation of multiple development sectors in a city (Taraporevala, 2018).

The SCM guidelines mandates government ownership of the SPVs in the form of combination of city governments and state governments. However, a study of 21 major cities India indicates that in as many as 19 cities elected councillors are not part of SPVs' board of directors (PRAJA, 2020). The SPVs are headed by the state government officials and city governments do not have much role in the decision-making processes of the SCM projects, thus eventually weakening the municipal governance structure. This makes poor people more vulnerable under the SCM as they depend on local political leaders and elected representatives to establish links with municipal power structures and to gain access to services (Benjamin, 2008; Jha *et.al.*, 2007).

Moreover, the SCM guidelines explicitly uphold the participatory ethos through emphasis on the citizen-driven smart city proposals from the beginning (MoUD, 2015). Such participatory imaginary is supposed to be achieved through citizen consultations, including active participation of groups of people, such as Residents Welfare Associations, Taxpayers Associations, Senior citizens and Slum Dwellers Associations. During consultations, priorities of citizens need to be identified and subsequently, citizen-driven solutions need to be generated. (MoUD, 2015). For example, one guideline asks: 'How well does the Vision come out of the needs, aspirations and wishes of the local people to make their city more liveable?' (MoUD, 2015). The SCM guidelines also call for the inclusion of 'details of process for co-creating every step (ideas, strategies, implementing mechanism and financial solutions) through an extensive consultation process' (MoUD, 2015). However, the actual implementation of the SCM portrays different picture. Private consultants have assumed central position in designing the smart city proposals and this, in turn, increases the risk of making these proposals more elitist (Das, 2019; Basu, 2019). In fact, the entire process "remained highly uneven and technology-centric, shaped by 'globalised' aspirations of urban smartness and by the upper and middle classes, leaving behind the voices and needs of poor and marginalised citizens" (Ghosh and Arora, 2019). There are some evidences that actual decision-making processes have fallen into a pattern of strict investment logic, resulting in preference to larger and costlier infrastructure over the needs of urban deprived communities (Baindur *et al.*, 2019)[8]. Moreover, the SCM is likely to create inequality within the cities as ABD projects, although covering a little over 7 percent of the area of the 99 cities and that too with concentration of affluent people and having better service coverage, account for 80 percent of the SCM budget (Taraporevala, 2018). Only 20 percent of the SCM budget is effectively left for the vast majority of the urban citizen with massive unfulfilled needs of basic urban infrastructure and services. Even under the pan city component, the cities are not allowed to make capital expenditure for infrastructure.

Regarding the financing of the SCM, the public sources emerge as the dominant sources with GoI's commitment of financial support to the extent of INR 48,000 crore (23.4 percent of Smart City Proposal value) over five years along with the requirement of equal matching amount to be contributed jointly by the state and city government. Apart from these, around INR 42,028 crore (21 percent) is expected from convergence with other Missions, INR 41,022 crore (20 percent) from Public Private Partnerships (PPP), around INR 9,843 crore (4.8 percent) from loans and rest from the other sources. Interestingly, the proposals of cities with the largest budgets (Bhubaneshwar, Jaipur, Indore, Raipur, Faridabad and Thane) lack details of funding sources for their proposed projects (Taraporevala, 2018). Especially, the smaller cities face the daunting task of developing more feasible budgets and revenue sources. Several of the projects undertaken under the SCM (parking facilities or real estate development or commercial real estate or uses of water meters) seek to build the financial corpus of the city (Taraporevala, 2018). This will likely to have regressive impact on urban poor's ability to access basic services. Further, given the SCM's emphasis on convergence of funds from other schemes, the possibility of transmission of inherent unequal nature of fund allocation for ABD projects into them will make all the policies more exclusionary.

Atal Mission for Rejuvenation and Urban Transformation (AMRUT)[9]

Acknowledging the importance of peoples' real need for basic urban services, AMRUT[10] aims to: (i) ensure that every household has access to a tap with assured supply of water and a sewerage connection; (ii) increase the amenity value of cities by developing greenery and well maintained open spaces (e.g. parks); and (iii) reduce pollution by switching to public transport or constructing facilities for non-motorised transport (e.g. walking and cycling) (GoI, 2015b). An incremental approach would be followed through a step-by-step process after achieving the benchmark of universal coverage. The Service Level Improvement Plans (SLIPs) would provide for provision of water and sewerage connections to all households. In the case of urban transport, the benchmark would be to reduce pollution in cities while construction and maintenance of storm water drains is expected to reduce and ultimately eliminate, flooding in cities, thereby making cities resilient.

AMRUT has replaced the previous project-by-project sanctions by approval of the State Annual Action Plan once a year by the MoUD where the States have to give project sanctions and approval at their end. In this way, States have been made equal partners in planning and implementation of projects, thereby actualizing the spirit of cooperative federalism. Further reforms would lead to improvement in service delivery, mobilisation of resources and making municipal functioning more transparent and functionaries more accountable, while capacity building would empower municipal functionaries and lead to timely completion of projects.

The total financial outlay for AMRUT is ₹ 50,000 crore for five years from FY 2015-16 to FY 2019-20. The funding under this mission would also provide incentive for reforms to the tune of 10% of the annual budgetary allocations. The pattern of funding would be one-third of the project cost as grant from GoI for cities with a population of above 10 lakh; one-half of the project cost as grant for cities/towns with population up to 10 lakh; and the remaining by State Governments / ULBs or through private investment. The tender would include O&M for five years based on user charges. For the purpose of calculation of the project cost, the O&M cost would be excluded; however, the States/ULBs would fund the O&M through an appropriate cost recovery mechanism in order to make them self-reliant and cost-effective.

The National Heritage Development and Augmentation Yojana (HRIDAY)[11]

HRIDAY seeks to promote an integrated, inclusive and sustainable development of heritage sites, focusing not just on maintenance of monuments but on advancement of the entire ecosystem including its citizens, tourists and local businesses. With the 32 UNESCO recognised natural and cultural heritage sites, ranking second in Asia and fifth in the world, the tourism potential of the country remains to be fully exploited and the new scheme seeks to assist in this regard. ₹ 500 crore would be provided to the 12 cities[12] selected in the first phase under the 'Central Scheme' of HRIDAY, and the central government would meet the entire expenditure under the scheme. The states and urban local bodies have also been encouraged to supplement their resources for rapid development of heritage cities and to put efforts aiming at blending 'nature and culture for a better future' (GoI, 2015a).

Pradhan Mantri Awas Yojana (PMAY) - Housing for All (HfA) (Urban)[13]

The President of India, in his address to the Joint Session of Parliament on June 9, 2014 announced that by the time India completed 75 years of its Independence, every family would have a pucca house with water connection, toilet facilities, 24×7 electricity supply and access. Towards this, Central Government launched a comprehensive mission "Pradhan Mantri Awas Yojana – Housing for All (Urban)". It seeks to address the housing requirement of urban poor including slum dwellers through slum rehabilitation of slum dwellers with participation of private developers using land as a resource; promotion of affordable housing for weaker section through credit linked subsidy; affordable housing in partnership with public and private sectors and provide subsidies for beneficiary-led individual house construction/enhancement. All statutory towns (4041) as per Census 2011 and towns notified subsequently would be eligible for coverage under the Mission.

Swachh Bharat Mission (SBM) Urban[14]

SBM Urban aims to achieve an Open-Defecation Free (ODF), clean and hygienic urban India. All statutory towns (4041) as per Census 2011 and towns notified subsequently would be eligible for coverage under the Mission. The Mission objectives are: (a) elimination of open defecation; (b) eradication of manual scavenging; (c) modern and scientific municipal solid waste management; (d) to effect behavioural change regarding healthy sanitation practices; (e) generate awareness about sanitation and its linkage with public health; (f) capacity augmentation for ULB's; (g) creation of an enabling environment for private sector participation in Capex and Opex. The Mission has the following components: (i) household toilets; including conversion of insanitary latrines into pour-flush latrines; (ii) community toilets; (iii) public toilets; (iv) solid waste management; (v) IEC and public awareness; (vi) capacity building and administrative and office expenses (A&OE).

The estimated cost of implementation of SBM (Urban) based on unit and per capita costs for its various components is ₹ 62,009 Crore. The Government of India share as per approved funding pattern amounts to ₹ 14,623 Crore. In addition, a minimum additional amount equivalent to 25% of GoI funding, amounting to ₹ 4,874 Crore would be contributed by the States as State/ULB share. The balance funds are proposed to be generated through various other sources of fund which are, but not limited to: (a) private sector participation; (b) additional resources from state government/ULB; (c) beneficiary share; (d) user charges; (e) land leveraging; (f) innovative revenue streams; (g) Swachh Bharat Kosh; (h) corporate social responsibility; (i) market borrowing and (j) external assistance.

Importantly, as opposed to the centralised "one-size-fits-all" approach of JNNURM, the recent policies provide, at least in paper, some degree of flexibility in the formulation, approval and implementation of projects at the state and local level (Sadoway *et al.*, 2018). As mentioned earlier, the AMRUT statement delineates specific criteria for selection of cities, reform conditionalities and financial provisions. The SLIPs, containing the details of all such criteria, are evaluated and approved by the states and then combined into State Annual Action Plan for approval by the MoUD. Similar, city specific plans under the SCM have greater scopes for variations in program design and implementation. Nonetheless, the operationalisation of these schemes portrays worrisome picture. For example, the provision of 'end to end support' by the Project Development and Management Consultants (PDMCs) for planning, design, management and monitoring of urban projects will likely to lead to the splintering of resources away from the purview of democratic accountability (Sadoway *et al.*, 2018).

4. Challenges and Prospects in Financing Cities' Amenities

To reduce the top-down implementation of policies, planners and policymakers have in recent years made a strong case for para-statal agencies and local governments to depend increasingly on their internal resources and institutional finance with the objective of 'bringing in efficiency and accountability in their functioning' (Kundu *et al.*, 1999; Kundu, 2006). However, decentralising the functions has its own set of challenges. For instance, the available financial resources and powers is not sufficient for augmenting resources of the local bodies, which must be backed by actual devolution of powers and responsibilities and their use by the local bodies, like the mobilisation of tax and non-tax resources. The management capacities of these bodies need to be strengthened by giving more technical personnel, training the existing staff and capacity building (Kundu *et al.*, 1999). In case of JNNURM, most of the ULBs, owing to their limited internal resource mobilisation capacities, failed to raise matching requisite financial contribution parallel to the Central Government grant that resulted in the discontinuation of flow of the central funds to them (Chattopadhyay & Tiwari, 2013). Even the funds under JNNURM to cities and towns for infrastructural development and housing for the poor were seen to be concentrated in comparatively financially stronger states and their larger cities (Chattopadhyay & Tiwari, 2013).

It is evident that the financial requirements for managing urban amenities and infrastructure in India on the scale needed were not able to be supported through current methods and institutional capacities. ULBs in India have continued to suffer from dwindling finances, which has been a matter of concern over the years, especially for the smaller cities. Total revenue of the city governments in India, on an average, accounts for only 1 percent of the country's GDP and these figures are substantially low compared to the estimated municipal revenue-GDP ratios of 8.6 percent for Canada and 8.1 percent for Germany (ICRIER, 2019). More alarmingly, the city governments' ability to raise their own sources of revenue has shown signs of worsening in recent years and that too with considerable inter-state and inter-category variations. In 2017-18, own revenue stood at 0.43 percent of GDP, the lowest in the last eight years (ICRIER, 2019). The smaller municipalities have performed far worse than Municipal Corporations in this respect. State governments in India have left the ULBs with limited taxing instruments and autonomy and ULBs, owing to their capacity constraint, have even failed to properly utilise the taxes at their disposal. Property tax is the mainstay of own revenue of the ULBs. The importance of PT in India has become all the more important especially after demonetisation, and implementation of Goods and Services Tax (GST). However, the revenue collections from PT are significantly low. At present, revenues from PT roughly constitute 0.15% of the gross domestic product (GDP) in India, which is far below the level of 1 percent estimated for recurrent taxes on immovable property in OECD countries (OECD Revenue Statistics 2018) and 3 to 4% contribution to GDP in case of the developed countries, like Canada and US. In 2017-18, property tax contributed about 60 percent to municipal tax revenue in India and among the different categories of city governments, municipal corporations of Gujarat, Maharashtra and Karnataka together accounted for 60 percent of the all India property tax revenue in 2017-18 (ICRIER, 2019). Even a modest increase in revenue from PT systems can help ULBs expand their municipal taxes to a large extent, which could enhance their developmental activities. Property tax is poorly administered in Indian cities, and its potential has not been harnessed. Poor assessment of properties, inefficient collection, and widespread exemptions have undermined the revenue potential of property tax (Chattopadhyay and Kumar, 2019). User charges are rarely levied to cover the cost of urban services. State governments, out of their fear of losing political power, have found to be, by and large, reluctant to increase both municipal taxing power as well as amount of shared taxes. Ad-hoc transfers from the Finance Commission have failed to address the expenditure needs of the ULBs. The situation is equally unsatisfactory on the expenditure side. The average municipal expenditure as a percentage of GDP stands at 0.82 percent and cities are spending way below the expenditure norms (ICRIER, 2019). More alarmingly, cities tend to spend more on per capita basis on general administration and salaries and wages. As a result, little funds are left for development purposes and this limits the city governments' capacity of providing basic urban services. Essentially, the cities often get entangled in a vicious circle where paucity of resources causes poor service delivery, leading to poor revenue generation. In essence, financing urban infrastructure and services is considered to be the most daunting challenge in the future (Chattopadhyay, 2015).

The problem of municipal revenue deficit can be addressed through the following steps: (a) increasing revenue from existing local taxes, and (b) strengthening the revenue-raising power of the city-level municipal governments or urban local bodies (ULBs) by broadening the sources of revenue base (Chattopadhyay and Kumar, 2019). The HPEC (2011) proposed a framework for financing the large amounts of urban expenditure with three major elements:

(i) Securing the revenue base of ULBs through 'exclusive taxes' and a guaranteed and predictable share of ULBs in tax revenue of state governments;
(ii) A significantly larger scale of financing from the Government of India; and
(iii) Reforms in governance and financing at ULB level to begin a move away from a weak financial base towards a framework which enhances the creditworthiness of the ULBs and improves their ability to generate and leverage revenue surpluses for accessing market funds.

It is clear that the budgeted funds alone would not be sufficient to entirely finance the development of infrastructure in Indian cities. Indeed, other modes of financing such as PPPs, infrastructure bonds and municipal bonds, and land monetisation need to be explored to generate funds for these cities and to diversify risks. Unlike the important role played by municipal bonds in United States and many developing countries (e.g. Russia, Mexico) in financing urban infrastructure, India has experienced very modest utilisation with virtual stagnation of municipal bond market. In the last twenty years, municipal bonds along with pooled financing issues mobilised roughly US $ 386 million (Srikumar, 2018). The availability of grant under the JNNURM for project financing could have contributed to the reluctance of the municipal governments in accessing the debt market. Such limited access could also be attributed to the supply side factors – weak financial health of the ULBs, lack of transparency in budgeting and accounting system of the ULBs and absence of specific statute addressing insolvency of ULBs. Moreover, the absence of any secondary market, interest rate limitation of 8 percent and unfavourable rules regarding income tax on interest earned by the bondholders[15] make municipal bond unattractive to the potential investors. In July 2015, SEBI notified a new regulatory framework to streamline the issuing of municipal bond in India and the provisions included investment grade rating for the ULBs, no default in the last 365 days, a mandated guarantee from the central or state government and maintenance of municipal accounts as per the National Municipal Accounts Manual. The credit rating has been completed for 463 cities out of 500 AMRUT cities and only 161 cities obtained investment grade rating (BBB – and above) with A – and above ratings for only 35 cities (MoHUA, 2018). The irony is that only financially stronger cities would find investors[16] as the major investors like pension funds, insurance funds are risk averse and prefer to invest in bonds with rating above AA. Moreover, even with investment grade rating, ULBs find it difficult to access bond market as their financial dependence on the state governments and thereby the financial health of the state government also influences the investors' decision.

Under the ongoing programmes of urban development in India, the public-private partnerships emerge as one of the major sources of fund. As per the CPR Smart City Database (2018), PPPs contributed approximately 25 percent of the total fund requirement. A detail analysis of 20 also indicated similar contribution of PPP in smart city capital expenditure, *albeit* with wide city-wise variations (Sarkar *et al.*, 2016). Only in case of Bhubaneshwar, Ahmedabad, Indore and Bhopal, PPPs contributed more than two-fifths of capital expenditure. Large scale PPPs have by and large been limited to projects involving construction of urban commercial infrastructure in India with the Government contribution primarily being in the form of land[17]. Urban social infrastructure (e.g., water supply, sanitation, solid waste management) generally receives lukewarm response from the private sectors primarily due to their inability to levy user charges reflecting the cost of service delivery. Moreover, lack of enabling PPP legislation, multiplicity of agencies, lack of ability to select and structure a PPP project, lack of political will towards project implementation and lack of citizen participation further complicate the entire process of project plan and implementation.

ULBs in India are also expected to utilise land as financial instrument to augment their resources[18]. Land pooling and readjustments provides another innovative technique of financing land and infrastructure, especially in the smaller towns (Sahasranaman, 2012). Under this method, smaller tracts of land can be pooled where ULBs can provide infrastructural facilities by using their own resources or borrowed fund. This would improve the value of the pooled land, a part of which can be used for public sale and the rest can be returned to the original landowners. However, lack of proper documentation of land holdings and institutional fragmentation characterizing the land use planning seriously undermine the Indian cities' potential to use land for augmenting their resources[19].

It is to be noted that ULBs in India urgently need an integrated policy and regulatory environment, in which they are able to enhance their capacities to generate resources from existing sources at their disposal and also can make better utilisation of innovative sources of infrastructure financing. The reform should start with functional and financial empowerment of the ULBs. Devolution of revenue raising power of the ULBs through taxation should be accompanied by the authority to set the tax rate and determine the tax base. For property tax, improvement in valuation techniques and efficient tax collection and management are essential. All measurable services for which consumers can be identified should be charged on the basis of costs. In order to insulate the urban poor, an independent regulatory mechanism could be useful for accurately assessing and monitoring of cost of service delivery and most importantly, adopting a cross subsidy model for levy of differential user charges across different user groups / segments to enable recovery of cost of service delivery at an overall level. The recommendations of the SFCs should be implemented by state governments to improve the financial health of municipal bodies. A proper accounting system via switch over to accrual-based accounting system should be made mandatory for all the municipalities. Adoption of a standardised budgeting framework, common accounting framework as per the National Municipal Accounts Manual and regular audit of financial data would infuse the much-needed accountability and transparency in the municipal financial management.

Because of the interconnectedness between financial health of municipalities and the aspects of municipal management as a whole in reshaping each other, a narrow focus on the financial management alone could result in an inadequate and lopsided view of the issues at hand (HPEC, 2011; Asher & Sheikh, 2014; Chattopadhyay, 2015). There are grave staff shortages, especially at the lower and medium levels at ULBs and the problem is compounded due to their shortage of skills. Competencies have to be developed and augmented particularly in relation to financing, especially with regard to PPPs, project management, and contracting out of services (Asher and Sheikh, 2014).

Active citizen participation in the monitoring and evaluation of municipal functions and expenditures would also be useful to establish financial and social accountability and operational transparency of the municipalities (Chattopadhyay, 2015). Most importantly, these public financial and administrative reforms would need to be initiated and sustained over a longer period of time and scope of experimentation with administrative and governance structures of the cities under programmes like SCM, AMRUT and so on should be exploited to enhance performance orientation and accountability at the city level.

In essence, there is a clear need of carrying out effective and stringent legal and administrative reforms and of enforcement of second-generation reforms on priority basis by states and ULBs. In order to deliver affordable, adequate and efficient housing amenities and municipal services, the ULBs need to work in an expansion or exponential mode, with continuous capacity building and revitalisation of administrative and financial energy, which will require roping in of specialised institutions and para-statal agencies. These institutions need to be more people friendly and should make optimum utilisation of local resources, and choose appropriate actions learning from past experiences across urban spaces, for arriving at apt decisions. Also, constant scrutiny of the existing programmes and policies, along with continuous technology up-gradation and R&D, will be also required for the development efforts to be sustainably effective (Kumar, 2015b).

5. Emerging Issues and Concluding Observations

'Basic Amenities for All' has been a dream long envisioned and worked upon, but 'All' appears to be a misnomer as there are still a large proportion of urban households that have been unable to secure adequate and affordable housing and the essential basic amenities, especially the households located in slums, small-size class of towns/cities and backward states, and those belonging to the lower strata of consumption expenditure (poor), wage labourers and marginalised sections of the society. This has rendered the SDGs unfulfilled and thus requires immediate policy action. The policies reviewed in this paper draw attention to some important governance issues influencing the implementation of urban reforms in India. Most of the ongoing urban policies and programmes, despite having scope for directly connecting with the urban citizen, followed a typical top down approach. The SCM has facilitated increasing dominance of private actors and their interests in formulation and implementation of urban plans, resulting in the weakening position of the democratically elected leaders of the city. The incorporation of voices of the marginalised and their needs and priorities in urban plans is central to achieving inclusive and sustainable cities. However, the participatory avenues have been found to be restricted to the upper- and middle-class people whose visions largely reflect that of the consultant driven city administration. All these have led to adoption of plan aiming at redevelopment of a certain pockets of existing cities, retrofit them with smart tools and provision of improved basic infrastructure provision and thus, ultimately would create 'smart' and 'not so smart' pockets within a city.

Development of smart, inclusive and sustainable cities and steps towards the achievement of SDGs require smart and empowered ULBs and para-statal institutions. Even after 25 years of the 74th CAA, functional and financial empowerment of the ULBs can at best be described as partial. They are devoid of any real decision-making power and perform only as implementing agencies of the central and state urban plan and policies. Capacity constraint at the local level might justify the involvement of the SPVs or development authorities on urban issues, but that should be in consonance and not exclusion of the elected representatives of the ULBs. This would then correct the under representation of the heterogeneous population in urban areas and ensure prioritisation of equitable and affordable distribution of basic urban services. Moreover, coordination with all the stakeholders, involved in the delivery of urban services, to efficiently monitor the households' demand and requirements along with the supply-side leakages would pace up the delivery of such services in timely manner keeping in view their quality, sources, seasonal planning, resources utilisation, environment and sustainability (Kumar, 2015b; Maringanti & Mukhopadhyay, 2015).

ULBs in India urgently need an integrated policy and regulatory environment, in which they can enhance their capacities to generate resources from existing sources at their disposal and also can make better utilisation of innovative sources of infrastructure financing. Possible reform actions to improve municipal finance are true local financial autonomy, sustainable finances supported by user charges, property tax reforms, restructuring of intergovernmental grants to incentivise reform with greater assistances for smaller cities, encouraging PPPs, deepening of the municipal bond market, local capacity building and strengthening regulatory framework of service delivery. Systemic and reliable real time information and data (e.g., service availability at each household level) has to be used for monitoring and evaluation and also for spatial and micro resource planning. As institutional reforms take shape to usher in better governance standards and as innovations yield efficiencies in service delivery, the creditworthiness of the ULBs and their ability to generate and leverage revenue surpluses for accessing market funds would improve and also the cost of service provision may come down. If the goal of spending less, spending well, and spending wisely is to be achieved by these ULBs, public financial and administrative reforms will need to be initiated and sustained over a longer period of time (Asher and Sheikh, 2014).

In essence, the universalisation of amenities and services in our cities is important with a special focus on redeveloping slums and squatter and informal settlements. The incremental service level benchmarks are another challenge along with the local resource utilisation. The use of technology will bring efficiency in service delivery and resources planning, but at the same time focus should be there to ensure that it is leading to equity especially in terms of essential amenities and services (also inter and intra city disparities), and non-exclusionary character of the cities. The paradigm shift in urban development necessitates specialised urban institutions for implementation, inclusivity and sustainability, with continual vigour, to address the needs of the people in our cities. Smart and empowered ULBs and para-statal institutions will cater to our current needs and challenges and also help to meet our future requirements and planning judiciously.

References

Ahluwalia, I G (2017). Urban Governance in India", *Journal of Urban Affairs*, DOI: 10.1080/07352166.2016.1271614

Asher, M. & S. Sheikh (2014). Financing Smart Cities: Key Requirements. *Pragati*, September 16, 2014 (http://pragati.nationalinterest.in/2014/09/financing-smart-cities-key-requirements/).

Avashia, V K and A Garg (2016). Urban Infrastructure and Governance Mission under JNNURM have the Reforms Delivered, Economic and Political Weekly, Vol. LI, No. 2: 41 -57.

Benjamin, S (2008). Occupancu Urbanism: Radicalizing Politics and Economy Beyond Policy and Programs, *International Journal of Urban and Regional Research*, 32 (3): 719-729.

Bhan, G and A Jana (2015). Reading Spatial Inequality in Urban India", *Economic & Political Weekly,* Vol. 1, No. 22, 49-54.

Chattopadhyay, Soumyadip and Arjun Kumar (2019). "Tapping the Revenue Potential of Property Tax in India", https://www.ideasforindia.in/topics/macroeconomics/tapping-the-revenue-potential-of-property-tax-in-india.html

Chattopadhyay, S and M Das (2018). Urban Service Delivery in West Bengal: Current Scenario and New Challenges", *Journal of Infrastructure Development*, 10 (1-2): 18-36.

Chattopadhyay, S. & D.M. Tiwari (2013). Reform Initiatives in Financing India's Urban Infrastruc-ture: The Case of JNNURM. *Urban India*, 33(2): 1–16.

Chattopadhyay, S (2017). Neoliberal Urban Transformation in Indian Cities: Paradoxes and Predicaments, *Progress in Development Studies*,17 (4): 307-321.

Chattopadhyay, S. (2015). Financing India's Urban Infrastructure: Current Practices and Reform Options. *Journal of Infrastructure Development*, 7(1): 55–75.

Das, D (2019). In Pursuit of being Smart? A Critical Analysis of India's Smart Cities Endeavour, *Urban Geography*, DOI: 10.1080/02723638.2019.1646049.

Deka, K (2019). Why the Smart Cities Mission Will Miss its Deadline, https://www.indiatoday.in/india-today-insight/story/why-the-smart-cities-mission-will-miss-its-deadline-1574728-2019-07-29.

Ghosh, P and S. Arora (2019). Smart as Democratically Transformative? An Analysis of 'Smart City' Sociotechnical Imaginary in India, *STEPS Working Paper 109*, Brighton: STEPS Centre.

Government of India (2008). *Handbook of Service Level Benchmarking*. New Delhi: Government of India, Ministry of Urban Development, 2008.

Government of India (2012). *Report of the Sub-Committee on Financing Urban Infrastructure in the 12th Plan*. New Delhi: Government of India, Ministry of Urban Development, March, 2012.

Government of India (2015a). *Operational Guidelines for HRIDAY: Heritage City Development & Augmentation Yojana*. New Delhi: Government of India, Ministry of Urban Development, January, 2015.

Government of India (2015b). *Atal Mission for Rejuvenation and Urban Transformation (AMRUT): Mission Statement & Guidelines*. New Delhi: Government of India, Ministry of Urban Development, June, 2015.

Government of India (2015c). *Smart Cities: Mission Statement & Guidelines*. New Delhi. Government of India, Ministry of Urban Development, June, 2015.

HPEC (2011). *Report on Indian Urban Infrastructure and Services*. New Delhi: Ministry of Urban Development, The High Powered Expert Committee (HPEC) for Estimating the Investment Requirements for Urban Infrastructure Services.

Indian Council for Research on International Economic Relations (2019). 'State of Municipal Finance in India', *Report prepared for the Fifteenth Finance Commission*, New Delhi.

Jha, S., V Rao and M Woolcock (2007). Governance in the Gullies: Democratic Responsiveness and Leadership in Delhi Slums, *World Development*, 35 (2): 230-246.

Kumar, A. (2013). Access to Basic Amenities in Urban India—An Analysis across Size Class of Towns/Cities. *Urban India*, 33(2): 127–140.

Kumar, A. (2015a). Housing Shortages in Urban India and Socio-Economic Facets. *Journal of Infrastructure Development*, 7(1): 19-34.

Kumar, A. (2015b). Housing Amenities in Urban India- Issues and Challenges. *Shelter*, 16(1): 7-14, Housing and Urban Development Corporation Limited (HUDCO) Human Settlement Management Institute (HSMI).

Kundu, A. (2006). *Trends and Patterns of Urbanisation and their Economic Implication* (India Infrastructure Report on Urban Infrastructure, 2006 by Infrastructure Development Finance Company). New Delhi: Oxford University Press.

Kundu, A. (2011). Politics and Economics of Urban Growth. *Economic & Political Weekly*, 46(20): 10–12.

Kundu, A. (2014). Exclusionary Growth, Poverty and India's Emerging Urban Structure. *Social Change*, 44(4): 541–566.

Kundu, A., S. Bagchi & D. Kundu (1999). Regional Distribution of Infrastructure and Basic Amenities in Urban India: Issues Concerning Empowerment of Local Bodies. *Economic & Political Weekly*, 34(28): 1893–1906.

Kundu, D. (2014). Urban Development Programmes in India: A Critique of the JNNURM, *Social Change*, 44(4): 615–632.

Kundu, D and A Banerjee (2018), Migration, Caste and Marginalised Sections Inequality in the Coverage of Basic Services in Urban India, *Economic and Political Weekly*, Vol. LIII, No. 2, January 13: 62-70.

Mitra, A and J P Nagar (2018). City Size, Deprivation and Other Indicators of Development: Evidence from India", *World Development*, 106, 273-283.

Maringanti, A. & P. Mukhopadhyay (2015). Data, Urbanisation and the City. *Economic & Political Weekly*, 50(22): 39–41.

Mathur, M. P. et al (2007). *Norms and Standards of Municipal Basic Services in India*. NIUA WP 07- 01, National Institute of Urban Affairs.

McKinsey Global Institute (2010). *India's Urban Awakening: Building Inclusive Cities, Sustaining Economic Growth*. New York: McKinsey and Company.

PRAJA (2020). National Consultation on Urban Governance Key Findings from 21 states, www.praja.org.

Rao, G and R Bird (2014). Governance and Fiscal Federalism" in Ahluwalia I J, R Kanburand P K Mohanty (eds.) *Urbanisation in India challenges, opportunities and the way forward*, Sage Publication, New Delhi, 203-229.

Sarkar, S, S Maitra and A Kumar (2016). Preparing Smart City Development Plan Based on Demographic and Socio Economic Analysis, *Institute for Human Development*, New Delhi, December.

Saroj, S K, S Goli, M Rana and B K Choudhury (In Press). Availability, Accessibility and Inequalities of Water, Sanitation and Hygiene (WASH) Services in Indian Metro Cities, *Sustainable Cities and Society.*

Sadoway, D, G Gopakumar, V Baindur and M G Badami (2018). JNNURM as a Window on Urban Governance Its Institutional Footprint, Antecedents and Legacy, *Economic and Political Weekly*, Vol. LIII, No. 2: 71-81.

Sridhar, K S and A Venugopalareddy (2010). *State of Urban Basic Services in India's Cities Spending and Financing*, Oxford University Press, New Delhi.

Taraporevala, P (2018). *Demystifying the Indian Smart City an Empirical Reading of the Smart City Mission*, Working Paper, Centre for Policy Research, New Delhi.

World Bank Group (2015). *Leveraging Urbanisation in South Asia: Managing Spatial Transformation for Prosperity and Livability* (South Asia Development Matters). Washington DC: The World Bank.

Notes

1. Goal 11 of the SDGs calls for ensuring access to adequate, safe and affordable housing and basic services for all and for upgrading the slums by 2030 (Available at: (https://sustainabledevelopment.un.org/)
2. As per 2011 Census, 31 percent of India's population live in the urban areas and by 2030 it is estimated that more than 40 percent of the Indian population will be living in cities.
3. Available at: *http://smartcities.gov.in/*
4. Retrofitting introduces planning in an existing built-up area to achieve smart city objectives, along with other objectives, to make the existing area more efficient and liveable. In retrofitting, an area consisting of more than 500 acres is identified by the city in consultation with citizens. Depending on the existing level of infrastructure services in the identified areas and the vision of the residents, the cities prepare a strategy to become smart. Since existing structures are largely to remain intact in this model, it is expected that more intensive infrastructure service levels and a large number of smart applications are packed into the retrofitted smart city. This strategy may also be completed in a shorter time frame, leading to its replication in another part of the city.
5. Redevelopment entails a replacement of the existing built-up environment and enable co-creation of a new layout with enhanced infrastructure using mixed land use and increased density. Redevelopment envisages an area of more than 50 acres, identified by Urban Local Bodies (ULBs) in consultation with citizens. For instance, a new layout plan of the identified area will be prepared with mixed land-use, higher FSI and high ground coverage. Two examples of the redevelopment model are the Saifee Burhani Upliftment Project in Mumbai (also called the Bhendi Bazaar Project) and the redevelopment of East Kidwai Nagar in New Delhi being undertaken by the National Building Construction Corporation.
6. Greenfield development introduces most of the Smart Solutions in a previously vacant area (more than 250 acres) using innovative planning, plan financing and plan implementation tools (e.g. land pooling/ land reconstitution) with provision for affordable housing, especially for the poor. Greenfield developments are required around cities in order to address the needs of the expanding population. One well known example is the GIFT City in Gujarat. Unlike retrofitting and redevelopment, greenfield developments could be located either within the limits of the ULB or within the limits of the local Urban Development Authority (UDA).
7. Pan-city development envisages application of selected Smart Solutions to the existing city-wide infrastructure. Application of Smart Solutions involve the

use of technology, information and data to make infrastructure and services better. For example, applying smart solutions in the transport sector (intelligent traffic management system) and reducing average commute time or cost of citizens will have positive effects on productivity and quality of life of citizens. Another example can be waste water recycling and smart metering which can make a huge contribution to better water management in the city.

8. For example, under urban transportation, nearly 40% of projects are focused on roads and parking lots, while only 20% of the budget is focused on public transportation and only 2% of the entire transportation budget is focused on buses (Taraporevala, 2018).
9. Available at: *http://amrut.gov.in/*
10. Five hundred cities are covered under the ambit of AMRUT under the following categories: (i) All Cities and Towns with a population of over one lakh with notified Municipalities, including Cantonment Boards (Civilian areas); (ii) All Capital Cities/Towns of States/ UTs, not covered in above; (iii) All Cities/ Towns classified as Heritage Cities by MoUD under the HRIDAY Scheme; (iv) Thirteen Cities and Towns on the stem of the main rivers with a population above 75,000 and less than 1 lakh; and (v) Ten Cities from hill states, islands and tourist destinations (not more than one from each State).
11. Available at: *http://hridayindia.in/*
12. 12 HRIDAY Cities- Ajmer (Rajasthan), Amaravati (Andhra Pradesh), Amritsar (Punjab), Badami (Karnataka), Dwaraka (Gujarat), Gaya (Bihar), Kanchipuram (Tamil Nadu), Mathura (Uttar Pradesh), Puri (Odisha), Varanasi (Uttar Pradesh), Velankanni (Tamil Nadu) and Warangal (Telangana).
13. Available at: *http://mhupa.gov.in/*
14. Available at: *http://swachhbharaturban.gov.in/*
15. The Finance Ministry declined to give tax free status to municipal bond, but the MoUD declared the provision of interest subsidy to cities issuing bonds.
16. Pune and Hyderabad raised INR 200 crores each, Bhopal raised INR 175 crores, Indore raised 140 crores and Amaravati raised INR 2000 crores through municipal bonds (MoHUA, 2018).
17. In three out of these four cities where PPP contributed major part of the CAPEX, the city plan incorporated monetisation of available pubic land in the chosen area for area development project (Sarkar *et al.*, 2016).
18. In three smart cities, Bhubaneshwar, Indore and Bhopal, the city plan incorporated monetisation of available pubic land in the chosen area for area development project (Sarkar *et al.*, 2016).
19. Municipal Corporation of Greater Mumbai lacks substantive power to lease land independently for raising revenue and this seriously limits the MCGM's capacity to undertake and finance city development.

13

Education Production Function: Does Health Matter?

Muktar Bala

Abstract

Most of the literatures estimating education production function focus on school, child, parents and peer influences. However, studies in clinical sciences suggest the possibility of a link between health and children's cognition. This study estimates the effects of children's physical and mental health on their academic performance. The study applies quantile regression to discern whether the health of the children may have differential impacts at different points on the children's performance distribution. A sample of 1,140 children was collected from rural areas of Niger State, Nigeria, a state located in the northern part of the country where evidence has shown that more than half of the children suffer from poor health. The results show that the children's physical and mental health affects their academic performance, but the effect is specific to the children at the lower and upper tails of the performance distribution. Other covariates that were found to impact the children's academic performance include parental involvement, school type and birth order, but the effect of birth order is specific to the children at the lower and upper quantile. Policies that would enhance the physical and mental health of the children are therefore suggested, particularly those that would target children who are at the lower and upper quantiles.

Key Words: *Physical Health, Mental Health, Academic Performance, Quantile Regression.*

Introduction

The link between health and cognition has long been established in the literature. Children that enjoy having some of the proximate determinants of health, such as having proper food intake often perform better on academic scale (Florence *et al.*, 2008; King *et al.*, 2005; Pollitt, 1993; Zaini *et al.*, 2005). It is also documented that children's health is associated with their level of concentration in class. Children that suffer from poor mental health are often preoccupied with irrelevant thoughts, which might divert their attention from class lessons and thus affecting their cognitive performance (Nolen-Hoeksema, 2000).

The recent demographic and health survey (DHS) shows that children suffer from poor health in Nigeria, but the situation defers between the northern and the southern part of the country. The DHS shows that 33.3% of the children in northern Nigeria are undernourished as compared to only 8% of similar children in the south (NPC & ICF, 2019). Similarly, empirical evidence has shown that over 37% of public school children in Northern Nigeria suffer from poor mental health as compared to 23.1% of similar children in the Southern (Abubakar-Abdullateef *et al.*, 2017; Akpan *et al.*, 2010). It therefore implies that child health problem is more prevalent in Northern than in Southern Nigeria.

One of the objectives of sustainable development goals (SDG) is to ensure quality education. Quality education entails acquiring skills and having cognitive abilities such as being proficient in mathematics and reading. Quality education is beneficial because it promotes socioeconomic mobility, escape from poverty, tolerance, living healthy and reducing inequality. It is reported that more than 55% of the global children and adolescence lack proficiency in mathematics and reading, and the condition is worst in sub-Saharan Africa and Asia (Abdin, 2018). Therefore, if health might affect cognition, understanding the association between health and cognitive performance may help in achieving the goals of SDG, particularly in sub-Saharan African countries like Nigeria (Abdin, 2018).

However, most of the previous studies that investigated the determinants of children's cognitive performance often overlooked the role of children's health (Animasaun & Abegunrin, 2017; Badasyan & Silva, 2018; Briggs & Ololube, 2015; Folorunso *et al.*, 2010; Li *et al.*, 2017; Mujumdar *et al.*, 2016). This study extends the current literature by considering health among the factors that might affect the academic performance of children. The study also uses quantile regression to determine whether health might have differential impact at different points on the children's performance distribution.

Health and academic Performance

Education, specifically cognitive skill, is the backbone of economic growth. However, in most developing countries, health, particularly child's health is an issue. Therefore, understanding the relationship between health and cognition may help government in making developmental policies. Studies that investigate the children's cognitive performance often focus on non-health variables (Animasaun & Abegunrin, 2017; Badasyan & Silva, 2018; Briggs & Ololube, 2015; Folorunso *et al.*, 2010; Li *et al.*, 2017; Mujumdar *et al.*, 2016). The studies that investigated the association between health and cognition often focused on the impacts of some aspects of health, such as food intake (Chenoweth, 2007; Florence *et al.*, 2008; Lieberman, 2003; Zaini *et al.*, 2005) or physical health indicators, such as the Anthropometric health indicators (Hall *et al.*, 2001; Mukudi, 2003). Although Anthropometric health indicators capture both children's health and nutrition, which might make them show better relationship between health and cognition than the studies that only measure the impacts of nutrition (Webb & Bhatia, 2005), most of the previous Anthropometric-cognition studies were based on average effects. Average effects may be biased if the children's health has differential effect on their academic performance distribution (Betts & Grogger, 2003). Moreover, studies that investigated the impact of physical and mental health on children's academic performance in one model are scarce. Most of the studies that determined mental health in relation to cognition often investigated the cognitive performance of children with poor mental health such as anxiety and depression, without including other covariates that are known to impacts children's academic performance (Khursid *et al.*, 2015). This study estimates education production function and adds physical and mental health among the variables that may affect the children's cognitive performance. The study also uses quantile regression to find out whether the physical and mental health of the children may have different effects at different points in the children's performance distribution.

Research Objective

This study seeks to investigate the effects of physical and mental health on the academic performance of children in Niger State, Nigeria by using education production function as the underpinning theory.

Methodology

Theoretical Framework: Education Production Function

The education production function of Hanushek (1971) opines that academic performance of child *i* is a function of the child's innate ability (Ia_i, parents' influence (PIn_i), school inputs (SI_i) and peer influence (PI_i). The original function is given in Equation (1):

$$A_i = f(Ia_i, PIn_i, SI_i, PI_i) \qquad ...(1)$$

However, Arshad (2012) asserts that separating peer influence and other effects, such as school and parents' effects is econometrically difficult, because a child may influence or be influenced by his/her peers. Therefore, variable on peers' effect was removed and replaced with birth order (BO_i) of child *i*. Birth order may affect children's academic performance in the sense that older children derive more benefit from the family's academic and financial resources because they lived in a smaller family size and lived longer time with parents than later-born children (Monfardini *et al.*, 2016). Also, previous test score (Pts_i) was used as a proxy for innate ability, as it removes the need for data on innate ability (Arshad, 2012). On school inputs, Ashley *et al.* (2014) reviewed an extensive literature covering developing countries and found that in developing countries, school input is determined by the ownership structure of the schools, with private school children out-performing those in the public schools. Therefore, school influence was replaced with school type (St_i) of child in this study. The health variables that were added include the physical health (Ph_i) and the mental health (Mh_i), while age (age_i) and gender ($gder_i$) were added as controls. The academic performance of child *i* is thus presented in the modified function that is shown in Equation (2):

$$A_i = f(Pts_i, PIn_i, St_i, Ph_i, Mh_i, BO_i, age_i, gder_i) \qquad \ldots(2)$$

Method of Analysis

To estimate the effects of the regressors of the model in Equation (2) on their regressand, the econometric model shown in Equation (3) was first estimated:

$$A_i = \beta_0 + \beta_1 Pts_i + \beta_2 PIn_i + \beta_3 St_i + \beta_4 Ph_i + \beta_5 Mh_i + \beta_6 BO_i + \beta_7 age_i + \beta_8 gder_i + \mu_i \quad \ldots(3)$$

where the βs are the coefficients of the explanatory variables and μ is the error term. The Ordinary Least Square (OLS) provides the best linear unbiased estimates (BLUE) of the parameters of the model in Equation (3) when the assumptions of linearity, homoscedasticity and independence of X values are met. On the other hand, quantile regression can be an alternative when some of the assumptions of OLS are not met (Koenker & Bassett, 1978). The coefficients of the explanatory variables are estimated at certain points in the distribution of the dependent variable in quantile regression. Equation (3) was first estimated using OLS and when the OLS assumptions were confirmed violated, quantile regression was later used. Three quantiles (0.39th, 0.50th and 0.75th) were used for the estimation.

The empirical model of the quantile regression is shown in Equation (4).

$$A_{i\tau} = \beta^{\tau}_0 + \beta^{\tau}_1 Pts_i + \beta^{\tau}_2 PIn_i + \beta^{\tau}_3 St_i + \beta^{\tau}_4 Ph_i + \beta^{\tau}_5 Mh_{i,} + \beta^{\tau}_6 BO_i + \beta^{\tau}_7 age_i + \beta^{\tau}_8 gder_i + \mu^{\tau}_i \quad ...(4)$$

The symbol, τ, is the quantile at which the parameters of the model were estimated. Equation (3) only differs from (4) by the τs, which show that the estimation of the coefficients of the model ($\beta^{\tau}{}_s$) occur at some points on the children's academic performance distribution.

Sampling Method and Data Collection Procedure

This study uses a sample of children from Niger, State, Nigeria. Niger State is located in the northern part of Nigeria where evidence has shown that there is prevalence of physical and mental health among children as compared to the southern part of the country. Niger state is classified into three senatorial zones, namely, Zone A, Zone B and Zone C. A multi-stage sampling approach was used in collecting the data for the study due to lack of sampling frame.

Three local governments were randomly selected in each zone. In each local government, six towns were also randomly selected. In each town, twenty-two households were selected randomly. The data for the study were then collected from each of the twenty-two houses in each town across the nine selected local governments in the three senatorial zones of the state. A total of 1,140 respondents were used for the analysis. Children and their parents constitute the respondents of the study. The children are those within the age brackets of 6-10 years. The age bracket of 6-10 years was chosen because academic performance data in Nigeria is available for children from primary one (six years), and the indicator of children physical health (Weight-for-age) that was used in this study is better for children that did not exceed the age of ten years.

Definition of Variables

Table 1: Definition of Variables

Variable	*Measurement*
Academic Performance	End-of-the-term Examination scores in English Language and Mathematics adjusted to 100% $(X^1/200)*100$
Parental involvement	A questionnaire[2] score $\leq 198 = 0$, while questionnaire score $>198 = 1$, denote low and high parental involvements respectively.

(*Contd...*)

Physical Health	Weight-for-age (WAZ) Z-score was used as the indicator of physical health of the children. WAZ was calculated using CDC[3] calculator. The values were classified[4] as adequate nutrition ($2 \leq$ Z-score $<$ $+2$) = 3, moderate malnutrition ($-3 \leq$ Z-score < -2) = 2 and severe malnutrition (Z-score < -3) = 1.
School Type	Private school = 1 and Public school = 0
Mental Health	Mental health was measured using SDQ[5]. An SDQ score of 17 and above was assigned 1, to denote poor mental health of the children, while 0, otherwise.
Birth order	An oldest male child was assigned the value of 1, while 0, otherwise and an oldest female child was assigned the value of 2, and 0, otherwise.
Previous test score	Child's previous term's examination scores in Maths & English
Age	Number of years since birth
Gender	Male child = 1,while female child = 0

1. X is the sum of scores in Mathematics and English Language,
2. The parental involvement questionnaire developed by Hoover-Dempsey and Sandler as revised by Walker *et al.* (2005). The parental involvement scores were dichotomized following Khajehpour and Ghazvini (2011),
3. CDC: Center for Disease Control & Prevention, a branch of the United Nations.
4. Webb and Baita (2005).
5. SDQ: Strength and Difficulties Questionnaire developed by Goodman (1997).

Results

Descriptive statistics

The descriptive investigations on the respondents (Table 1) revealed that a wide variation among the students in terms of their academic performance and previous test scores exists, with a minimum test score of around 3 marks and a maximum of around 100 marks. The age of the respondents is between 6 to 10 years.

Table 2: Characteristics of the Respondents

Variable	*Mean*	*SD*	*Min*	*Max*
Academic Performance	55.89	25.2	3	100
Previous test score	52.27	23.86	5.5	98.5
Age	7.9	1.29	6	10

Note: SD: standard deviation; Min: minimum; and Max: maximum.

Information on other variables (Table 2) shows that majority (82.81%) of the children under study received high parental involvement, and more than half of them (55.14%) attend public school. However, most of the children (86.63%) are not the eldest in their families and the population of male children (52.54) is not too different from that of the female children (47.46) in the sample.

Table 3: Characteristics of the Respondents (Dummy and Categorical Variables)

Variable	*Frequency*	*Percent*
Parental Involvement		
Low Parental Involvement	196	17.19
High Parental Involvement	944	82.81
School Type		
Private School	511	44.86
Public School	628	55.14
Birth Order		
Oldest Son	68	5.98
Oldest daughter	84	7.39
Non-Oldest Son nor Oldest daughter	985	86.63
Gender		
Male	599	52.54
Female	541	47.46

Regression result

Equation (4) was first estimated using OLS. Normality and homoscedasticity tests were conducted. Both the normality and homoscedasticity assumptions were noticed to have been violated, because the p-value of Shapiro-Wilk test and that of the White's tests were significant (Shapiro & Wilk, 1965; White, 1980). The results are shown in Table 4. The violation of the two assumptions of normality and homoscedaticity, therefore, justify the application of the quantile regression (Hao & Naiman, 2007).

Table 4: Normality and Heteroscedasticity Tests on the Residuals of the OLS Model

Tests			*p-value*
Shapiro-Wilk Test for Normality			
R			0.0000
White's Test for Heteroskedasticity	***chi²***	***df***	
Heteroskedasticity	116.33	58	0.0000
Skewness	25.25	10	0.0049
Kurtosis	8.33	1	0.0039
Total	149.91	69	0.0000

Note: Robust standard errors in parentheses *** p<0.01, ** p<0.05, and * p<0.1.

The result of the quantile regression is shown in Table 5. It shows that previous test score has positive and significant impact on the current academic performance of the children in both the OLS (β=1.035***) and across all the three quantiles in the quantile regression ($\beta_{0.39th}$ = 1.048***,

$\beta_{0.50th}$ = 1.048***, $\beta_{0.705th}$ = 1.048***). Also, children that receive high parental input perform academically better than their peers who receive low of such inputs. The estimate is positive and significant in both the OLS (β=1.841***) and across the three quantile estimates ($\beta_{0.39th}$ = .592***, $\beta_{0.50th}$ = 1.384***, $\beta_{0.705th}$ = 1.152***). Moreover, children that attend private school and are in the lower or upper quantile perform better than their peers in public schools ($\beta_{0.39th}$ = 0.431**, $\beta_{0.75th}$ = 0.501**).

On the physical health variables, children who are adequately nourished ($\beta_{0.75th}$ =1.794***) or moderately malnourished ($\beta_{0.75th}$ =1.408**) and are in the upper tail of the performance distribution perform academically better than their peers who are severely malnourished. Similarly, children who have poor mental health and are in the upper quantile perform academically lower than their peers that have good mental health ($\beta_{0.75th}$ = -0.723***). Also, oldest sons who are in the upper quantile perform academically lower than their younger counterparts ($\beta_{0.75th}$ = -0.747***), and eldest daughters who are in the lower tail of the performance distribution perform academically less than their younger ones ($\beta_{0.39th}$ = -0.611*).

Table 5: OLS and Quantile Estimates of the Determinants of Academic Performance of the LBC

	OLS	*Quantile Regression*		
	(1)	*(2)*	*(3)*	*(4)*
Variable		**0.39**	**0.5**	**0.75**
Entering Ability	1.035***	1.048***	1.048***	1.045***
	(0.00760)	(0.00530)	(0.00537)	(0.00567)
High P/Involvement	1.841***	1.592***	1.384***	1.152***
	(0.392)	(0.236)	(0.304)	(0.333)
Private School	0.375	0.431**	0.189	0.501**
	(0.240)	(0.186)	(0.194)	(0.211)
Physical Health				
M/Malnourished	0.431	-0.410	0.0513	1.794***
	(1.116)	(0.632)	(1.150)	(0.660)
A/Nourished	0.120	0.142	0.195	1.408**
	(0.888)	(0.513)	(1.147)	(0.603)
Poor Mental Health	-0.518	0.175	0.0148	-0.723***
	(0.354)	(0.224)	(0.215)	(0.217)
Birth Order				
Oldest Son	0.256	-0.263	-0.223	-0.747***
	(0.534)	(0.441)	(0.433)	(0.207)
Oldest Daughter	0.229	-0.611*	-0.101	-0.341
	(0.465)	(0.316)	(0.4780	(0.429)
Age of the Child	0.0704	0.106	0.0655	0.125
	(0.0911)	(0.0681)	(0.0711)	(0.0780)
Male Child	0.202	-0.0394	0.00926	0.116
	(0.239)	(0.1760	(0.172)	(0.232)

Note: Robust standard errors in parentheses *** p<0.01, ** p<0.05, and * p<0.1.

Discussion

The findings of this study are consistent with most of the previous study. For instance, the finding that children's previous academic performance affects their current academic scores is consistent with Khajehpour and Ghazvini (2011). Also, the result that children who receive high parental input perform better than their peers who receive less of such inputs is in line with Al-Alwan (2014), Chowa *et al.* (2013) as well as Marshall & Jackman (2015).

However, attending private school only improves the performance of children who are in the lower or upper tails of the performance distribution. This might be because private schools provide motivations in form of demotions for poor performance and prizes for good performance. The poor student might therefore be motivated to improve while the good students might strive to maintain their tempo. Similar result was found by Lamarche (2008).

The results also show that having good physical health, such being adequately nourished or moderately malnourished enhances the academic performance of children who are in the upper tail of the performance distribution. This might be because maintaining high academic performance requires lengthy period of reading, which might require being well fed and healthy. According to Benton (2010) and Mahoney *et al.* (2005), brain activity requires constant supply of energy, which might be possible only if a child is nutritionally stable. Similarly, the result on mental health shows that children with poor mental health and who are in the upper quantile of performance distribution do academically poorer than their counterparts that have good mental health. Although no clear explanation that could be ascribed to this finding, one might assume that if by coincidence the poor mental health affects the social relations of only the better performing children, then it might affect their academic performance. According to Brackett *et al.* (2011) poor mental health affects social relations and poor social relations may affect the supply of academic inputs to students. Finally, the result shows that oldest male children who are in the upper quantile of the academic performance ladder perform lower than their non-oldest counterparts and eldest female children who are in the lower tail perform less than their non-eldest peers. This might be because parents are more likely to give outside-the-home responsibilities to the more intelligent oldest male children and eldest female children are more likely to be given high responsibilities inform of domestic chores, regardless of their level of intelligence (Chang *et al.*, 2011; Guberman, 1996; Robson, 2004). Assigning responsibilities to children, when regular, might affect their home study hours and thus affecting their academic performance.

Conclusion and Recommendations

Based on the findings of this study, it could be concluded that both physical and mental health have a lot of bearing on the children's academic performance. Therefore studies that estimate children's academic performance using education production function should include health variables among the covariates. Secondly, government policies targeting child malnutrition, such as school feeding program, could enhance the academic performance of children in Niger State, especially if aimed at the high-performing malnourished children, such as those in the gifted schools. Thirdly, government policies that suggest the establishment of counseling units in schools in Niger State may improve the performance of children, particularly if targeted at the high-performing children with symptoms of poor mental health, such as those with behavioral, social and emotional issues.

References

Abdin, M. (2018). Sustainable Development Goal: Ensure inclusive and quality education for all and promote lifelong learning. https://www.un.org/sustainabledevelopment/wp-content/uploads/2017/02/4.pdf

Abubakar-Abdullateef, A., Adedokun, B., & Omigbodun, O. (2017). A comparative study of the prevalence and correlates of psychiatric disorders in Almajiris and public primary school pupils in Zaria, Northwest Nigeria. *Child and adolescent psychiatry and mental health*, *11*(1), p. 29.

Akpan, M. U., Ojinnaka, N. C., & Ekanem, E. (2010). Behavioural problems among school children in Nigeria. *South African Journal of Psychiatry*, *16*(2), pp. 50-55.

Al-Alwan, A. F. (2014). Modeling the relations among parental involvement, school engagement and academic performance of high school students. *International Education Studies*, *7*(4), 47-56.

Animasaun, I. L., & Abegunrin, O. A. (2017). Gender difference, self-efficacy, active learning strategies and academic achievement of undergraduate students in the Department of Mathematical Sciences, Federal University of Technology, Akure, Nigeria. *International Journal of Teaching and Case Studies*, *8*(4), 255-280.

Arshad, M. N. M. (2012). Estimation issues and mathematical derivation of educational production function. *International Journal of Economics, Management and Accounting*, *20*(2), pp. 149-186.

Ashley, L. D., Mcloughlin, C., Aslam, M., Engel, J., Wales, J., Rawal, S., ... & Rose, P. (2014). The role and impact of private schools in developing countries. *Education Rigorous Literature Review*.

Badasyan, N., & Silva, S. (2018). The impact of internet access at home and/or school on students' academic performance in urban areas in Brazil. *International Journal of Education Economics and Development*, *9*(2), 149-171.

Benton, D. (2010). The influence of dietary status on the cognitive performance of children. *Molecular Nutrition & Food Research*, *54*(4), 457-470.

Betts, J. R., & Grogger, J. (2003). The impact of grading standards on student achievement, educational attainment, and entry-level earnings. *Economics of Education Review*, *22*(4), 343-352.

Brackett, M. A., Rivers, S. E., & Salovey, P. (2011). Emotional intelligence: Implications for personal, social, academic, and workplace success. *Social and Personality Psychology Compass*, *5*(1), 88-103.

Briggs, T., & Ololube, N. P. (2015). Children's reading and writing success: the role of diligence and intelligence. *International Journal of Knowledge and Learning*, *10*(1), 78-93.

Chang, H., Dong, X. Y., & MacPhail, F. (2011). Labor migration and time use patterns of the left-behind children and elderly in rural China. *World Development*, *39*(12), 2199-2210.

Chenoweth, W. L. (2007). Vitamin B Complex Deficiency and Excess. In: R. M. Kliegman, H. B. Jenson, R. Behrman, B. F. Stanton (Eds) *Nelson Textbook of Pediatrics* (pp. 18-35). Philadelphia: Saunders.

Chowa, G. A., Masa, R. D., & Tucker, J. (2013). The effects of parental involvement on academic performance of Ghanaian youth: Testing measurement and relationships using structural equation modeling. *Children and Youth Services Review*, *35*(12), 2020-2030.

Florence, M. D., Asbridge, M., & Veugelers, P. J. (2008). Diet quality and academic performance. *Journal of School Health*, *78*(4), 209-215.

Folorunso, B. A., Aremo, A. G., & Abogan, P. O. (2010). Family characteristics, students' reading habits, environment and students' academic performance in Nigeria. *International Journal of Education Economics and Development*, *1*(4), 366-383.

Guberman, S. R. (1996). The development of everyday mathematics in Brazilian children with limited formal education. *Child Development*, *67*(4), 1609-1623.

Hall, A., Khanh, L. N., Son, T. H., Dung, N. Q., Lansdown, R. G., Dar, D. T., ... & Bundy, D. A. (2001). An association between chronic undernutrition and educational test scores in Vietnamese children. *European Journal of Clinical Nutrition*, *55*(9), 801-804.

Hao, L., & Naiman, D. Q. (2007). *Quantile regression: Quantitative applications in the social sciences.* No. 149, Thousand Oaks, California: Sage.

Khajehpour, M., & Ghazvini, S. D. (2011). The role of parental involvement affect in children's academic performance. *Procedia-Social and Behavioral Sciences*, *15*, 1204-1208. doi.org/10.1016/j.sbspro.2011.

Khurshid, S., Parveen, Q. M., Yousuf, M.I. & Chaudhry, A.G. (2015). Effects of depression on students' academic performance. *Science International, 27(2)*, 1619-1624.

King, G, McDougall, J., DeWit, D., Hong, S., Miller, L., Offord, D., ... & LaPorta, J. (2005). Pathways to children's academic performance and prosocial behavior: Roles of physical health status, environmental, family, and child factors. *International Journal of Disability.*

Koenker, R., & Bassett Jr, G (1978). Regression Quantiles. *Econometrica: Journal of the Econometric Society, 46*(1) 33-50.

Lamarche, C. (2008). Private school vouchers and student achievement: A fixed effects quantile regression evaluation. *Labour Economics, 15*(4), 575-590.

Li, J., Miranti, R., & Vidyattama, Y. (2017). What matters in education: a decomposition of educational outcomes with multiple measures. *Educational Research and Evaluation, 23*(1-2), pp. 3-25.

Lieberman, H. R. (2003). Nutrition, brain function and cognitive performance. *Appetite, 40*(3), 245-254.

Mahoney, C. R., Taylor, H. A., Kanarek, R. B., & Samuel, P. (2005). Effect of breakfast composition on cognitive processes in elementary school children. *Physiology & Behavior, 85*(5), 635-645.

Marshall, I. A., & Jackman, G A. (2015). Parental Involvement, Student Active Engagement and the Secondary Slump: Phenomenon-Evidence from a Three-Year Study in a Barbadian Secondary School. *International Education Studies, 8*(7), 84-96.

Monfardini, C., & See, S. G (2016). Birth order and child cognitive outcomes: an exploration of the parental time mechanism. *Education Economics, 24*(5), 481-495.

Mujumdar, S., Friesner, D., Schibik, T., & Harrington, C. (2016). Do tuition increases lower student academic performance?. *International Journal of Data Analysis Techniques and Strategies, 8*(3), 183-205.

Mukudi, E. (2003). Nutrition status, education participation, and school achievement among Kenyan middle-school children. *Nutrition, 19*(7), 612-616.

National Population Commission (NPC) [Nigeria] and ICF. 2019. Nigeria Demographic and Health Survey 2018 Key Indicators Report. Abuja, Nigeria, and Rockville, Maryland, USA: NPC and ICF.

Pollitt, E. (1993). Iron deficiency and cognitive function. *Annual Review of Nutrition, 13*(1), 521-537.

Robson, E. (2004). Children at work in rural northern Nigeria: patterns of age, space and gender. *Journal of Rural Studies, 20*(2), 193-210.

Shapiro, S. S., & Wilk, M. B. (1965). An analysis of variance test for normality (complete samples). *Biometrika, 52*(3/4), 591-611.

Webb, P., & Bhatia, R. A. (2005). *Manual: Measuring and Interpreting Malnutrition and Mortality*. Rome: Nutritioni Servce, World Food Programme.

White, H. (1980). A heteroskedasticity-consistent covariance matrix estimator and a direct test for heteroskedasticity. *Econometrica: Journal of the Econometric Society, 48*(4), 817-838.

Zaini, M. A., Lim, C. T., Low, W. Y., & Harun, F. (2005). Effects of nutritional status on academic performance of Malaysian primary school children. *Asia-Pacific Journal of Public Health, 17*(2), 81-87.

14

Gender Bias in Education Expenditure among Religious and Social Groups: A Case Study for Below Class 10 Level in West Bengal

Chayanika Mitra

Abstract

This paper attempts to capture gender bias in education expenditure among the religious (Hindu, Muslim and Others) and the social groups (SC, ST and General) in the state of West Bengal. Oaxaca-Blinder decomposition technique is used to obtain gender bias for a specific demographic group. Further, an attempt has been made to identify the religious or social groups with acute problem of gender bias. In this work, 71st round (January, 2014-June, 2014) education expenditure data (individual level) provided by NSSO (National Sample Survey Office) are used.

Key Word: *Oaxaca-Blinder Decomposition, Gender Bias, West Bengal.*

1. Introduction

There exists a vast literature with evidences of gender discrimination against female household members in intra household allocation of goods and services at regional/national level in India. In the context of 'education', a substantial number of studies on India point to the existence of gender bias(e.g. Subramanian and Deaton (1991), Drèze and Kingdon (2001), Kingdon (1998, 2002, 2005), Kambhampati and Pal (2001),Tilak (2002), Pal (2004), Kambhampati (2008), Lancaster, Maitra, and Ray (2008), Zimmerman (2012) and Azam and Kingdon(2013), to name a few).

There are official evidences as well. The Govt. of India (2013) reports very low enrolment rate in the primary and secondary education level for female students compared to male students. Subrahmanian (2005),

Bandyopadhya and Subrahmanian (2008) suggested socio-economic reasons for the existence of gender bias in education in India. The topmost reasons for dropping out are lack of interest in studies, economic condition of the parents, lack of parental motivation, cost of schooling, migration of family and demand for child labour for domestic and other purposes. After dropping out from upper primary classes, students have been found to be generally helping the parents in earning money, either by getting involved in agriculture and allied activities or directly by doing work to earn money. Girls have been found to be more victimised as households consider investment on a girl child for education an additional monetary burden over and above the dowry and expenditure on marriage. On the other hand, investment on a boy child is considered more fruitful as he would turn out to be another bread earner for the household.

The present work is in line with the work by Borooah and Iyer (2005), who examined inter social group differentials using Oaxaca-Blinder decomposition technique under the multinomial logit model for school enrolment. Here, in addition to the social groups, religious groups are also studied using latest data on education expenditure provided by NSSO.

The plan of the paper is as follows. In Section 2, the model used in this paper is described. Section 3 presents the methodology used; Section 4 provides a brief description of the data used; Section 4 discusses the regression and decomposition results. Finally, Section 5 provides the concluding remarks.

2. Model Specification: the Oaxaca-Blinder Decomposition

To find the within and between group differentials, a decomposition technique analogous to the wage differential model of Brown et al. (1980) is used.

Two separate regression equations for the lth male and the lth female individual belonging to j^{th} demographic group are given by

$$\text{Male: } \ln[Y_j^{ml}] = X_j^{ml'} \beta_j^m + \varepsilon_j^m \qquad \text{...(1)}$$

$$\text{Female: } \ln[Y_j^{fl}] = X_j^{fl'} \beta_j^f + \varepsilon_j^f . \qquad \text{...(2)}$$

Here, Y is the expenditure for educational items; m and f are indexes for male and female students, respectively.

X is the vector of explanatory variables(personal characteristics) of students which includes log of monthly per capita expenditure

(Log(MPCE)), its squared term ((Log(MPCE))[1]), household size (hhsize), age of the student (Age), age at the time of entry to school (Entry_age), a dummy d_1 which takes the value 1 if education is free and 0, otherwise; another dummy d_2 which takes the value 1 if the student has a computer and 0, otherwise, and a constant term.

In this model, parameters of equations (1) and (2) are estimated separately for men and women based on the respective sets of personal characteristics. In early models, discrimination was measured as the difference between the intercepts in the two regressions. However, Blinder (1973) and others argued that the slope coefficients also contain information about discrimination. Oaxaca-Blinder decomposition enables to isolate the contributions of the explained factors (the difference between average of measured characteristics of explanatory variables of males and females) and that of unexplained factors (the differences in the estimated values of the regression coefficients between males and females). In this model, we have three religious groups (Hindu, Muslim and Others) and three social groups (SC, ST and General). In order to get overall mean of log of education expenditure for male and female students, the concept of composite mean is used.

Overall mean of log of education expenditure for male students = $\overline{lnY^m} = \sum_{j=H,M,O} \theta_j^m \overline{lnY_j^m}$

Overall mean of log of education expenditure for female students = $\overline{lnY^f} = \sum_{j=H,M,O} \theta_j^f \overline{lnY_j^f}$

Here, θ_j^m and θ_j^f are the fractions of total male and female observations belonging to the jth demographic group, respectively.

In other words, $\theta_j^m = \frac{\sum_{j=H,M,O} N_j^m}{N^m}$ and $\theta_j^f = \frac{\sum_{j=H,M,O} N_j^f}{N^f}$ such that $N^m + N^f = N$

Here, N=total number of observations

N^m= total number of male observations

N^f= total number of female observations

N_j^m= the number of male observations belonging to the jth demographic group, $j = H, M, O$.

N_j^f = the number of female observations belonging to the jth demographic group, $j = H, M, O$.

Since fitted regression lines pass through the means of the data, the difference between overall raw mean for male and female students can be decomposed like the following way:

$$\overline{lnY^m} - \overline{lnY^f} = \sum_{j=H,M,O} \theta_j^m \overline{lnY_j^m} - \sum_{j=H,M,O} \theta_j^f \overline{lnY_j^f}$$

$$= \sum_{j=H,M,O} \theta_j^m \overline{X_j^m}' \widehat{\beta_j^m} - \sum_{j=H,M,O} \theta_j^f \overline{X_j^f}' \widehat{\beta_j^f}$$

$$= \underbrace{\sum_{j=H,M,O} \theta_j^m (\overline{X_j^m} - \overline{X_j^f})' \widehat{\beta_j^m}}_{Explained\ Effect} + \underbrace{\sum_{j=H,M,O} \overline{X_j^f}' (\theta_j^m \widehat{\beta_j^m} - \theta_j^f \widehat{\beta_j^f})}_{Unexplained\ Effect} \qquad (3)$$

In case of social groups (SC, ST and General), the similar expression can be obtained:

$$\overline{lnY^m} - \overline{lnY^f} = \underbrace{\sum_{j=SC,ST,General} \theta_j^m (\overline{X_j^m} - \overline{X_j^f})' \widehat{\beta_j^m}}_{Explained\ Effect} +$$

$$\underbrace{\sum_{j=SC,ST,General} \overline{X_j^f}' (\theta_j^m \widehat{\beta_j^m} - \theta_j^f \widehat{\beta_j^f})}_{Unexplained\ Effect} \qquad (4)$$

Further, in order to identify the religious or social groups with acute problem of gender bias, a similar decomposition is done separately for each jth demographic group like the following way:

$$\overline{lnY_j^m} - \overline{lnY_j^f} = \overline{X_j^m}' \widehat{\beta_j^m} - \overline{X_j^f}' \widehat{\beta_j^f}$$

$$= \underbrace{(\overline{X_j^m} - \overline{X_j^f})' \widehat{\beta_j^f}}_{Endowment\ Effect} + \underbrace{\overline{X_j^f}' (\widehat{\beta_j^m} - \widehat{\beta_j^f})}_{Coefficient\ Effect} + \underbrace{(\overline{X_j^m} - \overline{X_j^f})' (\widehat{\beta_j^m} - \widehat{\beta_j^f})}_{Interaction\ Effect} \qquad (5)$$

'Endowment Effect' is the expenditure gap due to differences in the average characteristics between males and females. This is the "Explained" part. If males and females had the same endowments, this term is zero. In the "Unexplained" part, 'Coefficient Effect' represents the differential treatment of characteristics (due to difference by sex) when a particular set of characteristics is given. Interaction Effect accounts for the fact that the endowments effect and coefficients effect exist simultaneously between two groups.

3. Methodology

In this paper we examine the implications of this decomposition within two types of demographic groups, viz., 'Religious groups' and 'Social groups'. Religious groups include Hindu, Muslim and Others. Social groups include SC (Scheduled Caste), ST (Scheduled Tribes) and General.

To do this, the regression equations specified in equation (1) and equation (2) are estimated for male and female students separately for each

j^{th} demographic group. The components of the decomposition in (3) and (4) are then estimated for all demographic groups. Finally, using (5) these components are compared over all demographic groups to identify the demographic group where the magnitude of gender bias is strongest.

4. Description of the Data

The data set used here is the 71th round data on participation and expenditure on education conducted by the National Sample Survey Office (NSSO), Govt. of India, for the state of West Bengal. The span of the data set is January 2014-June 2014. The survey has been conducted over 29 states and 6 UTs. This is the latest data set available that contains detailed information on education expenditure. From this data set a complete profile of household education expenditure pattern at the individual level is available.

In West Bengal, the number of students at the class 10 level and below is 6079 (3279 in the rural sector and 2800 in the urban sector).

From the NSS item classification the items pertaining to 'education' exclusively for these students are: ITEMLIST [see Majumder and Mitra (2016)].[2]

5. Results and Discussion

In Table 1, the regression results for male and female students belonging to religious groups Hindu and Muslim[3] are reported separately for both sectors. The R^2 ranges between 0.3949 and 0.5361. It can be observed that the coefficients of Log(MPCE) and $[\text{Log(MPCE)}]^2$are positive, significant and negative, significant, respectively, for both religious groups in both sectors, thus having the expected signs. The coefficients of 'hhsize' are positive, significant for male students and negative, significant for female students in both sectors for both religious groups. That is, with increase in household size there is a cut down in educational expenses for female children, whereas this is not the case for male children. The coefficients of 'Entry_age' are significant, negative in both sectors for both religious groups, except for Muslim female students in the rural sector (non-significant). This indicates that, in general, higher entry age of students at schools leads to lesser expenditure in educational items. This finding can be explained in the following way: parents of the students starting school at higher age give less importance to their children's schooling and their educational needs as generally, children start their schooling at higher age when they were engaged in other activities (domestic, agricultural etc.) during actual school going age. This reasoning is further supported by the positive, significant coefficients of Age in both sectors for both religious groups. The coefficients of the dummy variables d_1 and d_2 are negative, significant in both sectors and for both religious groups implyingthat expenditure on children's education decreases if the education is free ($d_1=1$) and if the student has access to computers ($d_2=1$) as computer access reduces charges for items like photocopy and allied items.

Table 1: Regression Results for Religious Groups

Explanatory Variables	*Coefficients: Rural Sector*			
	Hindu (2102)		*Muslim (1124)*	
	Male (1130)	*Female (972)*	*Male (591)*	*Female (533)*
Log(MPCE)	0.040*	0.804*	1.845*	2.582*
$[\text{Log(MPCE)}]^2$	-0.062*	-0.022*	-0.080*	-0.244*
Hhsize	0.157*	-0.007*	-0.065*	-0.032*
Entry_age	-0.217*	-0.229*	-0.253*	0.010
Age	0.131*	0.155*	0.197*	0.153*
d_1	-0.560*	-0.515*	-0.284*	-0.495*
d_2	-0.021*	-0.011*	-0.010*	-0.001*
Constant	2.583*	2.013*	2.304*	1.315*
R^2	0.4327*	0.4466*	0.4245*	0.3949*
Explanatory Variables	***Coefficients: Urban Sector***			
	Hindu (2250)		*Muslim (517)*	
	Male (1241)	*Female (1009)*	*Male (264)*	*Female (253)*
Log(MPCE)	0.983*	0.405*	0.100*	0.085*
$[\text{Log(MPCE)}]^2$	-0.133*	-0.033*	-0.071*	-0.626*
Hhsize	0.110*	-0.018*	-0.061*	-0.027*
Entry_age	-0.154*	-0.045*	-0.253*	-0.211*
Age	0.077*	0.072*	0.050*	0.137*
d_1	-0.090*	-0.029*	-0.012*	-0.087*
d_2	-0.031*	-0.201*	-0.076*	-0.012*
Constant	3.509*	2.013*	2.612*	1.096*
R^2	0.5361*	0.4466*	0.4943*	0.4923*

* Significant at 5% level.

Note: 1. Figures in parentheses are the number of students.

2. The number of observations for "Other" religious groups is insufficient to do a meaningful analysis.

Table 2 describes the decomposition results based on the religious groups. The following observations are in order. *First,* the total differential (male expenditure - female expenditure) of mean expenditure is positive in both sectors. *Second,* it can be seen that the magnitude of the "Unexplained Effect" component is higher compared to the "Explained Effect" component for both sectors. This explains the fact that the treatment of characteristics by students differ by their sex. Thus, the unexplained part, which reflects differential returns to measured characteristics of males and females, has a larger contribution and hence points to discrimination, as noted earlier. *Third*, in terms of religious groups, the unexplained effect of the Muslim group is contributing highest in both rural (41.91%) and urban sector (64.61%). This indicates to the fact that the presence of the differential returns of males and females is acute for Muslim which implies the fact that the problem of gender bias is acute in the Muslim group compared to the Hindu group.

Table 2: The Decomposition Result Based on the Religious Groups

Rural Sector				***Urban Sector***			
Total Difference ($\overline{lnY^m} - \overline{lnY^f}$) 1.637				**Total Difference** ($\overline{lnY^m} - \overline{lnY^f}$) 1.509			
Explained Effect ($\Sigma_{j=H,M,O}\, \theta_j^m\, (\overline{X_j^m} - \overline{X_j^f})'\, \widehat{\beta_j^m}$) 0.376		**Unexplained Effect** ($\sum_{j=H,M,O} \overline{X_j^f}'\left(\theta_j^m \widehat{\beta_j^m} - \theta_j^f \widehat{\beta_j^f}\right)$) 1.261		**Explained Effect** ($\Sigma_{j=H,M,O}\, \theta_j^m\, (\overline{X_j^m} - \overline{X_j^f})'\, \widehat{\beta_j^m}$) 0.229		**Unexplained Effect** ($\Sigma_{j=H,M,O} \overline{X_j^f}'\left(\theta_j^m \widehat{\beta_j^m} - \theta_j^f \widehat{\beta_j^f}\right)$) 1.280	
HINDU 0.118 (7.20%)*	MUSLIM 0.258 (15.76%)	HINDU 0.575 (35.13%)	MUSLIM 0.686 (41.91%)	HINDU 0.102 (6.76%)	MUSLIM 0.127 (8.42%)	HINDU 0.305 (20.21%)	MUSLIM 0.975 (64.61%)

*Figures in the parentheses represent the percentage of contributions by these components to total differential ($\frac{\text{Numerical value of the component}}{\text{Total difference}} \times 100$).

In Table 3, the results of the decomposition for each religious group are presented. The following observations are in order. *First*, the total differential of mean expenditure (that is, male expenditure - female expenditure) is positive and higher for Muslims than Hindus in both sectors. *Second,* the major contributor to this difference is the 'Coefficient effect' for both religions and sectors. Since this component quantifies the differential treatment of characteristics, a positive value clearly points to pro male bias.[4] *Third,* the contribution of 'Coefficient effect' is highest for the Muslim group in the urban sector and followed by the Hindu group in the rural sector. Further, the fact that the 'Coefficient effect' is higher in the Muslim group indicates a higher degree of gender bias in this community with respect to education expenditure.

Table 4 presents the regression results relating to the social groups. Here the R^2 is ranges between 0.3649 and 0.6422. The number of observations in the ST group in the urban sector is insufficient to run a meaningful regression. It can be seen that the coefficients of Log(MPCE)

Table 3: The Decomposition Result within Religious Groups

Rural Sector						***Urban Sector***					
Hindu			***Muslim***			***Hindu***			***Muslim***		
Total Difference $(\overline{lnY^m} - \overline{lnY^f})$ 0.123			Total Difference 0.235			Total Difference 0.061			Total Difference 0.112		
Endowment Effect	Coefficient Effect	Interaction Effect	Endowment Effect	Coefficient Effect	Interaction Effect	Endowment Effect	Coefficient Effect	Interaction Effect	Endowment Effect	Coefficient Effect	Interaction Effect
0.005 (4.06%)*	0.108 (87.8%)	0.010 (8.14%)	0.103 (43.82%)	0.130 (55.32%)	0.002 (0.86%)	0.023 (37.07%)	0.035 (57.37%)	0.003 (5.60%)	0.011 (9.82%)	0.100 (89.29%)	0.001 (0.89%)

and $[Log(MPCE)]^2$ are positive, significant and negative, significant respectively for all social groups in both sectors. The coefficients of hhsize are positive and significant for both sexes in the ST group and negative and significant only for females in the SC group in the rural sector. For the urban sector the coefficient is significant only for male students in the SC group with a negative sign. Thus, in the General group hhsize does not seem to play any role, in the ST group in rural sector there is no differential role between males and females, but in the SC group the effect is negative for females in the rural sector and for males in the urban sector. The coefficients of Entry_age are negative, significant and coefficients of Age positive, significant across groups, sexes and sectors. This pattern is similar to that for the case of religious groups. The coefficients of the dummy variables d_1 and d_2 are negative, significant in both sectors and for both religious groups leading to similar explanations as in case of religious groups.

Table 4: Regression Results for Social Groups

Coefficients: Rural Sector						
Explanatory Variables	***SC (625)***		***ST (274)***		***General (1203)***	
	Male (346)	***Female (279)***	***Male (159)***	***Female (115)***	***Male (625)***	***Female (578)***
Log(MPCE)	1.821*	3.046*	0.904*	1.844*	1.877*	0.396*
$[Log(MPCE)]^2$	-0.481*	-0.157*	-0.129*	-0.509*	-0.196*	-0.098*
Hhsize	0.006	-0.043*	0.078*	0.043*	-0.036	-0.014
Entry_age	-0.209*	-0.163*	-0.089*	-0.238*	-0.222*	-0.072*
Age	0.172*	0.165*	0.145*	0.143*	0.126*	0.160*
d_1	-0.471*	-0.630*	-0.494*	-0.769*	-0.591*	-0.334*
d_2	-0.185*	-0.075*	-0.021*	-0.159*	-0.072*	-0.089*
Constant	4.337*	3.533*	2.527*	1.622*	1.241*	3.701*
R^2	0.4767	0.4574	0.3649	0.4569	0.4039	R^2=0.3964
Coefficients: Urban Sector						
Explanatory Variables	***SC (852)***		***ST (22)***		***General (1376)***	
	Male (489)	***Female (363)***	***Male (13)***	***Female (9)***	***Male (739)***	***Female (637)***
Log(MPCE)	2.401*	2.945*	NA	NA	1.248*	1.362*
$[Log(MPCE)]^2$	0.209*	-0.151*	NA	NA	-0.059*	-0.089*
Hhsize	-0.048*	-0.027	NA	NA	0.030	0.017
Entry_age	-0.122*	-0.167*	NA	NA	-0.188*	-0.105*
Age	0.072*	0.082*	NA	NA	0.074*	0.064*
d_1	-0.374*	-0.405*	NA	NA	-0.617*	0.454*
d_2	0.103*	0.156*	NA	NA	-0.011*	-0.134*
Constant	1.884*	2.604*	NA	NA	2.393*	2.218*
R^2	0.4481	0.3821			0.6166	0.6422

* Significant at 5% level.

Note: 1. Figures in parentheses are the number of students.

2. The number of observations for "ST" group in the urban sector is insufficient to do a meaningful analysis.

In Table 5, the components of the differentials based on social groups are reported. Among the components of total differential, the "Unexplained Effect" is highest contributor in both sectors across all social groups. In the rural sector, the contribution of "Unexplained Effect" by ST is highest (46.30%) where as that by SC is highest in the rural sector (70.54%). Hence, it indicates to the fact that pro male gender exists in both sectors across all social groups and the problem in acute in ST group in the rural sector and in SC group in the urban sector respectively.

Table 5: The Decomposition Based on Social Groups

Rural Sector						***Urban Sector***					
Total Difference $(\overline{lnY^m} - \overline{lnY^f})$ 1.572						**Total Difference** $(\overline{lnY^m} - \overline{lnY^f})$ 1.402					
Explained Effect $(\sum_{j=SC,ST,General} \theta_j^m (\overline{X_j^m} - \overline{X_j^f})' \widehat{\beta_j^m})$ 0.231			**Unexplained Effect** $(\sum_{j=SC,ST,General} \overline{X_j^f}' (\theta_j^m \widehat{\beta_j^m} - \theta_j^f \widehat{\beta_j^f}))$ 1.341			**Explained Effect** $(\sum_{j=SC,ST,General} \theta_j^m (\overline{X_j^m} - \overline{X_j^f})' \widehat{\beta_j^m})$ 0.198			**Unexplained Effect** $(\sum_{j=SC,ST,General} \overline{X_j^f}' (\theta_j^m \widehat{\beta_j^m} - \theta_j^f \widehat{\beta_j^f}))$ 1.204		
SC 0.029 (1.84%)*	ST 0.150 (9.54%)	General 0.052 (3.30%)	SC 0.249 (15.74%)	ST 0.729 (46.30%)	General 0.366 (23.28%)	SC 0.146 (10.41%)	ST NA	General 0.052 (3.71%)	SC 0.989 (70.54%)	ST NA	General 0.215 (15.34%)

*Figures in the parentheses represent the percentage of contributions by these components to total differential $(\frac{\text{Numerical value of the component}}{\text{Total difference}} \times 100)$.

In Table 6, the components of the decomposition for each social group are reported. Among the components of the decomposition of total differentials of mean expenditure on education between male and female students, the 'Coefficients effect' is the highest contributor for all social groups. This implies that there exists pro male bias in education expenditure across all social groups. Further, a comparison of the components over all three social groups in the rural sector and two groups in the urban sector shows that the total differential component is maximum for the ST group in the rural sector and for the SC group in the urban sector. The 'Coefficient effect' is maximum for ST in the rural sector and for SC in the urban sector. Hence, it can be concluded that the magnitude of gender bias is highest in the ST group in the rural sector and gender bias is higher in the SC group compared to the General group in the urban sector.

5. Conclusions

In this paper, the gender bias in education expenditure in the religious and social groups is examined using the 71st round education data provided by NSSO. The underlying methodology is the Oaxaca-Blinder decomposition

Table 6: The Decomposition Result within Social Groups

Sector	Group	Total Difference	Endowment Effect	Coefficient Effect	Interaction Effect
Rural Sector	*SC*	0.136	0.023 (16.91%)*	0.072 (52.94%)	0.041 (30.15%)
	ST	0.235	0.092 (39.15%)	0.128 (54.47%)	0.015 (6.38%)
	General	0.059	0.022 (37.29%)	0.032 (54.24%)	0.005 (8.47%)
Urban Sector	*SC*	0.151	0.061 (40.40%)	0.083 (54.97%)	0.007 (4.63%)
	ST		NA	NA	NA
	General	0.119	0.036 (30.25%)	0.072 (60.50%)	0.011 (9.25%)

* Figures in the parentheses represent the percentage of contributions by these components to total differential $\left(\frac{\text{Numerical value of the component}}{\text{Total difference}} \times 100\right)$.

technique. Evidence of pro male gender bias in found in both religious groups, with a higher magnitude for 'Muslims' in both sectors. For the social groups, pro male gender bias is evident in all groups, with ST in the rural sector and SC in the urban sector showing higher magnitudes.

(The author is grateful to Professor Amita Majumder for her valuable suggestions. The usual disclaimer applies)

References

Azam, Mehtabul and Kingdon, Geeta Gandhi (2013). Are girls the fairer sex in India? Revisiting intra-household allocation of education expenditure. *World Development 42: 143-164.*

Blinder, A.S., (1973). Wage discrimination: reduced form and structural estimates. *Journal of Human Resources 8, 436-455.*

Bandyopadhyay, M., & Subrahmanian, R. (2008). Gender equity in education: A review of trends and factors.

Borooah, V. K., andIyer, S. (2005). The decomposition of inter-group differences in a logit model: Extending the Oaxaca-Blinder approach with an application to school enrolment in India. *Journal of Economic and Social Measurement, 30*(4), 279-293.

Brown, R.S., Moon, M.andZoloth, S., (1980). Incorporating occupational attainment in studies of male-female differentials. *Journal of Human Resources 15, 3-28.*

Deaton, A. and Subramanian, Shankar (1991). Gender bias in Indian consumption pattern,*Sarvekshana 14, no. 4: 1-12.*

Dreze, Jean and Kingdon, Geeta Gandhi (2001). "School participation in rural India."*Review of Development Economics* 5(1): 1-24.

Government of India(2013). Survey for Assessment of Dropout Rates at Elementary Level in 21 States, Final Report, Edcil (India) Limited. A Government of India Enterprise.

Lancaster, Geoffrey, Maitra, Pushkarand Ray, Ranjan(2008). "Household expenditure patterns and gender bias: evidence from selected Indian states", *Oxford Development Studies,* 36(2), 133-157.

Kambhampati, Uma S. (2008). "Does household expenditure on education in India depend upon the returns to education?", *Henley Business School University Whiteknights Reading RG6 6AA United Kingdom.*

Kambhampati, U.S. and Pal, S. (2001). 'Role of Parental Literacy in Explaining Gender Difference: Evidence from Child Schooling in India', *European Journal of Development Research,*13(2),

Kingdon, Geeta Gandhi (1998). "Does the Labour Market Explain Lower Female Schooling in India?"*Journal ofDevelopment Studies*, 35(1), 39-65.

Kingdon, Geeta Gandhi (2002). 'The Gender Gap in Educational Attainment in India: How Much Can BeExplained?'*Journal of Development Studies,* 39(2), 25-53.

Kingdon, Geeta Gandhi (2005). "Where has all the bias gone? Detecting gender bias in the intrahousehold allocation of educational expenditure." *Economic Development and Cultural Change,* 53(2), 409-451.

Majumder, A.andMitra, C. (2017). Gender Bias in Education in West Bengal. *Journal of Quantitative Economics*, *15*(1), 173-196.

Majumder, A.andMitra, C. (2016). Gender bias in household education expenditure: the case of West Bengal. *Indian Growth and Development Review*, 9(2), 129-150.

Pal, S. (2004). How much of the gender difference in child school enrolment can be explained? Evidence from rural India. *Bulletin of Economic Research*, *56*(2), 133-158.

Subrahmanian, R. (2005). Gender equality in education: Definitions and measurements. *International Journal of Educational Development*, *25*(4), 395-407.

Tilak, J. B. (2002). "Education poverty in India", *Review of Development and Change,* 7(1), 1-44.

Zimmermann, Laura (2012). "Reconsidering gender bias in intra household allocation in India." *Journal of Development Studies,* 48(1), 151-163.

15

Social Determinants and Inequality in Immunisation in India

Nit Ranjan

Abstract

Unfortunately, religion and caste system in India continue to have unwarranted association with the immunisation coverage in India. These rigid institutions-by birth mostly, indirectly concomitant in low immunisation coverage also. This study used the NFHS-IV data of 2015-16, found the existence of inequity by religion and caste in uptake of three basic vaccines-BCG, three doses of DPT and measles, allied in prevailing low level of full immunisation. Extensive immunisation programme over the decade has resulted in rapid improvement in vaccination coverage for such children as well. However, Concentration Index based on mother education, health facilities and wealth quantiles emphasize the existence of inequity among Muslim, Scheduled Castes and Scheduled Tribes children. The logistic models show that lower interaction with health institutions and low level of mothers' formal education were associated with a lower chance of immunisation status for the children. Whereas, when these two factors improved, it resulted in a higher chance of full immunisation. Also, interactions of mothers with health institutions had a more prominent role as compared to mothers' formal education in enhancing the chances of higher immunisation status.

Key Words: *Immunisation, Inequity, Concentration Index, Mothers' Formal Education, Health Institutions*

Introduction

Over the period of time, India has developed a vast network of public health system. Within this, immunisation programme continues to share the burden in improving child survival rate, along with other programmes. Irrefutably, it remained one of the most cost-effective public health interventions, covered many bases of health infrastructure and distributed mostly free in public health facilities (WHO, 2000). With a long history of immunisation programme for children, India has achieved many milestone-Polios free, extending to vast geographical areas augmented with extensive supply chain network and extensive out-reach activities. However, in parallel, we have missed to achieve many goals like having full vaccination for basic vaccines-BCG, DPT and measles vaccines, and failed to cover more than 90 percent of children, which many neighbouring countries like Sri Lanka, Bhutan, Bangladesh, etc., have achieved in a much shorter period of time. These countries have followed similar vaccination programmes with extensive out-reach activities to provide timely vaccination to children. While, they have been able to achieve but we have failed miserably in many fronts in these levels, results in more than 20 percent of the child population not completely vaccinated for basic vaccines, even though India is a leading producer of vaccines in the world. Universal Immunisation Programme 1985 targeted to bring 80 percent of children under immunisation coverage by 1990 (Ko Keja et al., 1988, MoHFW-UIP) failed by more than a decade to achieve it undermined the frivolous nature of advancement it this.

Similar to other developing countries, India also countenances the problems of completely missing out one or two vaccine and not completing multiple dosages of vaccines. These factors have resulted in low full immunisation rate prevailing in India. These variations in vaccination intake emanated in inequity in immunisation status among children. So, the basic question is not limited to equity in uptake of individual vaccines but also to somehow stimulating the overall vaccination rate stretching to the geographical boundaries of India. In the past, to overcome the inequity in rural and urban divide, most of the outreach activities were centred on the rural areas (B. Kate and A. Thakur, 1988). As a result of which, immunisation rate in rural areas has increased and now analogous with urban areas. By virtue of this also, difference due to gender has reduced to minimal, which is also the good sign for child health programme especially in country like India. The presence of inequity between high and low birth order children has been sought in many literatures. Unfortunately, it continues to exist but to many reasons the proportion of high birth order children itself is reducing in nature over the time following the population dividend in India. And, so the shortcomings in vaccination of higher birth children as compared to low birth order children has significantly reduced over time.

Immunisation programmes stretched for more than three decades in India resulted in reducing inequity covering many based of socio-demographic problems. However, we have failed to achieve uniformity and equity in the two most important socioeconomic structures-Religion and Caste. In a nutshell way, through different pathways health shrives differ in the society. The substantial difference in use of health facilities observed with variability in demand by ethnicity, social and economic factors (Pabley et al., 1996). And, in most of the socioeconomic studies on immunisation in India has successfully established that full immunisation in Muslim as well as Scheduled Castes and Scheduled Tribes children remained low as compared to other religions or castes. More than this, it also has been argued that immunisation status has improved for this category over the period, and parents have low or minimum cultural resistance to immunisation and are willing to start vaccination (Incentive for immunisation-J-Pal Policy Briefcase, Nov 2011). Given this also, India continued to have low level of immunisation level for decades mostly failing to bring the immunisation level of these groups, which constitute a large section of the growing population. Religion and caste in India act as an instrumental proxy of structural social network especially in the village, with strong intra-group interaction and much less inter-group interaction. Women's interaction is higher in their respective social groups especially in village within castes and religions stratifications (Wendy, 2011). And this has been stimulated with low interaction with village health programme along with low empowered Muslim women in terms of educational level, financial autonomy and decision making. This resulted in extremely low immunisation rate for all vaccines.

A study in Madhya Pradesh shows that a low level of Muslim population and high level of Scheduled Tribes population had differential vaccination outcome in children. Mother having higher literacy results in better vaccination intake. And, this is too observed in case for Muslim children also. Muslim children had better immunisation levels mostly to those mothers who had higher level of formal education (De and Bhattacharya, 2002). Otherwise, children from these social groups had low immunisation status and found to have low intake of DPT vaccines mostly. However, impact of maternal education on child health remained debatable especially in case of immunisation, as knowledge and literacy are not the same as a result failed to complete the full doses of vaccines (Oladokun et al., 2010). While, the four possible pathways identified as-human, social and cultural capitals and more financial autonomy within households. Among these-human capital (health knowledge) and cultural capital (communication skills) became deterministic in child immunisation with secondary and above formal education of mother even after controlling for other socio-demographic and village and neighbourhood fixed effect (Vikram Kriti et al., 2012; Goodburn et al., 1990). Above this, overall high proportions of female literates in rural parts of district or in village or in community level, results in higher rate of child immunisation with socioeconomic developments (S. Parashar, 2005; Bicego and Boerma, 1993). However, formal education does not always result in better immunisation status and it depends heavily on information of immunisation with promotional and awareness programmes through interactions with health institutions over the time (Parthiban et al., 2014).

Shrivastawa et al. (2015) found that religions and castes had significant association with the child immunisation, along with mother's TT vaccine and ANC visits. In religion, Muslim children had 2.2 times higher odds of being non-vaccinated as compared to Hindu children, while other religion groups like-Sikh, Christian were not having any such association. On the other hand, children from scheduled castes and scheduled tribes continued to have high association with having either no or partial immunisation and the chances of full immunisation remained uncertain for large section even when mothers had access or some interactions with health institutions. Tandon and Gandhi (1992) study on vaccination for target groups (Scheduled Castes, Scheduled Tribes, Backward Castes and minorities) covering 19 rural, 8 tribal and 9 urban areas found that vaccination coverage varied between sixty to eighty percent. Limited outreach activities (locational access problem) were not able to break the resistance towards vaccines due to uncertainty about the availability of vaccines. This results in the lowest vaccines coverage among Scheduled Tribes children. Under Integrated Child Development Services (ICDS), BCG and DPT vaccines intake has shown positive results and coverage improved to 65 percent and 63 percent respectively. While, it fell sharply for children not covered under these programme (22 percent in BCG and 28 percent in DPT vaccines). Due to ICDS, vaccination coverage improved for target groups and was similar to those of higher castes in that areas. Whereas, overall average vaccination rates remained significantly low in the tribal areas.

Study in urban slum in Lucknow district found that only forty-four percent of children were fully vaccinated and Muslim children had higher percentage of partial and no vaccination. And, partial immunisation in Scheduled Caste and Scheduled Tribes children were largely due to missing DPT or measles vaccines dosages (Nath et al. 2007). The story of low immunisation rates for Muslim children is not limited to India only. Ojikutu (2012) study in Lagos (Nigeria) examined the belief, knowledge and perception of parents for child vaccination found a very high percentage of full vaccination among Christian children as compared to Muslim children, who had a lower level of complete immunisation despite having conducive belief and knowledge. Even, Bbaale (2013) study found similar findings for Muslim children in Uganda and they have initiated to vaccine programme but severely failed to complete the full dosages of DPT vaccines.

The literature has correctly addressed the fact that children from these social groups have unfavourable immunisation status and remained far away from the main stream. And, without bringing immunisation status of children from these section of society in India to a certain level, the improvement in average immunisation level of full immunisation will have limited success. This study helps to bridge the gap from identification of inequity, to analyze a vital force as complementary strategy to bring the equity in immunisation status within these groups and also improved the overall immunisation rate in India in coming year.

1A. Objective of the Study

The primary objective of this study is to identify the prevailing inequity in the immunisation level among children, by castes and religion. Secondly, to understand the influence of sociodemographic and mothers' interactions with health facilities on immunisation levels and characterised the nature of inequity among fully and not fully vaccinated children. And lastly, to study the complementary necessary condition required to bring equity in immunisation level with overall improvement in full immunisation level too.

1B. Definition

Immunisation levels are defined based on the different dosages of BCG, 3 doses of DPT and Measles vaccines received by the child age 12-23 months. Full immunisation levels are the cases where children have received all dosages of BCG, DPT and Measles vaccines, while others are categorised as not fully vaccinated. In this, when none of these vaccines was received by the child is termed as No immunisation. While, if few dosages of either BCG or DPT or Measles were received by the child defined as Partial immunisation. In this study, this category is further broken up into two distinct groups to capture the dropout scenario of DPT and not opting for specific vaccines. Selective immunisation is defined as the cases when any one or two of the vaccines among BCG, DPT and Measles were received by the child whereas, in Incomplete immunisation, BCG and Measles vaccines were received but the complete 3 dosages of DPT were not fully completed. The first one helps to identify the cases where one or two vaccines are completely missed out while the later one helps to identify the dropout rates of DPT vaccines.

1C. Data and Methodology

For the objective of the study, secondary data from National Family Health Surveys (NFHS-IV) is used to study the immunisation in India covering the period of 2015-16. This is the fourth in the series of national representative survey, widely used as it provides information on population, health and other topics for India and each State/Union Territory based on census stratification of 2011. This face to face survey covered 601,509 household including information of approximately around 699,686 women and 103,525 men. This survey collected information on vaccination details for all living children born in the five-year preceding the survey period. Information of vaccination is collected and documented from women questionnaire. If a vaccine card was available, field-staff was required to copy the information about the vaccines received by child. In case, mother was not able to show a vaccination card, the information on vaccines were collected based on memory recall. In this survey, the number of vaccination card has significantly increased but at aggregate level, the number of these cases remained in parallel.

The data set for dependent variable of immunisation status for children aged 12-23 months prepared as exhaustive in nature to avoid anomalies (Appendix Table 2). However, to study the prevailing inequity in immunisation using concentration index methodology, the binary independent variable-full and not full immunisation was considered. The independent variables characterised as household or individual information along with access to health facilities by mother. It consists of information related to place of residence (rural/urban), gender of the child (male/female), birth order (birth order<=2/birth order>=3), religion (Hindu, Muslim and Others), castes (SC/ST/OBC/Others), mothers' education level (no formal education/primary education(upto primary)/above primary education), and binary variables for information on health facilities like antenatal care visit during pregnancy (yes/no), mother tetanus vaccine (yes/no), place of delivery (institutional/non-institutional), facilitated by community health workers (yes/no) are constructed. Along with this, state specific wealth quantiles of households are considered: poor and the poorest wealth quantile are merged in one group (named-poor), medium quantile, and rich and the richest wealth quantile merged in one group (named-rich). These socioeconomic determinants cover most of the aspects of socioeconomic inequality prevailing in India in the context of health studies.

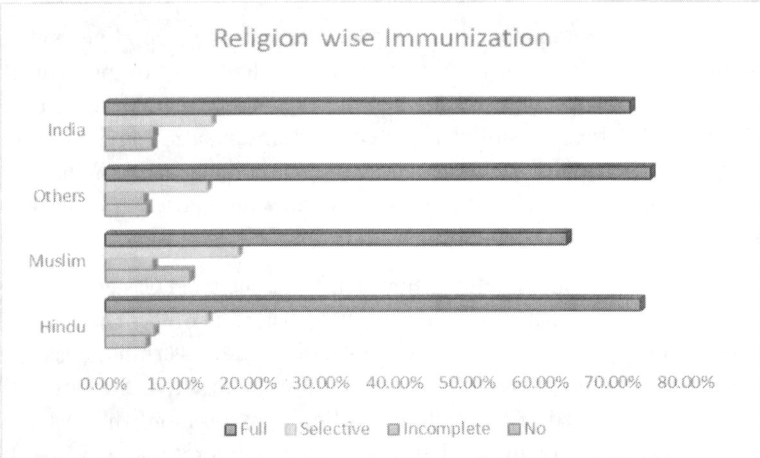

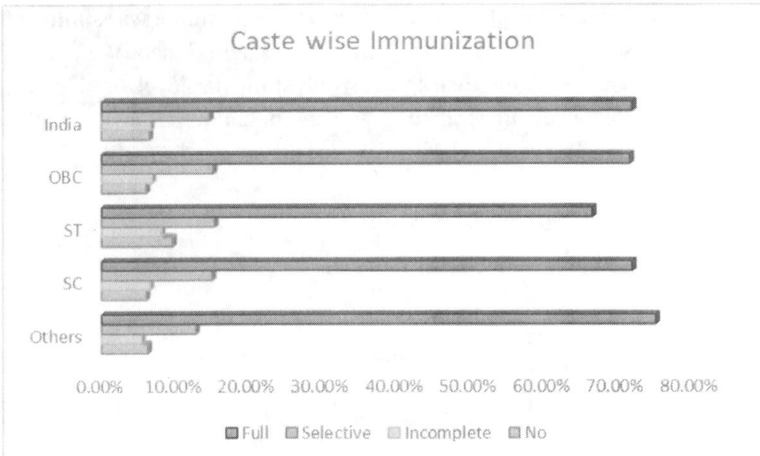

Graph 1: Immunisation Status by Religion & Caste

According to NFHS IV data (Graph 1: Immunisation Status by Religion & Caste), India achieved only 72 percent of full immunisation for children aged 12-23 months for these three basic vaccines-BCG, DPT1-3 and Measles. And, the level of disparity in immunisation status continued to prevail by religion and castes. Full immunisation rate for Hindu children was slightly higher than the national average and a little over 5 percent of them had not opted for any vaccines. Approximately, 14 percent of Hindu children had selective immunisation while 7 percent of these children had not completed the DPT vaccines when other two vaccines were opted (incomplete immunisation). It feels a little melancholy with advanced immunisation programme in India for decades, as more than 11 percent of Muslim children did not receive any vaccine and only 63 percent of them had full vaccination. Even when the vaccination started, more than 18 percent of them resulted in selective immunisation and roughly around 6.65 percent of children had incomplete immunisation. Whereas, children from 'Other' religions had slightly better immunisation status than Hindu children.

On the other hand, immunisation status of Scheduled Castes children was par as India level average but more than 20 percent of them had partial immunisation. Children from Scheduled Tribes had lower immunisation status, and only 66 percent of them had full immunisation. More than 9 percent of Scheduled Tribes children had no immunisation while having the highest percent of incomplete immunisation (more than 8 percent). The immunisation status of Other Backward Caste children was similar to Scheduled caste children while children from 'Other (General)' caste had better immunisation status than the rest. Overall, the level of selective immunisation remained higher than 15 percent for children from Scheduled Caste, Scheduled Tribes and OBC.

2. Multinomial Logistic Regression

Dependent variable is defined as follows,

$$Y = \begin{cases} 1, if\ No\ immunization; \\ 2, if\ Incomplete\ immunization; \\ 3, if\ Selective\ immunization; \\ 4, if\ Full\ immunization \end{cases}$$

This section helps to analyse the association between a set of predictors and a multi-category outcome (unordered). As there is no order between Incomplete and Selective immunisations assumed, this approach is adopted. Among four outcomes, full immunisation is considered as the reference category for developing the regression along with linearity assumption.

2A. Result

Table 3 (Appendix) and Graph 2, 3, 4 represent the statistical Multinomial Logit (Unordered Response) Models to study the association of independent (explanatory) variables on different levels of immunisation (No, Incomplete and Selective immunisations with respect to Full immunisation). The confidence interval of 95 percent is considered for rejecting or accepting null hypothesis of no association/effect of any explanatory variable in determining child immunisation status, i.e., the null hypothesis of no association/effect of the factor is rejected if p-value<0.05.

(a) No immunisation as references to full immunisation:

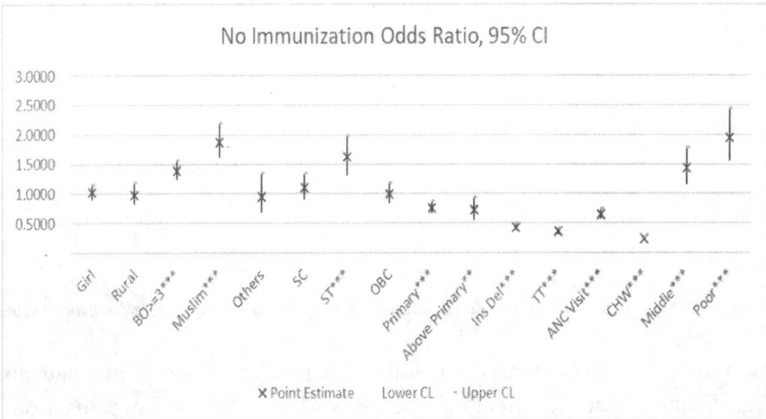

*** p<0.01, ** p<0.05, * p<0.1

Graph 2: Odds Ratio, 95% Confidence Interval by Variables – No Immunisation

From the model and confidence interval graph, it has been observed that gender of the child or the place of residence had no association with no immunisation, while birth order (>=3) children had higher odds (38.3%) of no immunisation as compared to low birth order children. In religions and castes, Muslim (87.4%) and Scheduled Tribes (61.4%) children had higher odds of no immunisation as compared to Hindu and 'Other' religions respectively. And, mothers' formal education-primary (24.3%) and above primary (28%) had lower odds of no immunisation as compared to the no formal education of mother. Child and mothers' health facilities like institutional delivery (57%), mother TT vaccines (64.5%), ANC visit (35.7%) and facilitated by community health workers (75.7%), presence of all these lowered the odds of no immunisation as compared to their respective references. Whereas, children from middle (42.6%) and poor (94%) wealth quantile household had higher odds of no immunisation than rich wealth quantile households.

(b) Incomplete immunisation as references to full immunisation:

Girl children had slightly lower odds (12.5%) of incomplete immunisation as compared to boy children, while place of residence had no such association. In castes, children from Scheduled Castes (19%), Scheduled Tribes (50%) and OBC (25%) had higher odds of incomplete

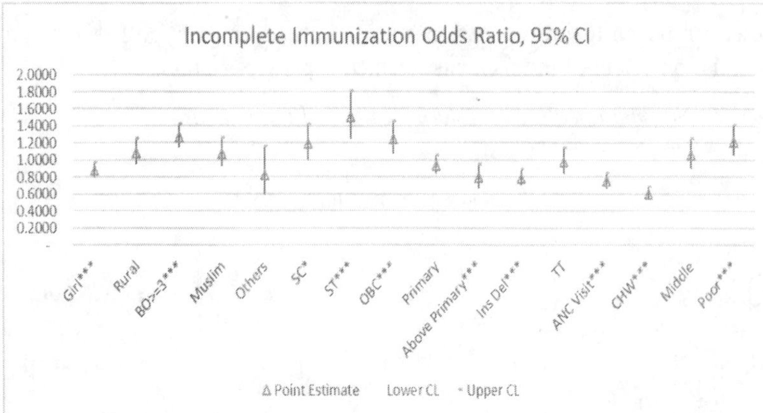

*** p<0.01, ** p<0.05, * p<0.1

Graph 3: Odds Ratio, 95% Confidence Interval by Variables – Incomplete Immunisation

immunisation as compared to 'Other', while religious group had no significant impact in changing the odds of incomplete immunisation. Children whose mothers having above primary education had lower odds (21%) of incomplete immunisation as compared to children with mothers with no formal education. In child and mother health facilities-institutional delivery (21.6%), ANC visit (25%) and facilitated by CHWs (40%) had lower the odds of incomplete immunisation as compared to respective references. And also, children from poor wealth quantile have higher odds (21.5%) of incomplete immunisation as compared to rich wealth quantile.

(c) Selective immunisation as references to full immunisation:

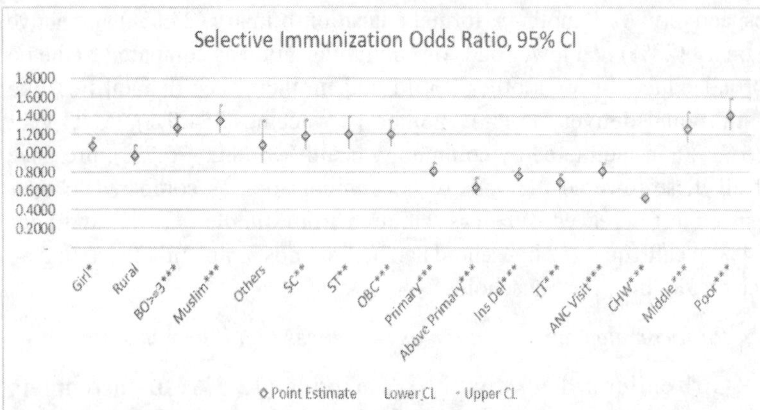

*** p<0.01, ** p<0.05, * p<0.1

Graph 4: Odds Ratio, 95% Confidence Interval by Variables – Selective Immunisation

In this model, gender and place of residence had no linear association with selective immunisation while birth order (>=3) had higher odds of selective immunisation as compared to lower birth order children. In religion and castes, children from Muslim (34.4%) and Scheduled Caste (18%) & Scheduled Tribes (20%) had higher odds of selective immunisation as compared to Hindu and Other castes respectively. Children of mothers with upto primary (18.7%) and above primary (36.5%) education level had lower odds of selective immunisation as compared to no formal education of mother. Institutional delivery (24%), TT vaccine (31%), ANC visit (19%) and facilitated by CHWs (47%) had lower the odds of selective immunisation as compared to respective references. Lastly, children from middle (26%) and poor (40%) wealth quantile households had higher odds of selective immunisation as compared to rich wealth quantile households.

The statistical model clearly identifies that immunisation status had no such association with gender or place of residence of child, while higher birth order children had some disadvantages and had worse immunisation status as compared to lower birth order children. This also emphasizes that children from Muslim, Scheduled Castes and Scheduled Tribes were associated with worse immunisation status. Mothers' formal education as well as child-mother care health facilities like-institutional delivery, mother TT vaccines, ANC visits and facilitated by CHWs had positive impact in improving the immunisation status. Lastly, children from poor and middle wealth quantile households were associated with lower immunisation status as compared to children from rich wealth quantile.

3. Concentration Index

Health facilities and mother's formal education had fundamental importance in improving the child immunisation status by lowering the odds of no, incomplete and selective immunisation. Along with that, religions and castes-wise difference were also persistent in immunisation status. Now, let us analyze that how the "fully immunised" children were concentrated with respect to mothers' formal education, access to health facilities and wealth groups for different religions and castes. Basically, we aim to find out that whether higher formal education, access to health facilities characteristics had relatively more fully immunised children or not at overall and by religions and castes as well. Wagstaff et al. (1997) research explores the inequality in health using concentration indices. Following the theoretical setup, rank variables-mothers' formal education, access to health facilities, wealth quantile index constructed while immunisation status is categorised as full and not full. This helps in assessing the presence of socioeconomic inequalities with immunisation, though it does not explore the reasons for inequality in immunisation.

Table 1: Concentration Index by Mothers' Formal Education, Health Facilities for Religion & Castes

	Conc. Index	*St.Err.*	*p-value*	*F-Stat*
	Mother's Formal Education			
Religion				
All	0.0507	0.002	0.000	
Hindu	0.0459	0.002	0.000	
Muslim	0.0589	0.008	0.000	
Others	0.0522	0.009	0.000	103.4***
Caste				
All	0.0507	0.002	0.000	
Others	0.0541	0.005	0.000	
SC	0.0360	0.005	0.000	
ST	0.0477	0.006	0.000	
OBC	0.0516	0.003	0.000	73.9***
	Health Facilities			
Religion				
All	0.0762	0.002	0.000	
Hindu	0.0692	0.002	0.000	
Muslim	0.0995	0.007	0.000	
Others	0.0781	0.010	0.000	105.8***
Caste				
All	0.0762	0.002	0.000	
Others	0.0549	0.005	0.000	
SC	0.0825	0.005	0.000	
ST	0.0980	0.006	0.000	
OBC	0.0776	0.003	0.000	79.9***
	Wealth Quantile			
Religion				
All	0.0435	0.002	0.000	
Hindu	0.0434	0.003	0.000	
Muslim	0.0499	0.008	0.000	
Others	0.0422	0.011	0.000	90.3***
Caste				
All	0.0435	0.002	0.000	
Others	0.0421	0.005	0.000	
SC	0.0301	0.005	0.000	
ST	0.0332	0.005	0.000	
OBC	0.0447	0.003	0.000	29.8***

*** $p<0.01$, ** $p<0.05$, * $p<0.1$

From the Table 1, it can be concluded that fully immunised children were more concentrated among mothers with higher level of formal education across all religions and castes. Interestingly, the concentration was more for Muslim (0.0589) children than Hindu (0.0459) children implying that mothers' higher formal education would result in more fully immunised children for Muslim than Hindu. Similarly, with mothers' formal education, Other Caste (0.0541) & Other Backward Caste (0.0516) would have more fully immunised children than Scheduled Castes (0.036), Scheduled Tribes (0.0477).

To understand the influence of health facilities in concentration of fully immunised children, a rank variable with four categories based on access to considered health facilities (ANC visit, TT, institutional delivery, CHW interaction) is constructed. Not having access to all such facilities would have lowest rank followed by any one or two facilities, any three facilities and lastly access of all having the highest rank of health facilities. Here as well, fully immunised children were more concentrated for mothers having more health facilities across all religions and castes. Muslim (0.0995) fully immunised children were more concentrated for mothers with more health facilities than Hindu (0.0692). Whereas, mothers with more health facilities had more fully immunised children for Scheduled Castes (0.0825), Scheduled Tribes (0.098) than Others (0.054), OBC (0.0776) castes.

Also, it is observed that fully immunised children were more concentrated in richer wealth quantile across religions and castes as well. The extent of concentration was higher more Other Backward Caste (0.0447), "Other" (0.0421) castes as compared to Scheduled Castes (0.0301) and Scheduled Tribes (0.0332). Among different religions, the concentration extent was more for Muslim (0.0499) than Hindu (0.0434).

Clearly, this indicates that mothers' formal education and access to health facilities would further improve the child immunisation status across religion and castes. Now, we would discuss the impact of interaction impact of mothers' formal education and access to health facilities on child immunisation for different castes and religions. Along with this, we would discuss whether access to health facilities and mother's formal education helped in reducing religions or castes-wise differences in child immunisation concomitantly, and to what extent.

4. Multinomial Logistic Model by Religion and Caste

Now, Multinomial Logistic Model is developed to understand the interaction of mothers' formal education and health services on immunisation status of children by religions and castes. This will examine the impact of these factors on the inequity in immunisation level and to understand the nature of influence to improve overall immunisation rates in India. For this, probabilities of different immunisation levels are calculated for each type of interaction and simplified the child and mother care variables as two distinct cases- mother having all these favourable health facilities outcome and otherwise.

4A. Religions

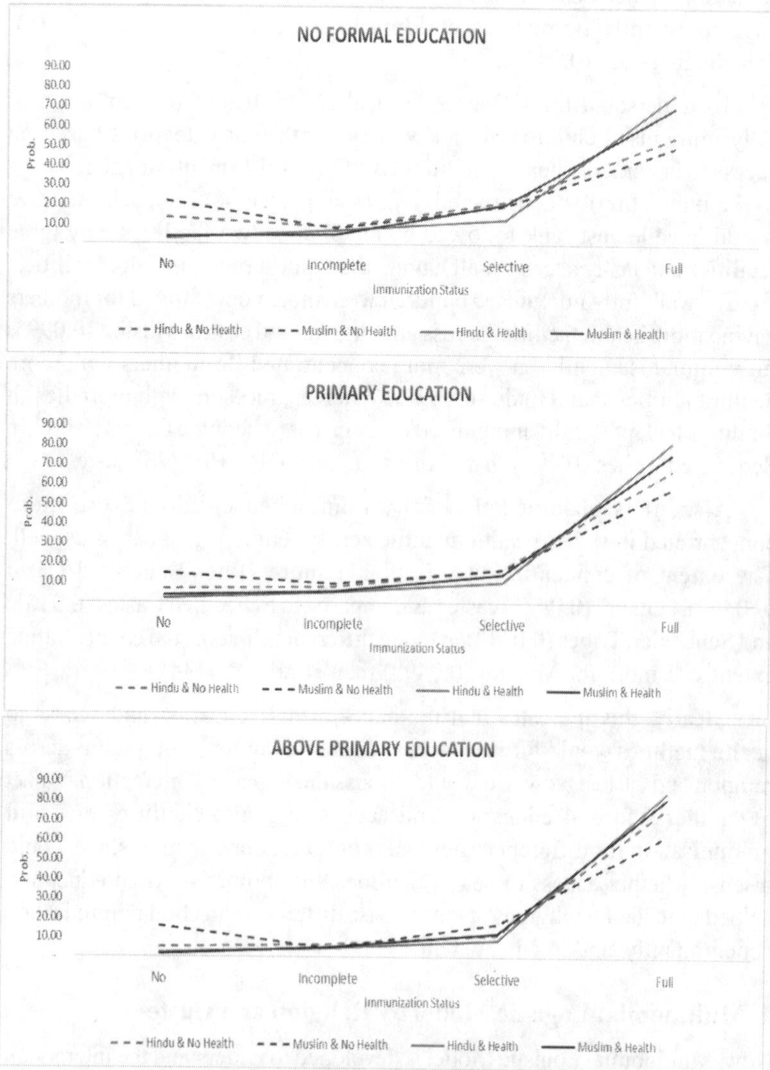

Graph 5: Probabilities of Immunisation Status for Formal Education and Health Facilities by Religion

When a mother had no or limited health facilities (instance other than all health facilities) with no formal education, the chances of no immunisation level were 22 and 14 percent for Muslim and Hindu children respectively. As the formal education level of mother improved, the chance of no immunisation reduced more significantly in case of Hindu than Muslim. While, the chances of full immunisation of Hindu and Muslim children were 55 and 50 percent with no formal education of mother, and it improved with formal education for both but had much better outcome in Hindu.

In the partial immunisation, the chances of incomplete immunisation reduced only with above primary education of mother for both Hindu and Muslim children. Within partial immunisation, the chance of selective immunisation reduced succeeding with increase in formal education of mother for Hindu. It reduced for Muslim also, but no such significant difference is observed between above primary and upto primary, which was otherwise observed in case of Hindu.

When mothers had all the health facilities (opted all these health facilities), the chances of no immunisation were low for both Hindu and Muslim children irrespective of mothers' education. Even with no formal education of mother, the chances of full immunisation for Hindu and Muslim children were 77 and 70 percent respectively, and it significantly improved. Also, the gap in the full immunisation level reduced with improvement in formal education of mother. Apart from this, in the presence of all the health services, the chances of incomplete immunisation remained low with improvement in formal education for both Muslim and Hindu children with minimal gap. However, the chance of selective immunisation reduced much faster in Hindu children with mothers' formal education as compared to Muslim children but the gap had reduced significantly. Above primary formal education with all health facilities, the chance of full immunisation Hindu and Muslim children were 84 and 81 percent respectively. This emphasis that the combined effect of formal education and health facilities, the religion-wise differences would also be reduced to a large extent, not completely though, and the uniformity and equity could be achieved.

Along with this (from Graph 6), the chances of full immunisation were much higher in the case of mothers having all health facilities with no formal education as compared to no or limited health facilities with primary education for both Hindu and Muslim children. Also, for both Muslim and Hindu children, the full immunisation were higher in case of mothers having health facilities with upto primary education as compared to no or limited

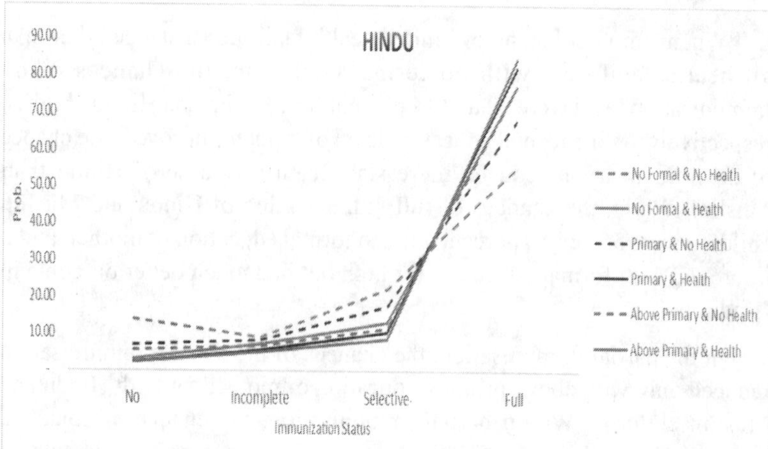

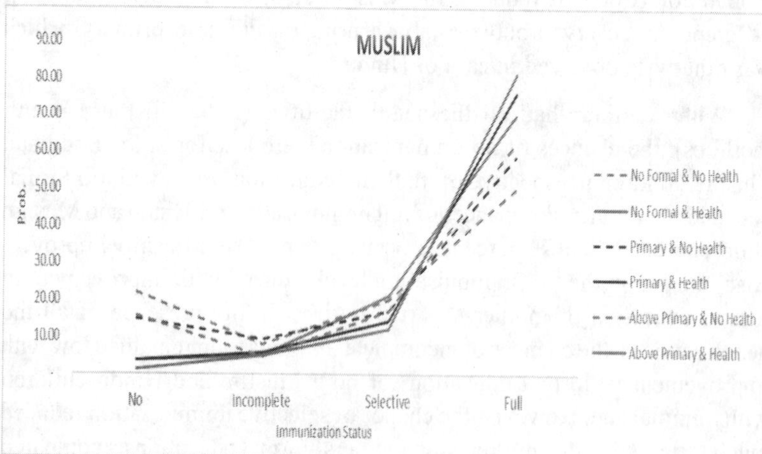

Graph 6: Probabilities of Immunisation Status for Formal Education and Health Facilities by Religion

health facilities with above primary education. This clearly established the fact that improvement in health facilities had more prominent impact in full immunisation level as compared to mothers' formal education. Along with all the health facilities, mother formal education further significantly improved the chance of full immunisation and inequity due to religion reduced largely with overall improvement in the chance of full immunisation.

4B. Castes

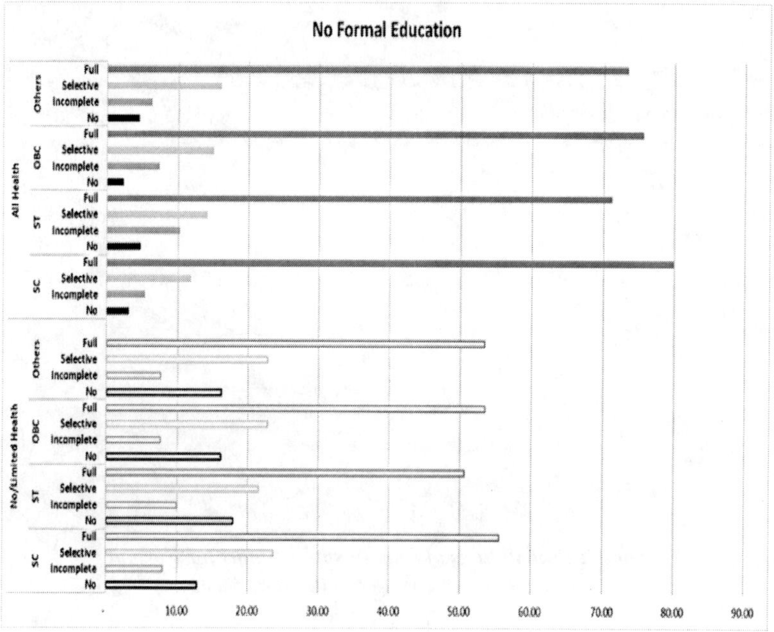
No Formal Education
All Health
No/Limited Health
Others
OBC
ST
SC
Full
Selective
Incomplete
No
10.00
20.00
30.00
40.00
50.00
60.00
70.00
80.00
90.00

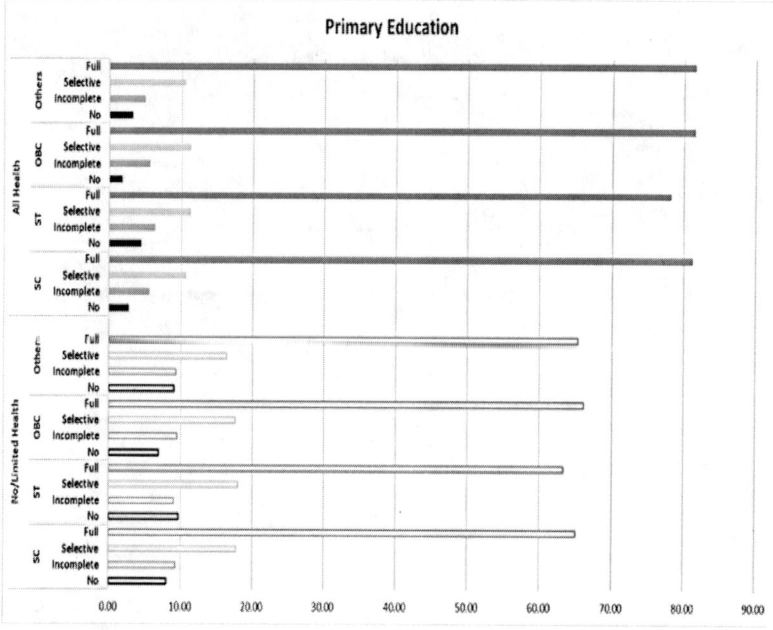
Primary Education
All Health
No/Limited Health
Others
OBC
ST
SC
Full
Selective
Incomplete
No
0.00
10.00
20.00
30.00
40.00
50.00
60.00
70.00
80.00
90.00

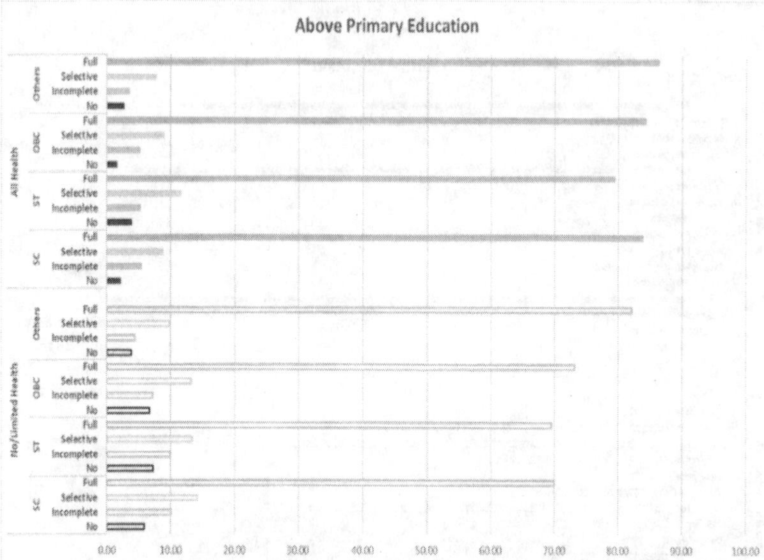

Graph 7: Probabilities of Immunisation Status for Formal Education and Health Facilities by Caste

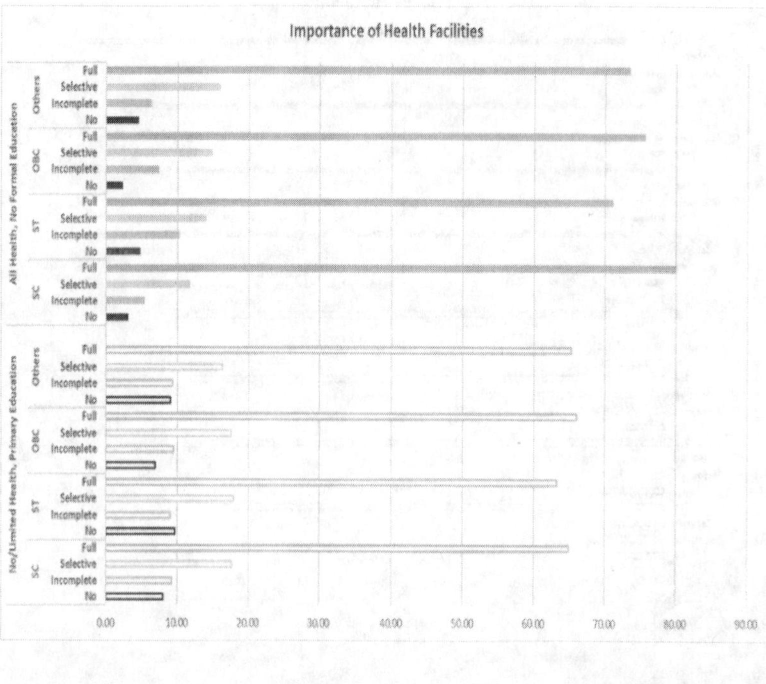

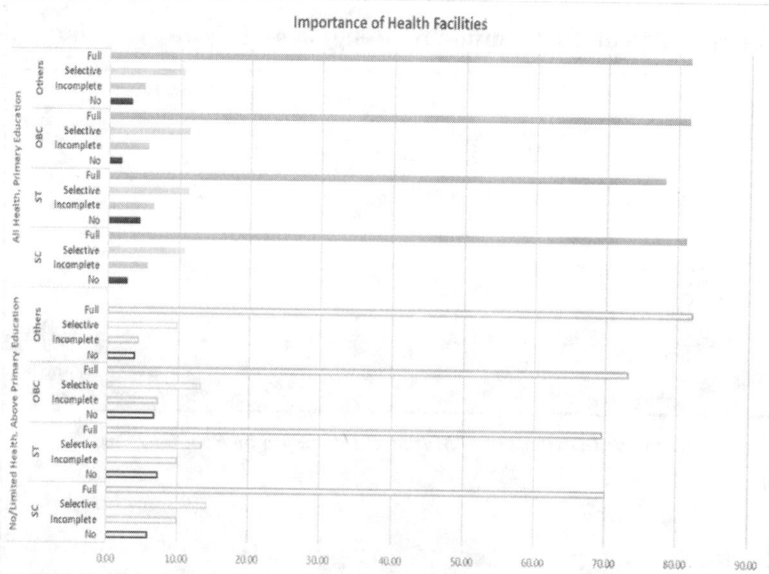

Graph 8: Probabilities of Immunisation Status for Formal Education and Health Facilities by Caste

The above Graph 7 shows that the chance of full immunisation improved across castes when mothers having all health facilities for all level of formal education of mother. Not only this, it also brought uniformity in immunisation state between castes with significant improvement in full immunisation chance and low chances of no, incomplete and partial immunisations. In this, formal education higher than primary education of mother reduced the chances of selection and incomplete immunisation for irrespective of nature of health facilities opted by mother. However, caste differences continued to persist.

Uniformity had achieved to a certain extent with above primary formal education and health facilities, except for Scheduled Tribes and are worse among other castes in best case scenario. On the other hand, similar to religion, the chance of fully immunised children was higher when mothers have all health facilities with no (primary) education as compared to no or limited health facilities with primary (above primary) formal education (Graph 8). In positive note, in most of these cases from Graph 7 and Graph 8, the immunisation status of Schedules Castes children was at par with "Others" caste.

5. Discussion on Distribution by Religion and Caste

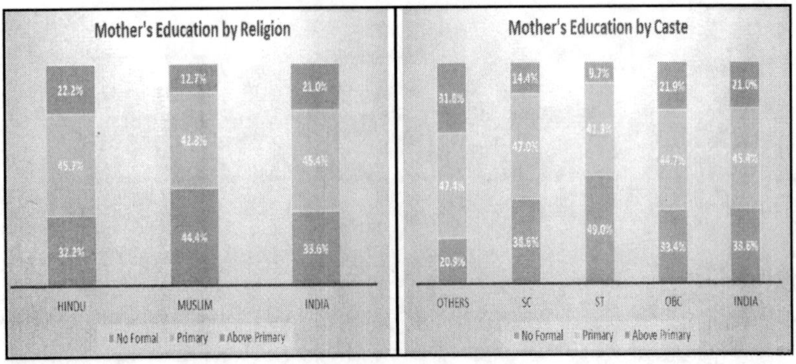

Graph 9: Distribution of Mothers' Education by Religion, Caste

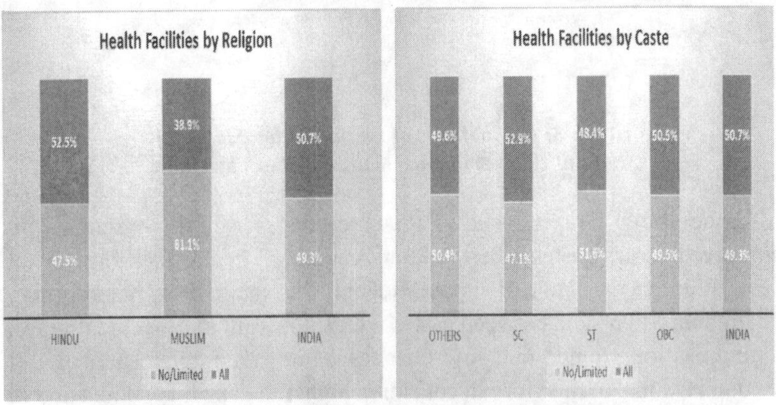

Graph 10: Distribution of Health Facilities by Religion, Caste

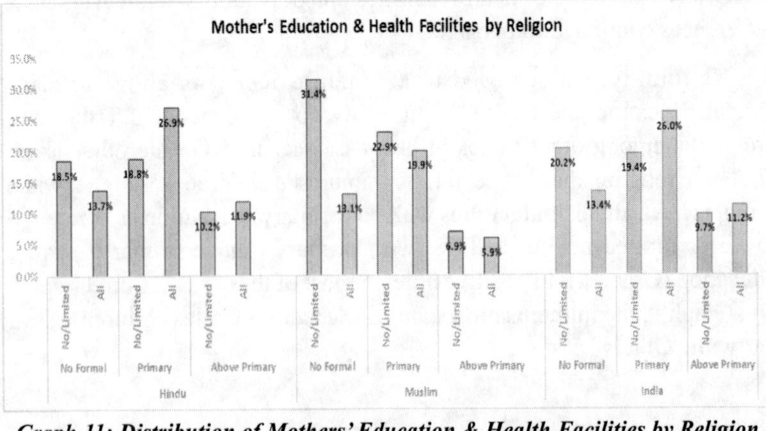

Graph 11: Distribution of Mothers' Education & Health Facilities by Religion

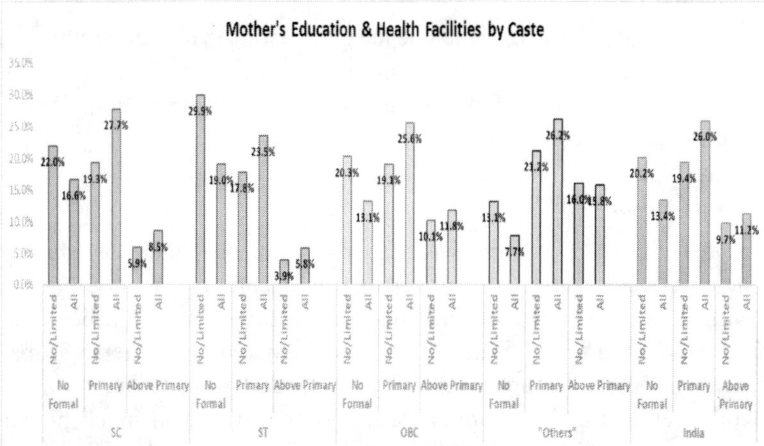

Graph 12: Distribution of Mothers' Education & Health Facilities by Caste

Above Graph 9 & Graph 10 are prepared with NFHS IV data following same definition as in this study, and show the unfavourable distribution of mother's formal educational level and access to health facilities for Muslim. Whereas, formal educational level of mothers from Scheduled Tribes remain low and almost 50 percent of them had no formal education and is followed by Scheduled Caste, OBC and "Others" caste. On the other hand, mothers' access to these health facilities had more or less even distribution for all castes.

In similar terms, Graph 11 exhibits that mothers having no formal education had high distribution of no or limited access to health facilities in Muslim, while it remained high as compared to mothers having all these health facilities for all formal education level. Whereas, the proportion of mother having all health facilities was higher than no or limited access to health facilities for primary and above primary formal education and it also derived the overall India level in same direction.

From Graph 12, no such specific difference is observed in distribution of access to health facilities and no or limited access to health facilities with mothers' formal education along castes in India. Apart for no formal education of mother, the proportion of no or limited access to health facilities was low with primary and above primary education. However, the gap between the no or limited access to health facilities with complete access to health facilities was significantly higher even proportionally for no formal education of mother.

This clearly shows the fundamental gap existing in our social structure even for access to health facilities and formal education of mother. And, these differences as one of many issues, resulted in unequal immunisation status for basic vaccines too.

6. Conclusion

Health facilities, with formal education of mother helped in reducing religion as well as caste-wise differences significantly. Apparently, mothers having access to all health facilities had relatively more influence in enhancing child immunisation status as compared to mothers' formal education. Both in religions and castes, the children whose mothers had all health facilities and no formal (primary) education had much higher probability of full immunisation as compared to those children whose mothers had no or limited access to health facilities and had primary (above primary) education.

Certainly, with no or limited access to health facilities, higher level of mother education enhanced the child immunisation along with lowering the religion-wise differences. The religion-wise differences in child immunisation reduced as mothers' education level had improved and access to all health facilities had been there, however, it was not eliminated completely. There still existed religion-wise differences in the chances of full immunisation between Hindu and Muslim children whose mothers had access to all health facilities and above primary education, but definitely, the improvement was quite noteworthy. On the other hand, along with high immunisation status, caste-wise differences in child immunisation reduced to marginal level with access to all health facilities and mothers' above primary education. However, in less privileged situations than mothers having access to all these health facilities and above primary education, caste-wise differences emerged. And so, the access to health facilities along with mothers' formal education enhanced the chance of children having full immunisation and above that brought the equality among children across all religions and castes.

Overall, to have less religion-wise differences and marginal caste-wise differences in child immunisation, access to all health facilities and mothers' above primary education were of essential need. It also showed that with the positive impact of mothers' formal education, health facilities, the influence of our embedded social structures which generally play an important and differentiating roles in other social issues, could be minimised to a significant extent in child immunisation status. Having such a privileged situation across all religions, castes is obviously desirable, but yet to achieve which is clearly shown in our demographic distribution. India needs to target on improving the overall education level and health facilities across all religions and castes, with more focus on those social structures who are lagging behind.

References

Bbaale, Edward, (2013). "Factors Influencing Childhood Immunisation in Uganda". Journal of Health, Population and Nutrition. Vol. 31, Issue No. 1, pp. 118-129.

Bicego, G and Boerma J T, (1993). "Maternal education and child survival: A comparative study of survey data from 17 countries. Social Science and Medicine, Vol. 36, issue 9, pp. 1207-1227.

De, Partha and Bhattacharya B N, (2002)." Determinants of child immunisation in four less- Developed states of north India". Journal of Child Health Care. Vol. 6, Issue 1, pp. 34-50.

Goodburn, E, G J Ebrahim and S Senapati, (1990). "Strategies educated mothers use to ensure the health of their children". Journal of Tropical Pediatrics; 36: 235–239.

Incentive for immunisation-J-Pal Policy Briefcase, Nov 2011.

Jamil, K., Bhuiya, A., Streatfield, K., & Chakrabarty, N. (1999). The immunisation programme in Bangladesh: impressive gains in coverage, but gaps remain. Health Policy and Planning, 14(1), 49-58.

Janssens Wendy, (2011). "Externalities in program Evaluation: The impact of a women's empowerment program on immunisation" Journal of the European Economic Association, Vol. 9, issue 6, pp. 1082-1113.

Kakwani, N, Wagstaff, A, Van Doorlsaer E. (1997). "Socioeconomic inequalities in health: measurement, computation and statistical inference" J Econometrics 466 1997;77:87–104.

Kate, B, Thakur, A, (1988). "Reasons of less coverage of immunisation under UI Programme". Indian J Public Health 1988, Vol. 32: 90.

Keja, Ko, Chan, Carole, Hayden, Gregory & Henderson, Ralph H. (1988). "Expanded Programme on Immunisation". World health statistics quarterly 1988; 41(2): 59-63.

Ministry of health and family welfare: Universal Immunisation Program.

Nath, B, Singh, JV and Awasthi, S. (2007). "A study on determinants of immunisation coverage among 12-23 months old children in urban slums of Lucknow district, India". Indian Journal Medical Sciences, 61:598-606.

Ojikutu, R K, (2012). "Beliefs, knowledge and perceptions of parents to paediatric immunisations in Lagos State, Nigeria". Journal of Management and Sustainability 2, 227.

Oladokun, R E, Adedokun, B O, Lawoyin, T O (2010). "Children not receiving adequate immunisation in Ibadan, Nigeria: What reasons and beliefs do their mothers have?". Nigerian Journal of Clinical Practice. Vol. 13, Issue 2, pp. 173–178.

Parthiban, K, Myde, C S, Rahe, M A, (2014). "An analysis of immunisation status of children in Chinnamanur and Cumbum area of Theni district, Tamil Nadu, India". Asian Journal of Epidemiology, Vol. 7, issue 1, pp. 23-27.

Parashar, S, (2005). "Moving beyond the mother-child dyad: women's education, child immunisation, and the importance of context in rural India". Social Science & Medicine, Vol. 61, issue-5, pp. 989-1000.

Pebley, A., Goldman, N., & Rodríguez, G. (1996). Prenatal and delivery care and childhood immunisation in Guatemala: do family and community matter? Demography, 33(2), 231-247.

Shrivastwa, N, Brenda, W G, Kolenic G E and et al. (2015). "Predictors of vaccination in India for children aged 12-36 months". American Journal of Preventive Medicine. Vol. 49, Issue 6, S-4, pp. S435-S444.

Tandon, B N and Gandhi, N. (1992). "Immunisation coverage in India for areas served by the Integrated Child Development Services programme. The Integrated Child Development Services Consultants". Bull World Health Organ, 70(4): 461-465.

Vikram Kriti, Vanneman, R. & Desai S.(2012). Linkages between maternal education and childhood immunisation in India. Social Science & Medicine, 75 (331-339).

The World Health Report 2000-Health System: Improving Performances, Geneva: WHO: 2000.

Appendix

Table 1: Definitions of Different Levels of Immunization Considered for the Study

1.	√	√	√	√	√	Full
2.	√	√	×	×	√	Incomplete
3.	√	√	√	×	√	
4.	√	×	×	×	×	Selective
5.	×	√	×	×	×	
6.	×	√	√	×	×	
7.	×	√	√	√	×	
8.	×	×	×	×	√	
9.	√	√	×	×	×	
10.	√	√	√	×	×	
11.	√	√	√	√	×	
12.	√	×	×	×	√	
13.	×	√	×	×	√	
14.	×	√	√	×	√	
15.	×	√	√	√	√	
16.	×	×	×	×	×	No

Table 2: Multinomial Logistic Regression

Variables	*Coef.*	*St.Err.*	*p-value*	*Sig*
No Immunization				
Girl	0.016	0.059	0.793	
Rural	-0.022	0.093	0.814	
Birth Order>=3	0.324	0.059	0.000	***
Muslim	0.628	0.078	0.000	***
Others Religion	-0.052	0.171	0.763	
SC	0.093	0.102	0.363	
ST	0.479	0.106	0.000	***
OBC	-0.003	0.087	0.969	
Mother Primary Education	-0.279	0.067	0.000	***
Mother Above Primary Education	-0.328	0.130	0.012	**
Institutional Delivery	-0.846	0.064	0.000	***
Mother Received TT	-1.037	0.074	0.000	***
Mother ANC Visited	-0.442	0.071	0.000	***
CHW Interaction	-1.413	0.061	0.000	***
Middle Wealth	0.355	0.112	0.002	***
Poor Wealth	0.666	0.113	0.000	***
Constant	-0.291	0.150	0.053	*
Incomplete Immunization				
Girl	-0.133	0.050	0.008	***
Rural	0.083	0.072	0.247	
Birth Order>=3	0.241	0.055	0.000	***
Muslim	0.074	0.078	0.345	
Others Religion	-0.196	0.175	0.261	
SC	0.174	0.089	0.050	*
ST	0.407	0.094	0.000	***
OBC	0.223	0.076	0.003	***
Mother Primary Education	-0.067	0.058	0.246	
Mother Above Primary Education	-0.237	0.088	0.007	***
Institutional Delivery	-0.243	0.061	0.000	***
Mother Received TT	-0.023	0.080	0.771	
Mother ANC Visited	-0.289	0.063	0.000	***
CHW Interaction	-0.514	0.064	0.000	***
Middle Wealth	0.058	0.083	0.483	
Poor Wealth	0.195	0.074	0.009	***
Constant	-1.816	0.134	0.000	***
Selective Immunization				
Girl	0.067	0.037	0.070	*
Rural	-0.035	0.056	0.533	
Birth Order>=3	0.241	0.042	0.000	***
Muslim	0.296	0.055	0.000	***
Others Religion	0.084	0.105	0.420	
SC	0.167	0.066	0.012	**
ST	0.183	0.074	0.014	**
OBC	0.179	0.057	0.002	***
Mother Primary Education	-0.207	0.044	0.000	***
Mother Above Primary Education	-0.454	0.069	0.000	***
Institutional Delivery	-0.279	0.044	0.000	***
Mother Received TT	-0.374	0.061	0.000	***
Mother ANC Visited	-0.215	0.049	0.000	***
CHW Interaction	-0.638	0.045	0.000	***
Middle Wealth	0.233	0.066	0.000	***
Poor Wealth	0.338	0.061	0.000	***
Constant	-0.698	0.107	0.000	***

(*Contd...*)

Mean dependent var	3.476	SD dependent var	0.923
Pseudo r-squared	0.068	Number of obs	47073.000
Chi-square	2477.403	Prob > chi2	0.000
Akaike crit. (AIC)	75215.368	Bayesian crit. (BIC)	75662.101

*** p<0.01, ** p<0.05, * p<0.1.

Table 4: Multinomial Logistic Regression with Interactions between Religion, Health Facilities & Mothers' Formal Education

Mother's Education, Health Facilities	Religion	No	Incomplete	Selective
No Formal Education No/Limited Health Facilities	Hindu			
	Muslim	0.561***	-0.101	0.07
	Others	0.036	-0.481	0.061
No Formal Education All Health Facilities	Hindu	-1.865***	-0.581***	-0.867***
	Muslim	-1.544***	-0.806***	-0.292***
	Others	-1.671***	-0.876**	-1.21***
Primary Education No/Limited Health Facilities	Hindu	-0.91***	-0.307***	-0.446***
	Muslim	-0.189	-0.19	-0.335***
	Others	-0.473*	-0.038	-0.181
Primary Education All Health Facilities	Hindu	-2.2***	-0.89***	-1.151***
	Muslim	-1.639***	-0.746***	-0.75***
	Others	-1.671***	-1.026***	-1.044***
Above Primary Education No/Limited Health Facilities	Hindu	-1.286***	-0.634***	-0.997***
	Muslim	-0.587	-0.766***	-0.396**
	Others	-2.158***	-1.262***	-0.908***
Above Primary Education All Health Facilities	Hindu	-2.26***	-1.044***	-1.384***
	Muslim	-2.688***	-0.957***	-0.986***
	Others	-3.126***	-1.68***	-1.753***
Constant		-1.382***	-1.817***	-0.91***

**** p<0.01, ** p<0.05, * p<0.1*

Table 5: Multinomial Logistic Regression with Interactions between Caste, Health Facilities & Mothers' Formal Education

Mother's Education, Health Facilities	Caste	No	Incomplete	Selective
No Formal Education No/Limited Health Facilities	SC			
	ST	0.431***	0.313**	-0.164
	OBC	0.27***	0.119	0.025
	"Others"	0.275**	-0.122	-0.189
No Formal Education All Health Facilities	SC	-1.79***	-0.761***	-1.064***
	ST	-1.251***	-0.308*	-0.764***
	OBC	-2.043***	-0.396***	-0.768***
	"Others"	-1.341***	-0.521**	-0.668***
Primary Education No/Limited Health Facilities	SC	-0.625***	-0.08	-0.442***
	ST	-0.407**	-0.033	-0.402***
	OBC	-0.792***	-0.166	-0.467***
	"Others"	-0.51***	-0.228	-0.527***
Primary Education All Health Facilities	SC	-1.932***	-0.743***	-1.175***
	ST	-1.415***	-0.574***	-1.085***
	OBC	-2.375***	-0.744***	-1.126***
	"Others"	-1.791***	-0.877***	-1.195***
Above Primary Education No/Limited Health Facilities	SC	-1.023***	-0.358	-0.743***
	ST	-0.798**	-0.009	-0.795***
	OBC	-0.929***	-0.384**	-0.859***
	"Others"	-1.605***	-0.992***	-1.275***
Above Primary Education All Health Facilities	SC	-2.224***	-0.798***	-1.419***
	ST	-1.567***	-0.773***	-1.075***
	OBC	-2.544***	-0.853***	-1.392***
	"Others"	-2.041***	-1.279***	-1.569***
Constant		-1.468***	-1.944***	-0.855***

*** $p<0.01$, ** $p<0.05$, * $p<0.1$

16

Crime and Socio-Economic Condition in India during 1990-2017: An Empirical Analysis

Poulomi Khasnobis,
Soumyanada Dinda

Abstract

This paper investigates the relationship between crimes and socio-economic factors in India highlighting the financial condition. It focuses on property (Robbery) and economic (Breach of Trust) crimes in India in the period of 1990-2017. Applying advanced econometrics techniques it examines nature of time series data. Unit root test suggests that all the variables follow integration of order one (i.e., I(1)) and consequently we examine co-integration test. Johansen co-integration test confirms the co-integrating relationship among variables. GDP per capita has no significant impact on property crime and it has positive impact on Economic crime. Inflation plays a vital role for increasing crimes. Real rate of interest is considered as proxy of financial factor and examine the connection between Crime and financial development. Higher education level helps to decrease economic crime (BOT) while more jobs leads to less property crime (robbery). Inflation helps to increase crime in society. Government should take some step to control unemployment by employment generation program, to increase education level and must concentrate on reducing inflation.

Key Words: *Crime, Socio-Economic Conditions, Breach of Trust, Robbery, Economic Development, Co-integration, VECM.*

Introduction

The rising criminal activity in various parts of the world is the greatest threat to the human civilisation. Crime destroys human life. People are not only victims; society also has to pay for it. Crime hampers business environment. Therefore, the government should design certain policy to control it. In this context it is required to identify socioeconomic conditions or factors which are responsible for crimes. There are mainly two factors 'push' and 'pull' acting behind the crimes. Social inequality acts as a push factors in the generation of crime and higher economic incentives constitute 'pull' factors of crime.

Becker (1974) was one of the first researcher who identified that crime depends on several social development factors. Economic development is hampered by illegal activities. Development and crime both are closely intertwined with each other. Some individuals become criminal because of their preference pattern between legal or illegal activities depending on the economic returns from those activities. Higher economic return is the influencing factor of crime (Ehrilichi, 1973). Crime does impose the various types of monetary and economic cost on individuals and society also, it also creates insecurity, propagates a sense of fear. The victims of crime are burdened with psychological setbacks (Cui and Hazra, 2017).

There are two types of crime in India, one is cognizable and another one is non-cognizable (Dutta and Hussain, 2009). In case of cognizable Crime police has taken action on receipt of complaints and non-cognizable crime left to be pursued by affected parties in court and police initiates investigation into such crimes with magisterial permission (Dutta and Hussain, 2009). Chakroborty (2014) categorised two types of crime mainly one is IPC, and SLL in India. IPC (Indian Penal Code) includes in property and violence crime likes illegal narcotics, gambling, etc., and SLL is special local laws. Many works focused on detecting factors of violent and property crime. Economic growth is influenced by crime rate (Ahmed et. al. 2014; Kathena and Shefeni, 2017). This relationship varies in different countries (Ragnasdottir, 2014). In India liberalisation leads to acceleration of growth however, crime did not reduce (Dutta and Hussain, 2009). Economic growth has no impact on property crime in India (Chakroborty, 2014). Property crime rate also depends on socio-economic factors like poverty, literacy rate, business cycle, demographics, criminal justice system, and family structure, unemployment etc (Allen, 1996). Unemployment rate, wage inequality and higher growth rate of the property variability mainly lead to property crime (Clarke and Feilding, 1999). Economic growth increases by 3.72% while robbery rate reduces from 2.09% to 1.1% in India (Kumar, 2013). Unemployment has a positive impact on crime (Melick, 2003). There is no significant relationship between Unemployment and aggregate property crime in Croatia. There is negative relationship between violent crime and unemployment (Recher 2016). Robbery and unemployment rates are not significant for other types of violent crime. Socio-economic factors like income inequality, unemployment rate, and poverty are responsible for specific types of crime such as property and violent crime (Berk Ozler, 2005; George Saridakis, 2004). Poverty and income inequality has negative impact on property crime (Allen, 1996; Poveda, 2012; Char Foon Tang, 2009; George Saridakis, 2004). Literacy rate has no significant role to play on property crime in India (Chakroborty, 2014). Ehrilichi model (1973) was considered first to point out the effectiveness of law and enforcement to control crime. This model estimates the efficiency of police and court activity against felony. When a person is charged with felony then the society is doubly affected, a personal loss to him and administrative cost for him. This model also points out the positive relationship between income inequality and property crime. The government should take actions to reduce the inequality and spend more resources on law enforcement. Police force is inefficient to reduce the property crime rate in India (Chakroborty, 2014).

In this study, we will analyze only property crime and Economic crime and their deducing factors in India. Property crime is closely associated with economic incentives. We will identify some offense under IPC viz. robbery, dacoity, burglary and theft, which are called Property Crime (because of damage to property). Here, we will consider two types of detecting factors, one is social factor and another is financial factor. Detecting social factors are education, unemployment, income inequality, migration etc. In this study, we focus on the impact of financial and socio-economic factors to control crime in emerging India. Objective of this study is to investigate the impact of social, economic development and financial factors on both property and economic crimes. According to NCRB (National Crime Records Bureau, the Government of India) property crime includes four criminal activities, viz., dacoity, robbery, theft and burglary; while Economic crime includes in three types of crime such as cheating, breach of trust and counterfeiting. In this paper, we select robbery and breach of trust as proxy variables of property and economic crime respectively. Both crimes are organised group crime. Robbery means when maximum five or less than five offenders are involved in occurrence of crime. Breach of trust (BOT) can be defined when such organisations violate the legal contract with their client and it is involved in money or property. Primary education enrollment and unemployment rate are social proxy variables. GDPPC, Inflation, real rate of interest are the proxy for economic development and financial factor, respectively.

Literature Review

In this section, we will review some related literature which have helped us finding research gap. Ahmed et al. (2014) investigated relationship between crime rate and economic growth in Pakistan by using time series data for 1980 to 2011. They concluded that crime has a negative but insignificant impact on growth in short run but it is significant in long run taking crime as independent variable and economic growth as dependent variable. They have suggested Pakistan should adopt various development programmes aiming to improvement of literacy rate, reduction of poverty and unemployment by raising job opportunity. Kathena and Shefeni (2017) have identified a relationship between economic growth and crime rate in Namibia, using secondary data. The co-integration test shows that there is no long run relationship between two variables crime and economic growth. Granger causality represents bidirectional causality running from economic growth to crime rate and vice versa. Impulse Response Function shows that increasing crime rate does indeed result in a declining economic growth. Since increasing crime rates lead to reduce economic growth then criminal justice forum should be adopted to help reducing crime and the fear of crime and their social and economic cost. Kumar (2013) has argued that reduction of homicide rate from 5.93 (1st quartile) to 4.59 (median) would enhance the annual growth rate of per capita net state domestic product by about 11% and a reduction of robbery rate to 1.1 from 2.09 would increase growth by 3.72%.

By using and analysing time series data (1971-2006), Nicolas and Alexandros (2009) argued that criminal offences depend on socio-economic determinants and justice system. They identified that unemployment rate, real consumption per employee, number of convict, net migration per 100.00 people are the socio-economic determinants of crime rate. The result shows that economic depression creates criminal activities and opportunities and economic prosperity created for gaining profit from illegitimate action. Conviction rates prove to be lower significance and migration rates are more insignificant than conviction rates. Enamorado et.al. (2015) explained that the impact of income inequality on crime in unique in the context of Mexico's drug war. Their study reveals that increase of more than 10 drugs related homicides per hundred thousand inhabitants due to 1-point increase of Gini coefficient across Mexican municipalities. Allen (1996) on the other hand, has shown that unemployment has a positive impact on crime. It also suggests existence of strong correlation between criminal justice and crime. Poverty and income inequality have negative impact on property crime while age and family structure has little impact on property crime. There are several other studies showing impact of crimes on economic growth and migration pattern and impact of poverty, income inequality, inflation, judicial system, population density, etc., on crime rate (Ray Burhman, et.al, 2006; Poveda, 2012; Tang, 2009; Ozler, 2005).

Richard Fowles and Mary Marva (1996) have found a robust relation between wage inequality and criminal activities in US, by using OLS and EBA technique with the help of cross-sectional data set for major MSAS over period 1975-1990. The result shows that wage inequality is very significant for violent crime but insignificant for property crime. Poverty and unemployment both factors are responsible for all types of crime. In another study, Khan et. al. (2015) using Pakistani data have found that higher education leads to lower crime and GDPPC, poverty and unemployment has positive and significant impact on crime. More income leads to more crime in Pakistan.

Data and Methodology

This study is based on secondary data. We have collected crime data from National Crime Records Bureau (NCRB) of India for the period of 1990-2017. Property crime includes four different types of crime which are robbery, dacoity, theft and burglary. Economic crime includes three types of crimes, which are cheating, breach of trust and counterfeiting. Here we choose 'robbery' and 'breach of trust' as proxy of property crime and economic offense respectively, as per the NCRB reports. Both crimes are organised crime activities. Robbery refers to at most five offenders are involved in occurrence. Breach of trust (BOT) refers to violation of the legal contract with their client at organisation levels and it is involved in money or property.

We have collected and used data for Inflation, primary education enrollment, unemployment, GDPPC from the World Bank[1] and data of real rate of interest have been collected from the RBI. Data[2] of Inflation (as measured by the consumer price index reflects the annual percentage change in the cost to the average consumer of acquiring a basket of goods and services), primary education enrollment (gross enrollment ratio is the ratio of total enrollment regardless of age, to the population), unemployment (Unemployment refers to the share of the labour force that is without work but available for and seeking employment), GDP per capita (gross domestic product divided by mid-year population, constant 2010 US dollar), and real rate of interest are collected (the lending interest rate adjusted for inflation as measured by the GDP deflator) from the World Bank (data were downloaded in October 2019).

Applying unit root test (ADF test) we examine the characteristics of data for stationary check for each variable. After confirmation of order one (i.e., I(1)), Johansen co-integration is applied for checking the existence of long run relationship among the variables. We applied VECM model for short run dynamics and impact of socioeconomic factors on Robbery and Breach of trust. In this context we use the following two models. Variables are GDP per capita (GDPPC), unemployment, education, real interest rate and inflation. Model 1 and Model 2 are differentiated due to incorporation of real rate of interest and inflation, respectively.

Robbery1 = f(EDU, GDPPC, real rate of interest, unemployment)
Robbery2 = f(EDU, GDPPC, Inflation, unemployment)
Breach of Trust1 = f(EDU, GDPPC, real rate of interest, unemployment)
Breach of Trust2 = f(EDU, GDPPC, Inflation, unemployment)

We have constructed the following model considering social, economic and financial development. In model 1, we have used four variables, which include three major development indicators like GDPPC for economic development, primary education enrollment, unemployment for social development and financial development (real rate of interest). In model 2, we take inflation instead of real rate of interest and other variables are same as in model 1.

Model specification for short run dynamics

Model 1:

$$CR_t = \alpha + \sum_{i=1}^{n} \beta_0 \Delta CR_{t-i} + \sum_{i=1}^{p} \beta_1 \Delta(GDPPC)_{t-i} + \sum_{i=1}^{q} \beta_2 \Delta(UNEMP)_{t-i} + \sum_{i=1}^{r} \beta_3 \Delta(P.EDU)_{t-i} + \sum_{i=1}^{u} \beta_4 \Delta(real\ rate\ of\ interest)_{t-i} + \gamma_1 EC_{t-1} + \mu_{1t}$$

and

Model 2:

$$CR_t = \alpha + \sum_{i=1}^{n} \beta_0 \Delta CR_{t-i} + \sum_{i=1}^{p} \beta_1 \Delta(GDPPC)_{t-i} + \sum_{i=1}^{q} \beta_2 \Delta(UNEMP)_{t-i} + \sum_{i=1}^{r} \beta_3 \Delta(P.EDU)_{t-i} + \sum_{i=1}^{s} \beta_5 \Delta(Inflation)_{t-i} + \gamma_2 EC_{t-1} + \mu_{2t}$$

Where μ_{1t} and μ_{2t} are random disturbance term, EC_{t-1} is error correction term, γ_1 and γ_2 are coefficient of error correction term and they are also known as adjustment coefficients which show how disequilibrium is adjusted in next period for maintaining the long run relationship.

Result and Discussion

Table 1 describes the summary statistics of major variables including robbery and breach of trust. All variables are converted to log form to avoid heterogeneity. We observe that average log value of robbery, breach of trust, unemployment, Inflation, real rate of interest, GDPPC and, primary education are 0.807, 0.431, 0.983, 2.02 and 1.53, 6.90 and 1.54, respectively. It may be observed that average property crime (robbery) is higher than average of economic crime (breach of trust).

Table 1: Descriptive Statistics

Variable	*obs*	*Mean*	*SD*	*Min*	*Max*
Ln Robbery	28	0.807	0.214	0.470	1.13
Ln Breach of Trust	28	0.431	0.152	0.182	0.74
Ln UNEMPLOYMENT	27	0.983	0.860	0.818	1.15
Ln Inflation	28	2.02	3.24	0.91	2.63
Ln real rate of interest	28	0.425	0.82	-0.32	0.79
Ln GDPPC	28	6.90	0.384	6.35	7.59
LnPrimaryeducation enrollment	25	1.54	0.85	1.50	1.56

Source: Calculation based on collected data (available at NCRB, World Bank and RBI)

Nature of data is examined and judged whether variables are stationary. Unit root test is applied for it and results are reported in Table 2.

Table: 2 Results of ADF Unit Root Test

Variable	*Lags*	*Level*	*1st difference*	*Remark*
Robbery[a]	6	-1.631	-4.29**	I(1)
Breach of Trust[a]	6	-1.78	-3.64**	I(1)
Primary education[a]	1	-0.75	-3.63**	I(1)
Inflation[a]	6	0.202	-5.80***	I(1)
Unemployment[b]	6	-2.734	-3.898**	I(1)
GDPPC[a]	6	2.78	-4.805***	I(1)
Real rate of interest[b]	6	-3.42	-7.27***	I(1)

Note: (a) Unit root test under intercept, (b) unit root test under the intercept with trend.

Table 2 represents the result of ADF unit root test (ADF). Result shows that all variables are non-stationary in their level data and stationary at 1st difference of all variables. Hence, all variable follow the integrated order of one, i.e., I(1). Next we examine co-integration test for all I(1) variables and results are presented in Table 3.

Table 3 shows the results of Johansen co-integration test. First coloumn of Table 3 presents number of co-integrating equation(s). Results of Trace statistics and maximum Eigen value of both models of both variables are displayed in Table 3. All results (Trace statistic and maximum Eigen value) indicate the existence of co-integration in both property and economic crimes (or robbery and breach of trust variables). Highly statistically significant results suggest that there is a co-integrating relation among variables. Johansen co-integration test indicates that there is statistically significant one co-integrating equation for each crime in our study. It indicates the long run relationship between crime and selected variables. All models confirm that there are long run relationships in robbery and breach of trust.

Table 3: Results of Johansen Co-integration Test

Crime: Robbery						
	Model 1			***Model 2***		
No. of CE	***Trace Statistics***	***C(5%)***	***P- value***	***Trace Statistics***	***C(5%)***	***P- value***
r = 0	91.24***	69.81	0.0004	101.25***	88.80	0.004
r≤1	46.10*	47.85	0.07	50.85	63.87	0.376
r≤2	17.32	29.79	0.616	30.66	42.91	0.463
r≤3	5.59	15.49	0.743	12.17	25.87	0.799
r≤4	0.444	3.84	0.504	2.24	12.51	0.951
No. of CE	***Eigen Value***	***C(5%)***	***P- value***	***Eigen Value***	***C(5%)***	***P- value***
r = 0	45.14***	33.87	0.001	50.40***	38.33	0.001
r≤1	28.78**	27.58	0.03	20.19	32.11	0.636
r≤2	11.72	21.13	0.574	18.48	25.82	0.341
r≤3	5.14	14.26	0.723	9.93	19.38	0.625
r≤4	0.444	3.84	0.504	2.24	12.51	0.951
Crime: Breach of Trust						
	Model 1			***Model 2***		
No. of CE	***Trace Statistics***	***C(5%)***	***P- value***	***Trace Statistics***	***C(5%)***	***P- value***
r = 0	102.14***	69.81	0.000	74.23**	69.81	0.021
r≤1	60.44***	47.85	0.002	39.55	47.85	0.238
r≤2	25.00	29.79	0.161	15.52	29.79	0.745
r≤3	9.32	15.49	0.33	5.15	15.49	0.792
r≤4	1.88	3.84	0.169	0.452	3.84	0.501
No. of CE	***Eigen Value***	***C(5%)***	***P- value***	***Eigen Value***	***C(5%)***	***P- value***
r = 0	41.70***	33.87	0.004	34.67	33.87**	0.040
r≤1	35.44***	27.58	0.004	24.03	27.58	0.133
r≤2	15.67	21.13	0.244	10.37	21.13	0.709
r≤3	7.43	14.26	0.438	4.70	14.26	0.779
r≤4	1.88	3.84	0.169	0.452	3.84	0.501

Note: (i) Results are based on intercept with no trend. (ii) '***', '**' and '*' denote statistical significant level at 1%, 5% and 10%, respectively.

Based on Johansen co-integration test, Table 4 presents long run relationship between selected crimes and socio-economic and financial variables. This result shows that GDPPC has no impact on robbery in both Model 1 and Model 2. Breach of Trust (BOT) is positively significant with GDPPC in Model 2. Model 1 shows inverse relation between crime and unemployment. Model 1 demonstrates that for breach of trust and robbery rate decline respectively around 1.32% and 3.92% as one unit rise of unemployment. However, Model 2 in case of robbery shows a direct relationship between unemployment and robbery. In Model 2, robbery increases in 4.66% with rise of each unit of unemployment. This result is same as in Pakistan (Gill and Khan, 2011). In Model 2, unemployment is insignificant for BOT. BOT falls at 2.92% in Model 2 with rising primary education enrollment while it is insignificant in Model 1. Education plays an insignificant role for robbery. Inflation is directly related to Robbery and BOT in long run. Inflation is associated with the cost of living in the society. It is difficult to maintain the standard of living as the price level increases and people may commit to crime. This result also same as in Malaysia (Tang, 2009). Real rate of interest rate is positively significant only for robbery while it is insignificant for BOT. We prefer Model 2 to Model 1 in terms of fitting criteria. In other word, incorporation of inflation in Model 2 is better than that of real rate of interest for representing economic condition for explaining crimes in this study.

Table 4: Estimated Co-integrating Vector (Long Run Relation)

Variables	*Robbery*		*Breach of Trust*	
	M-1	*M-2*	*M-1*	*M-2*
	Coef (t value)	*Coef (t value)*	*Coef (t-value)*	*Coef (t-value)*
lnGDPPC	0.149 (0.28)	-0.222 (-0.483)	0.300 (1.11)	-0.527** (-2.19)
ln primary edu enrollment	-3.65 (-1.44)	-3.59 (-1.62)	-1.50 (-1.22)	2.02** (1.97)
ln unemp	3.92*** (3.58)	-4.66*** (-4.62)	1.32** (2.35)	0.236 (0.580)
ln real rate of interest	-0.17*** (-3.16)		0.047 (1.60)	
Ln inflation		-1.52*** (-9.28)		-0.448*** (-4.82)
C	11.44	24.89	3.06	

Note: (i) Figures in parentheses are t-values. (ii) '***', '**' and '*' denote statistical significant level at 1%, 5% and 10%, respectively.

Table 5: Estimated Short-run Relationship

	Robbery		*Breach of Trust*	
	Model 1	***Model 2***	***M1***	***M2***
EC_{t-1}	-0.093** (-1.96)	-0.19*** (4.52)	-0.155** (-2.46)	-0.366*** (-4.07)
Δ Robbery(-1)	0.529** (2.20)	-0.100 (-0.411)		
Δ BOT(-1)			0.308 (1.36)	-0.097 (-0.406)
ΔGDPPC (-1)	-0.155 (-0.165)	-3.42*** (-3.61)	0.190 (0.320)	-1.30** (-2.23)
Δ p edu enrollment(-1)	1.15 (0.940)	0.642 (0.716)	1.22* (1.88)	2.34*** (3.86)
Δunemp (-1)	0.583 (1.17)	0.060 (0.173)	0.109 (0.361)	0.077 (0.332)
Δ Inflation(-1)		0.171*** (-3.61)		-0.070** (-2.42)
Δ real rate of interest(-1)	0.014 (0.843)		0.013 (1.17)	
C	-0.022 (-0.491)	0.116*** (2.71)	-0.0269 (-0.909)	0.022 (0.873)
AIC	-14.98	-17.15	-15.07	-17.83
SIC	-12.98	-15.16	-13.08	-15.83

Note: (i) Figures in parentheses are t-values. (ii) '***', '**' and '*' denote statistical significant level at 1%, 5% and 10%, respectively.

Table 5 presents the short run dynamics. The coefficient of error correction term is negative and significant. It indicates that there exists an error correction mechanism. The short run dynamics are statistically significant for robbery and BOT. Significant negative coefficient of error correction term suggests that there is convergence; in other words, if any departure from long run equilibrium, in short run it will come back to long run equilibrium path. Table 5 also shows the estimated short run relationships among variables. In short run, growth of GDPPC leads to lower the growth rate of both robbery and BOT in Model 2. Robbery rate and BOT both decline with rising income. Growth rate of robbery and BOT inversely related to that of inflation rate in short run.

It is observed that inflation, real rate of interest and unemployment significantly affect property crime (robbery) in long run while only inflation in short runs. Change of GDPPC or economic growth reduces robbery in short run.

It is also noted that breach of trust has linear relation with GDPPC, education and inflation in long run as well as in short run.

Concluding remarks

This study examines the relationship between crime and socio-economic factors in India during 1990-2017. The study observes long run relationship between crime and socioeconomic variables with short run dynamics. This paper shows that unemployment has negative impact on Breach of Trust and Robbery in Model 1. Unemployment have positive impact on robbery in both model but no impact on BOT. Education level reduces BOT but no impact on robbery rate. This is probably due to social upliftment. As education level rises in a country, then ethics of the people may raise. So, less people commits to the economic crime. GDPPC is insignificant for Robbery in both models; however, it has positive impact on BOT. Inflation rate plays an important role for increasing crimes in long run as well as in short run. From these findings we could suggest some policy to combat the robbery and breach of trust. Inflation rate certainly increases both robbery and breach of trust. Government should focus on price control to reduce crime. Through the increasing education level we can control economic crime and we can reduce robbery rate by creating more jobs or job opportunities.

There are some limitations of this study. Data are limited over time. Inequality is important factor which is used here. Regional variation is not captured in this study. Our next research agenda is to capture it.

References

Adekoya, F. A., Rajak, A. A. N., 2017. The Dynamic relationship between crime and economic growth in Nigeria. International Journal of Management and Economics. Vol. 53, Issue 1.

Ahmed, A., Ali, S., Ahmed, N., 2014. Crime and Economic Growth in Developing country. Journal of Basic and Applied Scientific Research, Vol. 4(4), pp. 31-41.

Allen, C. A., 1996. Socio Economic Condition and property crimes: A comparative Review test of the Professional Literature. American Journal of Economics and Sociology. Vol. 55, No. 3. pp. 293-308.

Becker, G. S. 1974. Crime and Punishment, NBER. ISBN No. 0-87014-2362-1.

Burnman, R., Feinberg, M, R. Husted, A, Thomas., 2004 Central city crime and Suburban Eco growth, Applied Economics, ISSN: 0003-6846, pp. 917-922.

Chakraborty, R. 2014. Deterrence Effect of Police on violent and property crime: An Empirical Investigation. https://www.ssrn.com/abstract=2488997.

Clarke, R and Feilding, N. (1999). Crime and Economic Growth, British Journal of Criminology. JSTOR, Vol. 39, No. 3, pp. 391-400.

Cui, Z., Hazra, D. 2017. Macro-Economic determinants of Crime: Evidence from India, SSRN Electronic Journal.

Dutta, M., and Hussain, Z. 2009. Determinants of Crime rates: Crime deterrence and growth in Post liberalised in India. MPRA.

Ehrlichi, I., 1973. Participation in Illegitimate Activities: A theoretical and Empirical Investigation. Journal of Political Economy, Vol. 81, No. 3, pp. 521-565.

Eide, E., Rubin, H. P., Shepard, M. J. 1999. Economics of Crime. http://ssrn.com/abstract=1912073., Vol. 2, No. 3.

Enamorado, T., Calva, L. F. L., Castelman, R. C., Winkler, H., 2015. Income inequality and violent crime: Evidence from Mexico Drug War. HiCN. Working paper 196.

Foon, T. C., 2009. Linkage Among Inflation, Unemployment and Crime in Malaysia. Journal of Economics and Management. ISSN 1823-836x. pp. 50-61.

Fowles, R., Merva, M., 1996. Wage inequality and criminal activity: An External Bounds Analysis for the US 1975-90. CRIMINOLOGY, Wiley Online Library, Vol. 34, Issue 3.

Glaeser, L. E., Sacredotes, B., 1996. Why is there more crime in city? NBER Working paper no. 5430.

Han, L., Bandopadhyay, S., Bhattecharya, S., 2013. Determinants violent and property crimes in England and Wales: A panel data Analysis. https://www.tandfonline.com/doi/full/10.1080/00036846.2013.806782

Iqbal, M., Jalil, H., 2010. Urbanisation and Crime: A Case Study of Pakistan. Pakistan Development Review.

Kathena, N, I., Sheefeni, J., 2017. Relationship between Economic Growth and Crime rate in Nambia. European Journal of Basic and Economic Science, Vol. 4, No. 1.

Khan, N., Ahmed, J., Nawaz, M., Zaman, K., 2015. The Socio-Economic determinants of Crime in Pakistan: New Evidence on an Old Debate. Arab Economic and Business Journal, Vol. (25)., pp. 73-81.

Kumar, S., 2013. Crime and Economic Growth: Evidence from India. MPRA.

Melick, D, Mathew, 2003. The relationship between 'Crime Unemployment and The Park Place Economist, Vol. 11, Issue 1.

NCRB data 1990-2017 available at https://ncrb.gov.in/hi/crime-india

Nikolas, D., Alexandros,G., 2009. The effects of socio economic determinants on crime rate: An Empirical research in case of Greece with co-integration Analysis. International Journal of Economic Science and Applied Research 2(2):51-64.

Poveda, C, A., 2012. Violence crime and Economic Development in Colombian City: A Dynamic Panel Data Analysis. Journal of International Development. Int DEV 24, pp. 809-827.

Ragnarsdottir, G. A., 2014. Investigating the long run causal relationship between crime and GDP in Sweeden.

Ray Burhman, et.al (2006). Central city crime and Suburban Eco growth, Applied Economics, pp. 917-922.

Recher, V., 2016. Tougher than the Rest? Relationship between unemployment and crime in Croatia. EIZ Working paper no. 1602.

Soh, C. B. M., 2012. " Crime and Urbanisation: Revisited in Malaysian Case"; Social and Behavioral Sciences 42(2012)., pp. 291-299.

Tang, C.F. 2009. 'Linkage Among Inflation, Unemployment and Crime in Malaysia', Journal of Economics and Management, pp. 50-61.

Witt, R., Clarke, A., Feilding, N., 1999. Crime and Economic Growth. British Journal of Criminology. Vol. 39, No. 3, pp. 391-400.

World Bank data are available at

https://data.worldbank.org/indicator/FP.CPI.TOTL.ZG?locations=IN,

https://data.worldbank.org/indicator/FR.INR.RINR

https://data.worldbank.org/indicator/NY.GDP.PCAP.CD?locations=IN,

https://data.worldbank.org/indicator/SE.PRM.ENRR?locations=IN,

https://data.worldbank.org/indicator/SL.UEM.TOTL.ZS,

Appendix

Table A1: Lag Length Selection

Model 1						
Lag length criteria Robbery						
LAG	***LOGL***	***LR***	***FPE***	***AIC***	***SC***	***HQ***
0	50.83	NA	1.07e-08	-4.16	-3.91	-4.10
1	175.62	181.51	1.32e-12*	-13.23*	-11.75*	-12.88*
Lag length criteria for Breach of trust						
LAG	LOGL	LR	FPE	AIC	SC	HQ
0	63.93	NA	3.24e-09	-5.35	-5.10	-5.29
1	181.2	170.60	7.91e-13*	-13.74*	-12.25*	-13.39*
Model 2						
Lag length criteria Robbery						
LAG	***LOGL***	***LR***	***FPE***	***AIC***	***SC***	***HQ***
0	66.70	NA	2.52e-09	-5.60	-5.36	-5.55
1	201.02	195.37*	1.31e-13*	-15.54*	-14.06*	-15.19*
Lag length criteria for Breach of trust						
LAG	LOGL	LR	FPE	AIC	SC	HQ
0	78.72	NA	8.45e-10	-6.70	-6.45	-6.64
1	203.08	180.87*	1.08e-13*	-15.73*	-14.24*	-15.38*

Table A1 represents the optimum lag length selection. As per AIC we selects the optimum lag length. Optimum lag length is 1 in all models for robbery and BOT.

Table A2: Diagnostic Test

	Robbery		*Breach of trust*	
	M1	*M2*	*M1*	*M2*
Serial correlation (LM test)	0.151 (0.703)	1.24 (0.285)	1.04 (0.326)	0.500 (0.491)
Heteroskedasticity (Breusch pagan test)	0.692 (0.714)	1.10 (0.439)	0.477 (0.870)	0.574 (0.802)

p value in ()

Table A2 shows the diagnostic test result likes LM test; heteroscedasticity proves there is no problem of serial correlation, heteroscedasticity. Cum sum parameter stability test indicates stable equilibrium in Model 1 and 2 for both robbery and breach of trust (BOT).

Robbery (M-1)

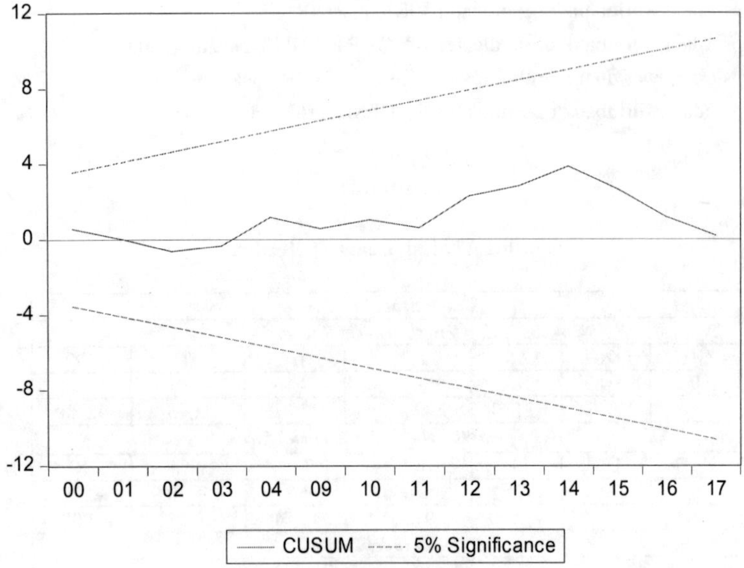

BOT (M1)

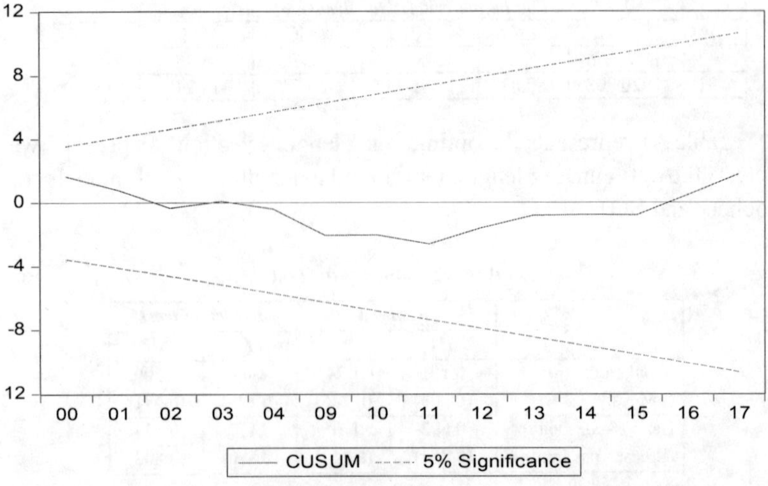

ROB(M2)

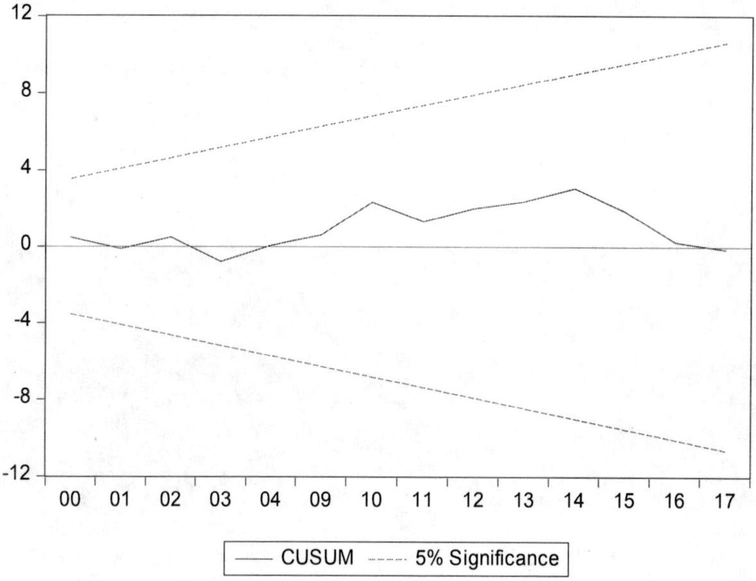
12
8
4
0
-4
-8
-12
00 01 02 03 04 09 10 11 12 13 14 15 16 17
CUSUM
5% Significance

BOT (M2)

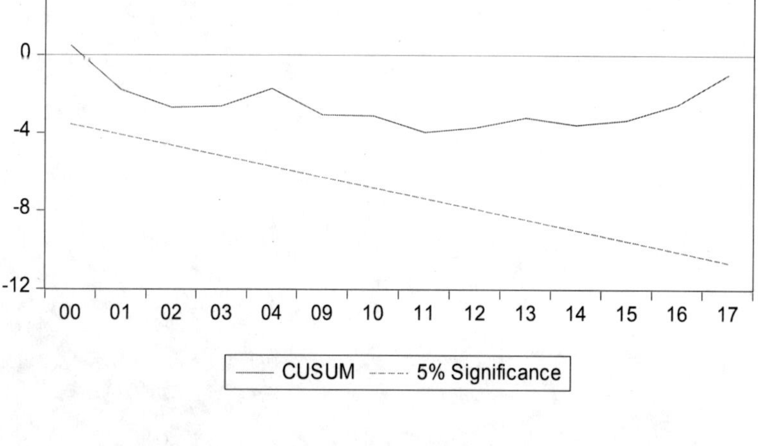
12
8
4
0
-4
-8
-12
00 01 02 03 04 09 10 11 12 13 14 15 16 17
CUSUM
5% Significance

Index

D

N

Q

R

T

U